Yard and Garden FURNITURE

2ND EDITION

Plans and Step-by-Step Instructions to Create 20 Useful Outdoor Projects

Bill Hylton

CRE**A**TIVE
HOMEOWNER®

CREATIVE HOMEOWNER®

Copyright © 2020 Bill Hylton and Creative Homeowner

This book may not be reproduced, either in part or in its entirety, in any form, by any means, without written permission from the publisher, with the exception of brief excerpts for purposes of radio, television, or published review. All rights, including the right of translation, are reserved. Note: Be sure to familiarize yourself with manufacturer's instructions for tools, equipment, and materials before beginning a project. Although all possible measures have been taken to ensure the accuracy of the material presented, neither the author nor the publisher is liable in case of misinterpretation of directions, misapplication, or typographical error.

Creative Homeowner® is a registered trademark of New Design Originals Corporation.

Yard and Garden Furniture, 2nd Edition

Editor: David Schiff

Designer: David Fisk

ISBN 978-1-58011-850-7

The Cataloging-in-Publication Data is on file with the Library of Congress.

We are always looking for talented authors. To submit an idea, please send a brief inquiry to acquisitions@foxchapelpublishing.com.

Printed in China

Current Printing (last digit)

10 9 8 7 6 5 4 3

Creative Homeowner®, www.creativehomeowner.com, is an imprint of New Design Originals Corporation and distributed exclusively in North America by Fox Chapel Publishing Company, Inc., 800-457-9112, 903 Square Street, Mount Joy, PA 17552, and in the United Kingdom by Grantham Book Service, Trent Road, Grantham, Lincolnshire, NG31 7XQ.

METRIC CONVERSION

Length

1 inch	2.54 cm
1 foot	30.48 cm
1 yard	91.44 cm
1 mile	1.61 km

Area

1 square inch	6.45 cm^2
1 square foot	92.90 cm^2
1 square yard	0.84 m^2
1 acre	4046.86 m^2
1 square mile	2.59 km^2

Volume

1 cubic inch	16.39 cm^3
1 cubic foot	0.03 m^3
1 cubic yard	0.77 m^3

Common Lumber Equivalents

Sizes: Metric cross sections are so close to their nearest U.S. sizes, as noted below, that for most purposes they may be considered equivalents.

Dimensional	1 x 2	19 x 38 mm
lumber	1 x 4	19 x 89 mm
	2 x 2	38 x 38 mm
	2 x 4	38 x 89 mm
	2 x 6	38 x 140 mm
	2 x 8	38 x 184 mm
	2 x 10	38 x 235 mm
	2 x 12	38 x 286 mm
Sheet	4 x 8 ft.	1200 x 2400 mm
sizes mm	4 x 10 ft.	1200 x 3000
Sheet	¼ in.	6 mm
thicknesses	⅜ in.	9 mm
	½ in.	12 mm
	¾ in.	19 mm

Capacity

1 fluid ounce	29.57 mL
1 pint	473.18 mL
1 quart	1.14 liters
1 gallon	3.79 liters

Temperature

Celsius = (Fahrenheit − 32) x $\frac{5}{9}$

°F	°C
0	−18
10	−12.22
20	−6.67
30	−1.11
32	0
40	4.44
50	10.00
60	15.56
70	21.11
80	26.67
90	32.22
100	37.78

SAFETY

Though all the designs and methods in this book have been reviewed for safety, it is not possible to overstate the importance of using the safest possible construction methods. What follows are reminders—some do's and don'ts of work procedures and tool safety that apply to construction projects in general. They are not substitutes for your own common sense.

■ Always use caution, care, and good judgment when following the instructions and procedures described in this book.

■ Always be sure that the electrical setup is safe, that no circuit is overloaded, and that all power tools and outlets are properly grounded. Do not use power tools in wet locations.

■ Always read container labels on paints, solvents, and other products; provide ventilation; and observe all other warnings.

■ Always read the manufacturer's instructions for using a tool, especially the warnings.

■ Use hold-downs and push sticks whenever possible when working on a table saw. Avoid working short pieces if you can.

■ Always remove the key from any drill chuck (portable or press) before starting the drill.

■ Always pay deliberate attention to how a tool works so that you can avoid being injured.

■ Always know the limitations of your tools. Do not try to force them to do what they were not designed to do.

■ Always make sure that any adjustment is locked before proceeding. For example, always check the rip fence on a table saw or the bevel adjustment on a portable saw before starting to work.

■ Always clamp small pieces to a stable work surface when working on them with a power tool.

■ Always wear the appropriate rubber or work gloves when handling chemicals, moving or stacking lumber, or doing heavy construction.

■ Always wear a disposable or permanent dust mask when you create dust by sawing or sanding. Use a special filtering respirator when working with toxic substances and solvents.

■ Always wear eye protection, especially when using power tools or driving nails with a hammer. A mis-hit can cause a nail to fly at you.

■ Never work while wearing loose clothing, hanging hair, open cuffs, or jewelry.

■ Always be aware that there is seldom enough time for your body's reflexes to save you from injury from a power tool in a dangerous situation; everything happens too fast. Be alert!

■ Always keep your hands away from the business ends of blades, cutters, and bits.

■ Always hold a circular saw firmly, usually with one hand on the trigger handle and the other on the secondary support handle.

■ Always use a drill with an auxiliary handle to control the torque when large-size bits are used.

■ Always move a router across a workpiece so that the bit rotation pushes the tool toward the fence rather than away from it.

■ Never work with power tools when you are tired or under the influence of alcohol or drugs.

■ Never cut tiny pieces of wood using a power saw. Always cut small pieces off larger pieces that are securely clamped or fastened to a stable work surface.

■ Never change a saw blade, drill bit, or router bit unless the tool's power cord is unplugged. Do not depend on the switch being off; you might accidentally hit it.

■ Never work in insufficient lighting.

■ Never work with dull tools. Have them sharpened, or learn how to sharpen them yourself.

■ Never use a power tool on a workpiece—large or small—that is not firmly supported.

■ Never saw a workpiece that spans a large distance between horses without close support on each side of the cut; the piece can bend, close on and jam the blade, and cause saw kickback.

■ Never support a workpiece from underneath with your leg or other part of your body when sawing or drilling.

■ Never carry sharp or pointed tools, such as utility knives, awls, or chisels, in your pocket. If you want to carry such tools, use a special-purpose tool belt with leather pockets and holders.

INTRODUCTION

92

64

84

146

164

116

38

Tools & Techniques

The Builder's Notes for any project in this book might spotlight a specialized tool or procedure that is essential for that project, but they also assume that you know the general stuff—cutting boards and driving screws, for example. Chances are that you already have some of the tools required, but as you tackle these projects, you may need to expand your collection. The following information will assist you in both choosing and using your tools.

Hand Tools

No matter how much electricity you have coming into your shop, and no matter how extensive your collection of power tools is, you really do need a few hand-powered tools. You'll use most of these tools for other projects around the house as well, not just for woodworking.

Your basic kit **(Photo 1)** should include a few sizes of screwdrivers, both Phillips and flat-blade, a light claw hammer (12 ounces is about right), and a socket wrench with a selection of sockets. Pliers, a couple adjustable wrenches, a hack-saw for metal, and a backsaw for wood round out the collection.

A modest selection of traditional woodworking hand tools will also come in very handy for refining the fit of joints, trimming inside corners of rabbets, and dozens of other odd jobs. **(Photo 2)** A set of four chisels (³/₈-, ¹/₂-, ³/₄-, and 1-inch widths) and a block plane are easy to find and don't cost a lot. Keep the blades sharp so they'll always be ready to use.

Layout Tools

The very first tool you are likely to use on any project is one for measuring or layout. **(Photo 3)** You'll probably use a measuring tape most. A 12-foot tape is long enough for the projects in this book, and it is a convenient size to fit in your pocket or hook on your belt.

Rules. For the most part, rules are simple-looking strips of metal, but they are very precise tools too. Once your stock has been cut into rough-length pieces, layout work is often done with a metal rule.

Bench rules range in length from 6 to 48 inches. A 6-inch rule works well for laying out joints and setting the cutting depth on routers and saws. A 6-inch rule often has graduations marked across the ends, which makes setting depths easier.

Perhaps the handiest rule for layout work is the hook rule, available in 6-, 12-, 18-, and 24-inch lengths. As with a measuring tape, you hook the end of the workpiece for easy, accurate layouts.

An oddball rule that some woodworkers find useful is the center-finding rule (not shown). It has a zero point at the center of the

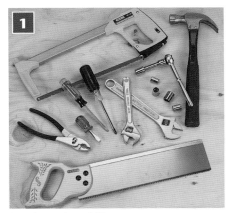

Handyman's tool kit

Woodworker's hand tool kit

rule, and measurements reading from that point out to both ends.

Rules are available in a variety of calibrations, including fractional inches, decimal inches and metric. A rule with one calibration on one edge and a different one on the opposite edge is an invitation to confusion. Better to get a rule reading left to right on one edge and a right to left on the other. With that arrangement, you can read the scale, regardless of how you pick up the rule or which direction you need to measure.

Combination Square. This is an excellent all-purpose square, which will get a lot of use. The square shown has a

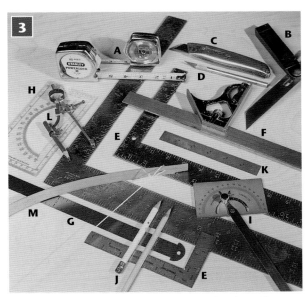

Layout tools: **A** *measuring tapes;* **B** *sliding T-bevel;* **C** *utility knife;* **D** *razor knife;* **E** *metal squares;* **F** *combination square;* **G** *hook rule;* **H** *protractor;* **I** *engineer's protractor;* **J** *pencils;* **K** *6-inch rule;* **L** *compass;* **M** *shop-made bow.*

12-inch blade, but lengths range from 6 inches up to 24 inches. The head, which can be moved and locked at any place along the blade, has machined edges at 90 and 45 degrees to the blade. The primary use of the combination square is as a try square—marking lines across boards, checking for flatness and squareness—but you can also use it as a marking gauge and a depth gauge.

Steel Squares. These all-steel, L-shaped tools have a long "blade" and a short "tongue," which meet in a right angle at the "heel." All edges of these squares are graduated in various scales. The largest of the steel squares is the framing square, used by builders for laying out stairs and rafters and other elements of a house's framework. The smallest is handy for layout work of a much smaller scale.

To use a steel square for layout, you hold the blade against a board's edge with the tongue extending across the board's face and mark along the tongue. You'll use it to make sure the corners are square, and the long blade is useful for determining whether or not a surface is flat.

Sliding T-bevel. For laying out angles, you ought to have this adjustable tool. It has a metal blade with a 45-degree miter on one end, joined to a wood or metal handle with a thumbscrew. Loosening the thumbscrew allows you to change the angle between the blade and the handle. You can lay out angles set from a protractor or transfer an angle from one place on the work to another.

To ensure your crosscuts are square, use an angle square (often referred to by the brand name Speed Square) as a guide. Hold the square against the work's edge, then guide the saw along it. To do this with both hands on the saw, clamp the square to the work.

Compass. This commonplace drafting tool makes it easy to lay out arcs and circles. But it can also be used, as dividers are, for transferring measurements from a rule to the work or from one spot on the work to another, or for dividing lengths into equal parts.

Protractors. This familiar semicircular measure calibrated in degrees is good for setting a sliding T-bevel or to read an angle from a plan or blueprint, but it is actually less useful in woodworking than an engineer's protractor, which combines the blade from the bevel with a protractor's degree scale. With this protractor, you set the blade to an angle on the scale, then use it directly on the work to lay out the angle.

Shop-Made Bow. For laying out curves, there's nothing so handy as a thin strip of wood from the scrap pile. You can usually bend it to a pleasing arc, then trace along it on the work while it's held by your assistant. If you're working alone, you can tie string to the ends—like an archer's bow—to hold the arc.

Marking Tools. The pencil is the most common and popular tool for marking cut lines, locations for holes, and all other manner of layout markings. A marking knife (or a utility or razor knife) makes more-precise layout marks.

Circular Saw

The circular saw is your basic wood-cutting power tool. If you don't have a power miter saw and a table saw, you can use the circular saw for crosscutting and ripping stock. **(Photo 4)**

Circular saws make straight cuts, and it's difficult to alter your direction once you begin cutting. Line up the notch in the saw's base on the layout line, and guide the cut by watching either the blade or the notch.

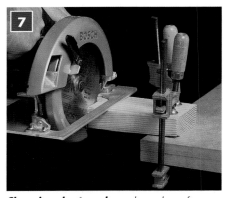

Clamping short work, as shown here, frees both hands to hold the saw. Operate your circular saw with both hands whenever possible. It is the safest way to work and yields the most accurate results.

You may not think of a circular saw as a tool for ripping, but it is essentially an upside-down, handheld, mini table saw. All you need for perfectly accurate rip cuts is a guide. An accessory edge guide comes with some saws, and the plans for a shop-made guide are on page 9.

The saw's base has a notch in the front edge, which you can use to follow a cutting line or to make sure you line up squarely at the beginning of a cut. The saw doesn't gladly change direction, even slightly, once a cut has begun. If you try to correct your course, the saw will shriek, maybe stall, and often burn the sides of the cut. A cutting guide may help you get started straight. With some practice, however, aligning the saw when starting a crosscut becomes second

Proper blade depth—$\frac{1}{8}$ in. below the bottom of the work—minimizes kickback by limiting the area of the blade that's in the kerf. It also reduces the amount of the blade that's exposed if the saw does kick back.

nature. **(Photo 5)** Clamping a carpenter's square to the work to guide the saw can be a big help.

Be sure to understand and follow all the manufacturer's safety instructions when you use your circular saw. Learn to set the depth of cut appropriately, and always clamp pieces that might move during the cut. **(Photos 6 and 7)**

When you shop for a saw, look at the motor's amp rating, which is a fairly reliable indicator of power. For saws using $7\frac{1}{4}$-inch blades, a 13-amp motor should provide plenty of power. A lower-amp motor will bog down when cutting hardwood, particleboard, and other dense materials.

Examine the saw's base, or shoe plate, carefully. Some saws have stamped-steel bases with relatively small footprints. These are good for remodelers, for whom maneuverability of the saw is important. But most woodworkers do lots of sawing "on the flat." Here, a substantial base is a plus, because it's easier to guide against a straightedge.

Check out the controls and adjustment knobs. See how they feel in your hands, how precisely they function. They should operate easily, lock firmly, and exhibit no play.

Circular Saw Guide

While you can just clamp any straight board to the work and use it to guide the saw's shoe, getting it offset correctly from the cut line and still exactly parallel with it can be pretty frustrating. This jig solves the problem because you clamp its edge directly on the cut line. A second board on

CIRCULAR SAW GUIDE

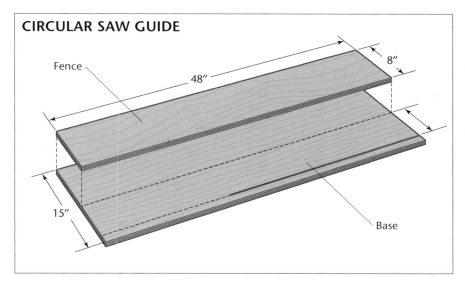

Fence

48"

8"

15"

Base

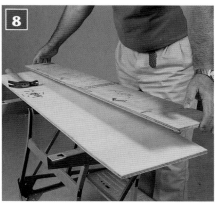

To assemble your circular saw guide, *nail or screw the narrow strip on top of the wide one. The factory edge, which is on the narrow strip, must be on the inside. (It's the edge nearest the hammer in the photo.)*

factory edge of the piece that will become the fence, and make sure it is the edge that ultimately guides the saw.

Begin by cutting two strips of ½-inch A-C or B-C plywood. (Ordinary fir plywood is fine for this purpose, but you do want a smooth surface for the saw to ride on. Don't use CDX grade.) Cut the first strip, which has the factory edge, 8 inches wide; this is the jig's fence. The second strip, the base, is 15 inches wide. You can cut the strips freehand; a perfectly straight cut isn't necessary.

Glue and screw the fence to the base, with the factory-cut edge facing the middle of the base. **(Photo 8)** Clamp the assembly to a workbench or across sawhorses, with the edge overhanging so that you can cut it without damaging the workbench or sawhorses. Using the factory-cut edge as a saw guide, cut off the end of the wide strip to complete the jig. **(Photo 9)**

To use this guide, align the edge of the jig on the cut line, and clamp or screw the jig to the work. Use at least two clamps. Set the saw on the jig's base, with its shoe against the guide fence. Switch on the saw and make a clean, perfectly straight cut.

Mounting the guide to a board for ripping is only slightly more involved. The guide is wider than individual boards, even 1x12s and 2x12s, so you have to screw the guide to the workpiece, and support the free end of the guide with a second board.

Power Miter Saws

Power miter saws have crosscut, mitered, and beveled their way onto the roster of primary woodshop tools, supplanting the loose and cranky radial arm saw as the tool of choice for breaking down rough stock. In addition to the rough stuff, they handle delicate finish cuts, making precise miter cuts, even compound miter cuts, then quickly adjusting back to square.

The most basic model is the "conventional" miter saw, which looks like a circular saw mounted above a small table on a spring-loaded hinge. The saw body rotates from a straight crosscut to a 45-degree miter cut in either direction. To make a cut, you grasp the handle, squeeze the trigger switch, and rock the blade into the stock in a chopping motion. The majority of the saws on the market use a 10-inch blade. Most will crosscut a 2x6 and miter a 2x4 at 45 degrees. It is a simple, functional saw.

To make compound miters, cuts that are simultaneously miters and bevels, you need the more sophisticated compound miter saw. It has a rotating table but also a pivot to enable the head to be tilted 45 degrees (or more) to one or both sides. Size ranges up to 12 inches, and cut capacities are similar to those of conventional miter saws.

The most sophisticated of the miter saws is the sliding compound miter saw. **(Photo 10)** Like the compound saw, the head assembly rotates and tilts (some models both left and right) for compound cutting. But it also slides forward and back on a rail system, thus increasing the crosscutting capacity to about 12 inches. To make a cut, you pull the elevated blade toward you, pivot it down into the stock, then push it back toward the fence.

Complete the guide *by ripping the base to width with your circular saw. Just rest the saw base on the guide base, with its edge against the fence, as shown here. Rip the waste off, and your guide is ready for use.*

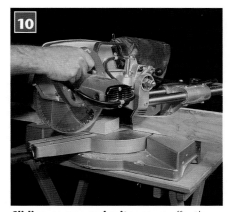

Sliding compound miter saws *offer the largest cutting capacities of all the power miters saws. The motor slides toward the operator, then pivots down into the work and cuts on the way back to the fence.*

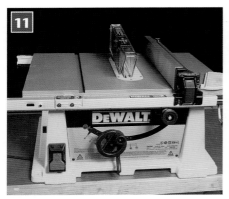

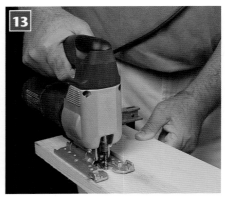

A good bench-top table saw is essential for some of the projects in this book. The low-price models sometimes lack the accuracy needed for this work, but a mid-price model will be fine.

It takes a steady, practiced hand to make precision freehand cuts with a saber saw. The saw is used for making internal cuts and trimming workpieces that are to be shaped with a template and a router.

The saber saw makes excellent rip cuts and crosscuts. To ensure they are perfectly straight, guide the saw along a straightedge clamped to the workpiece. Don't push the saw to cut too fast, or the blade may deflect.

cut, you pull the elevated blade toward you, pivot it down into the stock, then push it back toward the fence.

As you shop for one of these saws, look for smooth-working miter and bevel adjustments and easy-to-read scales. Miter-saw work will often require frequent setting changes. Large, accessible adjustment mechanisms make a big differ-

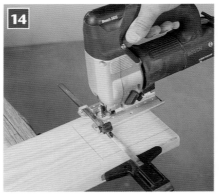

The edge guide is an inexpensive accessory that's handy for making cuts parallel with an edge. The guide is attached to the saw's base. Its shoe rides along the edge of the work, making rip cuts a breeze.

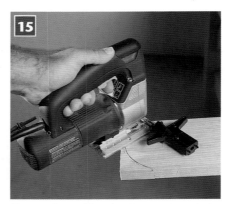

Better edge guides often incorporate a pivot pin, so it can be used as a trammel to guide the saber saw in cutting arcs. There's just a single pivot point, and you move the saw to adjust the radius of the cut.

On the safety front, the OFF switch must be large and easy to reach. The blade guard should swing out of the way during blade changing. Because it must be removed for some operations, look for a blade guard that's easy to remove and reinstall.

Buy a high-quality carbide tip combination blade, and use it to do all your cutting.

ence. In addition, detents (or stops) at common angles such as 0, 22$\frac{1}{2}$, and 45 degrees are useful. On a sliding compound saw, look for an adjustable depth stop, so you can use the saw to make dadoes and lap-joints.

On the safety front, look for a blade guard that retracts smoothly as you pivot the blade into the work. Look too for an electric brake that stops the blade when you release the on-off switch.

Table Saws

In the typical woodworking shop, the table saw is the queen. Buy a good one early on, and equip it with a first-rate blade, a good fence, and as big an outfeed table as your shop allows.

For the occasional woodworker, the bench-top table saw may be the best model to consider. Serious hobbyists usually opt for the midrange contractor's model, and a professional will undoubtedly buy a cabinet saw. The prices range from less than $200 for the bottom-of-the-line bench-top saw to more than $3,000 for a nicely outfitted cabinet saw. There are good contractor's saws in the $300 to $400 range. **(Photo 11)**

When shopping for a saw, look for sturdy handwheels, knobs, and locking devices that operate easily. The blade height and bevel should adjust without any play; a lock should hold the bevel setting. Degree scales should be easy to read, and there should be adjustable stops at 45 and 90 degrees.

Saber Saw

The saber saw is "the poor man's band saw." It can be used for straight-line crosscuts and rips, but its forte is the freehand curve. **(Photo 12)** Because the saber saw's blade isn't a loop like the band saw's, it doesn't have a "throat capacity" limitation, so it makes cuts no band saw can. The workpiece can be any width or length. You can cut around the outside of a workpiece, but you can make a closed-loop internal cut as well. With a straightedge guiding the cut, a saber saw makes decent rip cuts. **(Photo 13)** And because you bring the tool to the workpiece, not the other way around, a board's width, length, bulk, or weight won't prevent you from cutting it. With a long blade, it can make cuts in boards as thick as 2½ inches.

The saber saw cuts with a narrow strip of a blade. The number of teeth per inch and the "set" of the teeth have a lot to do with the aggressiveness with which a particular blade cuts. But so does the oscillation setting of the saw.

When first introduced, the saber saw cut with a straightforward up-and-down action. Known as "straight-line" action, this is still best for smooth, tearout-free cutting, but it can be slow going on rip cuts and in dense materials. To accelerate the saw's cutting speed, orbital cutting action has been added. In this mode, the blade churns forward and backward as it strokes up and down, cutting more aggressively, but more roughly. On most saws, you can switch the orbital action on or off; on the best, you can ratchet it on by degrees.

There are two styles of saber saws, the top handle and the barrel grip. The top handle is by far the most common. It has a loop handle positioned above and in line with the motor. A trigger switch is incorporated into the handle. Those who favor this style consider it more comfortable and say it affords increased control when cutting thick or dense materials.

The barrel-grip saber saw doesn't have a handle. As long as your hand isn't too small, you simply grip the motor housing. The switch typically is on the side of the housing. Having your hand low and behind the blade makes it easier to feed the saw aggressively, say the barrel-grip's partisans, and having your hand closer to the work makes it easier to cut tight curves.

When shopping for a saber saw, look for one that has variable speed, adjustable orbital action, a tilting base with stops at 45 and 90 degrees, and a blade-changing system you can deal with.

Also look for a good edge guide. **(Photo 14)** Some models include a pivot-point feature, making a mini-trammel for the saber saw. **(Photo 15)**

One last feature to consider is a dust-collection port. While saber saws don't generate a lot of dirt, their cutting action puts chips in front of the blade, where they pile up and obscure the cut line. Many models have a chip blower to clear them. Some models have a vacuum port so the sawdust can be sucked away by a shop vacuum.

Power Plane

Where hand planes left off, power planes have picked up. Hand planes are still used by fine woodworkers, but few carpenters have ever mastered them, and hobby woodworkers tend to be intimidated by the routine sharpening, tuning, and adjusting they require. A hand plane relies on a sharp iron, finely tuned adjustments of throat, frog, chip breaker, and iron, and lots of muscle to smooth an edge.

A power plane, on the other hand, has a pair of throw away knives and just one adjustment knob, and uses an electric motor to power the cut. **(Photo 16)** Just set the plane's front shoe on the work, pull the trigger, and feed the tool steadily—better too slow than too fast—along the wood. The only adjustment is the depth of cut. Turning the front hand-grip alters the vertical position of portion of the base in front of the knives, and that controls how much material can be sliced away. Usually, a single pass can smooth a rough-cut edge.

Unlike a belt sander, which is also used to smooth wood, a power plane does not abraid the surface to remove scratches, dents, gouges, and other blemishes; instead it slices off a layer of wood, leaving a clean, smooth surface. It won't hog out a hollow if you leave it running in one spot (as will a belt sander), but like that belt sander and a lot of other power tools, it can remove a lot of material very quickly and with little effort. You do have to pay close attention, use a conservative touch, and align the tool for each pass very carefully. Otherwise, you can quickly give an undesired contour to an edge or face.

Routers

The router is woodworking's most versatile power tool. It will surface stock, cut joints, profile edges, and knock out duplicate parts following a template or pattern. With the right trammel, it will cut arcs, circles, and even ellipses.

There are two types of routers: fixed-base and plunge. **(Photo 17)** With a fixed-base router, you set the depth of cut and don't change it while the router is running. The plunge router allows on-the-fly cutting depth changes.

Depending upon how involved you get with woodworking, you'll probably want to own several routers, along with a selec-

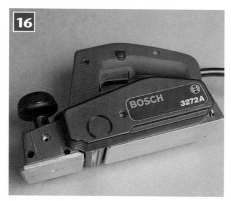

A power plane shaves boards with rotating cutters mounted underneath the body of the tool. The knob on top controls the depth of cut. A quick pass slices off just enough wood to transfer a rough edge into a smooth one.

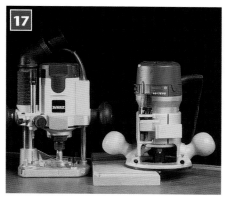

You'll probably want to get both types of routers; a plunge router, left, and a fixed-base router, right. If you can only get one, buy the fixed-base model: the low center of gravity keeps it more stable on some cuts.

tion of bits and accessories. Having more than one of these tools is almost essential for doing a few of the projects in this book.

The fixed-base model is less glitzy, perhaps, than a plunge router, but it is still the first you should buy. And if you feel you can only buy one, make it a fixed-base model. A fixed-base router is generally compact, has a low center of gravity, and is the more stable tool for the majority of the routing you'll do. Its handles are low enough that you can grip them firmly and still have the heels of your hands braced against the work. Any job that does not require those on-the-fly changes in cutting depth should be done with a fixed-base router. This includes edge profiling and cutting dadoes, grooves, and rabbets.

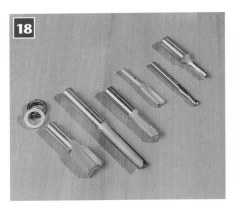

Straight bits (left to right): ¾-in. two-flute; 3 in. long ½-in. two-flute; ½-in. two-flute; ⅜-in. two-flute; ¼-in. solid-carbide up-spiral; ¼-in. two-flute on ½-in. shank. The bearings at left fit onto the ½-in. shanks.

Pattern bits: (left to right): 1⅛-in.-dia. 1½-in. cutting-length; ¾-in.-dia. 1½-in. cutting-length; ½-in.-dia. 1-in. cutting-length. **Flush trimming bits:** ¼-in.-dia. 2-in. cutting-length; ½-in.-dia. 1-in. cutting-length.

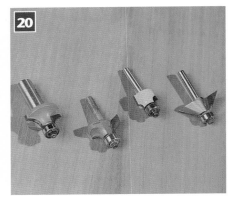

These bits are useful for softening the edges of seat slats, armrests, and tabletop edges. Useful roundover bits include: ⅜-in.-radius r.o. bit; ¼-in.-radius r.o. bit; ⅛-in.-radius r.o. bit; and a chamfering bit.

With the plunge router you lower the spinning bit into the work in a controlled manner, so you can begin and end a cut in the middle of a board. The trade-off is balance. The motor rides up and down on a pair of spring-loaded posts rising from the router base. To plunge the router, you release a lock and conscientiously push down on the handles.

At rest, the handles are 4 to 6 inches above the work, and even in the middle of a cut, with the router plunged to the max, you may have difficulty bracing the machine because the handles are so high above the work.

Nevertheless, a plunge router is ideal for cutting mortises and stopped grooves.

Weight and bulk are the main drawbacks of a powerful router. A router rated at 1 to 1¾ horsepower, regardless of type, will tip the scales at about 8 pounds. A powerful 3-horsepower model can weigh as much as 18 pounds. Because a big machine often is too unwieldy for common handheld operations, many woodworkers end up with an easy-to-maneuver 1½-horsepower model for handheld operations, and a plunge router of similar size for mortising.

The collet is a tiny, but vital, part of the router. Although it weighs only an ounce or two, this is the part that holds the cutter on the end of the motor's armature shaft. Four types are in use, the best of which is called the self-releasing collet. The double-taper collet and one-piece collet are OK and are still used on older designs. The worst type is the split-arbor; this is the sign of a cheesy router. The collet is integral to the motor's armature, and if the collet is damaged, you must replace the armature.

It's best if you focus on routers that come with both ½- and ¼-inch collets. Large diameter and very long cutters especially should have ½-inch shanks, and you need to get a router that will take them. At the same time, avoid models

COLLETS

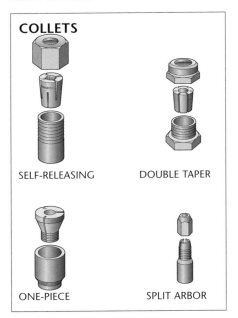

SELF-RELEASING   DOUBLE TAPER

ONE-PIECE   SPLIT ARBOR

COLLET TECHNIQUES   GETTING A GRIP 250

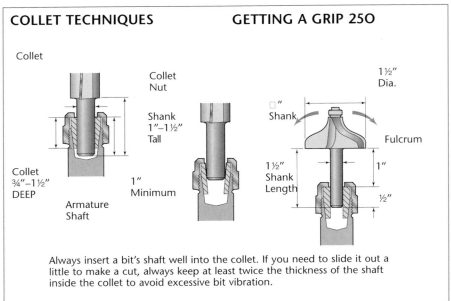

Always insert a bit's shaft well into the collet. If you need to slide it out a little to make a cut, always keep at least twice the thickness of the shaft inside the collet to avoid excessive bit vibration.

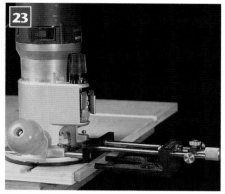

Strange as it may seem, that seemingly huge router is guided by the bearing on the end of the bit. The router is spinning the bit, but the bearing is controlling the cut and preventing it from straying.

To guide a router across a board to cut dadoes, use a straight board as a fence. To correct for imperfections in the base's shape, keep one spot on the base against the fence, rather than see-sawing the tool as you cut.

The edge guide guides the router for grooves and mortises. A state-of-the-art guide, like the Micro-Fence shown here, has very tight tolerances and secure lockdowns, and adapts to several brands of routers.

that don't provide a true ¼-inch collet, but use a sleeve to fit ¼-inch shanks in the ½-inch collet.

Routers cruise at 22,000 rpm, a speed that's fine for bits less than 1 inch in diameter but way too fast for 2- or 3-inch-diameter bits. Electronic variable speed (EVS) is an important feature on the more powerful models. EVS allows you to dial back the router's rpms, making it safer to use large-diameter bits. It also provides a "soft start" feature, which brings the motor up to speed gradually, eliminating the disconcerting jerk of accelerating from 0 to 22,000 rpm in a split second. Finally, EVS maintains the router's rpms under load.

EVS is seldom available on low-horsepower routers, in part because it isn't needed on them. They aren't suited for use with the large-diameter bits.

Aside from bits, you should also buy an edge guide and template guides.

An edge guide attaches to the router and slides along the edge of the workpiece to guide the bit. It is particularly useful for cutting rabbets and grooves, and, with a plunge router, for cutting mortises.

Template guides, sometimes called guide bushings or guide collars, are essential for doing template and inlay work. Many router jigs—half-blind dovetail jigs, for example—call for the use of template bushings to guide the router. You will need them to build some of the furniture in this book.

Router Bits
The most important part of any routing operation is the bit. The more bits you

have, the more you can do different jobs with the basic machine.

There are zillions of bits out there, made in the United States, Canada, Italy, Israel, and Asia. They're sold in hardware stores and building centers, and you can buy them through mail-order catalogs or on the Internet.

Virtually every bit made and sold these days has a carbide-tip (or is solid carbide). In every performance aspect, bits with carbide cutting edges are superior to high-speed steel bits. An extremely hard material (close to the hardness of diamonds), carbide is relatively insensitive to heat, so it won't lose its temper when it gets hot.

The drawbacks of carbide are brittleness and high cost. It is those weaknesses that spawned the carbide-tip bit. The shank and body of most bits are machined from steel (because it is strong and inexpensive), then slips of carbide—the cutting edges—are brazed to the bit.

The cost and quality of router bits range widely. One manufacturer's bit may cost two or three times what a comparable profile made by another manufacturer costs. The difference may stem from where the bits are made or how they're made. It may stem from how they're marketed. When shopping for a bit, look for visible signs of quality: the thickness of the carbide, how evenly it is brazed to the bit body, and the smoothness of the cutting edge. These aren't necessarily the most important aspects of bit quality, but they are things you can see. If they're poor, the likelihood is that the invisible aspects will also be poor.

Of the quality aspects you can't see, the most critical are the roundness of the shank and the overall balance of the bit. You can't tell about the bit's balance until you use it. If the shank isn't perfectly round, or if the bit isn't perfectly balanced, it will vibrate. When you cut with it, it'll chatter. Vibration is hard on the router, the bit, and the cut. Straight bits make most dadoes and mortise cuts. **(Photo 18)** For trimming parts to match templates, you'll need pattern and flush-trimming bits. **(Photo 19)** Roundover bits are used for softening edges and adding edge treatments. **(Photo 20)**

Using a Router Safely and Effectively
Before you jump into router woodworking, you should know some basics that will make your work safer, easier, and more satisfying.

The most important is that a router is almost never used without some sort of guide, such as a pilot bearing. **(Photo 21)** The guide can be as simple as a straight board for the base to ride against. **(Photo 22)** Some routers come with an edge guide to guide cuts. **(Photo 23)**

Even before you switch on the router, it's essential to know in which direction to feed it. You need to know so you can put the fence in the correct place, for example, or so you can stand in the right place and be prepared to move in the correct direction.

Suppose you haven't thought about this at all. You chuck a bit in the collet of your new router, and take it for a spin.

Tools & Techniques

Where you position the T-square in relation to the cut depends on which router and bit you are using. Make a setup gauge for each bit-and-router combination you use for cutting dadoes.

One well-placed clamp is all it takes to secure the T-square to the work, and the work to the workbench. Butt the crossbar of the T-square to the edge of the work, slide the guide into alignment, then clamp.

ROUTER T-SQUARE

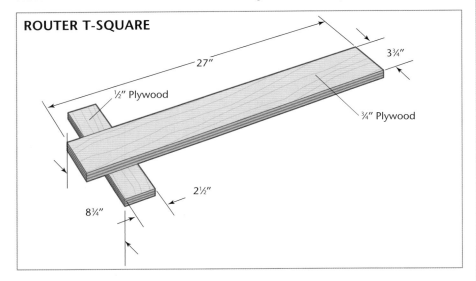

27"

3¾"

½" Plywood

¾" Plywood

2½"

8¾"

AVOIDING CHIP-OUT & TEAR-OUT

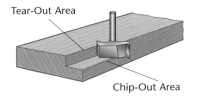

Tear-Out Area

Chip-Out Area

TEAR-OUT PROBLEM

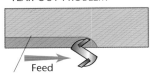

Feed

Cutting edge chops across grain, lifting wood fibers.

Solution 1

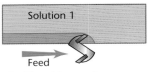

Feed

Avoid problem grain.

Solution 2

Feed

Cut on the board's edge, rather than the face.

CHIP-OUT PROBLEM

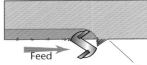

Feed

Wood fibers splinter as cutting edge exits wood.

Solution 1

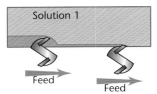

Feed   Feed

A shallow cut in the same direction reduces chip-out.

Solution 2

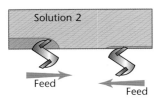

Feed   Feed

A shallow cut from the opposite direction also works.

You notice that the router seems to want to go in a direction, so you let it. Hey, you think, this isn't too bad. Then zziippp, the bit suddenly grabs and GOES, pulling the router and you along. You've just been introduced to the most fundamental of router feed direction rules:

Move the router opposite the way it would go if you let it.

If you do let the router go where it wants, you'll probably do OK ... for a while. But sooner or later the dynamics of the tool will really surface. If you are profiling an edge, the bit will push away from the wood, leaving you with a ragged, uncompleted cut. No harm done,

really. You just climb back on that horse and finish the cut. But if you are forging across a board, guided by a fence, the cut will veer away from the straightedge, going where you don't want it, very possibly ruining the workpiece.

All commercially available routers turn the same way. If you hold the router with the bit down, in standard hand-held operating orientation, the bit will turn clockwise. With an unpiloted cutter and an unguided router, the rotation of the cutter will drag the tool to your left as you push it away from you. As you pull it toward you, it will veer to your right.

You can use this dynamic to your advantage. Because you usually use a guide, feed the router so the cutter rotation pushes it against the guide.

Yard and Garden Furniture

From this statement come more specific ones, such as, "When you push the router the fence must be on the left; when you pull, the fence must be on the right," or "When you rout around the outside of a frame, go counterclockwise; when you rout around the inside of a frame, go clockwise."

Beyond feeding the router in the correct direction, you can do other things to avoid problems. You must begin with straight, flat stock, with faces parallel and edges parallel, and with faces at right angles to edges. In all the common handheld operations, the router rests on the stock while it works, and its guidance devices typically ride along an edge of the stock. Imperfections in the stock surfaces will telegraph directly into the cuts.

As you set up an operation, you should be as methodical as you can. The more precise you expect a cut to be, the more precise you have to be in setting up. In every case, you have a vertical adjustment to make to the router to establish how deeply the cutter will penetrate into the work. In some cases, you also have a horizontal adjustment to make—setting an edge guide or positioning a guide fence on the work and clamping it. The workpiece has to be secured. Maybe a template must be stuck or clamped to the workpiece.

All of these preparations offer opportunities for something to go wrong. The trick in routing—as in all woodworking—is to

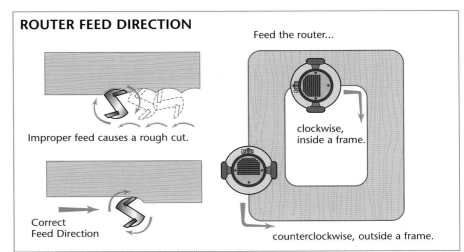

ROUTER FEED DIRECTION

Feed the router...

Improper feed causes a rough cut.

Correct Feed Direction

clockwise, inside a frame.

counterclockwise, outside a frame.

get the setup right. If not the first time, at least before you actually cut wood.

T-Square

Dadoes and grooves are fundamental joinery cuts, and they are easy to make with a router and straight bit. But as with every router operation, a guide is needed to keep the cut headed down the straight path you want. A T-square for the purpose is easy to make and use.

The big advantage a T-square has over a simple straightedge is that the setup and clamping are easy. Instead of a layout line the full length of the dado, usually a single pencil mark is enough.

(Photo 24) If the fence is perpendicular to the crossbar, you can be sure the dado will be square to the edge. In addition, the crossbar acts as a brace, allowing you to secure the typical T-square with a single clamp. **(Photo 25)**

To make one, glue and screw two straight-and-true scraps together in a T-shape. One piece, called the crossbar or the head, butts against the edge of the workpiece, and the other, called the fence, guide, or blade, extends at a right angle across the workpiece surface. The drawing "Router T-Square" on page 14, shows the dimensions for the T-square I used when building the projects in this book.

MAKING T-SQUARE SETUP GAUGE

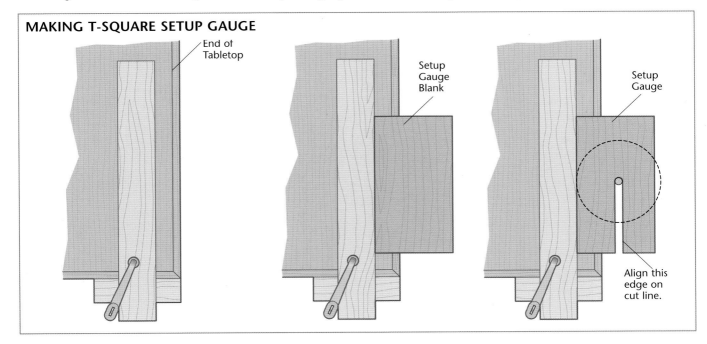

End of Tabletop

Setup Gauge Blank

Setup Gauge

Align this edge on cut line.

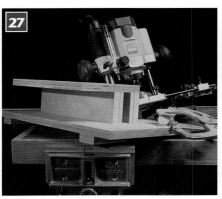

The mortise-and-tenon joint *is used extensively in the projects throughout this book. You'll use it to attach table legs to aprons, seat rails to chairs, and slats to the frames that form backrests for chairs.*

This easy-to-build jig helps you *cut all the mortises you'll need for the furniture projects in this book. Once the workpiece is clamped to one fence, the router rides on the top edges of the fences to make the cut.*

Put the workpiece into the jig, *and clamp it to the back. If your bit reaches, the work can sit on the bottom of the fixture. A Vise-Grip® C-clamp, which you operate with one hand, makes changing workpieces fast.*

Cutting Mortise-and-Tenon Joints

The mortise-and-tenon is woodworking's essential frame joint. If you want to get very far beyond nailed-together projects, you have to master this joint. This is especially true when it comes to making several of the tables and chairs in this book. **(Photo 26)** Fortunately, it isn't all that difficult, provided you have a good plunge router and a couple of easy-to-make jigs.

The typical sequence is to make the mortises, then the tenons. That way, the tenons can be sized to fit the mortises. This is a lot easier than trying to produce a mortise to fit a preexisting tenon.

Routing Mortises

The key to successfully routing mortises is to use a good plunge router, a good edge guide, and a good jig to hold the workpiece.

A useful, practical, and easy-to-make mortising jig is the miter-box-like construction shown here. **(Photo 27)** The entire jig is made of ³⁄₄-inch plywood and is assembled with 2-inch drywall screws.

As simple as it is, you must construct the jig with care. The bottom must be parallel to the top edge of the back, as must the top edge of the side. In use, the workpiece is set in the trough and clamped to the jig's back. The router is supported by the back and side of the jig, and its edge guide references the outer face of the back. Thus you build the jig so the axis of the router is supported perfectly perpendicular to the plane of the

desired mortise. If the side is slightly lower than the back, the router will be canted, and so will the mortises it cuts. If one end of the side is lower than the other, the mortises again will be out of alignment.

To use the jig, you clamp it in a bench vise. The workpiece used to set up the jig and the router must have the full mortise laid out on it, including a setup line. This line, exactly halfway between the ends of the mortise, is aligned with a matching setup line scribed on the jig. **(Photo 28)**

All the other workpieces only need to have the setup line marked on them, so they can be positioned consistently in the jig. The setup of the equipment will guarantee all the mortises will be the same length, depth, and width.

Position the first workpiece in the trough, align the setup line on it with that on the jig, and clamp the work to the jig back. **(Photo 29)** Chuck the appropriate bit in the router's collet. Set the router in place, and position the bit over the laid-

MORTISING JIG PLAN

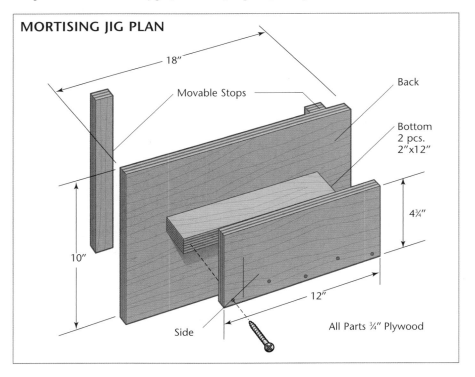

18"

Movable Stops

Back

Bottom
2 pcs.
2"x12"

10"

4³⁄₄"

12"

Side

All Parts ³⁄₄" Plywood

USING THE MORTISING JIG, VIEW FROM ABOVE

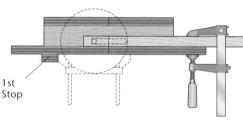

Centerline on Jig   Stock

Clamp the stock, aligning the center-line of the mortise with line on jig.

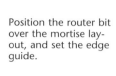

Edge Guide

Position the router bit over the mortise lay-out, and set the edge guide.

1st Stop

Move bit to one end of the layout, and attach first stop the the fence.

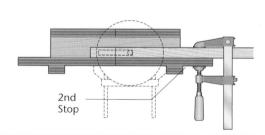

2nd Stop

Move the bit to the other end, and attach the second stop. You're ready to rout the mortise.

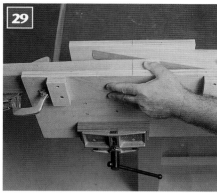

29

It is difficult to get a clamp *onto the short end of a workpiece when the mortise must be near the end. Instead, slide a wedge between the workpiece and the side, forcing the work tight against the fixture's back.*

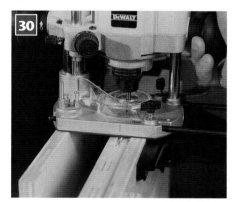

30

The side and back *support a plunge router nicely. The edge guide rides on the fixture's back. The block attached to the back stops the router at the end of the cut, preventing it from cutting a mortise that's too long.*

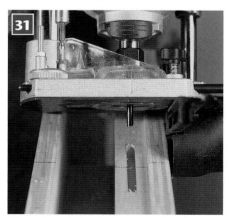

31

When the mortise is done, *turn the work around, and rout again. This makes the mortise a bit wider, but will also center it on the board. Routing it exactly on center in one pass is practically impossible to do.*

out mortise. Set the edge guide to fix the bit's position.

Next bottom the bit against the work, zero out the router's depth adjuster, and reset it for the depth of the mortise that you want.

Finally, set the stops that prevent you from making the mortise too long. **(Photo 30)** Move the bit so it aligns with one end of the mortise. Butt a scrap of wood against the appropriate end of the edge guide and screw it to the jig's back. When done correctly, the stop will not allow the router to move and cut beyond the end of the mortise. Move the router to the other end of the mortise, align the bit carefully, then screw a second stop to the jig's back.

Before cutting the mortise, determine the correct direction to feed the router.

You want to feed the router, remember, so that the bit's rotation will help pull the guide toward the jig. Move the router to the appropriate end of the mortise, switch it on, and plunge the bit about $1/8$ inch into the work. Make a cut, and retract the bit. Return to the starting point, plunge the bit a little deeper and make another cutting pass. Keep repeating this process until you've cut the mortise to full depth.

If the mortise is intended to be centered on the work, here's a little trick that will guarantee it will be so. After routing the mortise full depth, unclamp the work and turn it around. Align the setup lines and clamp the work. Rerout the mortise. **(Photo 31)** While it now will be wider than the bit, it will be centered. You haven't cut the tenons, and when you do, you

Tools & Techniques

This jig helps you cut all the tenons that fit into the mortises. You can make it out of scrape pieces of lumber and sheet goods you might have in the shop, and adapt it to cut all the various sizes of tenons you'll need.

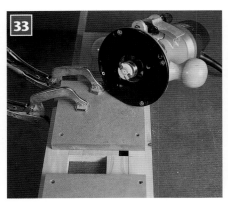

With the work and the jig clamped to the benchtop, you're ready to make the first cut. The adjustable stop (right) controls the size of the tenon cut into the workpiece (above the stop, underneath the jig).

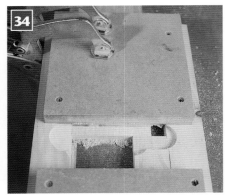

Lay the jig over the work, and clamp the whole works to the bench. Set the cutting depth on your router, and make the cut. The cut takes just a second or two to complete. The fences and the stop will also be routed.

If you have a lot of identical tenons to cut, use carpet tape to stick a positioning stop to the auxiliary top. With the stop butted tight to the work's end, the edge of the top should be directly on the layout line.

TENONING JIG PLAN

¾" Hardwood Fence

½" Plywood or MDF

3"

10"

9½"

1½"

¾" Hardwood Stop

16"

¾" Hardwood Fence

simply cut them to the thickness necessary to fit the mortise.

Routing Tenons

You can also use the router to make the tenon that fits inside the mortise. The challenge is to produce a tenoned workpiece that has crisp shoulders, all in the same plane, all perfectly square. There are two keys: One is using the right bit, the other is using a well-made jig. **(Photo 32)**

The bit I use is a dado-and-planer bit with a shank-mounted bearing. You can use any bottom-cleaning style bits, so long as the bit has a shank-mounted bearing to guide the cut.

The jig shown above is very simple to make and use. It's laid on top of the workpiece, with the edge of the jig's top dead

on the shoulder line for the tenon and the workpiece square and tight against the jig's fence. **(Photo 33)** The jig and work are clamped to the workbench. With the depth of cut properly set, run a router with an appropriate bit across the work. **(Photo 34)** The shank-mounted bearing rides on the jig's top edge, guiding the cutter. The fence backs up the cut, so you don't get tear-out. If you attach a stop (to position the workpieces) to the auxiliary top, change-over is speeded up. **(Photo 35)** You don't even have to lay out the tenons.

The jig can be made using scraps of hardwood and either plywood or MDF. The large top especially must be square and flat. The smaller top helps support the router. The stop is a job-specific fitting;

make a new one for each tenoning job, and screw it in place.

Router Trammel

Any number of the projects in this book call for you to cut circles or arcs. The Deck Table's top is round. The Porch Rocker's runners are arcs. The most common way to cut circles or arcs in woodworking is with a router and trammel.

Your router may have one among its accessories; sometimes a trammel is incorporated into a edge guide. But when you need a trammel right now, it's easy to cut out an oversized plywood baseplate, mount the router on one end—just stick it on with carpet tape—and drive a nail for a pivot at the other. **(Photo 36)** Locate the pivot point by measuring

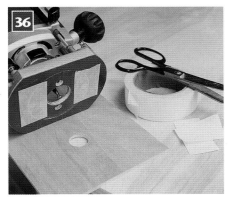

Two patches of carpet tape *(which is sticky on both sides) is all it takes to securely bond a router to a strip of ¹/₄-in. plywood, forming a trammel. Squeezing them together with a clamp improves the bond.*

from the appropriate side of the bit hole. **(Photo 37)**

A more elaborate and continuously adjustable trammel can usually be made to fit the same rods the router's edge guide uses. **(Photo 38)** One such trammel is shown in the drawing at right. This trammel won't leave a nail or screw hole as evidence of having been used. The critical part is the acrylic plastic pivot plate, which you stick to the work—temporarily—with carpet tape. The square plate has a hole at dead center. The pivot bolt in the trammel block projects just enough to catch in this pivot hole, but not enough to bottom in that hole and scratch the workpiece. The plastic plate is durable and bonds well to the tape. You adjust the radius of the circle at the router or at the trammel block.

Whatever trammel you use, cutting arcs and circles is the natural turf of the plunge router. **(Photo 38)** The plunger makes it easy to get the bit into the work, and to deepen the cut after each lap. Nevertheless, this doesn't mean you can only do this work with a plunge router. Especially if you are cutting an arc (as in making runners for a rocking chair), you can begin and end each pass with the bit clear of the work at one end of the arc or the other, and thus could easily use a fixed-base router.

When you are routing a circle or an arc using a trammel, in general you want to feed the tool in a counterclockwise direction. **(Photo 39)** This will keep you out of trouble. A clockwise feed yields a climb cut, which you don't want.

TENONING SEQUENCE

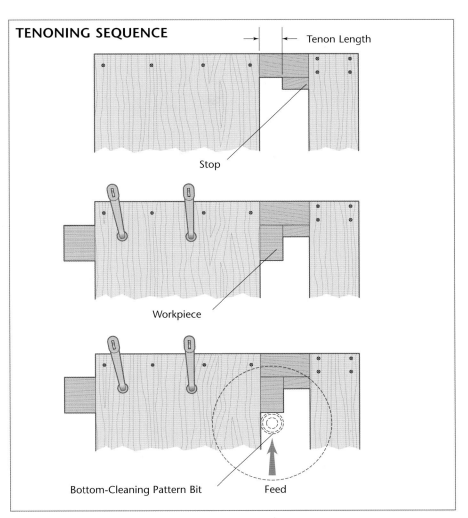

Tenon Length

Stop

Workpiece

Bottom-Cleaning Pattern Bit

Feed

TRAMMEL PLAN

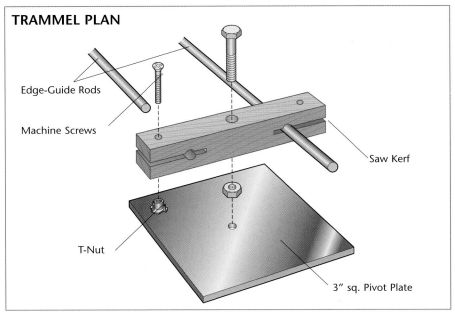

Edge-Guide Rods

Machine Screws

T-Nut

Saw Kerf

3" sq. Pivot Plate

To locate the pivot, measure from the bit with a ruler. Remember that the bit cuts a groove, and which side of it you measure from is different, depending on which side of the piece you are cutting.

Trammels are the key to cutting smooth arcs and circles in templates and workpieces. You can make your own trammels out of thin plywood, or there are several companies that make them to fit most routers.

Once you locate the pivot point and screw the trammel to the work, cutting the circle really is quite simple. Note that the arc is being cut in a counterclockwise direction, which keeps the bit in line.

This is a safety issue primarily because climb cuts are such grabby, galloping cuts. The worst situation happens when you are cutting a circle from a square. The bit is cutting a groove as it rounds off the corners of the square, but it's forming the edge elsewhere around the circumference. The bit can dig in and jerk the router as it exits the groove and begins making an edge cut. At the least, it will give you a start. But if the pivot isn't set securely, it can be jerked out of position.

Feed direction also becomes a quality issue because of chip-out. Chip-out occurs as the cutting edge of the bit sweeps off the wood, taking chips out of the edge. There's often a temptation to make a climb cut to avoid chip-out. In a climb cut, the cutting edge is sweeping into the wood, forcing the wood fibers in so there are no chips lifting out. A safer approach is to make a light finish cut in the proper, counterclockwise feed direction, to clean up the edge.

Templates

A template provides a quick and easy way to produce multiples of parts with somewhat complicated contours, like a leg with a kink in it, a curved rail for a chair, or a cut-out apron for a table or shelf. You can also use a template to make identical joinery cuts in part after part. Typically, a router is the tool that the template guides. **(Photo 40)**

Although computer-controlled routers are rapidly taking over such work in production settings, professional woodworkers still use templates to help them create stacks of identical parts. You can consistently contour the edges of workpieces by clamping a template to the blank for the part and then guiding the router around the perimeter of the template. Its bit will machine the workpiece to the same contour as the template. And every part cut using the template will be identical. This is how you make identical back legs for a set of four chairs, for example.

But the technique is a good one to use, even when you only have one or two parts to make. Routers can do very precise work when guided by a template. In addition, the material best suited for templates (medium-density fiberboard, otherwise known as MDF) is inexpensive and easily worked.

You may find it less laborious—not to mention less stressful—to make a template when the part you need for your project has a curved or otherwise complex

contour. If you goof, you haven't trashed a valuable board, you've just trashed a cheap piece of MDF.

Once you try any of these techniques, you'll recognize the ease and reliability of template-guided work. The potential is tremendous.

Two Guidance Setups

There are two different guide systems commonly used with templates in the home shop. In the first a collar or bushing attached to the base of the router rides along the template edge, guiding the router as it cuts. In the second system, a flush-trimming type of bit with a bearing either on the shank or on the bit tip is used to make the cut. The bearing rides along the template. Each system has its pros and cons.

Guide Bushings. This is what most woodworkers think of when template-guided work is discussed.

A guide bushing, sometimes called a template guide or guide collar, is a lot like a big washer with a short tube stuck in it. The bushing fits into the bit opening in the baseplate, and the bit projects through the tube. In use, the tube—called the collar—catches the edge of the template and rides along it. And the bit that's jutting through the collar makes the cut. Though it is slightly offset from the template, the cut nevertheless re-creates the template contour. **(Photo 41)**

While some router manufacturers provide a guide-bushing system specific to their routers, most have simply adopted the popular Porter-Cable system. In this design, the bushing drops into a rabbet around the bit opening so it will be flush with the baseplate surface. A threaded section projects up through the opening, and you turn a lock ring onto it, trapping the router's baseplate between the bushing and the lock ring, thus securing the bushing to the router. With this design, you can often change bushings without touching the bit. In fact, you may not even have to change the depth-of-cut setting. A big plus with this universal design, to me, is that you can buy guide bushings from a variety of sources. You aren't limited to the range of sizes made by the router manufacturer.

The size of the bushing is determined not by the overall diameter, which is the same for all bushings, but by the outside diameter of the protruding collar. You have to use a bushing with an inside

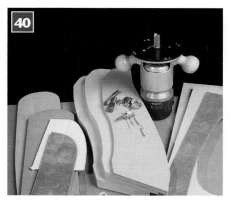

Templates help you make multiple copies of identical parts and give you the chance to shape a part in detail before you have to cut into expensive stock. MDF and some plywoods make good templates.

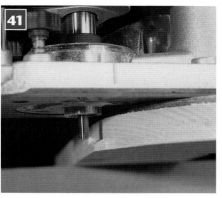

The advantage a template guide has is that it doesn't move as the depth of cut is changed. You can make a series of trimming cuts, increasing the depth of cut incrementally, until the full edge is trimmed.

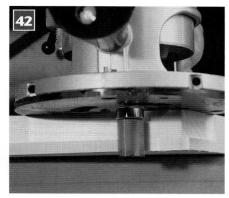

Sometimes a pattern bit isn't long enough to trim the full edge. First trim around the template, cutting as deep as you can, then remove the template, and make a pass with the bearing riding on the first cut.

diameter (I.D.) larger than the diameter of your bit. Most of the time, you'll find yourself using a collar that's at least $\frac{1}{8}$ inch bigger than the cutter.

You have to figure the offset into the size and shape of your template. The template cannot be the same size as the finished piece. See the "Calculating Offset" drawing, right, for details.

Here's an example: if you are using a $\frac{3}{4}$-inch-diameter bushing and a $\frac{3}{8}$-inch-diameter bit, the template offset will be $\frac{3}{16}$ inch. Remember, you've got to add the offset to each guiding edge of your template. In this example, to rout a 1x3-inch mortise, you'd need a template slot that measures $1\frac{3}{8}$x$3\frac{3}{8}$ inches.

Because of the need to accommodate the offset when laying out the template, setting up for template-guided routing does take extra time.

Pattern Bits. This simplest form of template-guided routing is done with either a flush-trimming bit or a pattern bit. Both have pilot bearings that are exactly the same as the bit's cutting diameter. There's no offset with these bits. On a flush-trimming bit, the bearing is at the tip of the bit. On a pattern bit, the bearing is on the shank, right above the flutes. **(Photo 42)**

Make the template (sometimes called a pattern) exactly the shape you want (limited only by the bit diameter). You don't even have to make a template in many cases. Instead, make the first of the actual parts especially carefully, then use it as the template and make as many more as you want. They'll all be the same.

Which System to Use?

Guide bushings offer several advantages over the piloted pattern bits.

Because they work in conjunction with your regular router bits, you save money—no special bits to buy.

But the BIG advantage is that the guide bushing is in a fixed position, regardless of the depth of cut. The bushing's design allows you to alter the depth of cut at will, and if you are using a plunge router, to change the cutting depth on the fly. Regardless of how much or how little you extend the bit, the guide is next to

the baseplate. This makes the system the only one you can use for plunge cuts. The guide is against the template, preventing the dynamics of the spinning bit from carrying it into the template itself as you plunge it into the work to begin the cut. This isn't the case with a pattern bit. Until the spinning bit has plunged deep enough to align the bearing with the template, you have little control over it.

With pattern and flush-trimming bits, on the other hand, the guide bearing changes position with every bit-height adjustment. With a flush-trimmer, the

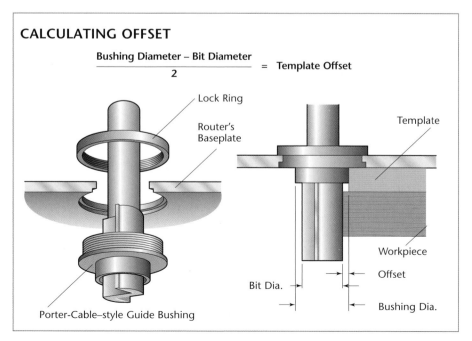

CALCULATING OFFSET

$$\frac{\text{Bushing Diameter} - \text{Bit Diameter}}{2} = \text{Template Offset}$$

Lock Ring

Router's Baseplate

Porter-Cable–style Guide Bushing

Template

Workpiece

Offset

Bit Dia.

Bushing Dia.

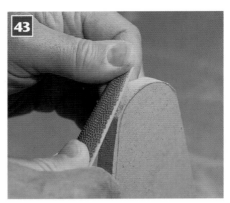

Although MDF is dense, it is easy to work. You can use a cabinetmaker's rasp, a file, or sandpaper to refine the edge, bringing it right to your layout lines. It's handwork, but it goes surprisingly quickly.

Having the right light will help you better see the imperfections and blemishes you are trying to remove when you sand. Set up a lamp so its light is directed across the surface of the piece that you are sanding.

cut has to go all the way through the workpiece on every pass, because the bearing is on the tip of the bit and the template is on the bottom of the work. With pattern bits, the guide is on top of the cutter. Unless the cutting edges are very short or the template very thick (or shimmed up somehow), you can't manage a shallow cut successfully.

The advantage these piloted bits have is in shaping parts, where you want to make a pattern that's exactly the size and contour you want. You don't have to struggle with the offset. The routine, with piloted bits, is to trim the workpiece as close to the template as possible with a saber saw, then make a series of very shallow cuts with the bit, until the bearing comes in contact with the template.

The advantage in tasks like template-guided mortising goes to the guide bushing system. The advantage in shaping parts goes to the bearing-guided bit system. What you'll find as you go through the projects in this book is that both systems are called into play, and often on a single template.

Materials for Templates

For templates, you want to use material that's easy to work, stable, flat, and inexpensive. You want something that is available in big pieces, and something that has crisp, dense edges. So sheet goods immediately come to mind: plywood, particleboard, hardboard, MDF.

Plywood works, but it has quite a few disadvantages and drawbacks. It isn't always flat, and it isn't always cheap, especially not the grades best suited for templates. When you cut it, the surface veneers chip and splinter, leaving fuzzy, potentially inaccurate edges. Moreover, the edges are not easily worked with a rasp, file, or sandpaper. Plywood often has voids in its interior plies, and when they emerge at the edge, they are hazards. If a bearing dips into one, you've got both a botched workpiece and a botched template.

Particleboard also works. It is available in a wider range of thicknesses than other sheet goods, and it is inexpensive. But the "particles" it's made of are pretty coarse, and it isn't particularly dense. Consequently, its edges are tough to really smooth, and they are easily dented by pilot bearings.

Hardboard has the advantages of being cheap, dense, smooth, and uniform. Thicknesses are accurate. But the edges get fuzzy when cut. And the maximum thickness, $1/4$ inch, is inadequate for a lot of applications.

Medium-density fiberboard, commonly called MDF, is extremely flat and smooth. Thicknesses are very precise. It is heavy, about half again as heavy as a comparable piece of plywood. The dense, homogeneous character of MDF gives it great stability, making it a particularly fine material for templates. A router bit's pilot bearing won't compress its dense edges. Nevertheless, it is easy to quickly shape an edge with a cabinetmaker's rasp, a file, or even coarse sandpaper. **(Photo 43)**

It isn't problem-free, of course. Left unsealed, it will wick up moisture and swell, causing permanent changes in dimensions. But a film finish (like quick-drying shellac or water-based polyurethane) will prevent it from absorbing moisture. Finally, MDF turns to powder when you machine it. I mean POWDER. The fine dust gets everywhere. A good dust mask is a must.

Sanding and Sanders

One of the great mysteries of woodworking is sanding. Everyone hates doing it, yet the typical hobby woodworker wastes a lot of effort on it. He sands and sands and sands, continuing to labor long after the job has actually been completed.

The goal of sanding is straightforward: you want to remove mill marks—those ripples left by surfacing equipment used at the sawmill—and smooth the wood. After the finish has been applied, you want the wood to look and feel smooth.

If you remember anything from this section, remember that you don't have to sand endlessly, through finer and finer grits of sandpaper. Sand only until the mill marks and other defects are gone and the wood is smooth. The goal is to achieve this as quickly as possible, with as little effort as possible. And when you get there, quit, because you are finished.

Remember, too, that you get the best results with the least effort if you do as much of the sanding as possible before assembly. You'll be able to clamp individual parts to your bench, where you'll be able to sand in a comfortable position, with good light, using any sanding tool you want. You'll also avoid the trials of sanding already-assembled right-angle joints, such as those between legs and rails, without introducing cross-grain scratches.

Sanding Basics

Before you actually begin sanding, you should know a little bit about the gritty stuff—sandpaper—that you'll be using.

Sandpaper is graded from coarse to fine in numbered grits. The sequence is 60, 80, 100, 120, 150, 180, 220, 240, 280, 320, 360, 400, 500, 600, 1000, 1500, and 2000. Don't be overwhelmed by the range. For woodworking, you should start with 80-grit paper and work grit by grit all the way up to 150 grit. Sanding the bare wood with finer grits—180 or 220—will give it a more polished appearance, but once a finish is applied, it won't really look any better.

A belt sander is an aggressive tool built to remove stock in a hurry. It's usually best for smoothing rough boards and removing mill marks. If you get a variable speed model, you can slow it down for more delicate work.

A good pad sander makes quick work of cleaning lumber. It typically uses one-quarter sheet of sandpaper, so this compact tool can get into fairly tight spots and can even sand some parts after assembly.

A random orbit sander has a pad that rotates as well as oscillates, so it smoothes a surface faster. Many models incorporate integral dust collection, actually drawing the dust up through holes in the sanding pad.

There are several types of sandpaper, but for woodworking tasks, you will almost always get the best results with garnet paper, which is orange-to-red in color, or aluminum-oxide paper, which is tan-to-brown. For sanding between coats of a finish, the best sandpaper to use is silicon carbide, which is available in stearated and wet-dry versions. Stearated silicon carbide paper, which is usually a gray color, contains a metallic soap (the stearate) as a lubricant to keep the grit from clogging with sanding dust. The wet/dry sandpaper, which is black, has the grit bonded to the paper with waterproof glue, allowing you to use water or some other fluid as a lubricant.

Whether you work by hand or with a power sander, there are really only two steps to sanding: removing the blemishes, then removing the scratches from step one.

Using a coarse grit sandpaper for the first step is appropriate. But you can reduce the work involved in the second step if you don't use a paper that's more coarse than necessary. In other words, don't automatically hit every board with a 60-grit sanding belt. If you can get the mill marks out quickly with 80 grit or 100 grit, use that instead, and you'll have one or two fewer grits to cycle through to smooth the board.

You need good light to get good results. Set up a task light at the end of your workbench, and adjust its angle so the light rakes across the work. Play around with it a little, and when the light is correctly set, you'll be surprised at obvious planer marks and scratches and other blemishes. **(Photo 44)**

Sand the workpiece with a coarse sandpaper to remove mill marks and the like. Just as soon as they are gone, stop. Brush the dust from the workpiece before changing to a finer grit. Be thorough. The dust will contain grit particles from the sandpaper you just used, and this grit will keep you from getting a uniform scratch pattern with the finer grit. Perform this cleanup after each sanding cycle.

Sand with the next finer grit, working until you can see no more improvement. The goal is to create a uniform pattern of scratches in the wood surface. You will always have scratches, because that's what the sandpaper does—it scratches the wood. But as you progress through finer grits, the scratches become tinier and closer together and fainter, and in essence, they disappear. So use that task light, and examine the work. Don't jump too quickly to a finer grit, a common mistake, but don't obsess over it either.

While you dare not skip any grits if you are sanding by hand, it is fairly common to leapfrog grits when doing the job with a power sander. The sander's greater speed makes up the difference.

Regardless of your final grit, you won't remove all of the tiny wood fibers that swell and make the wood rough to the touch if it gets wet. To eliminate these, you need to "sponge the wood" or "raise the grain" after your normal sanding. To do this, wet the wood, getting it thoroughly damp. Allow it to dry overnight. Then resand it, using sandpaper at least as fine as the last grit used. Don't overdo it. All you want to do is remove the raised fiber, nothing more.

Finally, don't be stingy with the sandpaper. The cutting efficiency of sandpaper declines quickly, and once it dulls, you are wasting your elbow grease. You'll shorten the time you spend sanding dramatically by changing sandpaper more often.

Sanding Tools

Many types of sanding tools are available. Detail sanders, quarter-sheet sanders, half-sheet sanders, stationary disk/belt sanders, edge sanders, and more. The three sanders, all portables, that make the most sense in a small start-up shop are the belt sander, the pad sander, and the random-orbit sander. With the belt sander, you can quickly remove the mill marks, both subtle and obvious, from lumber off the rack or just out of the thickness planer. The pad sander and the random-orbit sander both can help you deal with smoothing out the belt sander's scratches

Belt Sander. This common power tool has an abrasive belt mounted on rollers like the tracks on a bulldozer. Between the rollers is a flat platen, and it is this plate the determines how much of the abrasive belt is in contact with the work. **(Photo 45)** Belts and belt sanders are made in a variety of sizes, and the most common are 3 by 21 inches, 3 by 24 inches, and 4 by 24 inches.

Sanders are made in transverse and in-line configurations. In the transverse style, the motor is mounted crosswise. These models are taller and heavier, generally, than the in-line style. Weight isn't a bad thing in a belt sander. In the wood-

Quick-action bar clamps

Pipe clamps

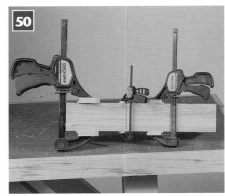
Trigger clamps

working shop, almost all your sanding will be performed with the machine flat on the work; you lift the tool on and off the work, but when it is running, its weight is supported by the work. The weight stabilizes it and helps it cut aggressively.

Aggressive sanding is what a belt sanders is all about. It can remove nicks and dents, snipe and other mill marks, and general roughness in nothing flat. The trade-off is that belt sanders require your full attention; a lapse in concentration and a wobble can result in a sizable trough or swale instead of a flat, smooth surface.

Pad Sander. The pad sander is much tamer than a belt sander, and in turn, it is much less effective at removing wood. But it is intended to complement an aggressive tool like the belt sander, not compete with it. It's a sander that you put into play for the last couple of sanding cycles.

A number of models are on the market. Larger ones take a third- or half-sheet of sandpaper. Palm sanders typically take a quarter-sheet of sandpaper. **(Photo 46)** The low-end pad sanders vibrate, but the better ones oscillate, orbiting between 10,000 and 20,000 times a minute. This orbital motion leaves swirls of scratches on the wood surface, which are all but invisible until you get the finish on. Then, of course, they are very obvious.

Here are some tricks to minimize the scratching. First, switch on the sander and let it build up speed before setting it on the wood. Then, don't press on the machine, because that slows it down. Keep the sander moving slowly back and forth in the direction of the grain. Finally, finish off the job by hand. Sand with fine sandpaper and a sanding block, in the direction of the grain.

Random-Orbit Sander. If what you want is a glassy-smooth surface, the belt sander isn't your choice. The random-orbit sander definitely is. The tool combines rotary and orbital actions so it can remove material quickly without being hard to control. Although the manufacturers claim these sanders can produce a scratch-free surface, even when sanding across the grain, it isn't entirely true.

Random-orbit sanders are made in several configurations, and whichever you buy should be influenced by the work you'll use it for.

The right-angle sander has the motor oriented horizontally. It transmits power to the sanding pad via bevel gears. If aggressive stock removal is what you need most, this is the model for you. It is more powerful than the others styles, but it also noisy and vibrates a lot. Because the motor is offset from the pad, right-angle sanders aren't particularly well balanced. Two-hand operation is a must; one hand grasps the motor housing, the other a handle that projects from the gearcase.

The palm-grip sander is, perhaps, the most familiar random-orbit sander, and it's the favorite of those planning to do mostly finish sanding with the tool. It is compact and is designed to be held in one hand. **(Photo 47)**

The secret of the random-orbit sander's scratch-free work is that its pad freewheels on a shaft that is eccentric from the driveshaft. Consequently, the pad's rotation (or orbit) is totally random; each new orbit cancels out scratches left from prior rotations.

A problem with the first generation of random-orbit sanders was that the sanding pad would pick up speed—rather dramatically so—when it was lifted from

the workpiece. Setting it back on the work was dicey; the sander would jerk around, often leaving noticeable swirl marks. The solution is a pad brake. Don't buy a sander without one.

Some random-orbit sanders are designed to use pressure-sensitive-adhesive backed (PSA-type) disks, while others take hook-and-loop disks. The advantage of the PSA disks is lower cost. But the adhesive often degrades in a hot environment, losing its stick. Dust can contaminate it. And on the other hand, the disks sometimes get stuck a little too securely to the sanding pad. Moreover, once the disk has been peeled off the pad, it can't be reapplied. Hook-and-loop disks, on the other hand, can be removed and reused easily.

Clamps

One of woodworking's oldest sayings is, "You can never have too many clamps." Well, OK. But there are so many styles and sizes and specialty designs are on the market, it is almost impossible to keep track of them all. You can easily be overcome with bewilderment.

The clamps used in constructing the outdoor furniture in this book are shown here. While there are less than a dozen styles, most are used in several sizes. It's enough to foster a sense that you do have altogether too many of the things— until you start to clamp up a big project.

Bar Clamp. The workhorse clamp in any woodshop is the fast-action bar clamp. **(Photo 48)** You'll find yourself using them to secure workpieces to the workbench, to mount temporary fences to machines or workpieces, for assembly work, and for countless other tasks.

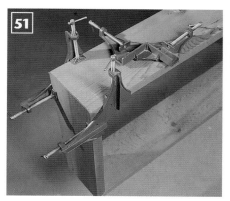

Corner clamps

Spring clamps

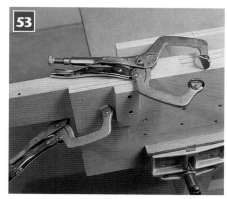

Vise-Grip® C-clamps

A quick-action clamp has a fixed jaw and an adjustable jaw, both mounted on a steel bar. The adjustable jaw has a threaded adjuster with a swivel foot and handle. You set the fixed jaw on the work, slide the adjustable one against the opposing surface, then turn the handle to tighten the clamp. Many of these clamps are sold with plastic pads to slip onto the contact surfaces on the jaws, so the pronounced tendency of these clamps to dent the work is minimized. Buy the pads separately if they aren't part of the clamp. In any event, to really protect the wood, you need to slip wood scraps, often called cauls, between the good wood and the clamp jaws.

The two variables in sizing these clamps are the opening capacity and the throat depth. The maximum possible span between the jaws is controlled by the bar length, and capacities range from 6 inches to 36 inches. The throat depth is the distance from the jaw tip to the bar, and it governs how far in on a board the clamp will reach. Typically, the clamp's

overall bulk is proportional to the throat depth; as the throat gets deeper, both the jaw and the bar get beefier. A clamp with a thicker and/or wider bar can exert more pressure with less flex.

The clamps applied across the box in the photo should give you a sense of the range and proportions of clamp sizes. The clamp at the left front corner is undoubtedly the most commonplace size. Its slightly deeper-throated kin at the right front is surprisingly useful because it can reach a little deeper, and clamp a little more securely.

Pipe Clamp. The pipe clamp is used primarily when edge-gluing boards to create wide panels and when assembling cabinets and the like. **(Photo 49)** The clamp consists of a pair of jaws that you mount on a length of steel plumbing pipe. One jaw, which incorporates a coarse-thread screw adjuster, is threaded onto one end of the pipe. The other jaw is infinitely adjustable along the pipe's length. Two sizes are available, those for ½-inch pipe (the red one in this photo)

and those for ¾-inch pipe (the orange one).

You buy the black or galvanized pipe separately. Buy 18- to 24-inch lengths for small glue-ups, 36-inch lengths for wide tabletops or casework, even longer lengths if you get into making truly wide tables. If you are on a tight budget, you can buy two or three different lengths of pipe for each jaw set you get, then switch pipes according to the demands of the task. To transform short pipe clamps into long ones, use pipe couplings to join two pipes end-to-end.

The black pipe is cheaper and more accurately sized. Because it is slightly softer, the adjustable jaw digs in better and its less likely to slip as you tighten the screw-jaw. Black pipe can leave black marks on the workpiece, which the galvanized pipe is less likely to do.

Trigger Clamp. Largely because they can be applied with one hand, Trigger clamps are very popular. **(Photo 50)** To tighten one on an assembly or workpiece, you simply squeeze the large trigger incor-

C-clamps

K-body clamps

Hand-screw clamps

Tools & Techniques

Cordless drills can handle almost any task that their corded ancestors did, without the hassle of a cord. Most come with two batteries so you'll always have one charged.

If you've already got one, a corded drill will also work fine for these furniture projects. For projects that are assembled in place, such as the Hammock Stand, just use a long extension cord to gain access to the work.

porated into the pistol-grip handle. This "walks" the adjustable jaw along the clamp's bar, pinching the work between it and the fixed jaw. This action allows you to hold parts together with one hand, while you apply the clamp with the other. Trigger clamps are available in various lengths up to 60 inches.

Corner Clamp. The ranks of clamps are filled with special-purpose designs. One such, useful in making a project or two in this book, is the corner clamp. **(Photo 51)** It has a right-angle fence and two screw-adjusted feet, one opposite each face of the fence. Its use is limited to holding two pieces at right angles to one another, hence the name. While the clamp won't "close" the joint for you, it will hold it closed while glue sets or while you drive fasteners into it.

Spring Clamp. A light-duty clamp that can be useful is the spring clamp. **(Photo 52)** The jaws are spread open simply by squeezing the two handles together, typically a one-handed operation. Position the jaws on the work, and release the handles. The jaws close firmly, even on work that doesn't have parallel faces. Spring clamps are plenty strong for holding things together during layout and assembly, and for glue-ups on small objects too. They are perfect for holding stop blocks, as shown on page 25.

Two types are available. The old standbys are made of metal with slip-on soft plastic pads on the tips and the handles. Composite plastic ones are also on the market. The soft jaws on these are more

substantial, providing delicate workpieces with better protection from pressure damage. A range of sizes is available in both styles.

Vise-Grip® Clamp. These may not seem to have a place in woodworking, but the style with C-clamp jaws do. **(Photo 53)** This clamp works with the familiar locking-grip action. Squeeze the plier handles in one hand to close and lock the jaws. Press the release trigger between thumb and a couple fingers to unlock the clamp, allowing its jaws to swing open freely. The type to use has swivel pressure-pads (and soft-plastic caps for the pads are available); it is available in three sizes (the middle size shown on page 25). The gap between the jaws is adjusted by turning the knurled knob projecting from one handle. Once the gap is established, you can close and open the clamp again and again; the jaws will always snap closed on the work with the same amount of pressure. This feature eliminates a lot of the clamping busywork that accompanies production-like work, such as clamping one workpiece after another in a mortising fixture.

C-Clamp. The oldest style of all-metal clamp, the C-clamp gets its name from its shape. **(Photo 54)** It exerts enormous clamping pressure. The sliding T-bar on the threaded adjuster allows you to crank it much tighter than if it simply had a spindle handle, like the typical quick-action clamp. One drawback here, of course, is the small contact area; the wood is almost guaranteed to be dented by the

pads on the screw and the clamp body, so you need to use cauls. Another drawback is that this type of clamp can be tedious to apply and remove, because the only way to do either job is by turning and turning and turning its T-handle. Quick-action and trigger clamps do most of the same jobs as a C-clamp, and though they aren't as strong, they are strong enough for most jobs, and they are much faster to apply and remove.

C-clamps are made in a wide array of sizes (lengths and throat depths) and variations. You ought to have a modest assortment of at least the smaller sizes—clamps with 2-inch, 3-inch, and 4-inch openings are shown on page 25. These are great for immobilizing stop blocks, particularly if they are likely to be butted roughly by board after board.

K-Body Clamp. The K-body clamp, made only by Bessey, is a hybrid of the pipe clamp and the quick-action clamp. **(Photo 55)** It looks like the latter style, but with very blocky, plastic-covered jaws.

To apply the clamp, you capture the work between the two jaws, sliding the adjustable jaw snug. Then you twist the handle to increase the clamp pressure. The main difference is in those flat-faced jaws. They are square to the bar and parallel to each other, and they remain that way even under heavy pressure. Pressure is distributed evenly along the full $17/16$ by 5-inch face of each jaw, not concentrated in small pads, as is the case with a quick-action clamp. The adjustable jaw isn't sloppy; it doesn't wiggle as you snug it against a workpiece, as does a pipe clamp's jaw.

The upshot is that when two or more boards are clamped edge to edge in K-body clamps, they are more likely to stay flat and aligned than when you clamp them with pipe clamps. You can use the clamps more easily to help square an assembly because the clamp itself is better aligned. The jaws are much less likely to dent or crush the edges of the work. The plastic shells on the jaws make them resistant to glue.

Not to be overlooked is their stability, the blocky jaws provide secure footing for the clamps; they'll stand on their own, either horizontally or vertically. You can set them on your benchtop, and they won't roll over when you lay the work on the bars.

The trade-off is a substantial price tag, one that's 30 percent or more higher than comparable sized quick-action clamps,

If your drill has a ⅜-in. chuck, you'll need to buy larger-diameter bits with stepped-down shanks, so that they'll fit your drill's chuck. Brad-point bits have a pointed tip to keep them from walking.

Forstner bits cut flat-bottomed, smooth-walled holes. They are great for counterbores in soft wood. The Forstner isn't really a good general-purpose bit, because it cuts slowly and tends to clog with chips.

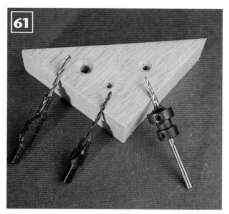

The quickest way to drill pilot holes is with a drill-countersink combo. These have a countersink bit fitted over a twist drill bit. You'll need two sizes for the projects in this book—the 6- and 8-gauge screw sizes.

and easily two to three times more than a pipe clamp.

Hand-Screw Clamp. The modern hand screw clamp is a clear descendant of an ancient, all-wood clamp. **(Photo 56)** In the original version, threaded wooden spindles link two wooden jaws, and by turning both spindles at the same time, you can open and close the jaws.

In the descendant, the spindles are metal with wooden grips, and they are threaded through nuts captured in the jaws. The nuts can pivot, so that in addition to simply opening and closing the jaws, you can offset one from the other, and you can adjust them so they are at an angle to one another. The jaws continue to be made of wood, and this makes them much less likely to mar your workpieces. Waxing them from time to time won't hinder their purchase on the work, but it will prevent glue from bonding to them.

Hand-screw clamps are not all-purpose clamps, but they are particularly good for laminations, the type shown in the photo on page 25. The jaws are long and flat, and thus you can apply intense pressure on broad areas (as opposed to isolated points). In the example shown, the pressure is applied evenly from edge to edge.

Sizes range from the baby No. 5/0, with 4-inch jaws that open a maximum of 2 inches, up to the Papa Bear No. 6, with 20-inch jaws

that open to 10 inches. As the jaw size increases, the spindle length does too.

Drill/Driver and Bits

It's probably the least-expensive power tool in the shop, but it's used on virtually every project. We call them drills but use them to drive screws as well. You've got to have at least one in your shop, and many

TOOL TIP

You're going to break a screw or two during the course of any construction project, even if you drill pilot holes. When it happens, use a pair of Vise-Grip® pliers to grab the shank and turn it out of the hole.

woodworkers have three or more, in both corded and cordless versions.

Look at cordless models first, **(Photo 57)** since they have a better combination of features than corded models. **(Photo 58)** The latter tend to be engineered either as drills or as screwdrivers. Cordless models, on the other hand, combine these functions in one tool. They also eliminate the cord to the outlet, freeing you to move around the shop, nosing in, over, under, and around the project you've assembled.

The power of cordless tools seems to be constantly increasing. The first cordless drills depended on 7.2-volt batteries for juice. Then it jumped to 12 volts, then 14.4, and now 20-volt and even 24-volt tools are for sale. With each increase in voltage, you'll find increases in speed and torque. The more work you expect from your drill, the more you will value the extra power of a powerful battery.

Other improvements incorporated into cordless drills include the adjustable clutch and the electronic brake. The former allows you to dial in a torque setting for driving screws; when the preset torque level is hit, the clutch disengages and the chuck stops turning. There's always a "locked-in" setting for drilling, of course. The electronic brake stops the chuck as soon as you release the trigger. No more waiting for the drill bit to

Tools & Techniques

Use a plug cutter to make wooden plugs to cover up the screw heads on your projects. The cutter is not easy to use with a handheld drill. Best results come with a drill mounted in a stand or a drill press.

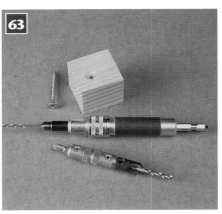

Drill-and-driver sets speed assembly. Chuck the socket into your drill. Drill the pilot hole, then pop the bit holder out of the socket, turn it end-for-end, and reinsert it. The screwdriver bit will now be in position.

stop spinning before you can position it for the next hole.

Another improvement that seems to have accompanied the cordless drill's development is the keyless chuck, which allows you to loosen and tight the chuck by hand.

The big shortcoming of the portable drill, of course, is the variable results of handheld operations. If you need a hole drilled at a precise angle, you need to use a guide, either shop-made or manufactured. The doweling jig may be the most-common drill guide, but there are also attachments that help hold a portable drill at an angle.

Twist Drill. The twist drill bit is the all-purpose hole-maker with which everyone is familiar. The same bit you use to drill holes in wood will also work in plastic and metal. **(Photo 59)** Twist drills are available individually and in sets, in fractional, decimal, wire, letter, and metric sizes, and in several different lengths. The jobber length, which varies from about 2 inches up to 4 inches, is the most common. The big sets, which include all the fractional sizes from $1/16$ to $1/2$-inch by 64ths, all the letter sizes, and all the wire sizes, run to 115 bits. You don't need anywhere near that many, and probably will find a 29-piece set of fractional sizes ($1/16$ through

$1/2$-inch) more than adequate.

Forstner Bit. The design of the Forstner bit combines a tiny center point with cutting rims and chisel-like cutting edges. **(Photo 60)** The point locates the hole, the rims score its circumference, and the cutting edges essentially plane its bottom. The result is a flat-bottomed, smooth-walled hole. There are times when you

TOOL TIP

Carpet tape is sticky on both sides, so it's perfect for attaching templates to blanks. Keep a roll on hand, and a pair of scissors right next to it. All it takes is a couple of squares to secure most templates.

need this type of hole, and this is the bit that will produce it for you. I find it does a great job on counterbores in the woods best-suited for outdoor uses (which tend to be soft).

The Forstner isn't really a good general-purpose bit, because it cuts slowly and tends to clog with chips. You need to withdraw the bit from the hole frequently to clear chips. The range of sizes begins at $1/4$ inch and jumps in $1/16$-inch increments to 1 inch, then jumps in $1/8$-inch increments to $3^{1}/2$ inches. The larger bits can be very difficult to control in a hand-held drill.

Countersink Bits. The most expeditious way to drill pilot holes for screws is with a combination drill-countersink. **(Photo 61)** These assemblies have countersink-counterbore cutter fitted over a twist drill bit. You can adjust how far out of the cutter body the bit extends, and you can replace the drill bit. (The bits break readily where they emerge from the cutter body.) The assemblies are labeled according to screw gauges, and for the projects in this book, you really need only the Nos. 6 and 8 bits. The most commonly available styles use regular bits, and they work fine for decking screws, which aren't tapered. The unit on the left does have a tapered drill bit; it is available in woodworking specialty stores and through mail order.

Plug Cutter. If you want to conceal the screws used to assemble your outdoor furniture, you'll need a plug cutter. **(Photo 62)** The cutter bores into the face or edge grain of wood scraps to produce plugs that blend right into the surrounding material. Because the plug is tapered, it's easy to insert into a counterbore. The deeper into the hole you push it, the tighter it gets. (Dowels don't work nearly as well, because they aren't tapered, and because they become unattractive little end-grain islands in your project's expanses of face grain.) The $3/8$-inch-diameter size plug cutter is right for decking screws of all lengths. The style shown here is usually found in home centers, although other styles are available through specialty stores and mail order. The cutter is not easy to use with a handheld drill. Try a drill mounted in a stand or a drill press.

Screwdriver Bits. Few people drive screws by hand these days. The cordless drill/driver does it for us, using special screwdriver bits. You can still buy Phillips bits, but power drills tend to chew these up and strip screws. This led to the invention of square-drive screws which are better, but have now been mostly surplanted by star-drive screws which hold the bit very securely and almost never strip.

Drill-and-Drive Set. These sets are handy when assembling furniture. **(Photo 63)** Instead of using two drill/drivers, one to drill pilot holes, the other to drive the screws, you need only a single drill and one of these sets. You chuck the tool socket in the drill. A bit holder, with a combination pilot drill-countersink in one end and a screwdriver bit in the other, fits into the socket. Drill the pilot hole, then pop the bit holder out of the socket, turn it end-for-end, and reinsert it. The screwdriver bit will now be at the ready. You can easily make the switch with one hand, while holding the drill in the other.

RESOURCE GUIDE

Bosch Power Tools
S-B Power Tool Company
4300 West Peterson Avenue
Chicago, IL 60646-5999
1-877-267-2499
www.boschtools.com
Manufacturer of power tools and accessories (including router bits); sells through distributors.

DeWalt Industrial Tools Co.
Consumer Service Div.
626 Hanover Pike
Hampstead, MD 21074
1-800-433-9258
www.dewalt.com
Manufacturer of power tools; sells through distributors.

Jepson Power Inc.
90 Grand Avenue. Apt. E1
Hackensack, NJ 07601
201-916-4709
www.jepsontpower.com
Manufacturer of power tools and accessories; sells through distributors.

Lee Valley Tools, Ltd.
PO Box 1780
Ogdensburg, NY 13669-6780
1-800-871-8158
www.leevalley.com
Manufacturer and direct-mail retailer of woodworking tools, hardware, finishing supplies, and more.

Makita
Makita USA
14930 Northam Street
La Mirada, CA 90638
1-800-462-5482
www.makitatools.com
Manufacturer of power tools and accessories; sells through distributors.

McFeely's
1620 Wythe Road
PO Box 11169
Lynchburg, VA 24506-1169
1-800-443-7937
www.mcfeelys.com
Sells a variety of fasteners, drill and router bits, finishing supplies, and other tools.

Milwaukee
13135 W. Lisbon Road
Brookfield, WI 53005
1-800-729-3878
Milwaukeetool.com
Manufacturer of power tools and accessories; sells through distributors.

Porter-Cable
4825 Highway 45 North
PO Box 2468
Jackson, TN 38302-2468
1-800-487-8665
www.portercable.com
Manufacturer of power tools; sells through distributors.

Rockler Woodworking and Hardware
4365 Willow Drive
Medina, MN 55340
1-800-279-4441
www.rockler.com
Sells a broad range of tools, hardware, and finishing supplies through the mail and operates a number of retail stores.

Ryobi Power Tools
One World Technologies Inc.
P.O. Box 1207
Anderson , SC 29625
www.ryobitools.com
Manufacturer of power tools and accessories; sells through distributors.

Whiteside Machine Company
4506 Shook Road
Claremont, NC 28610
1-800-225-3982
www.whitesiderouterbits.com
Manufacturer of router bits; sells through distributors and on-line.

Woodcraft
210 Wood County Industrial Park
PO Box 1686
Parkersburg, WV 26102-1686
1-800-535-4482
www.woodcraft.com
Retailer of woodworking tools and accessories, hardware, supplies; sells online, via direct mail and through 72 retail outlets.

Materials

Tables and chairs you make for your patio, deck, and yard can be just as elegant as furniture you make for your house. But outdoor furniture has to withstand exposure to the morning dew, harsh afternoon sunlight, drenching spring rains, and maybe even winter weather. For the furniture you build to survive outside, you need to use sound construction techniques and build your projects with wood, glue, and fasteners that can stand up to the weather.

Yard and Garden Furniture

WOOD

You need to work with wood that is strong, warp-free, and attractive. For these projects, the wood also has to stand up to fungi, insects, moisture, and sunlight. Some woods, such as redwood, cedar and teak, have natural characteristics that make them good candidates for outdoor furniture. But you may not be able to find them in your local lumberyard or home center, or you may find inferior grades of the wood that can make woodworking difficult.

At a typical home center, you'll probably find that your choice of species is limited. And the wood they do have may be damp, warped, cupped, and riddled with knots. **(Photo 1)** You can sometimes work around knots, but the need to work exclusively with straight, flat boards is absolutely fundamental. What looked like a small bow at the lumber yard will come back to haunt you when you're cutting joints back in the shop. Lumber that's cupped or crooked or has any kind of twist can make a project very difficult, if not impossible to complete.

Outdoor Grades

No matter what wood you select, try to use the heartwood, which comes from the core of the tree. This wood is denser, stronger, more stable, and generally more decay-resistant than the surrounding sapwood. As its name suggests, sapwood conducts water and minerals from the roots to the leaves, so it contains a lot of moisture. Heartwood isn't as laden with moisture, and stays remarkably stable even through large swings in humidity that affect outdoor furniture.

In the real world, many boards have both heartwood and sapwood in them, so be choosy and avoid boards that are all or mostly sapwood. **(Photo 2)**

If you are shopping for redwood, it's easy to pick the heartwood because it's specified in the redwood grading system. For example, the best grade is called Clear All Heart. It's free of knots and is all heartwood. Clear is next best, covering boards that are free of knots but contain some sapwood.

Grading systems used for other types of

Lumber quality is a key component of any furniture project. You may be able to work around minor defects in a few boards, but it's difficult to deal with wood with open knots, cupping, wanes, or damage along the edges.

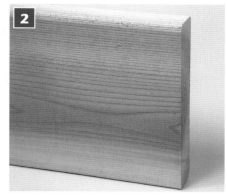

Buy heartwood for your outdoor furniture projects. It has the more attractive color and better decay resistance. Avoid boards that are all sapwood or have a significant percentage of sapwood, like this one.

lumber aren't as forthcoming. The softwood and hardwood lumber systems use different classifications and names but grade lumber according to the volume and character of knots and blemishes. But you don't have to pore over grading charts. Just zero in on clear stock. You'll pay extra for a top-quality grade, but your furniture project will look better and be easier to build.

You can combine different woods and finishes for striking effects.

Lumber Outlets

To find the clear grades you need, you may have to call around to see who stocks, or will order premium grade lumber. This is what I did to get the lumber for the furniture projects in the book.

Several projects are made of lumber that you should be able to find locally,

even in a home center. Some of the wood is stocked primarily for house framing, which means it is available in predictable thicknesses, widths, and lengths. By calling around, I found western red cedar, cypress, Douglas fir, eastern white pine, meranti, and other woods. I bought most of it from small, locally owned lumberyards that compete with the huge national chains by stocking some out-of-the-ordinary materials for decks, particularly cypress and meranti.

A committed woodworker, whether a hobbyist or a professional, might buy lumber from a specialty lumber dealer or even directly from a small local sawmill. The selection of species is likely to be broader. But you may be able to find good "outdoor" woods such as cypress and cedar at a local outlet.

In specialty outlets, you will find native hardwoods, some of which are great outdoor woods. And you might find several imported woods, such as Honduran mahogany, teak, and ipe. This lumber will probably be drier (down to 7 or 8 percent moisture content) and more stable in your projects as a result.

These boards are likely stockpiled in rough-sawn condition, in what is known as random widths and lengths. The thickness is pretty consistent, and will be expressed in quarter terms. For example,

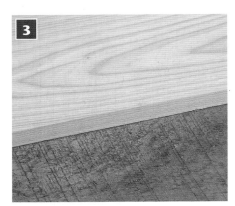

The edges of your lumber need to be square and true, and the thickness must be uniform. If you buy rough-cut boards, you'll need to have them dressed, or do the job yourself with a jointer and thickness-planer.

Allow your lumber to acclimate to the conditions in your shop by creating a stickered stack. Use 2x4s to keep the lumber off a concrete floor, and insert strips of wood, called stickers, between the layers.

a 1-inch-thick board will be listed as ⁴/₄ and called four-quarters, and a 2-inch-thick board will be listed as ⁸/₄ and called eight-quarters. The widths and the lengths will vary. At this kind of supply house, you will probably find prices determined by the board foot. This measurement covers length, width, and thickness. For example, one board foot is a piece of lumber that is 12 inches square and 1 inch thick. To add to the possible confusion, it's a nominal measurement, and as the stockperson tallies up your purchase, he'll round up.

Because this wood is rough-sawn, you will have to pay either the supplier or a local shop to dress it, or have a shop yourself that is equipped with a jointer

and a thickness-planer. You need these tools to put a square and uniform edge on your lumber **(Photo 3)** and to make all similar lumber in a project the same thickness. If you don't true up rough-cut lumber, you have no way of making tight joints or joining several narrow boards into a tabletop.

Lumber Storage

Allow at least a few days for your lumber to adjust to the humidity level in your shop. If you buy construction grades, they should have a moisture content no higher than 19 percent. But the lumber may be wetter or dryer than your shop and need some time to reach what's called equilibrium moisture content. You don't want to cut tight joints only to have them open up as the wood gives off excess moisture and twists.

For best results, stack your lumber off the floor with strips of wood between each layer to maximize air circulation. **(Photo 4)** Even a few days in a conditioned space can make quite a difference in wood that may have been stored under a shed roof.

Generally, low-density woods, such as cedar and redwood, have less tendency to warp, check, and change dimensions than high-density domestic woods, such as white oak and southern pine. However, some remarkably dense tropical species are quite stable.

Lumber Species

To keep the project manageable, all the material used in the furniture projects were purchased already dressed to the standard sizes. Here's a rundown about the species I used, as well as a few you might choose.

Cypress. (Photo 5) The heartwood varies in color, but typically is a warm tan with some darker streaks. If left unfinished, it will weather to a charcoal or black color with tan highlights. This relatively lightweight wood is strong, moderately hard, and straight grained. The best grades have a smooth texture and an almost waxy feel. Flatsawn grain can be flaky and separate along the annular rings when wet, so try to buy quarter-sawn stock that has straight grain. Standard, flat-sawn lumber has end grain roughly parallel with the board face, which makes the wood more likely to cup. More-expensive quarter-sawn lumber has end grain roughly perpendicular to the board, which makes it more stable.

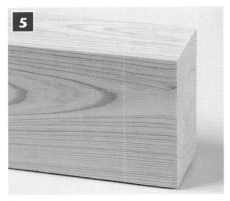

Cypress

Although cypress is resinous, it glues well, sands easily, and accepts finishes without a problem.

The lumber is sawed from the bald cypress tree, which grows in damp bottomlands along the southeastern coast and up the Mississippi basin as far as southern Illinois. It may be most available in the east and midwest.

The best stock for your outdoor furniture is, of course, the heartwood of old-growth trees. But old-growth lumber of any species is scarce. A fair amount of premium cypress is being cut from lost logs that are raised from swamp- and river-bottoms.

You may hear a variety of cypress names. Most of them stem from the color of the heartwood. White cypress is pale yellow, red cypress is reddish brown, and black cypress is dark green. Pecky cypress, prized for paneling, gets its name from a tunneling fungus that sometimes attacks older trees, creating galleries in the wood.

Douglas fir. (Photo 6) A resinous member of the pine family, and a softwood, Douglas fir (also known as Doug Fir) is relatively hard and strong. It is usually considered a construction timber, but it also serves well for furniture

The wood's clearly delineated grain pattern alternates between light areas of soft, fine-textured wood and darker streaks of more dense grain. Flatsawn boards commonly display a cathedral-shaped figure, while quarter-sawn boards, sold as VG (for vertical grain) yield a closely spaced pinstripe pattern.

The wood can be brittle and tend to splinter, which is a common problem on decking. But if you use sharp cutters, it machines well. However, drilling pilot

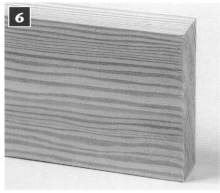

Douglas Fir

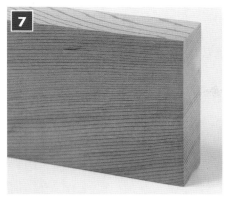

Western Red Cedar

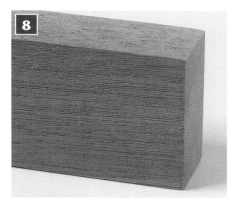

Meranti Mahogany

holes for screws is essential to avoid splitting the wood. It also glues well, and finishes easily with stains and clear finishes. You might have more trouble getting paint to adhere to it.

Western red cedar. (Photo 7) Because it is highly resistant to decay and rot, western red cedar has been used traditionally by Native Americans in the Pacific Northwest for totem poles, dugout canoes, and other outdoor applications. The wood is a dull red color when first cut, but loses most of its reddishness when exposed to the air and turns a handsome brown. The sapwood is quite white, and cedar boards may contain both sapwood and heartwood. It has a distinctive spicy odor that's quite different from the more pleasant odor of eastern red cedar. You'll find that prolonged or heavy exposure to the dust can be irritating.

The wood is light and very soft. Though it works easily, sharp tools are essential. It is prone to split. It is rather coarse in texture, but straight grained and very stable. Cedar is rich in tannins, so it is unwise to use any hardware containing iron.

Lumberyards typically stock common grades, but clear material seems to be readily available, though at a premium price. I used cedar for several projects, including the planter bench, the recliner, and the tree bench.

Meranti mahogany. (Photo 8) This wood is closely related to lauan (best known as a constituent of inexpensive plywood) and Philippine mahogany. Although collectively known as lauan, the meranti category is separated into white, yellow, light red, red, and dark red. The heavier dark red material has greater strength and is rated as moderately decay resistant.

Applying the name mahogany to these woods is basically a marketing gimmick. The color of the best boards resembles South American (true and genuine) mahoganies, but that's pretty much as

Some woods, such as cedar, fit into the landscape without a finish.

far as it goes. The texture is fairly coarse, the color highly variable, and the stability, which I thought was pretty good, doesn't match that of the true mahoganies.

I have mixed feelings about the wood after using it on several of the projects. The sizing was generous. The two-by boards were really $1\frac{1}{2}$ inches, as opposed to $1\frac{3}{8}$ inches with cedar and cypress. The $\frac{5}{4}$ meranti was $1\frac{1}{16}$ inches.

The color was highly variable, from almost burgundy to a mousy tan. I don't know if that is a result of getting a mix of species or a mix of heartwood and sapwood. Generally, the more attractive pink-red boards were all pink-red, and the mousy boards were uniformly dull.

The grain texture is relatively coarse, even after a fair amount of sanding. When I brushed on the spar varnish finish, some areas of the wood sucked it in like a blotter. It took four coats to achieve a reasonably uniform finish.

Pressure-treated southern yellow pine. (Photo 9) This pressure-treated (PT) wood is infused with wood-preserving chemicals to resist rot and insect damage. The preservatives are forced under pressure throughout the wood, which provides more protection than surface treatments. Although some pressure-treated wood can be difficult to work (and a bit shy of standard lumber dimensions) the rot-resistance makes it very popular for decks and other outdoor applications.

The main drawback is the chemical content. Although most experts say it can't leach out, woodworkers are warned to wear a dust mask (and safety glasses, as always) to keep from inhaling the sawdust when cutting. Also, remember that you can't burn the scraps.

Materials

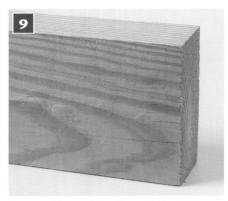

9

Pressure-Treated Southern Yellow Pine

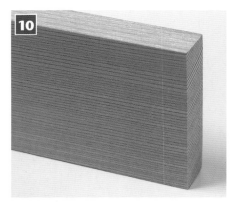

10

Redwood

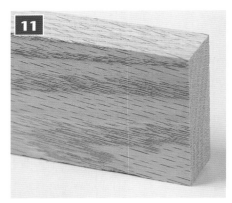

11

White Oak

If you don't like the green tinge of PT, you can stain it or even paint it. But it's difficult to conceal the grain of southern yellow pine, the wood most commonly treated. (You may find other treated species, including other pines, Douglas fir, western larch, Sitka spruce, western hemlock, western red cedar, northern white cedar, and white fir.)

Pressure-treated wood is good for ground contact, but it tends to twist and warp and throw big splinters. I used it on some projects—the planter boxes that actually hold damp soil for example—but concealed the green tinge and racy grain beneath paint.

Redwood. (Photo 10) Old-growth, all-heart redwood is expensive but an ideal outdoor wood. A bright red-orange when freshly cut, it darkens to a brownish red and weathers to a silvery gray. The wood is lightweight, soft and easy to work, but very stable with a smooth texture and straight grain. And it is highly resistant to insect and fungal invasion.

Just a relatively few years ago, this wonderful old-growth redwood was readily available and inexpensive. But the supply of ancient trees has dwindled dramatically, and now most old-growth redwoods are protected from logging. As a result, interest in recycled old-growth wood is booming. Entrepreneurs are dismantling old buildings and other structures that were framed

with old-growth redwood and resawing the beams into lumber.

Redwood does regenerate rapidly, but wood from second-growth trees can't match the lumber from old-growth trees. The color is lighter, the growth rings are more widely spaced, and the wood isn't as durable.

Nevertheless, currently available grades are still more than adequate for outdoor furniture. In fact, redwood may be your best choice for workability, good looks, and natural durability.

White oak. (Photo 11) More than 50 oak species grow in North America

Cypress makes furniture with a rich variation in the wood hues.

and are divided into two primary groups: red oak and white oak, which is stronger, harder, more durable, and better suited for outdoor furniture. White oak also is more moisture resistant than red oak.

The wood has a somewhat coarse texture to begin with. But if you plan to use spar varnish as a finish, you can smooth the texture by using wood filler, followed by a sanding sealer before varnishing. Don't let iron hardware come in contact with white oak. Like cedar and redwood, it has a high tannin content, and iron hardware will turn the wood black.

You can find oak in some home centers nicely surfaced and sized, but only in the nominal one-by thickness. Most of the outdoor furniture projects in the book call for some $5/4$ stock or some two-by stock. At a hardwoods yard, you should be able to find these other thicknesses, though in a rough-sawn state.

Teak. (Photo 12) This tropical hardwood is the ultimate in durability, stability, strength, smoothness, and ability to hold fasteners. I've seen rough-sawn boards at a local lumber dealer, but at $17 a board-foot, it's out of my league. Teak is so extraordinarily expensive because unrestrained logging has made it very scarce in the wild. Fortunately, this desirable hardwood responds well to plantation management, and today most teak comes from sustainable-yield plantations in Southeast Asia and South and Central America.

The heartwood, which is all that's imported, is yellow-brown to dark brown with occasional chocolate-brown to black streaks. It is straight grained and generally

Yard and Garden Furniture

Teak

Honduras Mahogany

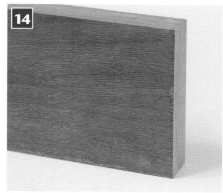

Ipé

easy to work. Freshly machined surfaces feel gummy because of a silica-based oil in the pores. Though the oil helps repel moisture, it can also inhibit glue adhesion, so you need to wipe joining surfaces with lacquer thinner or acetone immediately prior to applying the glue.

Honduran mahogany. (Photo 13) A fabulous wood for indoors and out, genuine mahogany has been in high demand for fine furniture since early in the eighteenth century. It is tough and highly stable, more so than any of the world's major timbers. The grain is open, much like walnut's, and the texture can range from fine to coarse. Its color varies: the heartwood is often yellowish when freshly cut, but soon afterward it turns reddish, pinkish, or salmon. With age, the color deepens to a rich red or brown.

Although it grows widely in the South and Central American tropics, true mahogany is becoming scarce, which is reflected in its high price. And it does seem a little frivolous to use this wonderful wood to build picnic tables. But maybe that's just me.

Ipé. (Photo 14) This Brazilian hardwood (pronounced "ee-pay") is another old wood that has found a new audience. Importers are promoting its use for decking, but you have little reason not to use it to make outdoor furniture. It is very similar to teak in appearance and weathering characteristics, but it is less expensive. Though heavy and extremely hard, it machines

well. Like teak, it has a lot of silica in the pores, so it is hard on cutting edges.

ADHESIVES

It may be difficult to find a single type of glue that will work in every situation when building outdoor furniture. But you have a half-dozen water-resistant or waterproof glues to use. Some are packaged ready to apply, while others need to be mixed.

I used at least four types building the projects. You may opt to use exactly the same ones or choose a different type with

Meranti *is one of many tropical hardwoods used on yard furniture.*

advantages that suit your needs, such as a longer set time.

A visit to a hardware store or home center will reveal that glues rated for outdoor use are typically more expensive than

general-purpose glues.

As you read labels on glue packages, you may come across water-resistance ratings of types I or II. A type I glue is rated to survive standard strength tests after repeated cycles of drying and dunking in boiling water. A type II glue is rated to resist separation after repeated wet-dry cycles in room-temperature water, but is not strength tested. Because most of the glued connections on the projects are backed up with joinery and mechanical fasteners, either type should do. Here is a brief rundown of the basic types:

Plastic resin. (Photo 15) This glue, sometimes called urea-formaldehyde glue, is highly moisture resistant and an excellent choice for outdoor projects. Open working time is a generous 20 to 30 minutes, so it's a good choice for complex glue-up jobs. The minimum clamping time is 12 hours. This glue produces good bond strength and good creep-resistance. In a tightly-sealed container, it also has a very long shelf life.

The glue is packaged as a powder, and you have to mix it. Once mixed, it has a pot life of four hours at 70 degrees Fahrenheit and 1½ hours at 90 degrees. But the powder contains toxins, so you need to wear a dust mask when mixing. And the mixed glue can irritate your skin, so you ought to wear protective gloves, too. After the glue has cured, it sands easily, but the dust is toxic. Another drawback is that the glue has a

Materials

Plastic resin glue *mixes up with water.*

Yellow glue *cleans up easily with water.*

Polyurethane glue *foams into gaps.*

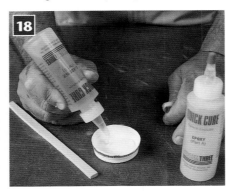

Mix epoxy glue *in small batches.*

high minimum application temperature of 70 degrees Fahrenheit. Plastic resin glue just won't cure in a cold shop.

Yellow glue. (Photo 16) The polyvinyl acetates (PVAs), which include the familiar white and yellow glues, are popular because they're strong, versatile, and cheap. No mixing is required, the bottle the glue comes in usually serves as an applicator, and required clamping times are short. It also has a reasonably long shelf life.

For outdoor projects, you want Type II yellow glue, which is highly water resistant though not completely waterproof.

Like regular yellow woodworking glue, Type II yellow glue can be used at temperatures as low as 55 degrees. It sets up fast, giving you only about 5 to 10 minutes between application and clamping.

Like other yellow glues, it tends to be very "grabby," too. If, for example, you have to line up multiple tenons in mortises before a complex assembly can be drawn closed, you might prefer the longer open time of polyurethane glue or plastic resin glue.

Clamp the assembly at least 1 hour. As the glue cures, the glue line becomes

nearly invisible.

Clean up, before the glue cures, is with water. A glue brush can be cleaned and reused many times. A wet—not just damp, but wet—rag can be used to wipe away squeeze-out before it skins over, while a chisel or scraper can do the job after that. The dried glue sands well and won't gum up sandpaper.

After a bottle is opened, the glue has a shelf life of at least a year. It will freeze, and freezing can degrade the product.

Polyurethane. (Photo 17) This glue is versatile, strong, and reasonably convenient to use. But it has some peculiar characteristics.

It offers an unusually long open time—as much as 40 minutes according to one maker—although you may not need it because you have to apply it to only one half of a joint. But the glue needs moisture to catalyze. So unless the wood has a high moisture content—and pressure-treated wood would be in that category—you have to moisten one of the joint surfaces with a damp cloth.

Clamping time is one to four hours,

depending on the ambient temperature (minimum application temperature is a fairly high 68 degrees Fahrenheit), and the glue cures fully within 24 hours. The result is a strong, creep-resistant and waterproof bond.

Remove squeeze-out by wiping the wet glue from the wood with mineral spirits or by scraping the dried glue. If you get some on your hands and don't remove it quickly (with rubbing alcohol) you'll carry stains for days. Note, too, that polyurethane glue presents a health hazard to asthmatics and those who tend to be highly allergic. Even if you don't have a problem, use it with ample ventilation.

Polyurethane glue expands as it sets up. That can fill an open seam—but can also push apart joints that aren't properly clamped. The shelf life is only two or three months.

Epoxy. (Photo 18) Epoxy is a two-part liquid system consisting of a resin and a hardener that create a solid bond. When cured, it's an incredibly strong, gap-filling glue that is waterproof and resists creeping. The open time and the full cure time of epoxy depend on the hardener and the temperature. A fast hardener used on a hot summer day may give you a pot life of only a couple of minutes. A slow hardener used in a cold shop may allow you to work with mixed epoxy for more than an hour.

It's so strong that you don't need to clamp joints. In fact, you can actually weaken a joint by applying too much pressure. You can simply hold parts steady with blocks or even tape. But squeeze-out from over-clamping or using too much glue can be a nightmare.

Cured epoxy won't come off anything very easily after it has completely dried. You can clean up squeeze-out with lacquer thinner while it is wet or scrape it off while it's still soft. Once it hardens, you can usually get under epoxy with a chisel, but you'll take some wood with it. You generally want to avoid skin contact with uncured epoxy and to avoid breathing dust from sanding.

OUTDOOR FASTENERS

You need corrosion-resistant fasteners to make outdoor furniture, which means screws and bolts, not nails. Consider self-drilling screws **(Photo 19)** that are less likely to cause splits, and star drives **(Photo 20)** that apply force more efficiently. Here is a brief rundown of a few of the options.

Galvanized steel. Most stock exterior-grade fasteners are galvanized. Hot-dipping is the best galvanizing method for nails, but not for screws because the process can clog the threads. Mechanically plated screws are generally suitable for decks and some furniture projects. But the iron content stains redwood and cedar. Electroplated screws have been improved with polymer coatings, but the coating is thin and can wear off even as you drive the screw.

Ceramic-coated. Ceramic-coated screws are a good alternative for woods with high tannin content such as cedar or redwood. They are typically found in green or beige.

Brass. These screws look great, and brass won't rust, streak, or react with tannic acids the way steel does. It will eventually oxidize and turn green. The one major problem is that it's soft. Brass screws break easily. To avoid this problem, drill a pilot hole, drive a steel screw into the hole, withdraw the steel screw and replace it with a brass one.

Silicon bronze. These screws look like brass, but the alloy won't oxidize or corrode as easily. And they're stronger, so they won't strip out of a hole or snap off. But they cost about twice as much as stainless steel.

Stainless steel. These screws and bolts are the strongest and most durable on the market. While they will eventually tarnish and develop a reddish cast, they won't stain wood or react with the tannins in redwood and cedar. They cost twice as much as coated steel.

WOOD FINISHES

Moisture, sunlight, swings in temperature, and insects can ruin your projects if you leave them unprotected. That's where the finish comes in.

Most provide some protection from moisture, the sun, and fungi, but each finish is better at some of these jobs than at others. Frequency and ease of maintenance also vary with types of finish. Here is a look at some of the options, aside from using a rot-resistant wood with no finish and watching it weather.

Paint. Paint does the best overall job of protecting wood outdoors because it has more pigment than other finishes. Of course it also conceals the wood. But while paint provides good protection on vertical surfaces like house siding, it is usually short-lived on horizontal surfaces like

Self-drilling screws are less likely to splinter.

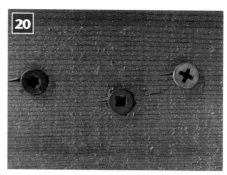

Star-drive screws (left) hold bits more securely than square- or philips drive bits.

Pigmented white shellac hides knots.

Most exterior finishes simply roll on.

tables and chair seats. And once the film is ruptured, moisture, mold, and insects can penetrate.

If you do paint, use a good latex primer and top coat with mildewcide and fungicide additives. They are easy to apply, quick drying, and easy to clean up with water. Also use a stain killer to hide knots. **(Photo 21)**

Solid-color stains. Heavy-bodied stains (either latex or oil based) also conceal the wood because they have much more pigment than other stains. As a result, they form a film like paint, and the oil-based stains can even peel like paint. But because the stain is thinner than paint, the surface can be recoated many more times before it needs stripping.

Varnishes. Exterior-grade varnish has blockers instead of pigments to reduce UV damage. Marine spar varnish formulated with a tung-oil phenolic resin is made to protect boats, so it is more than adequate for furniture. But it does darken the wood.

The newer version, polyurethane spar varnish, has the flexibility and light resistance needed for exterior use, and it's

considerably less yellow than the old marine spar varnish.

Semitransparent stains. These moderately pigmented stains let some wood grain show through and still retard UV damage. They do not form a film like paint, but penetrate the surface, which keeps them from peeling.

Penetrating stains are oil-based or alkyd-based. Latex stains also are available, but they do not penetrate the wood surfaces as do the oil-based stains. Although a penetrating stain will last only a couple of years, it is easy to reapply using a roller. **(Photo 22)**

Water repellents. These finishes contain a small amount of wax, a resin or drying oil, a solvent, and a fungicide. Because this is only a surface treatment, the fungicide will not prevent rot, only surface mildew and fungi. The first application may be short lived.

When a discoloration appears, clean it with liquid household bleach and detergent solution; then reapply the finish. After the wood has weathered, the treatments are more enduring.

Materials

Slat Table & Benches

This table and bench set is stylish and practical. The three-piece combination looks great on a grassy terrace, a brick patio, a deck, or wherever you like to settle down with friends. The solid cedar looks great in a clear finish, and it weathers extremely well. The set features a spacious tabletop with plenty of room for six or more. The wide benches are comfortable, too, and won't unexpectedly tip over when you shift position. Where the carpentry

is concerned, you'll find that if you can deal with miter joints, you can deal with this project. Sometimes miter joints can be finicky to cut and assemble. But if you follow basic procedures, taking the time to make a few test cuts before tackling the real stock, you can create tight, well-crafted joints. In fact, making miters is about the most difficult part of this very straightforward furniture project—where first-rate looks depend as much on quality materials as woodworking techniques. The overall design is remarkably simple, and the joinery is almost foolproof. What makes or breaks this set is the straightness of the legs, the smoothness of the aprons, and the alignment and finish of the top slat boards. You don't want bowed, cupped, or twisted surfaces, or boards with too many wanes or knots. Most of the lumber shows, so select good-looking material.

EXPLODED VIEW

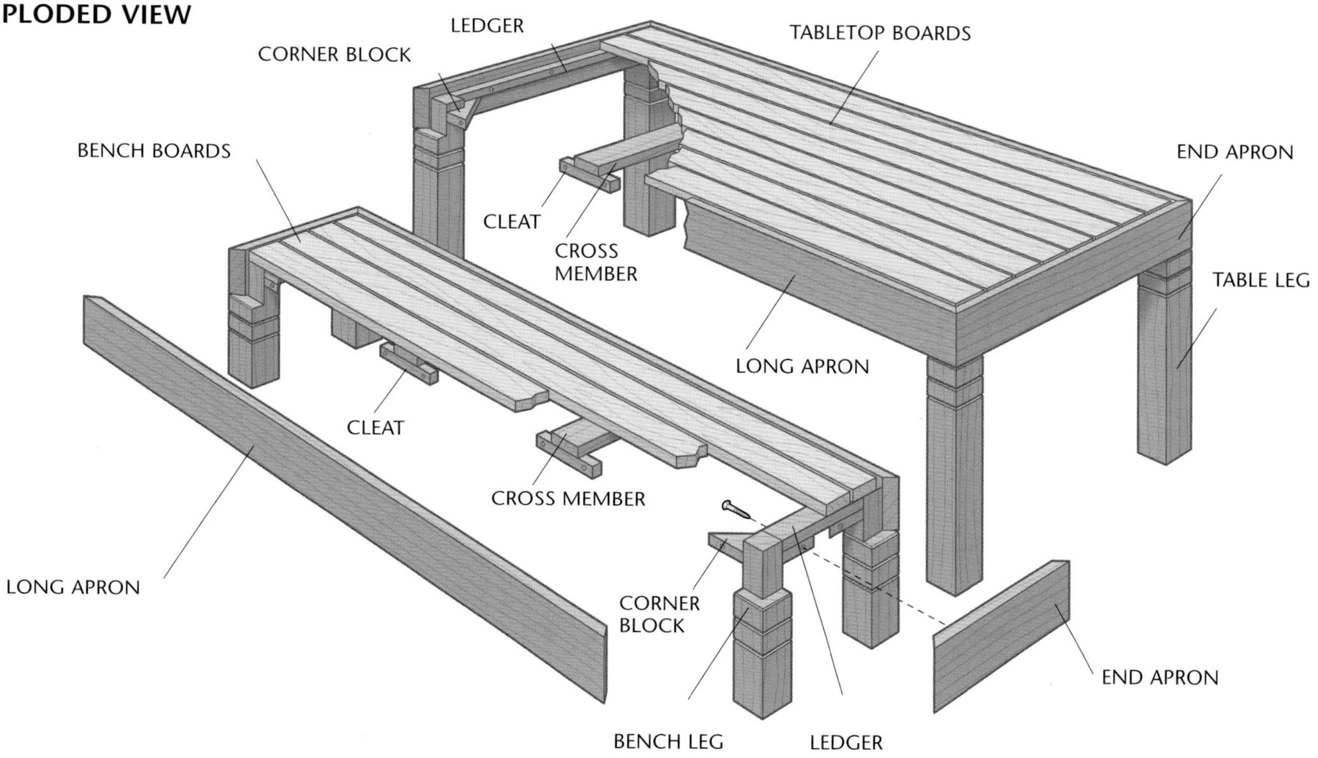

CUTTING LIST (Some parts are left long during construction.)

	Part	Number	Thickness	Width	Length	Stock
Table	Table legs	4	$3\frac{1}{2}$"	$3\frac{1}{2}$"	30"	4x4 cedar
	Long aprons	2	1"	$5\frac{1}{2}$"	72"	$\frac{5}{4}$x6 cedar
	End aprons	2	1"	$5\frac{1}{2}$"	$31\frac{1}{8}$"	$\frac{5}{4}$x6 cedar
	Cross members	2	1"	$5\frac{1}{2}$"	$29\frac{1}{8}$"	$\frac{5}{4}$x6 cedar
	Cleats	4	$\frac{3}{4}$"	$3\frac{1}{2}$"	7"	1x4 cedar
	Ledgers	2	1"	1"	$24\frac{1}{8}$"	$\frac{5}{4}$ cedar
	Corner blocks	4	1"	$3\frac{1}{2}$"	$8\frac{11}{16}$"	$\frac{5}{4}$x4 pine
	Tabletop boards	8	$\frac{3}{4}$"	$3\frac{1}{2}$"	70"	1x4 cedar
Benches	Bench legs	8	$3\frac{1}{2}$"	$3\frac{1}{2}$"	$15\frac{5}{16}$"	4x4 cedar
	Long aprons	4	1"	$5\frac{1}{2}$"	72"	$\frac{5}{4}$x6 cedar
	End aprons	4	1"	$5\frac{1}{2}$"	$16\frac{5}{8}$"	$\frac{5}{4}$x6 cedar
	Cross members	4	1"	$5\frac{1}{2}$"	$24\frac{5}{8}$"	$\frac{5}{4}$x6 cedar
	Cleats	8	$\frac{3}{4}$"	$3\frac{1}{2}$"	7"	1x4 cedar
	Ledgers	4	1"	1"	$9\frac{5}{8}$"	$\frac{5}{4}$ cedar
	Corner blocks	8	1"	$3\frac{1}{2}$"	$8\frac{11}{16}$"	$\frac{5}{4}$x4 pine
	Bench boards	8	$\frac{3}{4}$"	$3\frac{1}{2}$"	70"	1x4 cedar

SHOPPING LIST

- 3 pcs. 4x4 8' cedar
- 5 pcs. $\frac{5}{4}$x6 12' cedar
- 10 pcs. 1x4 12' cedar
- 1 pc. $\frac{5}{4}$x4 8' pine
- $1\frac{5}{8}$" stainless-steel deck screws
- 2" stainless-steel deck screws
- 2 tubes waterproof construction adhesive

ELEVATIONS

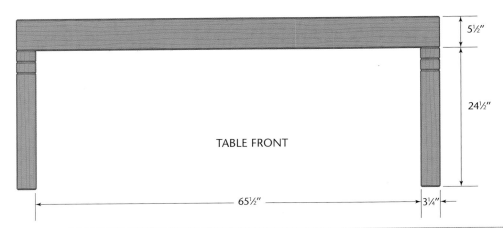

TABLE FRONT

5½"

24½"

65½"

3¼"

BUILDER'S NOTES

This is a project where it really pays to select your wood carefully. I used Western red cedar, which is generally soft and splintery. That means if you catch a splinter at the edge while you rout or sand, it can tear out a major divot. This can happen with many different materials, but it is especially troublesome with cedar.

Materials

Western red cedar is straight-grained and lightweight, with significant color alterations between the reddish brown heartwood and lighter sapwood. Unless you pay a premium to get heartwood only, you will have a mixture of heartwood and sapwood in your stock.

The relatively light weight is a bonus here: although the table and benches are fairly big, they are easy to move. The wood is strong enough, but the softness can be a problem, leading to dents as you work and clamp the wood. Cutting tools, especially chisels and planes, must be sharp to slice the cedar fibers. You'll know immediately when some

honing is due, because the fibers will tear, bunch up, and crush over the tool edge.

Your local lumber emporium probably won't have the top grade of cedar in stock, but will likely order it for you. The short wait in delivery will pay off as you work the better material and in the appearance of the final product.

With cedar, you will want to use stainless-steel fasteners. Galvanized hardware will eventually react with the cedar to produce black stains. Stainless-steel screws are pricey but well worth it. You could use ceramic-coated screws but I think the stainless screw heads look classier.

Instead of using glue for this project, try construction adhesive. Select one labeled for outdoor use. Typically, such adhesives are designed to remain slightly flexible—not flexible enough to allow the parts to shift or come unstuck, but just enough to accommodate wood movement. Use a caulking gun to run a narrow bead along one piece. There's no need to load up the joint and cover both pieces.

Tools and Techniques

For this project you need the usual assortment of tools—circular saw, saber saw, drill-driver, router, and sanders.

The most complicated cuts are beveled crosscuts that produce the miter joints used to assemble the aprons. You can make them with a circular saw. The key to success is patience in setting up. You can't simply tilt the saw and set the angle on its gauge. You need to make a series of test cuts, and assemble the test pieces to see whether the joints are tight and square. Typically, a miter will open at either the inside or outside edges when the pieces are square, indicating that the bevel angles are off. It's also useful to have a set of corner clamps at your disposal. With these clamps (sold in sets) you can hold two pieces at right angles. They won't pull the joint closed, but once set, they will hold the joint after you get it closed.

Corner clamps may not be used frequently, but once in a while, they are just the right clamps for a job. This is one of those jobs. They are

inexpensive, and a single set of four is all you'll need for the project.

Finish

The finish you use here depends on what you want the finished piece to look like. But you must also consider durability and the level of maintenance that will be required.

I used expensive, high-grade cedar that was free of obvious blemishes and defects. I wanted to be able to see the wood.

Spar varnish would display the wood, but to me, the gloss of this finish wasn't right for the look of the set. Also, you need to apply three or more coats of spar varnish to the wood, along with a maintenance coat every couple of years. Maintenance is not my strong suit.

Reluctant to hide my expensive cedar under a layer or two of solid pig-ment, I passed on paint and solid color stain. A semi-transparent stain provided beauty and protection.

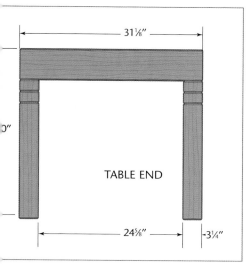

TABLE END

31⅛"

24⅝"   3¼"

STEP-BY-STEP

Selecting Stock

Building the table and benches will give you a taste of real production work. Except for a few minor differences, such as the number of top boards required and the lengths of the legs, end aprons, and cross members, building the benches is exactly like building the table. That means you could cut all your boards at once. But most do-it-yourselfers will find it a bit easier to build each of the three units as individual projects. That will be less confusing than working simultaneously on three assemblies.

Before you start cutting, it pays to sort through your entire stock of wood, stacking three separate piles: one for the table and one for each of the benches. Although many of the boards are the same size (or awfully close), this gives you the opportunity to sort by wood hue and grain. The tabletop, which is the most visible surface, should get the cream of the crop.

You might even take the trouble to create an artistic blend of different boards, such as using a darker strip down the center and progressively lighter hues toward the edges.

Cutting the Aprons

The basic framework of the table (and the benches) is formed by the aprons, which are mitered together into a box frame. You'll join the legs to the assembled aprons with lap joints. Building the table begins with the apron assembly.

Miter joints can be difficult to cut accurately. The cuts are easiest to make with a power miter saw. But no matter how good your saw is, the angle scale is likely to be a little off. The best approach is to make test cuts on two scrap pieces with the blade set at 45 degrees. Afterward, fit them together to determine whether the joint is tight when the pieces are square. Adjust the saw as necessary, making more test cuts until you have a tight joint. Then cut the

The key element in this project is the miter joint, which makes trim corners on the table and benches. For best results, make test cuts on scrap wood, assemble test joints, and refine your cuts as needed.

good stuff. **(Photo 1)** One trick is to insert a wood shaving under your workpiece to create a slight undercut. This allows the visible front edge of the miter to close just a hair before the rest of the joint closes.

You need six 72-inch aprons. If you work carefully, you should be able to get them from three 12-foot cedar boards. The end aprons for the table and both the benches will come from a fourth board.

Examine your stock, and pick the best edges for the top of the aprons. Mark them so that you get the top edges oriented the same way during the final assembly.

PLAN VIEW

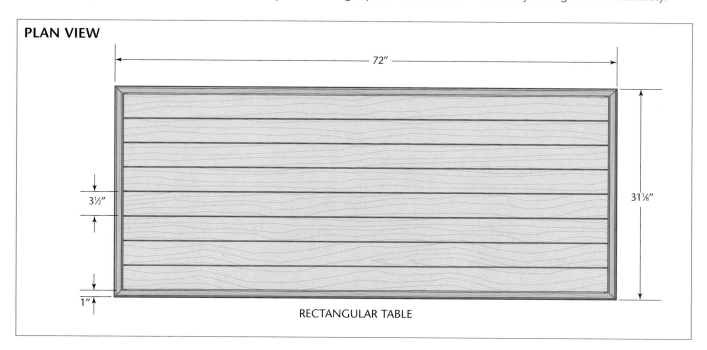

72"

31⅛"

3½"

1"

RECTANGULAR TABLE

Set up your pair of corner clamps on one of the aprons. Apply a bead of adhesive, and slide the second apron into the clamps. Then press the joint closed, and tighten the clamps. Try to avoid glue squeeze-out.

Make sure that one pair of joints is properly aligned, closed, and clamped securely before you move on to the second set of miters. Join the two subassemblies into a complete apron framework.

An auxiliary baseplate makes balancing the router easier on the narrow edge. This is especially true at corners. This auxiliary plate, made of scrap plywood, is simply stuck in place with carpet tape.

Assembling the Aprons

This is a two-step process. First, join a long apron to a short one, using corner clamps. Second, join two of these units, again using the corner clamps, to complete the apron assembly. If you pace your work, you can get all of the apron assemblies put together using only a single, four-piece set of corner clamps.

Miter joints are easy to assemble if you approach the process correctly. You simply have to get the corner clamps adjusted during a dry assembly, which is nothing more than a test fit without glue or fasteners. This way you can spend all the time you want adjusting the positions of the clamps. Then you can leave them clamped to one apron, remove the other, and start the final assembly.

Apply a bead of construction adhesive to the miter. Reinsert the apron in the clamps—pressing the joint closed as tightly as you can—then retighten the clamps. **(Photo 2)**

Now drill pilot holes and drive two 2-inch screws into the joint from each direction. You can enhance the appearance of your project if you take the time to lay out the screw positions consistently on each joint. Once you've driven the screws, you can remove the clamps and set the assembly aside while the adhesive sets. Once you have the partial assemblies together, you can go back to join the pairs into complete assemblies. **(Photo 3)**

Chamfer the Apron Edges

To soften the look of the slat table, you can chamfer the edges of the aprons inside and out. Chuck a chamfering bit

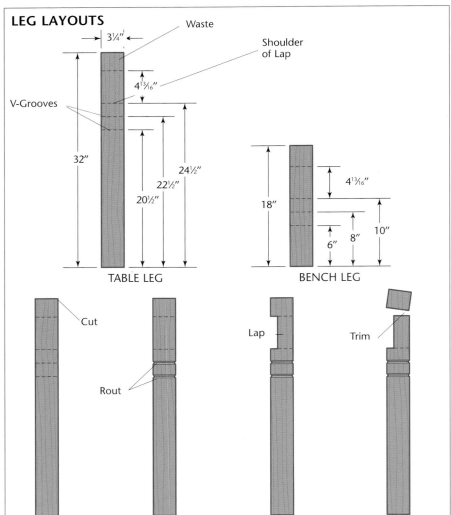

LEG LAYOUTS

Waste

Shoulder of Lap

$3\frac{1}{4}$"

$4\frac{13}{16}$"

V-Grooves

32"

$24\frac{1}{2}$"

$22\frac{1}{2}$"

$20\frac{1}{2}$"

TABLE LEG

$4\frac{13}{16}$"

18"

10"

8"

6"

BENCH LEG

Cut

Rout

Lap

Trim

in your router, and set the depth of cut by making a few test cuts on scrap. When you have a chamfer that suits, rest the router on the edge of the apron, and guide it around the entire assembly, cutting a chamfer on the outer edge. **(Photo 4)**

Now shift its position, and cut a chamfer around the inner edge. Then turn the assembly over, and repeat the process on the bottom.

Cutting the Legs

You have to keep a number of things in mind as you lay out the legs and make your cuts on the 4x4 cedar leg stock.

First, you want the legs to be straight, true, and relatively free of unattractive defects, so you need to examine your stock carefully as you lay out the legs. You have three 8-footers, and no matter how you take the legs from them, you will have a fair amount of waste. Use this excess to work around defects and blemishes.

If a particular blemish just can't be avoided, you can turn it to the inside. Remember that because the benches are lower, blemishes on the inside of those legs will be less obvious.

Second, no matter how you cut the joinery on the legs, it will be useful to have at least a couple of inches of waste at the top end. You want to add 2 or 3 inches to the lengths specified on the cutting list.

No matter what power saw you use—chop saw or circular saw—to cut the legs, you'll most likely have to cut about halfway through the 4x4 stock, then roll it over, and make a second pass to complete the cut. **(Photo 5)**

Routing the V-grooves

Each leg is embellished with a pair of V-grooves cut across all four faces. Measure from the bottom of the leg, and lay out the centerlines of the grooves. You can make the cuts using a V-grooving bit in the router.

Chuck the bit in the router, and adjust the depth of cut, making test cuts on scrap to evaluate the setting. The grooves should be about ¼ inch deep. Use a square to guide the router.

Cutting Laps on the Legs

Use a circular saw to cut the shoulders and slice away most of the waste. Then use a chisel to clean up the bottom of the cut. If you have the right bit, you can use a router to level and smooth the bottom

To cut completely through the leg with a standard circular saw, make two cuts—one on each opposing side of the stock. After the first cut, roll the stock over, alligning the blade with the kerf, and make a second cut.

After you break away the strips of waste left standing between the saw kerfs (a hammer does the job), use a chisel to pare away the remaining ridges of waste and smooth the bottom of the cut.

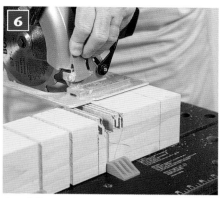

Carefully set the depth of cut on your circular saw to match exactly the thickness of the apron stock. Cut the shoulder of the lap first, using a square. Then make a series of cuts about ⅛ in. apart to clear the waste.

Mark the screw locations by holding a screw over a clamped leg and drawing a line down the inner face of the leg to guide your pilot holes. The screws should bite well into the apron but not break through.

of the cut, but it isn't really necessary. To locate the shoulder of the lap, you measure from the bottom of the leg. Make the lap about ½ inch shorter than the width of the aprons—5 inches wide, in other words. Leave the excess stock at full dimension.

Adjust the circular saw cutting depth against a scrap of apron stock so that the blade cuts as deep as the apron is thick. Cut the shoulder, right on the mark. Then make repeated cuts to remove the waste. **(Photo 6)** When the rough cuts are complete on both faces, use a chisel to pare away the unevenness typically left by the saw. **(Photo 7)** The final operation is to chamfer the shoulders of the laps and the foot of the leg. Use a chamfering bit in a router and try to match the V-grooves with the chamfers.

Joining the Legs and Aprons

Trim the legs to length. Ideally, the lapped section of the leg should be 11/16 inch shorter than the apron width, so when the leg and apron are joined, a tabletop resting on the leg top will be flush with the top edges of the apron. Typically, one-by cedar is 11/16 inch thick. Each leg is joined to the apron assembly with construction adhesive and four 2-inch stainless-steel screws. Apply a bead of adhesive to both faces of the lap, and set the leg in place.

You need to drive the screws at an angle into the aprons to make sure that they don't poke through. **(Photo 8)**

To make an angled pilot, you generally have to start drilling straight into the wood, then swing the drill to the desired angle once the drill bit has bitten partway into the wood.

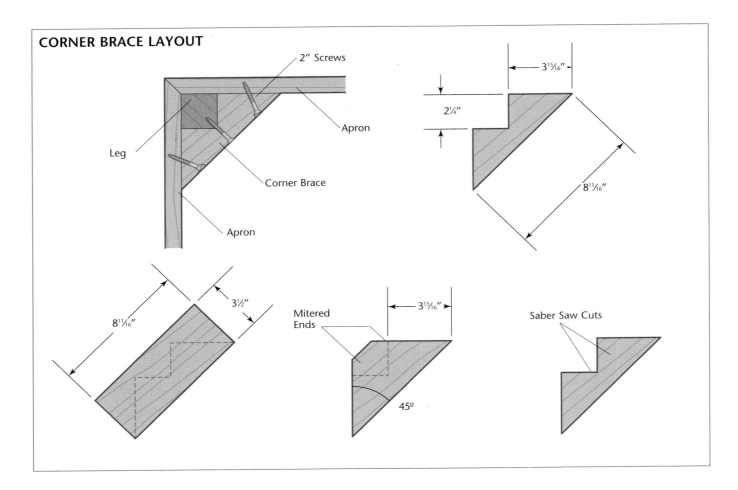

CORNER BRACE LAYOUT

Cutting the Corner Braces

The corner braces reinforce the joint between leg and apron. You can cut these braces from pine, fir, or other stock you might have around the home shop. The stock can be either 5/4 or two-by.

The ends of the braces are mitered at 45 degrees. To save time, you can miter them as you cut them from the raw stock.

To lay out the notch for the leg, just set it in place against the top of the leg, and scribe along the leg on the brace. Cut the notch with a saber saw.

Cutting the Cross Members

The cross members fit between the long aprons and help support the tabletop and seat boards. While the cutting list specifies these as 5/4x6 cedar, you can use other, less-expensive stock if you desire.

These pieces rest on scraps of the table-top stock that are glued and screwed to the aprons. The cross members in turn are glued and screwed to the scraps. Position the cross members as shown in the "Table Bottom View" drawing.

Installing the Corner Braces

The next step is to fasten the corner braces to the aprons and legs. The brace should be located near the middle of the lapped section, below the ledger, as indicated in the "Exploded View" drawing on page 39.

The exact position of the brace isn't critical; I placed each brace about midway up the lapped section of the leg. Apply a dab of adhesive to the edges of the brace that contact the apron and the leg, and press it in place. It should hold long enough for you to drill at least one pilot and drive a screw. Predrill a hole, and drive the first screw straight into the middle of the brace so the screw penetrates the upper section of the leg. I used a 2-inch screw here. Then predrill two more holes, and drive 1 5/8-inch screws through the corner brace into the aprons. **(Photo 9)**

Fastening the Ledgers

The ends of the tabletop and seat boards are supported on the ends of the legs and on a 1-inch-wide ledger glued and screwed to the end apron between the legs. Again, this piece doesn't have to be cedar. Whatever stock you select for the ledgers, cut them to fit between the legs and fasten them in place.

Installing the Tabletop

Cut the boards to fit. Chamfer all the upper edges, across the ends as well as along the long sides. To maintain a uniform space between the boards, you can use scraps of 1/4-inch plywood as spacers.

To avoid surprises, it is a good idea to set all the boards in place, putting spacers between them at the cross members (which will support the spacers) to see how the overall spacing works out. You don't want to glue and screw six of eight boards in place and discover that you've got extra-wide gaps between the last two and the apron.

9

Set the corner braces in position with a small bead of adhesive on the edges. Press the brace against the leg and aprons. Then drill pilot holes into each apron and into the leg, and drive stainless-steel screws.

TABLE BOTTOM VIEW

21"   21"   21"

When you have the spacing worked out, fasten the boards one at a time. Apply a dab of adhesive to the underside of the board where it contacts the ledger and the cross members. Drive a screw up through the ledger and the cross member into each board.

Finishing

Use an exterior-grade finish to protect your work. I applied semitransparent stain to enhance the color of the cedar and to protect it from ultraviolet rays. The manufacturer of the oil-based product I used suggested applying two coats,

with a minimum drying time of 24 hours between coats. You can also find water-based semitransparent stains, which dry far more quickly, so a finish can be completed in one day.

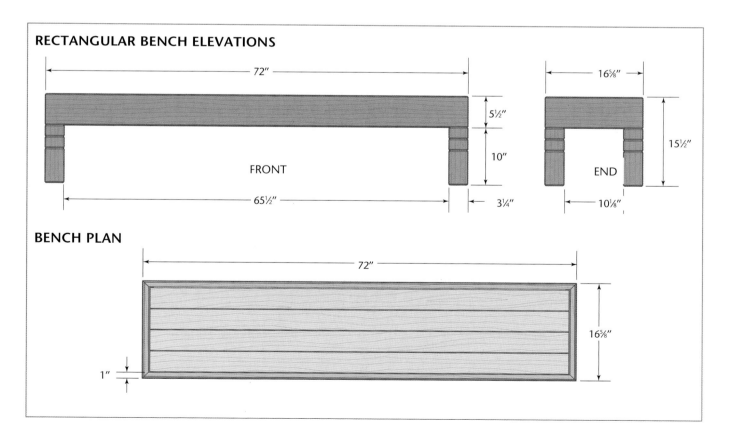

RECTANGULAR BENCH ELEVATIONS

72"

5½"

10"

FRONT

65½"   3¼"

16⅝"

15½"

END

10⅛"

BENCH PLAN

72"

16⅝"

1"

Round Deck Table

This table is just the right shape and size for casual entertaining and conversation with a few close friends. Maybe it's the lack of corners, but a round table just seems more intimate than one with straight lines. At just under 4 feet in diameter, this model achieves a practical compromise between intimacy and roominess for snacks or even for a full dinner. If your deck is only a modest size or you have only a small patch of flat lawn where you can eat out, the

table is perfect. It should be able to handle four people with enough room for complete place-settings. And you'll still be close enough to carry on conversation in a normal tone of voice. One dilemma common to round tables is finding the right compromise between solid footing for the table and leg room for the people sitting around it. A pedestal base generally provides the easiest access and the most legroom. But a pedestal support can make the table unsteady. So in this project the leg arrangement provides clear leg space for four, and keeps the top from rocking with legs out at the perimeter. The table may look a little lonely without chairs. But if you don't have some in mind already, you may want to make a few based on the Deck Chair project on pages 54 through 63. Build four, with or without arms, and you'll have a unique and attractive outdoor dining set.

EXPLODED VIEW

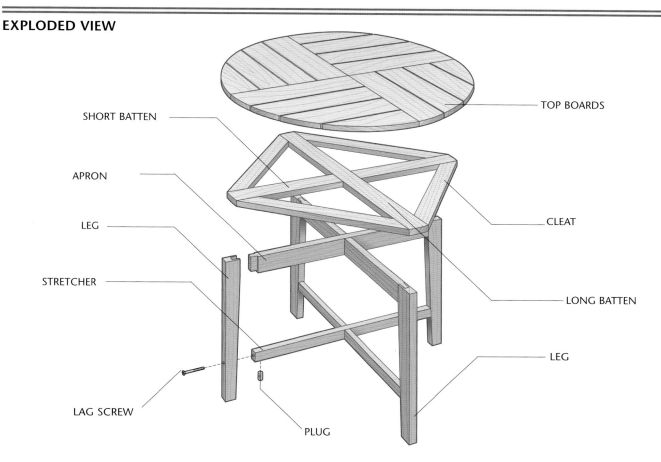

TOP BOARDS
SHORT BATTEN
APRON
LEG
STRETCHER
LAG SCREW
PLUG
CLEAT
LONG BATTEN
LEG

CUTTING LIST

Part	Number	Thickness	Width	Length	Meranti Stock
Legs	4	$1\frac{1}{2}$"	$3\frac{1}{2}$"	30"	2 x 4
Aprons	2	1"	$3\frac{1}{2}$"	$37\frac{1}{2}$"	$\frac{5}{4}$ x 6
Stretchers	2	1"	$1\frac{1}{2}$"	36"	$\frac{5}{4}$ x 6
Long batten	1	1"	$3\frac{1}{2}$"	$45\frac{1}{2}$"	$\frac{5}{4}$ x 6
Short battens	2	1"	$3\frac{1}{2}$"	21"	$\frac{5}{4}$ x 6
Cleats	4	1"	$3\frac{1}{2}$"	$29\frac{5}{8}$"	$\frac{5}{4}$ x 6
Top boards	4	1"	$5\frac{1}{2}$"	$22\frac{3}{4}$"	$\frac{5}{4}$ x 6
Top boards	4	1"	$5\frac{1}{2}$"	22"	$\frac{5}{4}$ x 6
Top boards	4	1"	$5\frac{1}{2}$"	$19\frac{5}{8}$"	$\frac{5}{4}$ x 6
Top boards	4	1"	$5\frac{1}{2}$"	$14\frac{13}{16}$"	$\frac{5}{4}$ x 6
Plugs	4	$\frac{1}{2}$" dia.	—	1"	birch dowel

SHOPPING LIST

- 1 pc. 2x4 10' meranti

- 7 pcs. $\frac{5}{4}$x6 8' meranti

- 1 pc. $\frac{1}{2}$" dia. 36" birch dowel

- 4 stainless-steel lag screws with washers, $\frac{1}{4}$"x4"

- $1\frac{5}{8}$" deck screws

- 2" deck screws

Round Deck Table

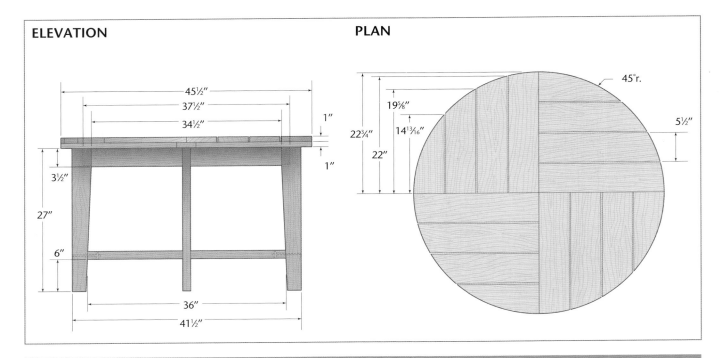

ELEVATION

PLAN

BUILDER'S NOTES

This table has a kind of pinwheel-pattern top that picks up on the design of deck boards and turns it into a focal-point piece where you can gather with friends.

Materials
You can use any of the durable outdoor woods that are available in two-by and ⁵⁄₄ stock. I used meranti, a variety of lauan harvested in Southeast Asia. Most of it goes into plywood, but boards are being marketed more aggressively in the U.S. for deck-building and other outdoor uses. Calling it meranti mahogany is part of the effort to promote the wood as premium-grade stock. But the wood is not related to the true, finely textured and stabile mahoganies from Central and South America.

It's ersatz character notwithstanding, I found the meranti a pleasure to work with. The boards seemed lightweight and quite soft, but consistently twist-free. That's important on the tabletop and on key joints between the stretchers and the legs where I used a long screw driven through the leg into the end of the stretcher. Because threads don't hold very well in end grain, I drilled holes in the bottom edges of the stretchers and glued dowels into the holes. With this combination, the screw penetrates the dowel, and its threads have some long grain to grab. I used the longest lag screws I could find at the local hardware store. One alternative is to drill deep counterbores in the legs and use shorter screws.

Tools and Techniques
For this project you need a circular saw, saber saw, and drill-driver. A plunge router is handy for cutting the mortises, but you can use a drill and chisel. A standard router is important for cutting the tabletop to its final circular shape.

Several bits used in building this table may be out-of-the-ordinary for the home shop. Two are drill bits, the others are router bits. Although the typical ¼-inch-diameter twist drill bit is about 4 inches long, I used one that's 12 inches long to bore bolt holes through the legs into the stretchers. (A hardware store that caters to tradespeople should have these long bits in stock.)

To drill the holes in the stretchers for the ½-inch dowels, you will need a drill bit that's slightly smaller than ½ inch in diameter. Dowels are notorious for being undersized, and if you drill ½-inch holes for the ½-inch dowels, you'll probably find them too loose to glue well. I used a ¹⁵⁄₃₂-inch bit, a size common in 30-piece drill-bit sets. A good hardware store will have this bit available individually, so don't buy 30 bits to get just this one size.

Two out-of-the-ordinary router bits are used to produce the mortises and tenons used to join the legs and aprons. (Find details on routing mortises and tenons in "Cutting Mortise-and-Tenon Joints," page 16.)

Finish
Unless you use stock from a dealer specializing in furniture-grade hardwoods, you'll be working with wood intended for construction that will need more than a light once-over with a pad sander. Go at it with a belt sander first; then finish up with that pad sander.

The best time to sand parts is just after they've been cut, and before they are joined. That's much easier than sanding assembled pieces. Start with a 50- or 60-grit belt. Brush or vacuum the resulting dust from the wood; switch to a 100- or 120-grit belt; and resand. Finally, use a pad or random-orbit sander with 150-grit paper. Then clean up the dust once again, and apply your finish.

STEP-BY-STEP

Cutting the Legs

You can cut all four legs from a single 10-foot 2x4. But don't start by cutting your 2x4 into four pieces. Instead, cut it in half, making a clean square cut. Then trim just enough from each original end to make them square.

Now, measuring from each end of both pieces, lay out the four tapered legs. The dimensions of the taper I used are shown in the drawing. Cut the tapers with your circular saw, trimming the piece just to the outside of the layout lines. Then crosscut each two-leg blank in half, leaving each leg slightly long. You can clean up the long sawed edge with a belt sander or with a hand or power plane. I used a router fitted with a long flush-trimming bit. **(Photo 1)**

Cutting Support Pieces

The aprons, stretchers, and battens are cut from the $^5/_4$ stock. In the meranti I used, I found the $^5/_4$ stocked in nominal 6-inch widths intended for decking. The lumberyard was willing to rip the stock to narrower dimensions, which helped. If the place you shop is not this helpful and you do not have a table saw, you can handle the job with a circular saw. The trick is to use a guide board that keeps the saw running true.

The guide system may seem to cause more problems than it solves because the guide will be wider than the stock, which should make it just about impossible to

clamp in place. So here's what I suggest. Crosscut each board that you need to rip, making it longer by an inch or so. Align the guide for the rip cut; then attach it to the workpiece with a screw at either end. **(Photo 2)** You don't have to worry about damaging the work because the screw holes will be trimmed off when you crosscut the piece to final length. (Another alternative is to run the screw into the back of the board.) When you rip a board to a uniform width, you could use the rip bar that comes with most circular saws, although some are less than sturdy. I like the guide-strip method because you get a true cut and there are no clamps in your way. **(Photo 3)** Of course, you have to use it on an angled rip like the leg taper. I also used it to take both aprons and both stretchers from the same 8-foot board, while the three battens came from another 8-footer.

Routing the Leg Mortises

The aprons and legs are joined with mortise-and-tenon joints. You can do this job several ways, but one of the easiest is to use a plunge router equipped with an edge guide. Using this approach, clamp the leg in a mortising fixture that you make yourself.

To set up the router and edge guide, you need to lay out a mortise on one of the legs. Take the layout from "Leg Layout" (below left) "Mortise & Tenon Joint" (page 50). In addition to scribing the sides, top, and bottom of the mortise, mark a center-line across it, as indicated in the drawing. This line is used to locate the leg in the fixture, and it is the only layout mark needed on the other three legs. Note that although the top of the mortise eventually will be open, at this point the leg is slightly long, and the extra length is at the top. You'll get better results if you rout a uniform mortise around the centerline, and open it later on in the process when you trim the legs to final length.

Clamp the mortising fixture in your workbench vise, or in another clamping work surface. Position the leg in the fixture, aligning the centerline on the leg with the line on the fixture, and clamp it.

Now set up the router. First, fit a $^1/_2$-inch straight bit in the plunge router. This establishes the width of the mortise. Second, after setting the router on the fixture and bottoming the bit against the leg, adjust the plunge depth to $1^1/_2$ inches. Every mortise will now be the same depth.

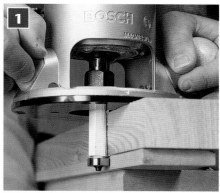

Smooth the sawed taper on the legs with a router and a long flush-trimming bit. A piece of MDF placed underneath guides the cut as the bearing on the tip of the bit rides along the MDF edge.

Drive a drywall screw at each end of the guide strip to hold the work. A long screw pins both pieces to your sawhorse, installs as easily as a series of clamps, and won't interfere with the path of your circular saw.

Make a clean and easy rip cut with a straight-edged guide strip screwed securely in place. A carbide-tipped combination blade should leave an edge smooth enough to need only moderate finishing.

LEG LAYOUT

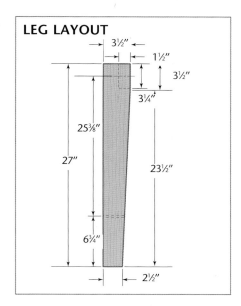

3½"
1½"
3½"
3¼"
25⅜"
27"
23½"
6¾"
2½"

Third, mount the edge guide. Set the router on the fixture and very carefully align the bit over the mortise layout. Bring the guide against the side of the fixture and lock it down. Every mortise will now be the same distance from (and parallel with) the leg's face. Finally, move the bit to the bottom line of the mortise. Set a scrap against the end of the edge guide and attach it to the fixture with a drywall screw. This built-in stop prevents you from cutting a mortise that is too long.

With the set-up complete, rout the first mortise. Be sure you feed in the proper direction. Plunge the bit, feed the router to cut, then retract the bit and return the router to the starting position. Make a series of cuts, each about ¼ inch deeper than the previous one.

When you have reached the final depth, unclamp the leg, turn it end-for-end, and reclamp it. Repeat the mortising cut to center the mortise on the leg. You can probably complete this in a single pass, two at most.

Rout the remaining three mortises in the same way. Because of the way the fixture and the router are set up, all the legs will have identical mortises.

Finally, measure from the foot, and trim each leg to the same, final length. It pays to get these measurements exactly the same. This step will remove the top wall from the mortise, opening it at the top. If necessary, use a file to remove any fillet that remains.

Cutting the Apron Tenons
The goal here is to make tenons that will perfectly fit the mortises that have already be cut. As with the mortises, there are numerous ways to cut tenons.

A good approach is to use a router and a homemade jig. Find plans for the jig in "Routing Tenons," page 18.

I used a basic six-step sequence. First, you need to collect your router, the appropriate bit, the tenoning jig, the aprons, layout tools, and a couple of clamps. Then lay out the shoulders of each tenon according to the dimensions on the drawings.

Second, fit the bit in the router, and adjust the depth of cut to be about ³/₁₆ inch more than the thickness of the tenoning jig's base. The bit's shank-mounted bearing must ride against the jig base.

Third, to prove the depth-of-cut setting, use a scrap of the apron stock. Apply a couple of clamps, simultaneously securing the jig on the work and both pieces to the workbench.

Fourth, make a cut, routing the first tenon cheek.

Fifth, unclamp the work, and turn the test piece over. Align the jig, clamp it, and rout the second cheek.

Sixth, test the fit of your sample tenon in a mortise. If the tenon is too thick, adjust the router, and make a second round of cuts on the same test tenon.

When you are satisfied with the fit (parts should fit snugly without being forced into place), move on to the working stock.

Position the jig on the apron, making sure the edge of the jig's base is directly on the tenon shoulder line. As you form each tenon, be sure to rout across the apron's bottom edge. The bottom corners of each tenon must be rounded to match the corners of the routed mortise. You can round the corners using a chisel or a file. **(Photo 4)**

Use a wood file (or a chisel if you're careful), *to round off the square edges on the tenons. You need to create the same shape made by the router bit on the mortise, or square off all the mortises instead.*

Cutting the Edge Laps
The two aprons and the two stretchers are connected with a joint called an edge lap. It is very much like a cross lap, but the cuts are made into the edges of the pieces, not the faces. You notch the edge of each of the mating pieces, cutting through half the width. When assembled, the pieces cross at 90 degrees, and their edges are flush. In this project, one apron/stretcher is notched in its upper edge, the other in its lower edge.

Lay out the laps using a rule, a square, and a scrap of working stock. Because these laps are square to the faces, you can cut both at the same time. Use a circular saw with the blade depth adjusted to cut halfway through the stock. Cut the shoulders; then make closely spaced cuts to remove as much of the interior waste as possible. Clean the bottoms of the notches with a chisel.

Because a different depth setting is required for the aprons, cut them separately. The aprons have already been tenoned, so when you cut the laps, make sure you orient one right-side up and the other upside down.

Assemble the Legs and Aprons
Glue two legs to one apron and two legs to the other apron using a waterproof glue. Spread a thin coat of glue on the inside of the mortise and on the tenon with a cheap bristle brush. Keep these coats thin and even to avoid a lot of squeeze-out and cleanup once the pieces are joined. Clamp each assembly with two pipe clamps, one on each side of the assembly. **(Photo 5)**

MORTISE & TENON JOINT

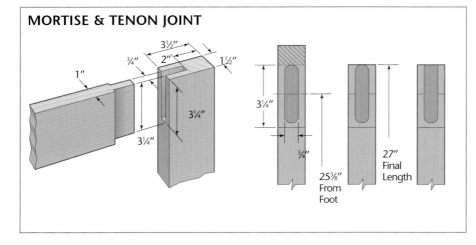

3½"
¾"
2"
1½"
1"
3¼"
3¼"
3¼"
¾"
25⅜" From Foot
27" Final Length

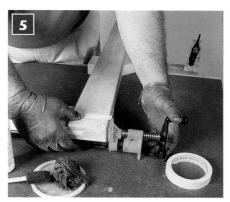

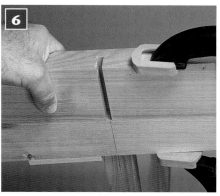

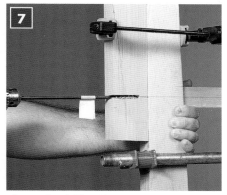

To prevent the clamp jaws from denting the edges of the legs, tape scraps of wood, called cauls, to the legs. Tighten the first clamp beneath the assembly; then add a second clamp on top to balance the pressure.

Make a jig to guide your long drill bit by routing a ⅞-in.-deep, ¼-in.-wide dado at right angles across a scrap of 2x4, stopping it ¾ in. shy of the edge. You can keep the bit in the dado while you drill.

Clamp the drill guide to the leg with the center of the dado aligned on the axis of the lag hole. Mark the hole depth with a flag on the bit. When the flag gets to the edge of your guide, the hole is deep enough.

Installing the Stretchers

Begin with the miter cuts, which make the angle between the stretcher and the leg the same as the angle between the apron and the leg. Place the body of a beveled square against the apron, and adjust the blade against the leg to capture the apron-to-leg angle. Transfer the angle to the stretchers.

Next, drill holes for the dowels into the bottom edges of the stretchers, and set up to glue a dowel in each one. The idea here is to provide better bite for screws that hold the pieces together. The holes should be just under ½ inch in diameter and about 1 inch deep. The center should be about ¾ inch from the end of the stretcher.

Test-fit the leg-and-apron units upside down on the workbench or a pair of sawhorses. Make sure the aprons are square to each other; then clamp this assembly to the bench or horses. Set the stretchers in place,

and align them so they are an equal distance from each foot. Apply pipe clamps to the ends of the legs, and apply just enough pressure to pinch the stretchers in position.

Now you must drill pilot holes through the legs for the assembly screws and, at the same time, penetrate ¼ inch or so into the stretcher. Using a rule and square, lay out the path of the bolt on the surface of each leg and the adjacent stretcher. Because proper alignment of the stretcher lag screw holes is so important, take a moment to make this jig to guide your long drill bit. Rout a ⅞-inch-deep, ¼-inch-wide dado at right angles across a scrap of 2x4, stopping it about ¾ inch shy of the edge. **(Photo 6)** Rest the jig on scrap, and drill through the material remaining at the end of the dado. You can keep the shank of the bit against the bottom of the dado while you drill. Then chuck a long

¼-inch-diameter twist bit in your drill, and drill a hole through the leg and just into the stretcher. If you drill too far into the stretcher, the screw won't hold.

The final operation is to extend each pilot hole into the stretcher. Clamp the drill guide to the leg, with the center of the dado aligned on the axis of the lag hole. Switch to a ³⁄₁₆-inch-diameter bit, and extend the hole about 1½ to 2 inches. To control the depth of the hole, measure from the tip of the bit, and wrap a piece of tape around the bit. When the tape flag gets to the edge of your guide, the hole is deep enough. **(Photo 7)**

Assembly is as simple as gluing and screwing the parts together. Apply water-resistant glue to the end of the stretcher, and set it in place, resting on the temporary support blocks. Turn the lags through the pilot holes in the legs, until they just

EDGE-LAP JOINTS

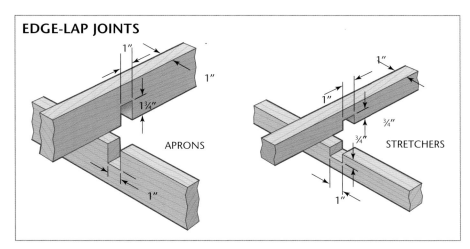

1″
1″
1″
1¾″
1″
APRONS

1″
1″
¾″
¾″
1″
STRETCHERS

LEG ELEVATION

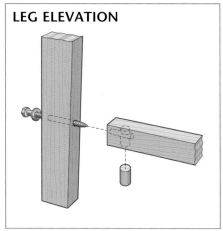

Clamp scraps of MDF or plywood to the aprons to keep them square as you install the battens. Screws driven through the long batten into both aprons help to hold the leg assembly square after the clamps are off.

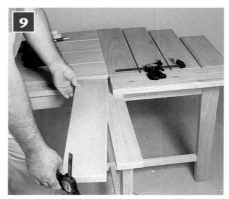

Use the long tabletop boards to align the shorter ones. Make a centerline on the batten (marked in red) to aid your setup. Position and clamp the board, and drive screws up through the batten to secure it.

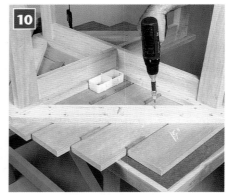

Turn the table over on you work surface, and insert hardboard scraps between the boards to maintain spacing. Make sure the boards are parallel; then screw on the cleat that ties the tabletop together.

engage the stretchers. Now apply the pipe clamps, pinching the stretchers between the legs, and turn the lags the rest of the way into the holes until they are tight. After the glue sets up, you can remove the pipe clamps and the support blocks.

Attaching the Battens

The battens are the link between the legs and the tabletop. You attach them to the aprons with screws, then attach the tabletop by driving screws through the battens into the top boards. The battens also lock the leg-and-apron assembles in proper alignment.

Mount the long batten first. Center it over an apron. Drill pilot holes, and drive 3-inch deck screws through the batten into the legs and into the aprons. Driving screws through this first batten into the apron that's at right angles to it will help keep the aprons square to each other. **(Photo 8)**

Attach the short battens in a similar manner. Make sure these battens are butted tightly against the edges of the long batten.

Cutting the Tabletop Parts

Although the finished tabletop is round, the boards that form it are square-cut to begin with. Each quadrant is composed of four $5/4$x6 boards, and each board is rough-cut to a different length. To make up all the quadrants you need to cut four boards of each length.

To start, you need to cut and miter the four cleats that extend from batten to batten. These are screwed to the undersides

of the tabletop boards, and they keep the quadrant assemblies together.

After cutting the boards to length (and sanding them), ease their edges with a $1/8$-inch or $3/16$-inch roundover bit in a router. You can do all the upper edges or just the long edges that won't be tight against an adjoining board. The idea is to eliminate relatively sharp edges that could make you uncomfortable when you use the table.

Assembling the Tabletop

Use the four long boards to align the other three boards in each quadrant. To do this, screw at least two of these boards to the leg assembly. You need to scribe alignment lines for the long boards on the battens. I used a chalk line, but a pencil line drawn along a straightedge works just fine. **(Photo 9)**

Install the first board. Apply some glue (or construction adhesive) at the appropriate spots on the battens. Align a long board on the line with its corner nudging the centerpoint of the table. Clamp it, and then drill pilot holes, and drive $1^{5}/8$-inch galvanized screws through the battens into the underside of the board. Remove the clamps.

Repeat the sequence to install the second long board. You can go on and install the remaining two long boards at this time. Or you can jump ahead now and install the three shorter boards to fill in a quadrant.

Attach the shorter boards with the table upside down on the workbench. The assembly will rest on the long boards, so

you can slide the ends of the shorter ones underneath the battens. Apply glue or adhesive to the boards where they will contact the battens. Butt the ends of these boards against one long board, and align them parallel with the other. You can use spacers made of scraps of $1/4$-inch-thick hardboard to align the boards and set a consistent gap between them. Drill pilot holes, and drive screws through the batten into the boards. Then lay the cleat in place, and check its fit. Remove the cleat and apply glue to it. Replace it, drill pilot holes, and drive two or three screws through it into each board it crosses. **(Photo 10)** After the first quadrant is done, move to the second, and then the third and fourth.

If you are interested in other tabletop options, you can follow the same basic cutting and assembly sequence but substitute different lumber. For example, you can use tongue-and-groove boards, different types of lumber in a pattern of alternating boards, or lumber that matches your deck.

Routing the Tabletop Shape

This is a trammel operation, which means that you hook your router to a pivoting arm that can guide it in a large-diameter cut. (Find plans for a trammel in "Router Trammel," page 19). Typically, you use a screw as the secure pivot point for a trammel. But if you feel that a screw hole in the center of the tabletop will degrade it, make yourself a pivot base. Use carpet tape to bond a scrap of wood to the tabletop, and drive the screw into it.

Use a trammel-mounted router to form the final circular shape, working counterclockwise. Keep the router moving so that the wood doesn't burn, and limit the cutting depth to about ⅛ to ¼ in. per pass.

A plunge router will make it easier to begin the cut and to increase the cut depth after each circuit. But if you set the trammel so that the bit's cutting edge is just tangent to the end of one of the longest tabletop boards, you should be able to handle the cut with a fixed-base router. Another option is to use a string and pencil to scribe your circle. Once that's done you can make a rough cut just slightly outside the line using a saber saw. That can save you some adjustment time with the trammel making repeated passes to gradually trim down the longest boards.

The biggest potential problem is blow-out that breaks away chips at the edges of the boards. The solution to this common splintering problem is to back up the edges. If you used ¼-inch spacers to establish the gap between boards, all you have to do is wedge those spacers between the boards along the path the bit will take. (Make index-card shims to wedge the spacers in place, if necessary.) With the spacers in place, the cut will be continuous, and you won't have splintering at the edges to contend with.

The tabletop diameter is 45½ inches. Use a trammel and pencil to lay out the cut line on the tabletop. With that marked, wedge the spacers into the gaps along the line. Make sure that they are flush with the top surfaces of the tabletop boards so that they don't get in the way of the router.

Attach the trammel to your router base, and chuck a ½-inch straight bit in your router. If you are using a plunge router, adjust the plunge depth to allow it to cut

completely through the tabletop (and at four places, the underlying battens). If you are using a fixed-base router, set the cut depth to about ¼ inch. Adjust the trammel to a radius of 22¾ inches, measuring from the pivot to the near point of the bit. Set the router on the tabletop, and drive the pivot screw into the centerpoint (or into the pivot block, if you've elected to use one).

Make the cut in several passes. The first pass should be cut to a depth of no more than ¼ inch. Then you can increase the depth of cut by about that amount with each pass. Feed the router counterclockwise. **(Photo 11)**

After the tabletop cut is completed, remove the trammel from the router, and switch to a roundover bit. Round over the edge of the tabletop. Remove the spacers, and do any touch-up sanding that's needed.

Finishing

Use an exterior-grade finish to protect your work. I applied several coats of a solvent-based marine spar varnish, fol-

lowing the directions on the can. The result is a high-gloss finish that is durable enough to withstand exposure.

For the first coat on bare wood, the manufacturer recommended thinning the varnish with 15 percent mineral spirits. To do this, I cut the top off a 1-quart plastic soda bottle and used a kitchen measuring pitcher graduated in ounces, and water. I marked my make-shift varnish container to hold a total of 5 ounces of the thinned varnish, with a mark at 4½ ounces. I filled the container with varnish to the 4½-ounce mark, then topped it up just over the 5-ounce mark with mineral spirits. After stirring, I applied the finish to the wood after dusting and vacuuming.

When this thinned coat is dry, you should lightly sand the entire piece even though it may seem that you are removing the varnish. Then you need to dust and vacuum again. After that, you can apply a full-strength coat. Lightly sand the table after that coat dries; dust and vacuum again, and apply a second full-strength coat.

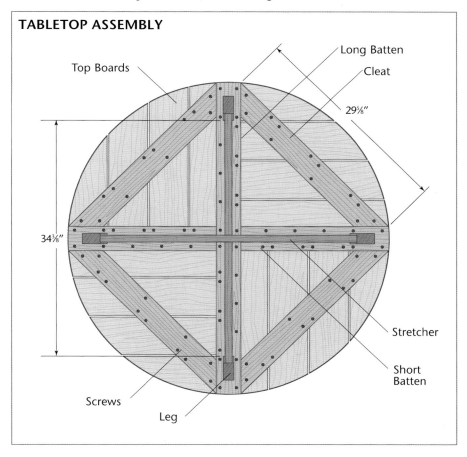

TABLETOP ASSEMBLY

Top Boards

Long Batten

Cleat

29⅝"

34⅜"

Stretcher

Short Batten

Screws

Leg

Deck Chair

At first glance, this deck chair may appear to be as finished as the kind of chairs you might use inside the house. It is a classic, and calls for a higher degree of woodworking skills than some of the bolt-together projects. But overall, the deck chair is a project that do-it-yourselfers can handle. You just need to work methodically and take the directions step by step. If you decide to build a set of chairs (anywhere from two to a full set of eight), you will have to

slow down at some points to build multiple parts. You'll find that this kind of production work is possible (even in a home shop) if you take advantage of the template plans included for this project. Sure, it takes some extra time and material to make the templates. But you'll save even more time in the end, and produce nearly identical parts to make your collection a true set. You'll find that the design of this piece follows basic rules-of-thumb for scaling a chair.

For example, the seat is about 16 inches high, which is comfortable for the average person. The 16-inch seat depth provides good thigh support without putting pressure on the backs of the knees. The backrest is reclined about 9 degrees, but because you'll probably use this chair at a table, the seat is level. When you're done, you'll have a set of chairs to complement the Round Deck Table.

EXPLODED VIEW

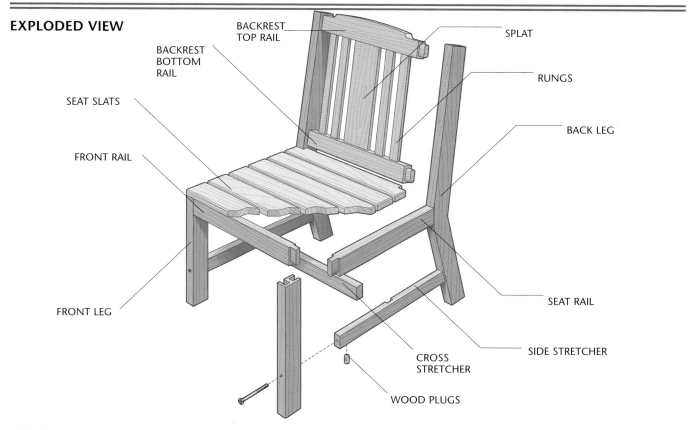

BACKREST TOP RAIL

BACKREST BOTTOM RAIL

SEAT SLATS

FRONT RAIL

FRONT LEG

SPLAT

RUNGS

BACK LEG

SEAT RAIL

SIDE STRETCHER

CROSS STRETCHER

WOOD PLUGS

CUTTING LIST FOR CHAIR (Second number for model with arms)

Part	Number	Thickness	Width	Length	Meranti Stock
Back legs	2	1½"	5½"	36"	2x6
Front legs	2	1½"	2¼"	16" (23")	2x6
Seat rails	2	1½"	2¼"	15¾"	2x6
Front rail	1	1"	2⅝"	18" (23")	¾x6
Side stretchers	2	1"	1½"	15⅞"	¾x6
Cross stretcher	1	1"	1½"	17¼" (22¼")	¾x6
Backrest top rail	1	1"	3½"	18" (23")	¾x6
Backrest bottom rail	1	1"	2½"	18"	¾x6
Splat	1	¾"	3½"	14¼"	1x6
Rungs	4 (6)	¾"	1¼"	14¼"	1x6
Seat slats	6	¾"	2½"	19" (24")	1x6
Armrests	2	1"	3"	20⁵⁄₁₆"	¾x6
Wood plugs	4 (6)	½" dia.	—	1¼"	birch dowel

SHOPPING LIST

For one chair
- 2 pcs. 2x6 8' meranti
- 1 pc. ¾x6 8' meranti
- 1 pc. 1x6 8' meranti
- 1 pc. ½"x36" dowel
- 1⅝" deck screws
- 3" deck screws

For one armchair
- 2 pcs. 2x6 8' meranti
- 1 pc. ¾x6 12' meranti
- 1 pc. 1x6 8' meranti
- 1 pc. ½"x36" dowel
- 1⅝" deck screws
- 3" deck screws

Deck Chair

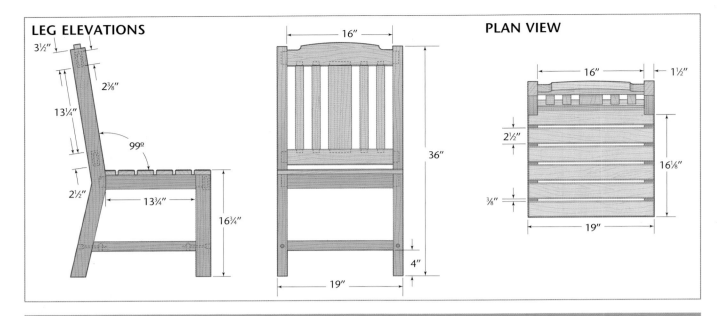

LEG ELEVATIONS

3½"

2⅜"

13¼"

99º

2½"

13¾"

16¾"

16"

36"

19"

4"

PLAN VIEW

16"

1½"

2½"

16⅛"

⅜"

19"

BUILDER'S NOTES

These chairs can stand by themselves, of course, although they are intended as companions for the Round Deck Table on page 46.

Materials

I used meranti on this project, a relative of luan imported from Southeast Asia. The wood is stable and reasonably resistant to weather, with a variable hue ranging from dark pink to light tan. It is easy to work, although the surface never quite gets glassy smooth after sanding.

You'll find that the shopping list calls for more stock than you will actually use in each chair. That's because you can't always buy stock lengths to suit. You may need to work around defects.

You need wood that's true and largely free of knots and other defects. When you can't pick and choose your boards it's wise to order extra material.

Tools and Techniques

Although there are always options, you will save time and effort on this project using a table saw and a plunge router plus a big flush-trimming bit and a dado-and-planer bit.

You'll use the table saw to do a lot of ripping because many of the chair parts are not standard widths. While it is possible to rip the stock you need without a table saw, it just isn't very efficient. A bench-top table saw should be adequate for the cuts required in this project. But you will have to slow your feed rate so you don't overload the motor. Ripping long pieces requires either an outfeed table or a helper to support the stock as it leaves the saw.

Ripping will leave slightly rough edges on the boards, but you can clean them up with a jointer, a plane, or by sanding.

You'll use the router to cut mortises and shape parts from templates—and I used a lot of simple templates. They wouldn't be worth the effort on one chair. But they can save you time and improve your results if you're making four or more. You can use them to

create multiples of the backrest rails and the back legs, and to cut accurate mortises in the legs and backrest rails. Good templates make layout much easier, reduce errors, and create nearly identical parts.

I cut the templates from ¾-inch medium-density fiberboard (MDF), which is a stock item at most big home centers. It's also inexpensive, so if you aren't satisfied with a template, you can toss it and start over without worrying too much about the waste.

To shape the parts, I used a fixed-base router fitted with one of two bits: a long, large-diameter pattern bit, which has the pilot bearing mounted on the shank, or a long, large-diameter flush-trimming bit, which has the bearing on the tip.

I set up the job by bonding the template to the work piece with carpet tape and clamping it in place. After trimming as much of the waste as possible with a saber saw, I use the router to pare away the remaining wood to

get a perfect match with the template. By using a cutter that is guided by a bearing, I was able to use a template cut to exactly the same dimensions as the finished piece of wood.

To cut the mortises with the help of a template, I used a plunge router fitted with a template guide. The step-by-step information that follows will provide details on the size of the template guide and the correct router bit to use for each mortise.

Ideally, you should have a plunge router and a fixed-based router. The fixed-based model is best for edge work, where you want stability. The plunge router is best for mortising where you need to make on-the-fly depth-of-cut changes.

Finish

I applied three coats of marine spar varnish. There are other possibilities, but you'll probably want to duplicate the finish of your matching table.

STEP-BY-STEP

Back-Leg Template

Each back leg for the chair is cut from a 36-inch-long piece of 2x6 stock. It would be easy to saw out a pair of legs with a saber saw if you were building a single chair. But if you are making a set of four chairs to go with the round deck table, you'll need eight back legs. That requires a lot of sawing, sanding, and mortising (for the backrest rails).

The best way to handle it is with templates. I made a template for shaping and mortising the back legs. A bonus is that you can use it for right and left legs, and for standard chairs or the optional model with arms.

I scaled the template shown in the drawing for use with a long flush-trimming bit. I made my template of ¾-inch MDF. You can also use ½-inch MDF or birch plywood, but using hardboard limits you to a ¼-inch template thickness, which is too thin in this case.

The "Back-Leg Template" drawing below provides complete dimensions and depicts the sequence of cuts you'll need to make to produce the template. First cut the leading edges of the leg. **(Photo 1)** Then rout the back edges, using an edge guide to ensure these edges are parallel with the front ones. **(Photo 2)** Finally, lay out and rout the slots for the backrest rail mortises. **(Photo 3)**

The next step is to cut the blanks for the back legs from a piece of 2x6 stock. Select the stock carefully, picking wood that is absolutely flat and true without any cupping or twisting. Crosscut a 36-inch-long piece for each back leg you will be making.

Use a piece of plywood with a straight edge to guide your angled cuts on the template. Cut the template close to the guide edge using a saber saw; then trim it to match the guide with a router and pattern bit.

Rout the back edge of the template using a plunge router fitted with an edge guide. It rides along the cut edge, ensuring that the cut is parallel. With ¾-in. MDF you need to make at least three passes.

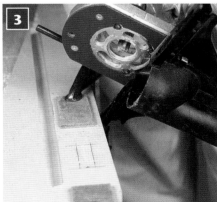

Rout the mortising slots in the template using a plunge router and edge guide. The hardboard stops clamped fore and aft of the layout will prevent the router from cutting beyond the layout lines for the mortise slot.

BACK-LEG TEMPLATE

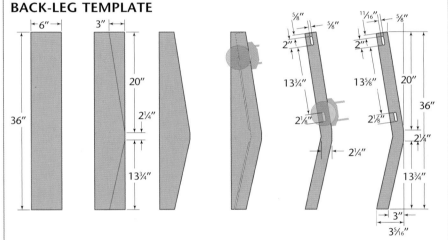
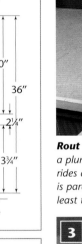

BACK-LEG LAYOUT

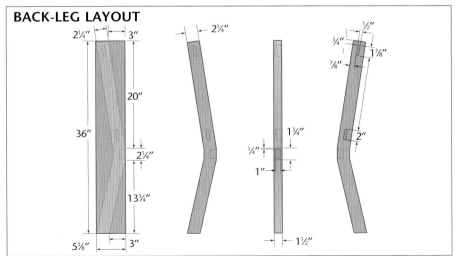

Deck Chair

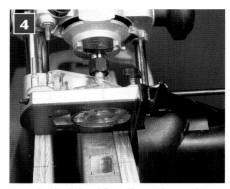

Rout half of the side rail mortise, and turn the workpiece around in the fixture, aligning your reference marks. Then rout the second half of the mortise. This will ensure that the mortise is perfectly centered.

Avoid confusion by laying out right and left legs for each chair at the outset. Set two leg blanks side by side. Trace around the template and mortise slots on one; then flip over the template to trace the second blank.

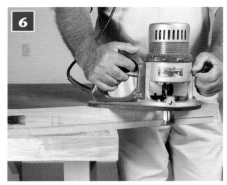

Use your router to trim the leg flush with the template. I used a flush-trimming bit guided by the template below the work. The oversize baseplate on this router extends under the D-handle to provide extra support.

Routing the Side-Rail Mortises

Join the seat rail to the front and back legs with mortise-and-tenon joints. To facilitate tenon-cutting, I designed the tenons to have $1/4$-inch-wide shoulders all around. (There is an exception to this rule later on when you get to the front legs.) To house the tenon in the back leg, create a 1-inch-wide, $1\frac{3}{4}$-inch-high, 1-inch-deep mortise. To cut it you need a plunge router, an edge guide, $5/8$-inch-diameter straight bit, and a version of the shop-made mortising fixture shown in "Routing Mortises," page 16.

As you lay out the mortises on the leg blanks, stack them together, and square layout marks across the lot of them. In addition, use the leg template to ensure that the mortises will be properly located in relation to the final shape of the leg.

When you set up, adjust the edge guide and the stops to produce a $5/8$-inch-wide mortise with a $1/4$-inch-wide shoulder. Cut that, and then turn the workpiece around in the fixture and repeat the cut to produce a mortise that is centered across the stock. **(Photo 4)** You may need to pare the end walls of the mortise flat with a chisel.

Shaping the Back Legs

Stick the template to the leg blank, and use it to guide your router as you shape the leg and excavate the mortises for the backrest rails. Remember that you need to make a left leg and a right leg for each chair. **(Photo 5)**

You can bond the template to the leg blank with a few small patches of carpet tape; improve the bond by squeezing the template and workpiece together with a quick clamp at each taped spot.

To position the template, use the foot, which is flush with the bottom edge of the blank, and the seat-rail flat, which is flush with the edge at the mortise, to align it on the leg blank. The best approach is to clamp the work at the edge of your workbench, cut a section, and then shift the leg position so that you can cut another. Always use two clamps to keep the work from shifting.

Cut away the bulk of the waste using a saber saw, but be sure not to nick the template. Then you can rout the work to match the template with either a pattern bit or a flush-trimming bit.

A pattern bit has the pilot bearing on the shank, so the router must ride on the template. A flush-trimming bit has the bearing on its tip, so the router must ride on the work, with the template on the bottom. **(Photo 6)** For best results, use a large-diameter bit with cutting edges at least $1\frac{1}{2}$ inches long.

Because of the angle, you will be cutting diagonally across the grain. To avoid tearout, the cutting edges should shear down on the grain as much as possible, rather than chopping across it.

After you cut the shape, cut the mortises using a plunge router. The template guide will fit the windows cut in the template and control the width and length of the cuts. But it's up to you to limit the depth of cut to 1 inch and avoid plunging the cuts through the work.

This is a cut where a dust extraction accessory is a plus. Without it, chips can pack the template opening and limit the

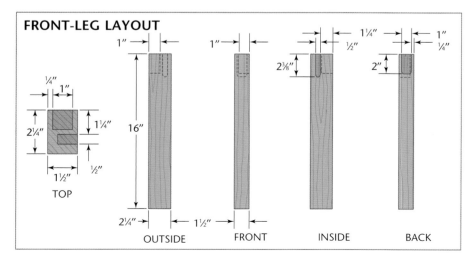

FRONT-LEG LAYOUT

TOP

1" · $1/4$" · $2\frac{1}{4}$" · $1\frac{1}{4}$" · $1/2$" · $1\frac{1}{2}$"

16"

$2\frac{1}{4}$" · $1\frac{1}{2}$"

OUTSIDE · FRONT · INSIDE · BACK

1" · 1" · $1\frac{1}{4}$" · $1/2$" · 1" · $1/4$" · $2\frac{3}{8}$" · 2"

Yard and Garden Furniture

Remove your router after a few passes to clear wood chips from the mortise. They expand into the template opening and pack into the ends of the slot. Vacuum out the chips, and make a final, full-depth pass.

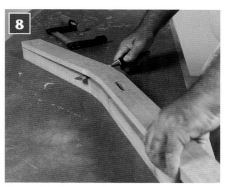

Use a chisel to gently pop the grip of the individual pieces of carpet tape one by one. Pry the template away from the workpiece in stages taking care not to gouge either one. You don't want to break the template.

The legs in front of the router have completed seat-rail mortises guided by the adjacent templates. The mortises are still closed. The leg at left has been trimmed to final length, creating open mortises.

router's movement. **(Photo 7)** If your router doesn't have a dust extractor, use a shop vacuum to remove the chips, and make a final pass to ensure that you've cut the mortise accurately.

When the leg is completed, carefully pry the template from the work with a chisel. **(Photo 8)** When you're ready to attch the template to the next workpiece, use fresh patches of carpet tape to ensure good adhesion. It may still seem pretty sticky, but don't take any chances.

Cutting the Front Legs

The front legs are cut from the same stock as the back legs. You need to rip each pair of legs to the width specified on the cutting list, but crosscut them $\frac{1}{2}$ to $\frac{3}{4}$ inch longer than the desired final length.

As with the back legs, you need to make a mirror-image pair for each chair. Each leg must be mortised for the seat-rail tenon and for the front-rail tenon. Bear in mind that the top rail edges are flush with the leg top in the assembled chair, which would leave only a $\frac{1}{4}$-inch of material between the mortise and the leg top. So I eliminated the shoulder from the top edges of the tenons and made the mortises open at the leg top. You can rout the mortises a little long, then trim the leg to final length. This means you don't have little fillets to pare away at the top of the mortise.

The locations and sizes of the mortises are shown in the "Front Leg Layout" drawing. The $\frac{3}{4}$-inch MDF templates I used to make the mortises are laid out in the "Front-Leg Mortise Template" drawing.

The first step is to make the seat-rail mortise. Because this mortise is centered on the leg, you can attach fences to the template and position the workpiece quickly and consistently.

The second template is for the front rail mortise. This template is flopped. depending on whether you are working on a right or a left leg. Cut the template to the same width as the leg and square up the foot end. Simply align the template on the leg by feel, making it flush with the edges and the foot.

I made both mortises with a $\frac{5}{8}$-inch outside diameter template guide and a $\frac{1}{2}$-inch straight bit. Both mortises are 1 inch deep. You can set up the router once and use it for all the mortises.

To make the seat rail mortise, set the leg blank on edge on the workbench and clamp the template on top of it. Set the router on the template with the guide inside the mortise window, switch it on, plunge the bit into the work, and rout around the perimeter of the window. Make several passes, cutting $\frac{1}{8}$ inch deeper on each pass. Vacuum the chips, and make a final full-depth pass to finish.

The second mortise in each leg is routed the same way, but the template has to be properly oriented and aligned by feel before you clamp it in place. To avoid confusion, work the legs in pairs so that you are sure about cutting the front-rail mortises in the proper places on each leg. **(Photo 9)** Trim each leg to it's final length.

FRONT-LEG MORTISE TEMPLATE

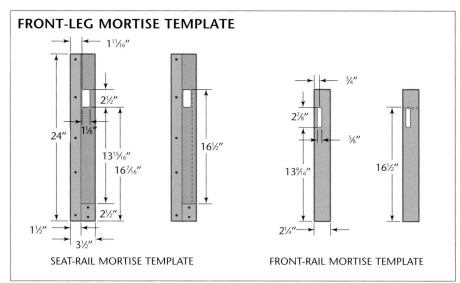

SEAT-RAIL MORTISE TEMPLATE

FRONT-RAIL MORTISE TEMPLATE

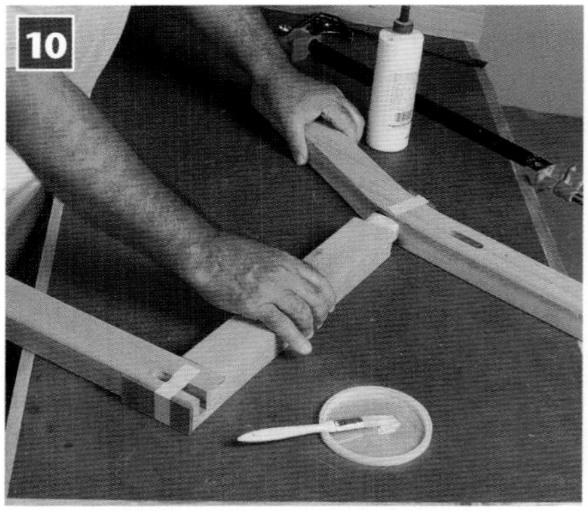
10

Apply an even coat of waterproof glue *in the mortise and on the tenons with a bristle brush. Then assemble the parts and apply clamps over ¼-in. plywood cauls taped in place to protect the legs.*

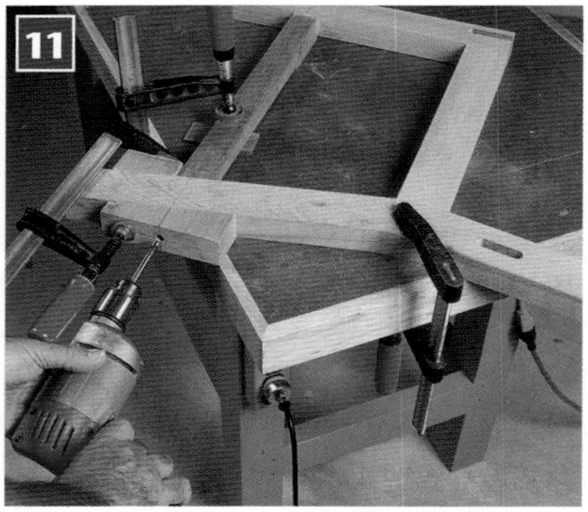
11

You can attach a boring guide *to help you drill the counterbores in the legs. Clamp the guide to the back leg using a wedge-shaped caul on the inner edge. The guide helps to keep the bit running true.*

BACKREST RAIL

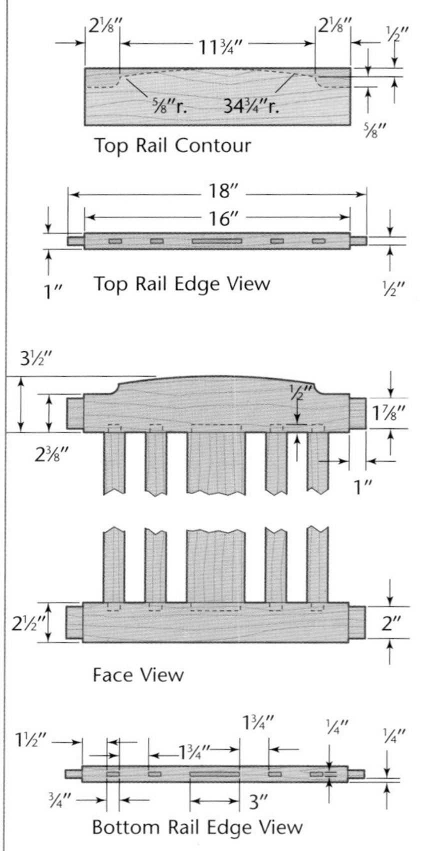

2⅛″
11¾″
2⅛″
½″
⅝″r.
34¾″r.
⅝″
Top Rail Contour
18″
16″
1″
Top Rail Edge View
½″
3½″
½″
1⅞″
2⅜″
1″
2½″
2″
Face View
1¾″
¼″
¼″
1½″
1¾″
¾″
3″
Bottom Rail Edge View

Tenoning the Seat Rails

After the mortises are prepared you need to cut tenons on the rails. You can use a router with the tenoning jig shown in "Routing Tenons," page 18. Remember that the tenon on the front end of the rail does not have a shoulder across the top edge. When you are done with the router, you will have a tenon with squared edges. The bottom edges will need to be rounded over with a file so the tenon will fit the mortises.

Assembling the Side Frames

Now you can assemble the parts you've created so far, starting with a dry run to ensure that everything fits. Use two pipe clamps per assembly; holding a back leg, a seat rail, and a front leg. You should be able to press the parts together. If you have to use more than a gentle tap with a mallet, the joints are too tight. Use this practice run to set the distance between the pipe clamp jaws. It's also wise to fasten protective cauls in place with masking tape so you don't have to fumble with them while you're applying the clamps.

Knock the assembly apart, and spread a thin, even coat of waterproof glue inside of the mortise and on the tenons. **(Photo 10)** Then assemble the parts, and apply a clamp across each side of the assembly.

Making the Side Stretchers

Cut the stretchers after the side frames are assembled. Set the side frame on the workbench, and lay out the location of the stretcher's bottom edge and the axis of the assembly screw hole on the front leg. Then use a framing square to transfer them to the back leg. Align a strip of stretcher stock on the marks; trace along the inner edges of the legs; and cut to the lines.

Now drill the counterbores and shank holes in the legs for the assembly screws. Clamp the side frame and stretcher in place, and use a ⅜-inch Forstner bit. If you are leery of doing this without a guide, make one. Use a ⅜-inch straight bit in your plunge router to make a deep hole into the end of a scrap of 2x6 stock. Then crosscut a 1½-inch long piece from the scrap, and clamp this guide to the front leg, aligning the guide hole with the counterbore. **(Photo 11)** Insert the Forstner bit in the hole, and drill as far as you can. Then remove the guide, and switch to a 3⁄16-inch twist drill bit to extend the hole.

The counterbored hole in the back leg is drilled about the same way. But a guide is more important here because your bit must address the leg surface at an angle. To make this guide, bore a hole in scrap with the plunge router, but crosscut the guide from the scrap on an angle to match the angle of the leg.

To improve the grip of the assembly screws in the end grain of the stretcher, give them some side grain to bite into. Drill holes into the bottom edges, and glue a dowel into each hole.

Cutting the Front and Backrest Rails, Splat, and Rungs

Cut these parts from 5⁄4 and 1-by stock. Some have to be ripped to width, as well. Cut these parts to the dimensions specified on the cutting list. Again, be choosy in selecting stock for these parts. You want them to be flat, square, and true.

Mortising the Backrest Rails

Join the splat and the rungs to the backrest rails with mortise-and-tenon joints. Cut the mortises first, according to the dimensions in the "Backrest Rail" drawing above. They are the same on both top and bottom rails, of course. You'll rout at least 10 mortises of different lenghts per chair. If you are making four chairs, as I did, you'll find that the job is easier using a template.

I made a template using more of that ¾-inch MDF, including mortising slots for each rung, the splat, and two extras that can be used in the armchair. **(Photo 12)** A screwed-in-place fence and a clamped-on stop make it easy to position the template on the edge of the rail blanks. Each slot is ⅝ inch wide and ⅛ inch longer than the mortise you cut with the slot. I made the template using a plunge router equipped with an edge guide and a ⅝-inch straight bit. I laid out the template carefully and

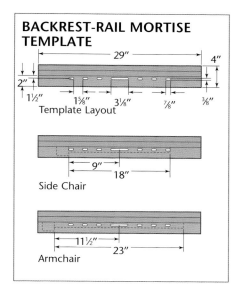

BACKREST-RAIL MORTISE TEMPLATE

29"
4"
2"
1½"
1⅝"
3⅛"
⅞"
⅜"
Template Layout

9"
18"
Side Chair

11½"
23"
Armchair

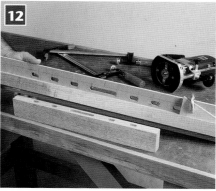

The backrest rail mortise template has a spaced slot for each mortise and a fixed fence to center them. A clamped-on stop holds the template end to end. Extra rung mortises help with the optional armchair rail.

To cut tenons on the rungs (there are four for each side chair), clamp several together and fit the assembly into a tenoning jig. Find jig plans and how-to help in the "Tools and Techniques" chapter.

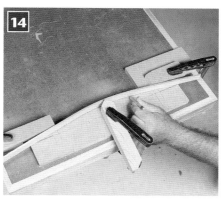

To create the backrest arch on your template, lay out the end points and the high point and clamp blocks at those points. Flex a thin ripping so it bows along the three points, and trace it's outline on the template.

Use a Forstner bit to make the small arc that adds an elegant twist to the contour of the crest rail. The 1¼-in.-diameter bit creates the basic shape, although you will need to sand and smooth the edges.

used stops clamped to the template blank to control the length of each slot I produced. I invested more time making the template than I would have routing all the mortises in one rail. But the time I saved in routing the rails using the template made it worthwhile.

To use the template, fit a ⅝-inch template guide into your plunge router, and chuck a ½-inch straight bit in the collet. Cut the rail blanks to size. Then adjust the position of the stop on the template so that the center of the long mortise slot (for the splat) is over the center of the rail blank. Stand the rail on edge, and set the template on top of it. Apply two clamps to hold the template on the rail and the parts on the workbench. This will cover two of the mortising slots, so you have to rout as many of the mortises as you can, then shift the clamps and continue.

Cutting the Tenons

To complete the chair-frame joinery, use the same router, bit, jig, and setup that you used to cut tenons on the seat rails. Use the setup to make a test tenon on a scrap of the working stock before you rout the parts and test-fit it to an appropriate mortise. If it fits, proceed to rout the parts.

Instead of cutting so many rungs one at a time, you may want to gang several rungs together and insert the group into a tenoning jig to cut them all at once. **(Photo 13)** Complete plans for this jig, including step-by-step construction tips, are shown in "Routing Tenons," page 18.

At this point you can cut a partial tenon on the backrest top rail—a tenon that will be far wider than the mortise is long. After the top edge of this part is shaped (in the next step), you must cut the top shoulder and trim the tenon with a backsaw.

To fit the routed mortises, you will need to round the corners of each tenon with a file or chisel.

Shaping the Backrest Top Rail

You can lay out the cut line on each top rail and make your cut with a saber saw. Another option is to make a template, stick it to the rail, and use a router to make the cut. This way you can be sure that every rail will have the same contour. Also, the router-cut rail edges will need little, if any, sanding.

Follow the "Backrest Rail" drawing to lay out the shape of the template. I used a flexible ripping held in shape with three clamped blocks to create the curve. **(Photo 14)** The template should be as long as the rails, including tenons. Then you can use a 1¼-inch-diameter Forstner bit to bore through the template **(Photo 15)**, making the radius between the top arc and the edge of the board near the tenon. Clamp the template to a rail, cut away the bulk of the waste with a saber saw, and rout the edge. With the edge contour-cut, the tenon will be a little closer to fitting. But to complete the tenon, you must cut the shoulder and trim the tenon to fit.

Assembling the Chair Frame

Assemble the sanded backrest parts, and join the subassembly to the two

STRETCHER ASSEMBLY

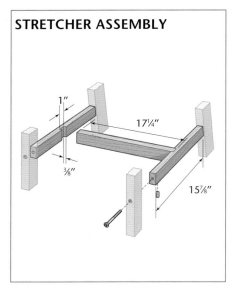

1"

17¼"

³⁄₈"

15⅞"

Clamp the bottom backrest rail; glue the tenons; and insert the rungs and the splat. Then add the top rail. Spread the glue thinly, so you don't have to contend with drips and runs. It's wise to try a test-fit first.

Set the second side frame onto the rails that have already been glued to the first side frame. Nestle the tenons into their mortises one by one; then apply clamps to pull the joints closed. Leave the clamps on overnight.

side assemblies. Try a test-fit first. Secure the bottom rail in the bench vise, and apply a thin coat of glue to the splat tenons and the rungs. As you finish applying glue to a part, insert its tenon in the rail, and then add the upper rail **(Photo 16)**. Free this assembly from your clamps or vise, and apply a few clamps to seat and secure the assembly. Leave the clamps in place for at least an hour. After removing the clamps from the backrest, put glue in the tenons one side rail and assemble the backrest to it. The glue the other side frame in place. **(Photo 17)** Stand up the assembly, and use pipe clamps paralleling each rail. Repeat this basic process for each chair

you must assemble.

Installing the Seat Slats

Each chair has six seat slats glued and screwed to the chair. You can drill counterbores with a Forstner bit and conceal the screw heads under wood plugs if you want. Cut the slats to the dimensions specified on the cutting list, and notch the back slat to fit between the back legs. **(Photo 18)** After you plan out the slat spacing, sand them smooth, adding any finishing touches, such as chamfered or rounded-over edges. Install the slats using glue and with screws driven through pilot holes. To plug counterbored screws, use a plug cutter in your drill to make plugs

from scraps of the working stock, gluing one into each counterbore. Try to set the plug grain parallel with the slat grain.

Installing the Stretchers

After you extend the pilot holes for the assembly screws well into the stretchers, set the stretchers in place; lay out the location of the cross stretcher, and mark it for length. Upend the chair on the workbench and clamp a scrap to each leg to support the side stretchers in the proper alignment. **(Photo 19)** Square up marks for the cross stretcher, then add about 3⁄4 inch to its length before cutting.

Next, dado the side stretchers for the cross stretcher. I set them side-by-side,

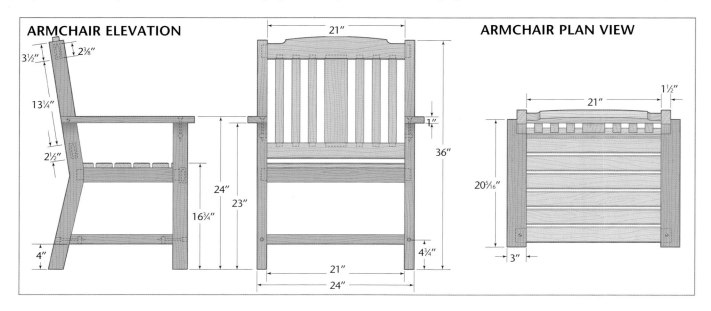

ARMCHAIR ELEVATION

3½"   2⅜"

13¼"

2½"

4"

21"

24"

23"

16¾"

1"

36"

21"

4¾"

24"

ARMCHAIR PLAN VIEW

1½"

21"

20⁵⁄₁₆"

3"

Set the back seat slat on the seat rails, snug it up against the back legs, and mark the notch areas. Then straighten out and square up your marks, and use a saber saw or sharp trim saw to make the cuts.

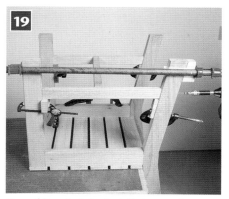

Upend the chair to install the stretcher assembly, and clamp a scrap to each leg to temporarily support the assembly. Then clamp two legs to pinch the side stretcher, and drive a 3-in. screw through each leg.

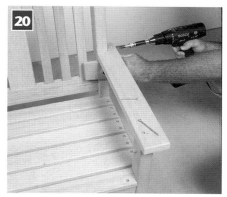

Drive the longer screw through the armrest face into the top of the leg and through the dowel for more holding power. The pilot for the second screw goes through the edge of the armrest into the back leg.

sandwiched between strips of scrap to prevent tearout from the router bit. I used a T-square to guide the router, and then cut a 3/8-inch-deep dado for the cross stretcher through both pieces. Now you can glue and clamp the cross stretcher between the two side stretchers and set the assembly back in place on the chair. Drive a 3-inch screw through each leg into the edge of a stretcher. Glue a wooden plug into each counterbore, trim it flush, and sand it. After a final sanding, vacuum the surfaces clean, and apply your finish.

The Armchair Option

The only differences on this version of the chair are the overall width, the length of the front legs, and, of course, the armrests. You cut the front legs to the optional dimensions specified in the cutting list, following the drawings to size and position the mortises for the side and front rails. Because the legs extend beyond the seat, these mortises are 1/4 inch shorter than those on the side chair. Also, the tenons on the side and front rails are shouldered all the way around.

The backrest on the armchair model has two extra rungs and the contour of the top rail is altered slightly. Both these differences are reflected in the "Armchair Backrest Rail" layout drawing, below right.

On the seat slats, you'll have to notch the back one, and the one between the front legs as well.

On the armrests, you should round over or chamfer the edges and notch the inside back corner to accommodate the back leg. You'll need to bevel the leading edge to match the angle of the leg. Secure each armrest with two screws driven through pilot holes. Because the screws in the front leg hit end grain, I glued a piece of 1/2-inch dowel in a hole drilled into the inner face of the leg. **(Photo 20)** To keep the armrest unblemished, I drilled a counterbore and covered the screw with a wood plug.

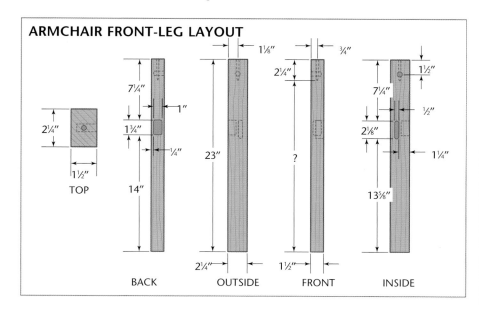

ARMCHAIR FRONT-LEG LAYOUT

BACK   OUTSIDE   FRONT   INSIDE

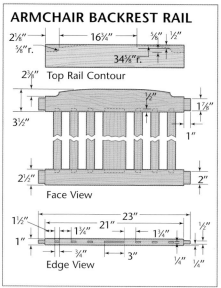

ARMCHAIR BACKREST RAIL

Top Rail Contour

Face View

Edge View

Adirondack Chair & Rest

Adirondack chairs are noted for their graceful, angular design. Remarkably, chairs built with this straightforward, nail-them-boards-together construction are comfortable. You just fall into that seat and lean back, and the aches and strife of the day tend to melt away. In the same curious way, Adirondack chairs are attractive, and they occasionally find themselves in rather stylish indoor settings. The name isn't just some market-

Yard and Garden Furniture

ing gimmick. The first such chair was constructed at the turn of the twentieth century in the general area of the Adirondack Mountains in upstate New York when backwoods camps furnished with elaborately rustic furniture were all the rage. The forerunner of this chair was one of the home-brewed solutions to a desire for comfortable seating in the camps. Soon it was a hallmark of Catskills resorts as well as Adirondack camps, and today you can find them all over the country. This particular Adirondack chair design has that original angularity combined with graceful curves and softened edges. The stringers of the chair and its companion footrest feature elegant curves that are at once attractive and intriguing. The design is distinctive; the chair is comfortable and practical; and the project is straightforward, so you can make one yourself.

EXPLODED VIEW

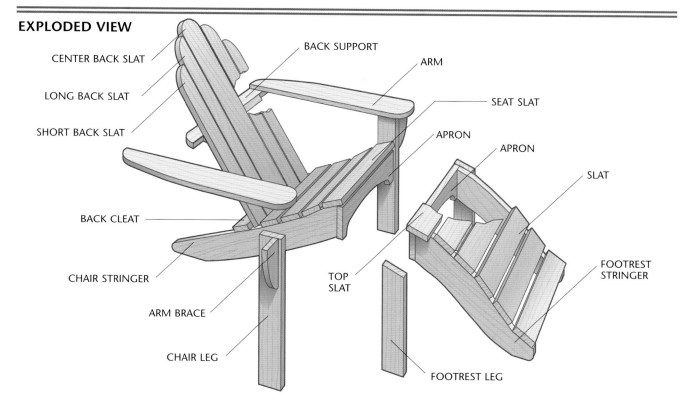

CUTTING LIST (Some parts are left long during construction.)					
Part	Number	Thickness	Width	Length	Pine Stock
Chair stringers	2	1 1/16"	7 1/4"	36"	5/4x8
Chair legs	2	1 1/16"	3 1/2"	21 1/2"	5/4x4
Chair apron	1	3/4"	5 1/2"	22 5/8"	1x6
Back cleat	1	1 1/16"	3 1/2"	22 5/8"	5/4x4
Back support	1	1 1/16"	3 1/2"	28 3/4"	5/4x4
Arms	2	3/4"	5 1/2"	29"	1x6
Center back slat	1	3/4"	5 1/2"	35 1/4"	1x6
Long back slats	2	3/4"	3 1/2"	33 3/8"	1x4
Short back slats	2	3/4"	3 1/2"	30 3/4"	1x4
Arm braces	2	1 1/16"	3"	8"	5/4x8
Footrest apron	1	3/4"	5 1/2"	22 5/8"	1x6
Seat slats	4	3/4"	3 1/2"	22 5/8"	1x4
Footrest stringers	2	1 1/16"	5 1/2"	23 3/4"	5/4x8
Legs	2	1 1/16"	3 1/2"	15 1/4"	5/4x4
Top slat	1	3/4"	3 1/2"	24 3/4"	1x4
Footrest slats	5	3/4"	3 1/2"	22 5/8"	1x4

SHOPPING LIST

- 1 pc. 5/4x8 12' pine
- 1 pc. 5/4x4 12' pine
- 4 pcs. 1x4 8' pine
- 1 pc. 1x6 8' pine
- 1 1/4" galvanized deck screws
- 1 5/8" galvanized deck screws

Adirondack Chair & Rest

CHAIR ELEVATIONS

CHAIR PLAN VIEW

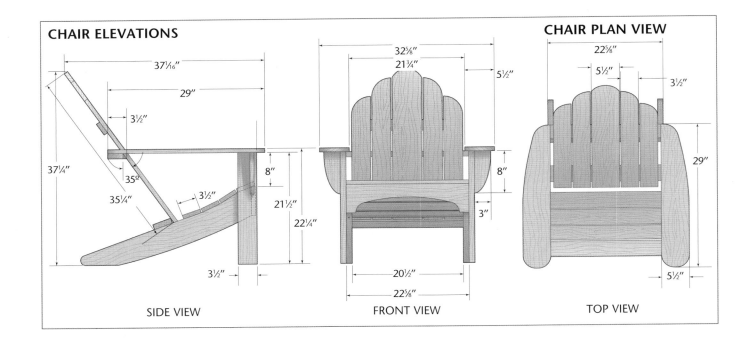

SIDE VIEW

FRONT VIEW

TOP VIEW

BUILDER'S NOTES

The original Adirondack chairs were made of clear hemlock and pine with a single wide board for the back and another for the seat. From the late 1920s on, after rapacious lumbering in the Adirondacks had cleared the really prime material from the region, chair makers used the now-familiar slatted construction.

Materials

You can use any of the common outdoor woods with clear finishes or paint. I used No. 2 common pine for most of the components, despite the knots. Overall, you should be selective and avoid boards with loose knots, knots on the edges, or pitch pockets. (I bought a clear board for each arm.)

One material you need that doesn't end up in the finished chair is hardboard, known to many by the brandname Masonite. I use it for templates—so you can lay out and cut some of the irregular pieces on an inexpensive and easily worked material. Then you can use the template again and again as a guide for the reproduction of duplicate parts.

The edges of your templates need to be free from nicks and bumps that can transfer to the cut. To reveal potential problems, lay the template on paper, and trace around it with a pencil. If at first you don't succeed, start over and make another template, which beats scrapping a piece of pine.

Tools and Techniques

You don't need a woodshop and stationary tools to make this chair. The usual portable power tools—circular saw, saber saw, router, drill-driver, sanders—will suffice. A handful of special bits, plus a drill and a router, can boost the quality of your work.

To help you shape the curvaceous parts, you may want to use templates to guide your router. Use either a straight-pattern bit or a flush-trimming bit with a pilot bearing that rides along the template. Whichever bit you choose, it must have cutting edges 1¼ inches long.

For drilling, countersinking, and counterboring pilot holes for the screws, you can use a combination pilot bit. It creates a hole scaled to the screw shank, plus a countersink for the screw- head. Once you drive the screw, you can fill the counterbore with putty or a wooden plug.

That leads to a plug cutter and a Forstner bit—tools to make your own wood plugs. Use the plug cutter to bore into a piece of the working stock. Don't bore all the way through. Instead, stick the blade of a screwdriver into the groove, and twist it to snap the plug free (or slice through the bases of several plugs at once using a saw).

I've found that the best bet is to begin pilot holes by drilling a counterbore with the Forstner bit, which cuts a clean, chip-free edge and leaves a dimple in the bottom of the hole. This centers the regular combination bit I use to drill the pilot and countersink holes.

Finish

You can use a clear sealer, but paint offers protection from damaging ultraviolet (UV) radiation and helps to reduce decay by sealing out moisture. Over time, the paint can crack, fade, and require recoating. But this is the case with any finish.

For best long-term results, make sure the wood surface is clean and dust-free. Prime first with a latex primer, and seal any knots with shellac or stain blocker. Use a couple of coats. This is not a guarantee that a knot won't bleed through the finish coat of paint, but it will definitely help. When the priming and stain-killing is completed, add your final, full-strength coats.

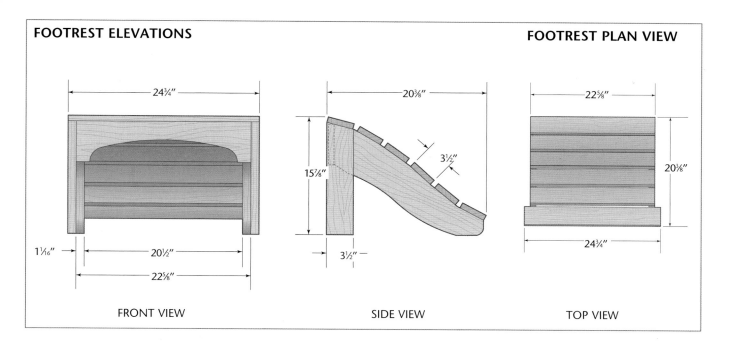

FOOTREST ELEVATIONS

FOOTREST PLAN VIEW

FRONT VIEW 24¾" 20½" 1¹⁄₁₆" 22⅝"

SIDE VIEW 20⅜" 15⅞" 3½" 3½"

TOP VIEW 22⅝" 20⅜" 24¾"

STEP-BY-STEP

Cutting the Parts

You can take two general approaches in building the Adirondack chair and matching footrest.

The cut-and-go approach is to lay out the curves directly on the various parts, cut to the line with a saber saw, sand the cut edges as best you can, and move on with the assembly. This is the fastest way to build the project, and if you have a knack for sawing curves, the results should be just fine. The risk is that you may cut one curve just a little bit differently than you cut the next—even when you need mirror-image parts.

That's why you may prefer the second approach: using templates to guide a router in cutting the curves. Of course, it takes time to build the templates and make sure that the edges are smooth. But the results will be consistently good, whether you've got the knack for cutting curves or not. Instead of trying to cut the curves on a ³⁄₄-inch-thick piece of wood, you produce them in inexpensive ¼-inch hardboard, which is a lot easier to throw out if you make a mistake. Once you've built a set of templates, you can make numerous identical parts with them. They should be nearly perfect duplicates, which require very little sanding. This is the best approach if you plan to build multiple units. Regardless of the approach, the basic sequence of cutting and assem-

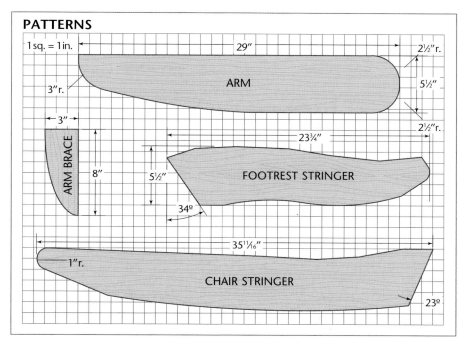

PATTERNS

1 sq. = 1 in.

ARM 29" 2½"r. 3"r. 5½" 2½"r.

ARM BRACE 3" 8"

FOOTREST STRINGER 23¾" 5½" 34°

CHAIR STRINGER 35¹¹⁄₁₆" 1"r. 23°

bling the parts is the same. In the directions that follow, the steps speak directly to the woodworker using the template approach because that's the one I used.

Router Templates

You need templates for the following seven parts: chair stringer, apron, arm, arm brace, center slat top, narrow slat top, and footrest stringer.

All can be made of ¼-inch hardboard or ½-inch medium-density fiberboard (MDF). (For general information on making templates, check page 20 in the Tools and Techniques chapter.) It can be somewhat difficult to see layout lines drawn on the dark hardboard surface. (**Photo 1**) But the character of the material is such that the bumps, dips, nicks, and general roughness associated with cut edges can

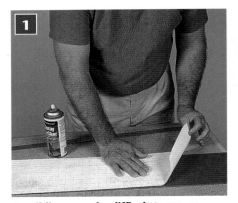

1

Pencil lines may be difficult to see on the dark brown color of hardboard. An option is to do your layouts on paper, then attach the paper to the hardboard with spray adhesive.

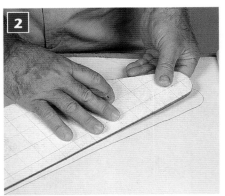

2

The true line of the template edge isn't always easy to see. To make sure it's right, trace along the edge on a piece of paper. The traced line will reveal ripples and nicks that need smoothing.

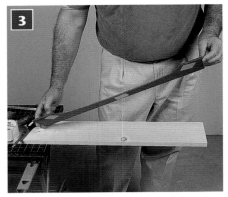

3

Make the apron from a long board. Extend it off the benchtop; then stick the template to it with carpet tape. That way you can cut the arch using a saber saw and router and not damage the bench.

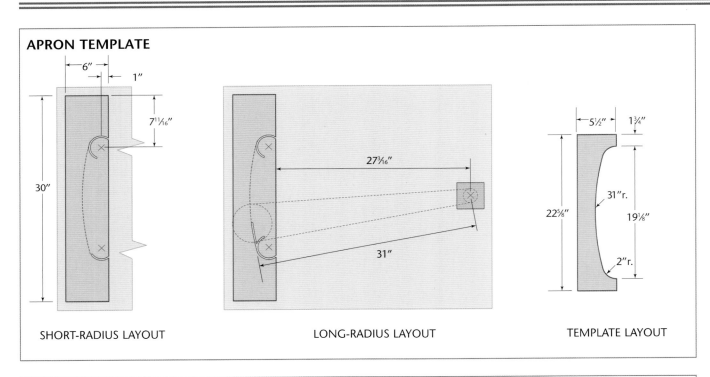

APRON TEMPLATE

SHORT-RADIUS LAYOUT

LONG-RADIUS LAYOUT

TEMPLATE LAYOUT

SLAT LAYOUTS

CENTER SLAT

TEMPLATE

FLANKING SLATS

TEMPLATE

Trim

4

Lay the chair leg on the workbench. Align the stringer on it, supporting its back end on a piece of scrap. After drilling pilot holes, drive 1¼-in. deck screws through the stringer into the leg.

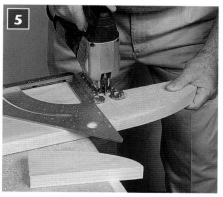

5

Lay out both arm braces on the end of a long piece of ⁵⁄₄x8 stock used for the chair stringers. Cut the curved edges, and cut them apart with a saber saw. To finish, crosscut them from the longer board.

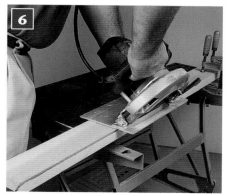

6

Cut the bevel on the back support before crosscutting the part to length. Rip the bevel, cutting just past the crosscut line. Switch off the saw, and when the blade stops, lift it from the work. Then cut to final length.

be filed and sanded out easily, smoothing the overall line.

Several of the templates are shaped primarily with a router and trammel. Little sanding is needed to make these ready to use. **(Photo 2)**

First you need to create full-size templates from my small-scale patterns. Do this by scaling up the grid-pattern drawings. One square on the grid equals one inch on the chair. It's wise to plot many points on the most complex curves and connect the dots to create the full-scale shape. When you are finished, bond the paper to the template with spray adhesive, and follow the paper layout as you cut. If you've elected not to use hardboard templates in building your chair, consider making cardboard patterns instead. You can tape them in place so that you can scribe around the pattern on the workpiece to lay out your parts.

Cutting the Lower Frame

These parts are the stringers, legs, apron, and back cleat. To make it easier to shape the cutout on the apron, hold off on crosscutting it from a longer board until after you shape it. The longer board helps to support your work. And afterward, you can easily cut it free. **(Photo 3)**

Begin by crosscutting the parts (except the apron, of course) to the cutting list dimensions. After sanding the contours to soften the edges, the legs and back cleat will be ready to be put together.

To shape the stringers and apron, use the templates (or your patterns) to trans-fer the layout to the blank, and cut out the parts with a saber saw.

If you are going to use the template, stick it to the workpiece with carpet tape, and cut about ⅛ inch shy of the edge with a saber saw. Then use your router fitted with either a flush-trimming bit or a straight-pattern bit to trim the workpiece to the template. If you use a flush- trimming bit, which has the pilot bearing on the tip, orient the workpiece so that the template is on the bottom. With a pattern bit, which has the bearing on the shank, the template should be on top. Lastly, use a roundover bit to soften the edges that will be exposed in the assembled unit, and sand smooth.

Assembling the Lower Frame

Start by joining a leg to each stringer. Be sure that you end up with a mating pair and not duplicates. Use waterproof glue and three 1¼-inch deck screws, driving the screws through the stringers into the legs. Countersink the pilot holes deeply enough for you to putty them or plug them.

Join the two leg-and-stringer assemblies with the back cleat and the apron. Again, use glue and deck screws, driving the screws into well-countersunk pilot holes to avoid splitting. **(Photo 4)**

Arms and Braces

Because they are relatively small, the best way to shape the arm braces is to rough-cut, then trim-rout the brace's arc on the ends of a fairly long piece of ⁵⁄₄ stock before you cut them free. Use the template you made at the beginning of the project to guide the router as it trims the arc to its final shape. **(Photo 5)**

Hold the brace against the leg, and drill two or three pilots through the leg into the brace. Apply glue to the edge of the brace, realign it, and drive 1⅝-inch screws.

Back Support

Cut the back support from ⁵⁄₄ stock. It has a 35-degree bevel along the front edge. It may be easiest to cut this bevel before crosscutting the support from a longer piece. **(Photo 6)**

To do this, lay the long piece of stock across a pair of sawhorses, mark the cross-cut line, and tilt the circular saw to the 35- degree angle. Cut from the end of the stock, going as far as the mark. Stop the saw and wait for the blade to stop. Then

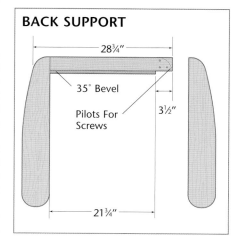

BACK SUPPORT

28¾"

35° Bevel

Pilots For Screws

3½"

21¾"

lift the saw from the stock, readjust the saw, and crosscut the support.

Form 3½-inch-wide notches at each end by trimming away the bevel. Leave the ends of the support square until you have fastened the arms in place.

Arms

Cut the arms from 1x6 stock (using knot-free pieces, if possible). Use the template to shape the arms; then use a router fitted with a roundover bit to soften the edges. Place the arms, upper faces down, and set the back support on top of them. Keep the curved ends flush with the ends of the back support, and be sure the arms are 21¾ inches apart at the front.

Apply waterproof glue to the mating surfaces. Drill countersunk pilot holes through the back support and into the

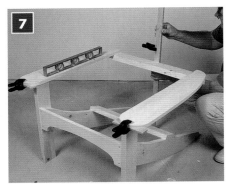

Level the arm assembly, and support it with a temporary leg screwed to its back edge. Scraps clamped to the arm control the overhang. After you attach the arms to the legs, remove the scrap leg.

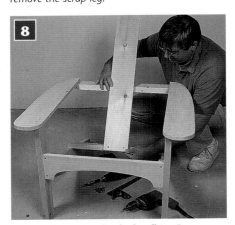

Mount the center back slat first. From behind the chair, align the slat. Drive a screw into the back cleat; then square up the slat and drive the second. Drive screws through the slat into the back support last.

arms. Then drive 1¼-inch deck screws into the pilots. Use a saber saw to trim the edges of the back support to the same curve as the arms. (Take the time to sand out the saw marks.)

Mounting the arms requires the use of temporary support. Screw a 6-inch-long scrap strip to the back edge of the back support. With a spring clamp, attach a second, long scrap strip to the first. These form an adjustable leg that will hold the arm assembly level while you fasten it to the legs and braces. **(Photo 7)** Set the arms on the legs, and get them aligned. Spring-clamp scraps under the arms and against the legs so the overhangs won't shift as you adjust the temporary leg. Adjust the leg until the arms are level. Drill and counter-sink pilot holes; then drive 1¼-inch screws, fastening the arms to the legs and braces.

Back Slats

Crosscut your stock to the lengths on the cutting list, and use the templates you made at the beginning of the project to cut and trim the tops of the specified radii.

Install the center slat first. **(Photo 8)** A good approach is to crouch behind the chair back so that you can pull the slat against the back cleat and back support. Align the bottom edge of the slat with the cleat, and center it. Then drill a pilot hole, and drive a 1¼-inch screw through the slat into the cleat. Make sure the slat is plumb; then drill pilot holes, and drive a few more deck screws. Next, screw the slat to the back support; then remove the temporary leg. Repeat the same general process to mount the remaining four slats.

Seat Slats

Cut the seat slats, sand them, and round-over the edges with your router. Spread glue on the edges of the stringers. Then position the slats with roughly equal spaces between them. Drill and countersink pilots, and drive 1⅝-inch deck screws. **(Photo 9)**

Cutting the Footrest

The footrest consists of a pair of legs, a pair of stringers, an apron, and six slats. The first slat, which must span the legs, is longer than the other five. You create the legs and slats with simple crosscuts.

On the other hand, you must shape the stringers. The bottom edge is a grace-ful S-curve. The top edge mimmicks the lower edge, but to accommodate the slats, it is composed of a series of flats strung together in a descending arc.

Begin making the stringers by clamp-ing a length of ⁵⁄₄x8 stock across a pair of sawhorses. Stick the template to the board. (If you use carpet tape, squeeze the template to the workpiece with a clamp to seal the bond.) Cut around the template using a saber saw. **(Photo 10)** Switch to your router, fitted with either a pattern bit or a flush-trimming bit, and rout around the template, trimming the stringer to size. You'll probably have to shift the way the work is clamped to make a complete circuit.

Carefully pry the template off the first stringer, and stick it to the second. Then you can cut it and rout it.

The last piece to shape is the apron. It is a twin of the chair apron, with the same graceful curve along the bottom edge, so you can use the same template to shape it.

With the pieces cut, soften the exposed edges using the router and a ¼-inch roun-dover bit. Then sand the parts.

Assembling the Footrest

Duplicate the basic sequence you followed to construct the chair. Glue and screw a stringer to each leg, making sure you assemble mir-ror images, not duplicates. Next, install the apron, which ties the two leg-and-stringer assemblies together. Set the unit on its feet, and glue and screw the slats in place with 1⅝-inch deck screws.

Finishing

Painting a project always seems like the easy way out. But the idea of just slap-ping on paint misrepresents both the work involved and the desired result. Don't take the job too lightly. To begin, use a plug cut-ter to make wooden plugs from scrap stock. Go over the entire chair and footrest, using waterproof glue to set the plugs in the counterbores to conceal the screws. **(Photo 11)** After the glue sets, cut the plugs close to flush using a flush-cutting saw or a chisel, and sand them smooth.

Clean all surfaces thoroughly; then prime. If you are going to use a color on the final coat, especially a dark color, make the primer easier to cover by adding a small amount of color tint. Under strong color, even a medium gray is better than stark white.

After the primer dries, seal the knots, using a stain blocker, fresh shellac, or pig-mented shellac. All dry quickly, so using a couple of coats won't prolong the work significantly. You can finish the project by applying the final paint coat.

AN ALTERNATIVE SEAT EDGE

If you don't want to build the matching footrest, you need to revise the front edge of the chair seat. As the drawings show, you can construct the chair so that the stringer projects beyond the front leg to carry additional slats. These provide extra support for the thighs. Here's how this alternative chair's construction is different: First, the stringers are longer. (You can make them with the extended pattern shown below.) But you make them the same way. Second,

there is no front apron. When it is time to install the stringer, you can install a temporary brace instead to hold the stringer-and-leg assemblies in the correct alignment as construction proceeds. Third, you need to cut and install two extra slats. The biggest difference, however, may be the savings in time and materials you realize in not building the footrest. But bear in mind that its graceful curve complements the overall Adirondack design.

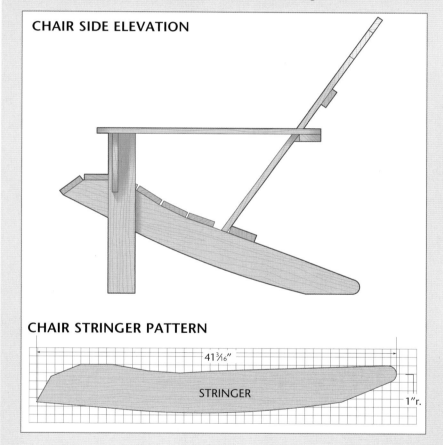

CHAIR SIDE ELEVATION

CHAIR STRINGER PATTERN

41³⁄₁₆"

STRINGER

1"r.

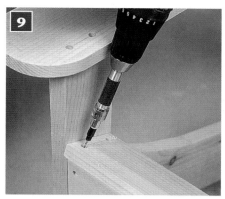

Drill and countersink pilot holes while holding the slat in place on the stringers. Center the pilot in the counterbore. A drill-and-drive accessory makes it easy to drill the pilot, then quickly drive a screw.

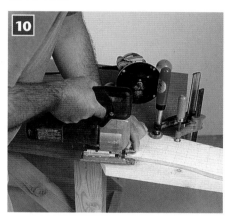

Place two clamps closely together to secure the work and prevent it from moving while you cut. You'll need to reset the clamps in order to cut all around the template-and-stringer workpiece.

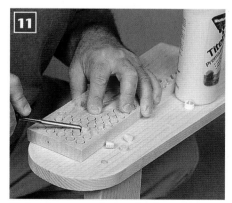

Make plugs out of scrap lumber with a plug cutter and a drill to hide the screw-heads. Break the plugs free with a screwdriver, or cut through the board to release several plugs at once.

Adirondack Side Table

ven though an Adirondack chair has wide arms, it's nice to have a matching side table. After all, you need room for food and drinks, books, newspapers, and a lot more to keep you happy on a summer afternoon. This table holds much more than the arms of a chair can, and it's designed to complement the Adirondack Chair project. It's just the right height and has an ample top. And even if you don't build them at the same time,

this table will look like part of the matched set of Adirondack pieces. The table repeats the design motifs of the chair, including the prime features of the furniture, such as the cutout aprons and the rounded-end slats. And like the chair, it's stylish enough to use indoors and out. The original designs were produced at the turn of the last century in the Adirondack Mountains in upstate New York. They served well on the wide porches of backwoods camps and gave the appearance of being very rustic even though the furniture was very comfortable. The style became a hallmark of Catskills resorts as well as Adirondack camps, and eventually spread across the country. This particular Adirondack table design has the same roots—a design of angles and edges that are softened with graceful curves. This a straightforward project that you can build with basic tools.

EXPLODED VIEW

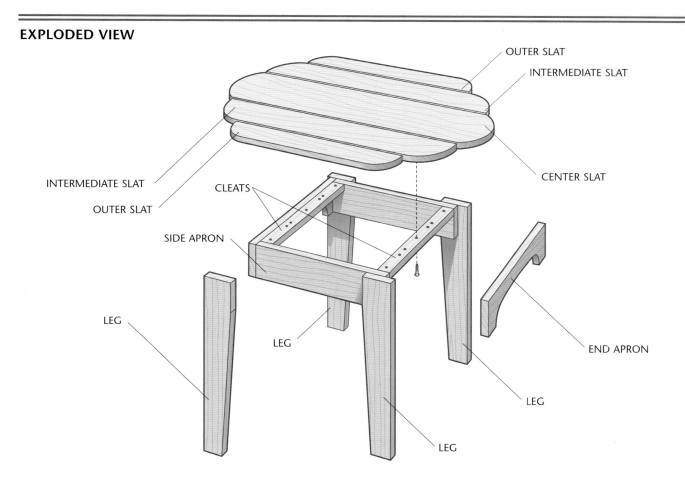

CUTTING LIST

Part	Number	Thickness	Width	Length	Pine Stock
Legs	4	¾"	3½"	17¼"	1x4
Side aprons	2	¾"	3½"	15¼"	1x4
End aprons	2	¾"	3½"	15"	1x4
Cleats	2	¾"	1½"	13½"	1x4
Center slat	1	¾"	5½"	30"	1x6
Intermediate slats	2	¾"	3½"	26½"	1x4
Outer slats	2	¾"	2½"	19½"	1x6

SHOPPING LIST

- 1 pc. 1x4 8' pine
- 1 pc. 1x4 10' pine
- 1 pc. 1x6 6' pine
- 1¼" galvanized deck screws

Adirondack Side Table

ELEVATIONS

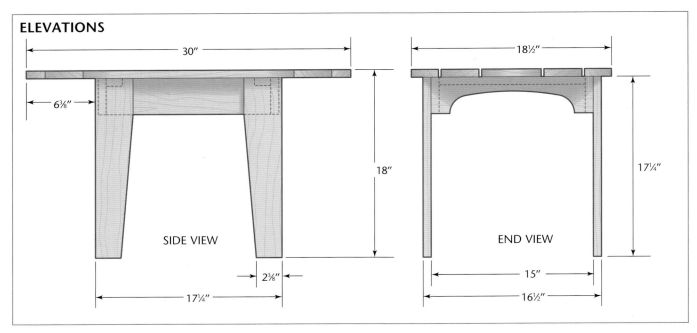

SIDE VIEW

END VIEW

PLAN VIEW

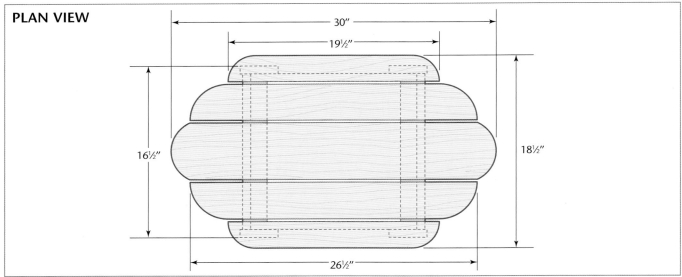

BUILDER'S NOTES

This side table is a companion to the Adirondack Chair in every way. It is built with the same wood, using the same tools and techniques.

You can use any of the common outdoor woods finished with an exterior clear sealer or paint. I used No. 2 common pine for most of the components, and splurged a little on a clear pine for the top boards.

Even good wood in this grade has a few knots, which you can seal under a coat of paint or allow to show through a clear finish. But you should avoid boards with loose knots, knots on the edges, or pitch pockets.

Although the table is basic, you may want to use the same template system that I used on the Adirondack Chair.

You can finesse the hardboard template until you get the curves just right, and cut another template if the first one doesn't work out. In the end, I think you will find that building templates is worth the time. Once you get the shape cut smoothly into the template, it becomes a simple matter to shape the curved parts of pine using your router.

You can also use the router to put a roundover edge on the boards. This step on the outside edges adds a nice finishing touch.

Yard and Garden Furniture

You can cut through the full thickness of the template stock in one pass. Set the router on the pivot with the bit off the stock. Then switch on the router, and swing it on the pivot to cut.

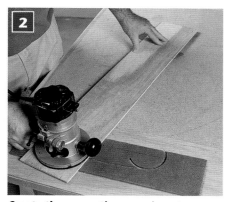

Create the connective arc using a trammel, a piece of ¼-in.-thick plywood attached to the router baseplate with carpet tape. The cut begins in one short-radius and ends in the other.

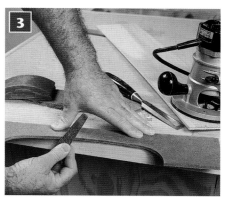

Smooth out any bumps or nicks in the template's guiding edge using a half-round file. Remove fuzzy hardboard edges with sandpaper. This will help the router make a clean cut in one pass.

STEP-BY-STEP

Router Templates

The ends of the tabletop boards are rounded. But the end aprons have an arched cutout that is formed from two different passes of the router. (You can also cut these curves using a saber saw, and sand down the rough edges with a belt sander.) To achieve a more precise and consistent job, you should use templates to shape the pieces with your router. With this system, the first step in making the table is to make the pattern-cutting templates.

If you've built the Adirondack Chair, you already have two of the three slat templates you need. If you don't have them, just use the dimensions in the template illustrations to make them. I used ¼-inch hardboard for the template stock and a router and trammel to cut the arcs.

Although the table's apron cutout looks similar to the chair's apron cutout, the dimensions are different. The length of the table apron is shorter and so is the cutout. That means you have to make two arcs and join them into the irregular curve of the arch. Here are some tips that you will find useful when it comes to making these shapes.

First, note that the radius of the minor arcs is shorter than the radius of most router baseplates. Therefore, you do not need a trammel to rout these arcs. Instead, drive small nails through the template stock at the arc center points. These serve as pivots. Measure from the

bit, and drill a hole in the router baseplate at the arc centerpoint. To rout the arc, set the router over a nail, and pivot the router on it. **(Photo 1)**

Second, it helps to attach the hardboard template stock to a larger piece of hardboard or plywood for the trammel cut. This base piece should be expendable because the router bit will cut into it when you're making the template.

Using this base will prevent damage to your workbench. It will also serve as a base for the pivot point needed in routing the connecting arc. **(Photo 2)**

Once you cut the template, it's wise to smooth the cut edges. I used a half-round file and sandpaper to finish the job. **(Photo 3)** This extra step will allow you to make a clean, smooth cut in one pass.

END APRON TEMPLATE

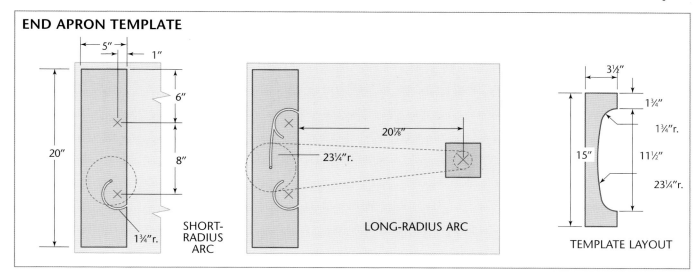

SHORT-RADIUS ARC

5″ 1″
6″
8″
20″
1¾″r.

LONG-RADIUS ARC

20⅛″
23¼″r.

TEMPLATE LAYOUT

3½″
1¾″
1¾″r.
15″
11½″
23¼″r.

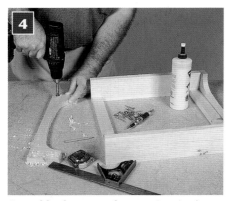

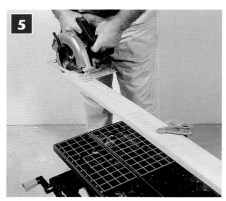

Assemble the apron frame using simple butt joints. Arrange the parts with the aprons upside down, cleats resting on the workbench. Drill pilot holes, apply water-proof glue, and drive screws.

Clamp a 1x4 board, and cut the leg taper, beginning at the foot and sawing toward the shoulder. Cut one leg, turn the board around, and cut the second. Then crosscut the board to produce two legs.

Apron Frame

This little table consists of a simple box frame with legs and top boards screwed down into position. The apron frame, which is the first subassembly you make, is composed of two end aprons that have the arched cutouts, two side aprons, and two cleats.

Lay out the four aprons on a length of 1x4 stock, with both end aprons in the middle and the side aprons flanking them on both sides. Don't cut the aprons apart. Instead, use the full length of the board for support in sawing and routing the cutouts in the end aprons. This tip can be applied in many operations and makes the job of trimming, ripping, or shaping both easier and safer. Because you have more wood to work with, you can clamp

the piece securely while you're working and make the final crosscut for length when you're done.

Lay the board across a pair of sawhorses or a workbench and clamp it. Position the template for making the first apron. Use either carpet tape or clamps to secure the template. Using a saber saw, cut as close to the template as possible, and complete the cutout contour by routing to the template edge with a pattern bit. (You can accomplish the same thing using a flush-trimming bit if you first turn the work over so that the template is on the bottom.)

After cutting the second apron, crosscut all four. Cut a 13½-inch length of the 1x4, and rip it roughly in half, forming the two cleats. (The exact width of these pieces

isn't critical.) Now sand all the parts, except for the cleats.

To assemble the frame, stand the aprons on edge, and arrange them in a box with the end aprons butted against the ends of the side aprons. Apply waterproof glue to the ends of the side aprons. Drill and countersink pilot holes through the face of the end aprons into the ends of the side aprons, and drive 1¼-inch screws. **(Photo 4)** Set the cleats in place, and attach them with glue and screws driven through the side aprons where they will be covered by the legs.

The Legs

In the same way that you worked on the aprons, shape the legs while they are still a part of a longer board. Cut all four legs from a single 1x4.

Lay out a leg at either end of the board. Lay the marked board across the sawhorses, and cut the taper on each of the two legs using your circular saw or a saber saw. **(Photo 5)** Once the shape is defined you can crosscut the legs from the board. Then lay out two more legs, cut the tapers, and crosscut them. When all four are cut, use a belt sander to smooth the surfaces.

Attach the legs to the apron frame as shown in the "Elevations" drawing and the "Table Bottom View" drawing. The tops of the legs are flush with the top edges of the frame, and the front edges are ¼ inch proud of the faces of the end aprons. Spread waterproof glue on the area of the leg that contacts the frame. With the frame upside down, position a leg, and clamp it securely while you drill and drive two or three screws through

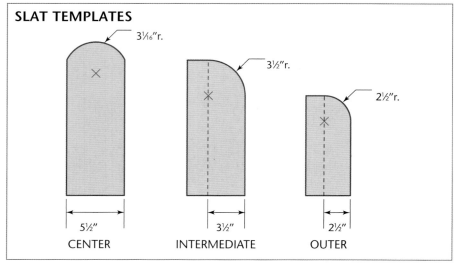

SLAT TEMPLATES

3¹⁄₁₆"r.

3½"r.

2½"r.

5½"
CENTER

3½"
INTERMEDIATE

2½"
OUTER

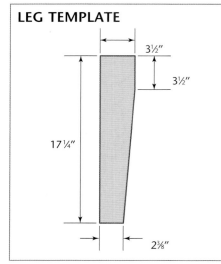

LEG TEMPLATE

3½"

3½"

17¼"

2⅜"

the frame into the leg, As soon as the screws are seated, you can remove the clamps and move on to the next leg, following the same basic procedure for all four boards.

The Top Boards

The tabletop is composed of five boards of three different widths and three different lengths. Radius both ends of each board using the slat templates.

Cut the boards to the lengths specified on the cutting list. The outermost boards, which are 2½ inches wide, should be cut from the 1x6 stock. Crosscut one board to the proper length; then rip it to width. If you have a table saw, this is a simple procedure. If you must use a circular saw and are uneasy about doing it freehand, use the shop-made guide shown in "Circular Saw Guide," page 9. Crosscut each board slightly overlong, and attach it to the guide with screws driven into areas of the board that will be trimmed off.

With the boards dimensioned, round off the ends using the templates to guide your work. Clamp the template in place to start, and cut close to the template edge using a saber saw, removing the bulk of the waste. When that's done, rout the board to match the template with either a flush-trimming bit (with the template on the bottom of the work) or a straight-pattern bit (with the template on top). The final operation is sanding the surfaces smooth.

Attaching the Top

Fasten the boards to the table framework with 1¼-inch screws. To leave the top boards free of fasteners, this design uses cleats so that you can drive the screws from below the surface into the bottom of the tabletop boards.

Lay out the top boards on your workbench or sawhorses. Use scraps of ¼-inch plywood as spacers so that the gaps between the boards are even. Gently set the table framework onto the boards and align it—without displacing any of the boards, of course. Then drill pilot holes, and drive 1¼-inch screws.

The outermost boards are positioned over the side aprons and legs. The mounting screws for these boards must be driven in pocket holes bored in the aprons. Use your combination drill- countersink bit to make these pilot holes. Begin drilling as though you intend to simply bore straight through the apron. But once the bit gets

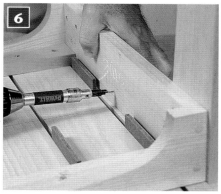

Make pocket holes for screws by beginning the hole straight on to give your bit purchase; then swing the drill to a sharp angle, and bore until the countersink creates the pocket shape.

Prime the knots with pigmented white shellac, generally called stain killer, to stop the resins exuded by the knots from bleeding through the paint. You may need two coats of this quick-drying sealer.

a purchase in the wood, swing the drill to a position about 20 to 25 degrees off vertical and continue boring. **(Photo 6)** The countersink element of the bit will create the pocket for the screwhead. Depending upon the position and angle of these holes, you may need to use screws longer than 1¼ inch. Just don't allow them to penetrate the top surface of the board.

Finishing

The first step is to conceal the heads of the screws that fasten the end aprons to the side aprons. You can putty them or cover

them using wooden plugs. Sand the plugs or putty flush and smooth. You should have already finish-sanded the rest of the table. If not, do it now, and then remove the dust from the table with a tack cloth or vacuum.

You can leave the knots and coat the table with clear sealer, of course, but I elected to paint. First, I coated the knots with stain killer, so the resin would not bleed through the paint. **(Photo 7)** Then I primed the wood with a latex primer, following the directions on the can. After the primer dried, I applied latex paint.

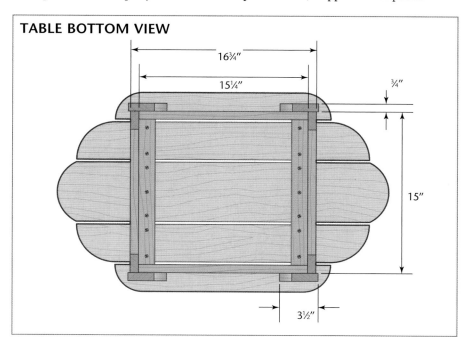

TABLE BOTTOM VIEW

16¾"

15¼"

¾"

15"

3½"

Adirondack Plant Stand

This plant stand rounds out the set of furniture in the Adirondack style that includes the chair with footrest and the side table. This isn't an historically accurate piece, but it is practical and easy to build. And it fits in beautifully with the other Adirondack projects, sharing the traditional design motifs that include the arch cutouts in the baseboard and sides, and the rounded-top slat construction. This stand will form an ensemble

for your deck, patio, porch, or terrace. Of course, you can use this stand with shelves inside your house, or add a finish that offers some protection from the weather and use it to display your plants. The three shelves are tiered to provide a desirable display. And the solid construction will support even a large, luxuriant plant. This particular stand was built of No. 2 common pine. I used it because the grade is relatively economical, widely available, and easy to work. The wood has knots, but they are hidden beneath sealer, primer, and paint. Even so, it pays to check the lumber thoroughly, looking for splits and wanes that can be difficult to finesse on a project where boards are fastened edge to edge. If you are willing to spend more for material, you can use clear pine, cedar, or another high-quality wood that will look good under a light stain or clear sealer.

EXPLODED VIEW

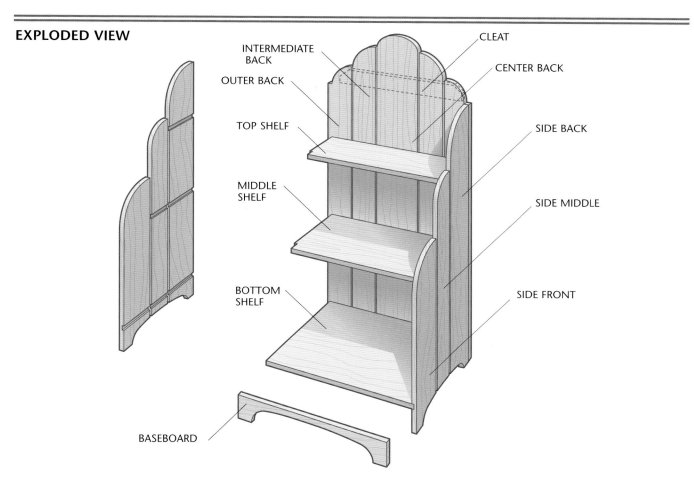

INTERMEDIATE BACK
OUTER BACK
TOP SHELF
MIDDLE SHELF
BOTTOM SHELF
BASEBOARD
CLEAT
CENTER BACK
SIDE BACK
SIDE MIDDLE
SIDE FRONT

CUTTING LIST (Some parts are left long during construction.)

Part	Number	Thickness	Width	Length	Pine Stock
Center back	1	¾″	5½″	43″	1x6
Intermediate backs	2	¾″	3½″	41¼″	1x4
Outer backs	2	¾″	3½″	37¾″	1x4
Side backs	2	¾″	5½″	35″	1x6
Side middles	2	¾″	3½″	28″	1x4
Side fronts	2	¾″	5½″	21″	1x6
Bottom shelf	1	¾″	15″	19½″	1x6
Middle shelf	1	¾″	10¼″	19½″	1x6
Top shelf	1	¾″	6½″	19½″	1x4
Baseboard	1	¾″	3½″	19″	1x4
Cleat	1	¾″	2½″	17¾″	1x4

SHOPPING LIST

- 1 pc. 1x4 8′ pine
- 2 pcs. 1x4 10′ pine
- 1 pc. 1x6 8′ pine
- 1 pc. 1x6 10′ pine
- 1⅝″ deck screws

Adirondack

ELEVATIONS

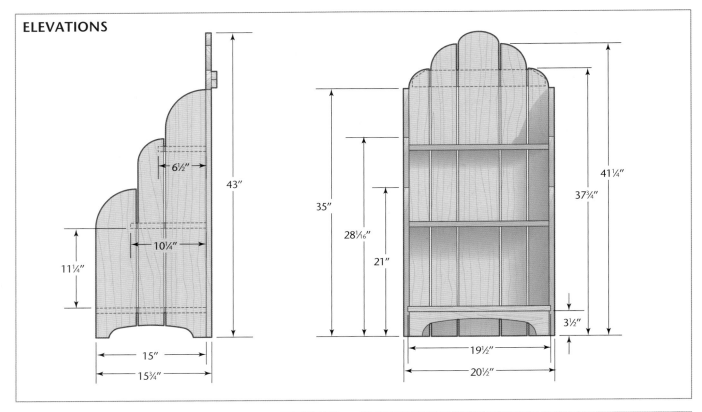

6½"

43"

10¼"

11¼"

15"

15¾"

41¼"

37¾"

35"

28¹⁄₁₆"

21"

3½"

19½"

20½"

PLAN VIEW

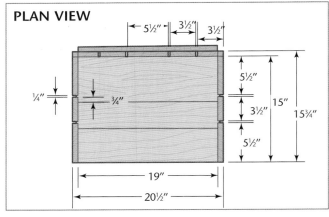

5½" 3½" 3½"

5½"

15" 15¾"

3½"

¼" ¾"

5½"

19"

20½"

CLEAT DETAIL

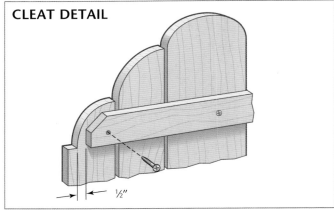

½"

BUILDER'S NOTES

Because it is a companion piece, the Adirondack Plant Stand uses the same basic materials and general construction techniques as the Adirondack Chair and Side Table. (You may want to refer to those projects for help with some of the cutting and

shaping details.) However, this piece certainly can stand alone. If you like the stand and don't need the chair, I recommend that you check through the Builder's Notes section for the Adirondack Chair project on page 66 for tips on working with pine,

using templates to guide the curved cuts this project requires, using wood plugs to conceal screwheads, and priming and painting the piece. You will want to pay extra attention to the most complicated joinery in this piece—making the dado

joints where the shelves tuck into the side slats. You could simply nail the shelves in place or add supporting cleats. But the dado system makes the piece stronger and better looking. Waterproof glue and deck screws hold everything together.

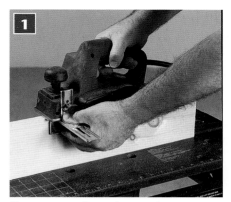

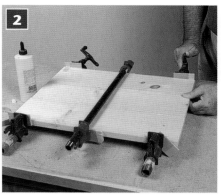

Use a power planer (or a stationary jointer-planer) to make your edge-glued joints tight, even though the edges of pine boards are often fairly flat and nearly true. A light pass with a power planer will do.

Use three pipe clamps on each shelf to minimize buckling. Set two across one face near the ends and the third across the opposite face at the center. Use wood scraps to prevent edge damage.

Sand across the seams after you scrape off any dried glue. Work your belt sander at a 45-deg. angle with a medium-grit paper to flatten the shelf. Then work with the grain, and finish with a fine-grit paper.

STEP-BY-STEP

Cutting the Parts

The plant stand is not difficult to construct. But you should mark the parts, which are many, as you cut so you don't mix up the pieces. Note: Leave the baseboard attached to one of the side pieces. This will make it easier to cut the arch. After that cutout is formed, you can crosscut it from the full piece.

This is a good time to do the majority of the sanding. You'll do a better job, and you won't have to deal with any obstructions and inside corners. Depending on the condition of the boards, you may want to hit them with the belt sander and a medium-grit paper. After dusting thoroughly, switch to 150-grit paper on a pad or random-orbit sander.

The shelves in this piece are wider than any stock boards you can buy at the lumberyard. That means you must edge-glue narrow boards to form the shelves. The bottom shelf is formed using three 1x6s, the middle shelf using two 1x6s, and the top shelf using two 1x4s. It's a good idea to cut these boards about 1 inch longer than specified on the cutting list so that you can square the ends after glue-up.

Gluing the Shelves

Unless you have a shop full of clamps, glue up the shelves one at a time. For best results, the mating edges of the boards should be jointed. You can do this with with a power planer or with a router. **(Photo 1)** The details of router-jointing

boards for glue-up are shown in the Garden Bench project on page 124.

You should use three pipe clamps to glue up the bottom shelf. In addition, you need scraps of wood to insert between each clamp jaw and the work, so the jaw doesn't crush the edge of the shelf as the clamp is tightened. Set out two clamps, and adjust them to loosely hold all three boards plus the scraps. Adjust the third clamp as well, but set it aside for now. Apply glue to the edges, set the board on the clamps' pipes, fit the scraps in place, and tighten the two clamps just enough to

hold the boards snugly. Now set the third clamp on top roughly centered between the other two. **(Photo 2)** As you start to tighten this clamp, fit the protective scraps in place. Make sure the surfaces are flush, and tighten this clamp completely. Then tighten the outer clamps.

Set the clamped-up shelf aside until the glue cures, and take the time to joint the other shelf boards. Once the glue dries, scrape off any excess using a sharp scraping tool, and finish the surface with a belt sander. **(Photo 3)** Work across the joints first, then with the grain.

BASEBOARD CUTOUTS & TEMPLATES

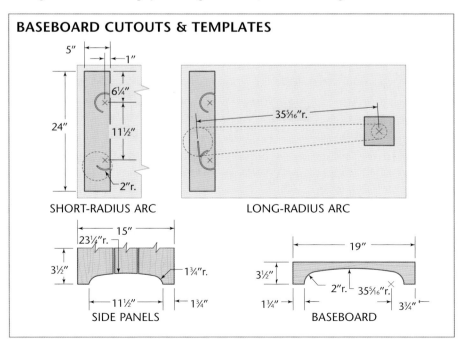

SHORT-RADIUS ARC — 5", 1", 6¼", 11½", 24", 2"r.

LONG-RADIUS ARC — 35⁵⁄₁₆"r.

SIDE PANELS — 15", 23¼"r., 3½", 1¾"r., 11½", 1¾"

BASEBOARD — 19", 3½", 2"r., 35⁵⁄₁₆"r., 1¾", 3¾"

Rough-cut the round shape on the ends of the side and back boards using a saber saw. Use two clamps to secure the template to the boards, and extend the boards beyond the work surface to make the cuts.

Trim the cut using a router fitted with a flush-trimming bit. Leave the template in place, but turn the workpiece over, and adjust the bit so the pilot bearing on the tip rides against the template edge.

Use two clamps to secure the ends of the board. Leave the board long, and apply the template with carpet tape or clamps. You need to keep the clamps at the ends so that you can freely rout the arc.

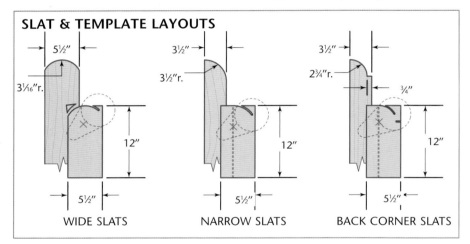

SLAT & TEMPLATE LAYOUTS

WIDE SLATS — 5½", 3¹¹⁄₁₆"r., 12", 5½"

NARROW SLATS — 3½", 3½"r., 12", 5½"

BACK CORNER SLATS — 3½", 2¾"r., ¾", 12", 5½"

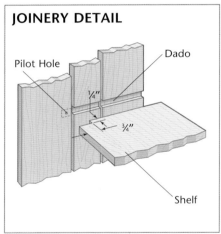

JOINERY DETAIL

Pilot Hole · Dado · ¼" · ¾" · Shelf

Making Templates

The tops of the side and back boards are rounded. The baseboard has an arched cutout, as do the side assemblies. All of these can be cut by hand using a saber saw, then sanded with a belt sander. But you can achieve a more precise and consistent job if you use templates and shape the edges with a router. If you've built the Adirondack chair, you already have two of the three slat templates. (Use ½-inch hardboard for the template stock.)

Although the cutouts on the sides and the baseboard look similar, the dimensions are different, and two templates are required. Both templates are created in the same way, but the length of the cutouts and the radii of the arcs are different. You can brush up on cutting and using templates in the Adirondack Side Table project on page 72.

Routing the Arcs

The back and side boards in this project are rounded off on top. All but three back boards have quarter arcs with a radius equal to the board width. The exceptions are the middle back board, which is fully rounded, and the two outer boards, which have a step on one side of the arc. The step is where the side backs join the back boards.

The quickest way to do the job is to use a saber saw and a router. Clamp your template to the stock, and round off the board with the saber saw, cutting very close to the edge of the template. **(Photo 4)** Then switch to the router and trim the arc, guided by the template. **(Photo 5)** Be careful when trimming the two outer back boards to ensure that you don't stray into the step. The Builder's Notes (on page 66) in the Adirondack Chair project has more

details on bit choices. If you've built the chair or table, you already know about this process.

Cut 11 side and back boards in all. Note that one is still paired with the baseboard, a situation that will not impair your ability to round its top.

The Baseboard

Once you cut the arch, crosscut the piece from the board to which it is still attached. Set up the board for the template-guided cuts. Cut close to the template edge using a saber saw. Then turn the assembly over, and use a router and a flush-trimming bit to cut the baseboard to match the template. **(Photo 6)** With the cutout completed, remove the template. Check the cutting list dimensions (adjust slightly as required), and crosscut the baseboard to final length.

Routing the Dadoes

The three boards from each side must be dadoed for the shelves. The board closest to the front is dadoed only for the bottom shelf. The narrow center board is dadoed for the bottom and the middle shelf. The wide board at the rear is dadoed for all three shelves. You could also dado the back boards, but on so narrow a span, dadoes on the side panels are more than enough to hold the shelves securely.

All the dadoes are routed through, which means they are cut from edge to edge. Use a ¾-inch straight bit in your router, and cut only ¼ inch deep; this is a depth that can be achieved comfortably in one pass without straining the router motor or chipping out the edges of your cuts. You can line up all the boards in one side using a framing square, and lay out the dadoes on all the boards at one time. But you may find it easier to cut the dadoes in one board at a time. Use a router T-square and check the "Tools and Techniques" chapter for plans and tips on using this router jig (page 15).

Assembling the Stand

Before you can actually glue and screw the parts together, you need to notch two of the shelves at their front corners, as shown in the Joinery Detail drawing. Begin this job by laying out two of the dadoed side boards, plus one of the undadoed side boards, spacing them ¼ inch apart. Set the shelves into the dadoes, and mark the corners for notching. **(Photo 7)** (You can use this same setup to lay out both ends of the shelves.) Cut the notches using a saber saw. Check the fit, and refine the cuts as necessary.

Go ahead now, and glue and screw the parts together. You may want to take the extra time to make a test fit first. This step can expose a few bad joints or rough cuts while it is still relatively easy to fix them. Once you are ready for final assembly, drill and countersink pilot holes for all the screws. If you intend to cover the screwheads with wooden plugs, which is what I did, begin each pilot by boring a counterbore with a Forstner bit. Then drill the pilot with a combination bit. Spread waterproof glue as you go, distributing a thin, even coat with a small brush. Apply it inside dadoes and on the shelf edges that will come in contact with the side and back boards. Squeeze-out can be a mess to clean up and can get in the way of paint or sealer, so don't overdo it. If glue

oozes out of the joints, clean it up with a wet cloth.

Begin by laying out three side boards. Fit ¼-inch-thick spacers between the boards, and pull them together with a clamp. Apply glue; then fit the shelves into their dadoes. Apply more glue, and set the second set of side boards, spacers between them, atop the shelf ends. Align the shelves square to the sides. Drive ¹⁵⁄₈-inch screws through the side boards into the shelf edges.

Add the first board next. Apply glue; then drive screws through it into the side board and the shelves. **(Photo 8)** Turn the unit over. Attach the other side boards, then the remaining back boards. Lastly, attach the back boards.

Side Cutouts

This is another template-guided router operation. Clamp the template to the side of the stand. Using a saber saw, cut close to the template edge, removing the bulk of the waste. **(Photo 9)**

Watch out for a potential problem with the gaps between the boards. That spacing can allow the router bit to blow out splinters along the edges of the boards. To prevent this, you need to back up the wood. I did this by planing temporary filler strips from scraps of the working stock. Cut short strips of wood with your saber saw; then plane them using a block plane until they just fit into the gap. Make the router cut, and remove the scraps when you're done.

Finishing

Finishing begins with good surface preparation. Start by running a putty knife over all the screwheads to make sure they are recessed. Then plug or putty over the heads. To plug the counterbores, glue a plug cut from the working stock into each counterbore. Orient the grain in the plug parallel with the grain in the stand. You can buy ready-made dowels and trim them to serve as plugs, or make your own using a plug cutter chucked in a drill. If you have a drill press, making your own plugs is even easier. After the glue sets, pare the protruding wood, and sand the plugs flush to the surface.

Do any touch-up sanding that's needed. Then clean the dust from the wood. Use a shop vacuum, or dust with a brush and follow up with a tack cloth.

Prime the raw wood with a latex primer. When it dries, seal knots with shellac or stain sealer. Lastly, apply the finish coat of paint.

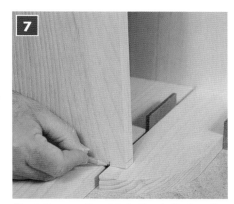

Mark the small notch in the shelf where it will project past the dado onto the surface of the last board. Set the assembly flat on a work surface, and use spacers to set the board in its final position.

Drive screws through the back boards into each shelf. You might want to mark a centerline as a guide. With the plant stand on its side, position side boards atop the shelf ends, and screw them in place as well.

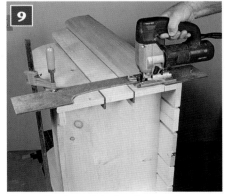

Clamp the template in place, and use a saber saw to trim most of the waste. Then use a router and pattern bit with a pilot bearing on the shank. Use filler strips between the boards to prevent splintering.

Planter Bench

The idea of this popular project is sensible and simple: hang a bench seat between a pair of planter boxes. This version of the planter bench has a traditional look, and it's easy to build. Although it is made of durable materials for outdoor use, the piece will require some routine maintenance to sustain its proud good looks—and a little in-season green-thumb attention to keep the flowers blooming. The planter boxes that support the cedar bench

Yard and Garden Furniture

are large enough and deep enough to support some impressive plantings. Hiding under the cedar is a pair of boxes made of pressure-treated plywood. If you are going to make a box to hold lots of damp, rich soil, this material is the one to use because preservatives in the wood make it almost rot-proof. One obvious drawback is its appearance. To address that, you can use paint. After you construct the boxes, but before you apply the cedar trim, paint the plywood to conceal the greenish color, and four small painted panels on each planter box are all you'll see in the completed project. The project is modular, so you can easily alter the length of your bench. Another option is to link several boxes with benches, and even use the assemblies to turn a corner on a deck. And if all you want is a planter without a bench, this may be your project, too. Just make the planter box.

EXPLODED VIEW

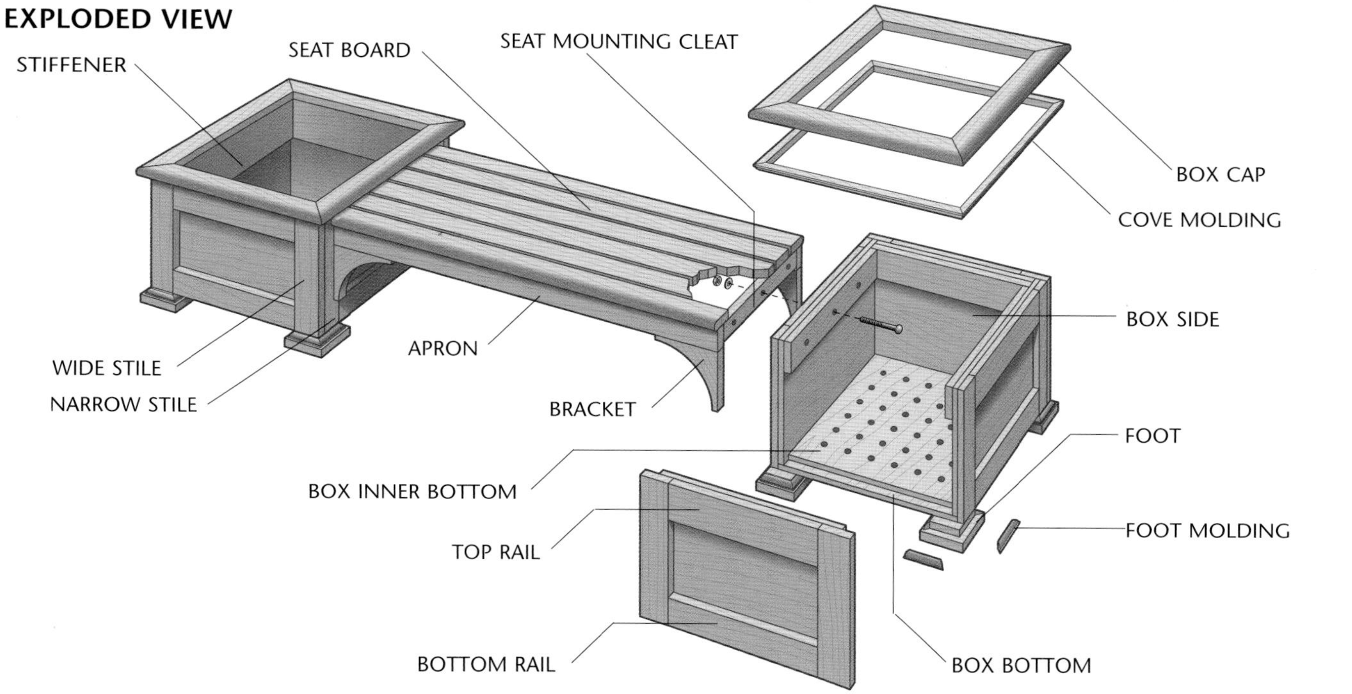

CUTTING LIST

Part	Number	Thickness	Width	Length	Stock
Box bottoms	2	¾"	22½"	22½"	PT plywood
Box inner bottoms	2	½"	21½"	21½"	PT plywood
Box sides	4	½"	14¼"	21½"	PT plywood
Box sides	4	½"	14¼"	22½"	PT plywood
Stiffeners	4	¾"	3½"	21½"	PT plywood
Stiffeners	4	¾"	3½"	20"	PT plywood
Wide stiles	8	¾"	3"	15"	1x cedar
Narrow stiles	8	¾"	2¼"	15"	1x cedar
Top rails	8	¾"	3¾"	18"	1x cedar
Bottom rails	8	¾"	3"	18"	1x cedar
Feet	4	1"	5"	5"	5/4x cedar
Foot moldings	4	¾"	4¼"	4¼"	1x cedar
Cap moldings	8	1"	2½"	26¼"	5/4x cedar
Cove moldings	8	¾"	¾"	25¼"	1x cedar
Seat mounting cleats	2	1"	1¾"	18"	5/4x cedar
Aprons	2	1"	2½"	50"	5/4x cedar
Brackets	4	1"	6"	6"	5/4x cedar
Seat boards	6	1"	3¼"	50"	5/4x cedar
Seat battens	2	¾"	3½"	18"	1x cedar

SHOPPING LIST

- 1 sheet ¾" pressure-treated plywood
- 1 sheet ½" pressure-treated plywood
- 6 pcs. 1x4 10' cedar
- 6 pcs. 5/4x4 10' cedar
- 1 pc. 5/4x6 8' cedar
- Construction adhesive
- 1¼" galvanized screws
- ¾" stainless-steel screws
- 1" stainless-steel screws
- 1¼" stainless-steel screws
- 1⅝" stainless-steel screws
- 2½" stainless-steel screws
- 2¼" stainless-steel finishing screws
- 6 Stainless-steel carriage bolts, ¼"x4", with nuts and washers

ELEVATIONS

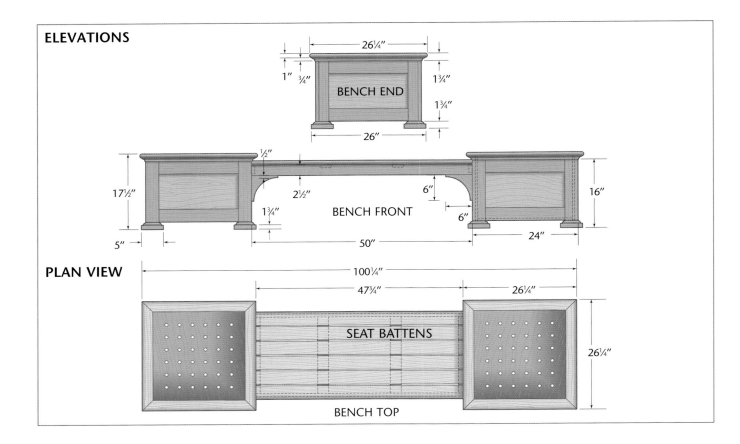

BENCH END

26¼"

1" ¾" 1¾" 1¾"

26"

BENCH FRONT

½" 17½" 2½" 6" 16" 1¾" 6"

5" 50" 24"

PLAN VIEW

100¼"

47¾" 26¼"

SEAT BATTENS

26¼"

BENCH TOP

BUILDER'S NOTES

With this project, you don't simply park yourself on a comfortable seat in the garden; you sit in the garden. The planters will be filled with a fertile soil, of course, so you have to take this into account in choosing your materials.

Materials

Tests at the USDA Forest Products Laboratory show that pressure-treated wood rated for ground contact won't rot even after 40 years. That's why I selected pressure-treated plywood for the planter boxes. But bear in mind that you need to protect yourself from the chemical preservatives while you work. Although the manufacturers insist the chemical treatment will not leach

out, it can spread in sawdust when you make cuts. So you need a good dust mask and a workable plan for capturing and properly disposing of the sawdust and scraps. (Don't burn them.)

I used cedar to dress up the planters and make the bench. It's attractive, weathers well, and is easy to work. To eliminate stains from steel fasteners, I used stainless-steel screws. (The galvanized screws on the shopping list are only for assembling the plywood boxes.) To attach the cap moldings I used finishing screws with a small head.

Tools and Techniques

Quite a bit of the stock for this project needs to be ripped to widths other than those that

are lumberyard standards. To make the feet, you need a beading bit for your router. It's like a round-over bit, except that the pilot bearing is undersized, so the cutter forms a step at the bearing-end of the quarter-round profile. If you have a ½-inch-radius roundover bit, buy a pilot bearing that's a ⅛-inch smaller in diameter than the one on the bit, and use the smaller bearing to make the cuts.

The same roundover bit (a ½-inch radius) comes into play a few steps further on, when you need to nose the edges of some seat boards. Here, the complete cut takes two passes, one with the router on the top surface of the board, the second with the router on the bottom surface. Each pass

removes stock from half the board thickness. On the first pass, the pilot rides along the lower half of the board's edge as the cutter shapes the upper half. When you turn the board over, you discover the bearing doesn't have a reference surface. It's been cut away. What to do? Use a router accessory called an edge guide.

Finish

For the outsides of the plywood boxes, I used ordinary white latex house paint. I applied two full-strength coats after sealing the knots and priming. I finished all the cedar with solvent-based marine spar varnish, which is more durable than its water-based counterpart.

STEP-BY-STEP

Cutting Box Panels

Under their cedar duds, the planter boxes are really nothing more than butt-jointed plywood boxes. Working within the caveats that apply to using pressure-treated wood, cut the plywood. (Remember, you should use eye protection and a dust mask to guard against the sawdust that is laden with wood- preservative chemicals.) Set out a pair of sawhorses, and lay scrap 2x4s or furring strips across them. Then lay the plywood on top. You can strike a line and follow it freehand using your circular saw. But to ensure straight cuts, its a good idea to make and use the circular saw guide described on page 9. **(Photo 1)**

Cut the parts to the dimensions specified on the cutting list, noting that the list assumes you are making two boxes. If you plan to make a two-bench unit, you have to make at least three boxes. Again, you should feel free to alter my basic plans if you want to customize the piece to suit your needs.

When you make the cuts, first check the depth of cut on your saw. You'll find that if you adjust the blade to cut just slightly deeper than the plywood, you can cut efficiently. And if you choose to use a support under the cut line, the blade will barely cut into it. **(Photo 2)** After completing the cuts, sweep up and bag the sawdust for disposal. (Remember, you should not burn sawdust or small scraps of pressure-treated lumber in a fireplace or woodstove.)

Drainage Holes

The two-piece bottom consists of a ½-inch plywood panel centered on the slightly larger ¾-inch piece. This creates a ½-inch-wide rabbet for the sides to sit in. Apply a bead of adhesive around the perimeter of the smaller piece and center it on the larger one. (You can use a scrap of ½-inch plywood as a gauge to make sure the top piece is centered all the way around.) Then apply three or four clamps. Turn the assembly over, and drive several galvanized decking screws through the underside to fasten the panels together.

Working on the top side, lay out a grid for locating the drainage holes. Draw three lines parallel with each side, making them 3 inches apart. At each intersection, drill a ¾-inch-diameter hole all the way through the bottom assembly. I used a spade bit for this job. Again, wear a dust

Support the complete sheet on 2x4s or furring strips that are laid across a pair of sawhorses when you break down large sheets of plywood into smaller pieces for the planter-box panels.

Set the blade on your saw to cut just through the box panel, and you will barely kerf the support. With this approach, the main sheet and the cut section will be supported as you cut.

BOX CONSTRUCTION

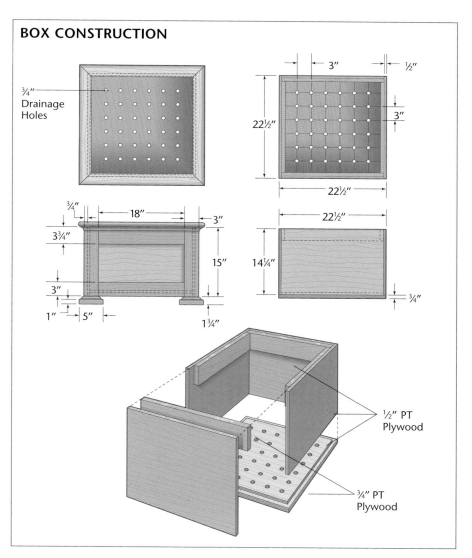

¾" Drainage Holes

3"   ½"
22½"
3"
22½"

¾"
18"   3"
3¾"
15"
22½"
14¼"
3"
1"   5"   1¾"
¾"

½" PT Plywood

¾" PT Plywood

3

Use a clamp to pull opposite sides into the rabbets formed when you glued up the bottom panels, and against the vertical edges of the third side. Then apply adhesive to the appropriate edges of the fourth side.

4

Work the fourth side back into the box, then drill pilot holes and drive screws to lock the parts together. Repeat the process on the other side of the box, then use the bottom panels as forms to make another box.

5

Glue and screw ¾-in. stiffeners around the inside of the box to reduce bowing. If the planter box side bows out, as it does here, orient any bow in the stiffener in the opposite direction.

BOX FACING CONSTRUCTION

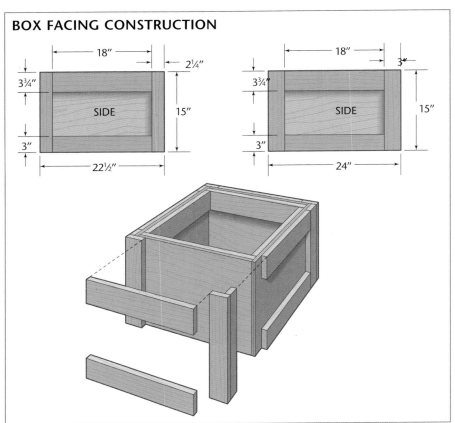

mask, and sweep up and bag the wood chips for disposal.

Assembling the Boxes

Join the four sides of the boxes using butt joints. Use the two identical bottom pieces as assembly forms when fastening the sides. With a clamp holding three sides of the box in the forms, apply adhesive to the appropriate edges of the fourth side, **(Photo 3)** and fasten it with screws or nails. **(Photo 4)** After the sides of both boxes are joined, install a bottom in each one.

You may find that the sides of the boxes are bowed a bit. To counter the bowing, cut strips of ¾-inch plywood (the stiffeners on the cutting list), and glue and screw them to the insides of the boxes. Orient each strip so that its bow is opposite to that of the side. **(Photo 5)**

After the boxes are assembled, prime and paint. I recommend latex for both the primer and paint. You don't need to coat the insides of the boxes.

Face Frames

Construct the frames with butt joints

between the stiles and rails and at the corners between the two adjoining stiles. The stiles you'll apply to the front and rear faces are 3 inches wide. Those applied to the ends are 2¼ inches wide, and when combined with the edges of the adjoining stiles, they form a 3-inch-wide surface. The best way to construct the frames is to cut and join the stiles, forming corner assemblies. Apply the corners to the boxes; then cut the rails to fit, and attach them. All the stiles should be 15 inches long, extending from the bottom edge of the box to the top edge. Crosscut the stiles from 1x4 stock, and then rip half of them down to 2¼ inches wide and the other half to 3 inches wide.

To form each corner assembly, glue a narrow stile to a wide one, edge to face, using construction adhesive. Clamp the assemblies, and set them aside overnight. (Be careful that you don't dent the soft cedar when you clamp these corner boards; use small scraps of wood to protect the wood from the clamps.) Sand the completed corners; then glue and screw them to the planter boxes. Apply beads of adhesive to the back of a corner, press

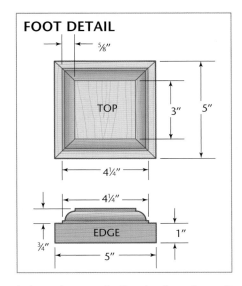

FOOT DETAIL

TOP

⅝″

3″ 5″

4¼″

4¼″

EDGE 1″

¾″

5″

be 4¼ inches square with a routed profile on three edges. Take one, and press it down on the nails, orienting the piece so that you can rout the fourth edge. The router will hold the workpiece down, and the nails will prevent it from twisting. To avoid splinters, work in from both edges, and end the cut in the center. **(Photo 8)** Crosscut the other two blocks from the working strip. You'll need to route the profile on two sides of these blocks.

Make the feet by bonding a top and bottom section together with adhesive. Then stick them to the planters at the corners. Drive a couple of screws through the planter into the foot and a couple through the foot into the planter.

Making Cap Molding

The cap molding is attached to the top edge of the planter box to finish it. It covers the plywood edges as well as the edges of the frame pieces. Rip the cap stock to the width specified on the cutting list. Check the dimensions of your planter, and adjust the cap molding as needed. (The molding should overlap the inner face of the box by ⅛ inch.) As you crosscut the pieces, miter the ends.

It's wise to test-fit the pieces on your benchtop (without glue), and check the fit of the miter joints. You want tight-fitting miters, even if that means the unit is slightly out of square. When the assembly looks right, attach it to the top of the

it into place, and align it; then clamp it temporarily. **(Photo 6)** Drive three or four stainless-steel screws through pilot holes in the plywood and into the back of each stile.

After you've attached all the stiles, measure and cut the rails. The top rails are partially covered by the cove molding, so you can use 1x4 stock and set the rails ¼-inch down from the top of the plywood. The bottom rails are 3 inches wide. Glue and screw them in place as you did the stiles.

Making Feet

Each foot is a two-ply construction glued and screwed to the bottom of the planter. The bottom layer is simply a 5-inch-square piece of ⁵⁄₄ cedar. The top layer is a 4½-inch square of one-by cedar. All edges get a quarter-round bead using a router and ¾-inch beading bit.

Cut the eight blocks needed for the bottom layer of the foot assemblies. Hold off on crosscutting the upper layer. Routing pieces this small can be tricky with a hand-held router. First, rip a 36-inch board to the desired width: 4¼ inches. Rout the profile on the long edges of this board and across both ends as well. Make a small-workpiece holder about a foot long with three nails driven through it in a triangular pattern at one end. The points of the nails should protrude about ⅜ inch. **(Photo 7)** Tack a fence across the board about 3½ to 4 inches from one end. Clamp this fixture to your workbench so that the nail end is right at or slightly over the edge.

Crosscut the first two blocks from each end of your working strip. They should

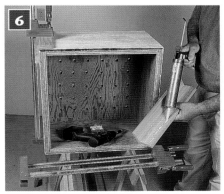

Attach the corner face-frame assemblies *in pairs. Run adhesive on the backs, set them in place, clamp the assemblies tight, and drive stainless steel screws through the box sides into the backs of the assemblies.*

Hold the small feet pieces for routing *by pressing them onto a trio of exposed nail points. The router holds the soft cedar on the nails, which keep the block from kicking out from under the tool.*

Work the router *from the corners towards the middle of the foot. If you rout from corner to corner when cutting an edge profile, the bit tends to blow out splinters as it exits the wood.*

Apply adhesive *to the mitered ends and the planter box's top edges to get tight miter joints on the cap molding. Fit the section in place and screw through the edge of one molding piece into the adjoining piece.*

Planter Bench

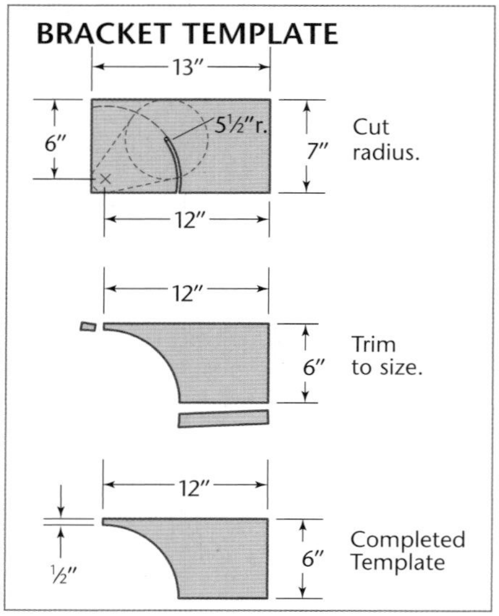
BRACKET TEMPLATE
13″
6″
5½″r.
7″
Cut radius.
12″
12″
6″
Trim to size.
12″
½″
6″
Completed Template

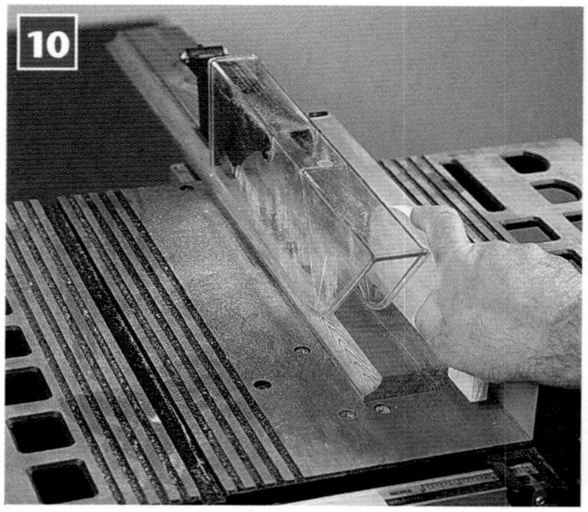
10

***Rout the cove molding profile** on both edges of a board; then rip the molding from the board. You can make molding from scraps of stock if the pieces are long enough and have knot-free edges.*

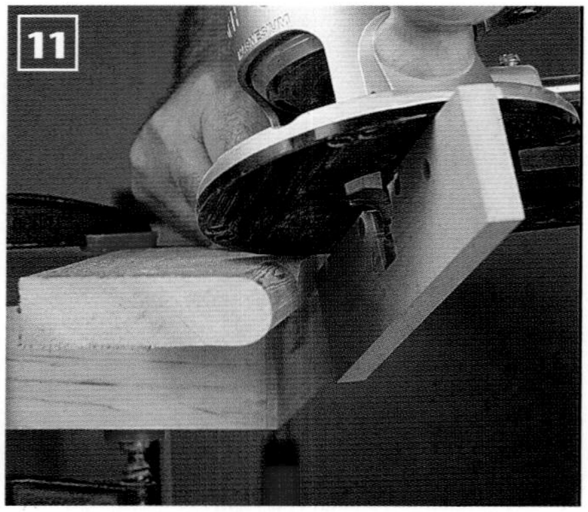
11

***Bullnose the outer bench seat boards** using a roundover bit and an edge guide. When the pilot bearing hangs below the quarter-round profile on the second pass, the guide orients the bit correctly.*

planter box. Apply adhesive to the top edges of the planter box, and press the strips in place. **(Photo 9)** There are many things you can do to get tight miter joints (aside from making accurate cuts), and one of the most important is using clamps. Just be sure that the clamp surfaces don't mar your wood. Lastly, drive three or four stainless-steel finishing screws through each molding piece into the top edges of the planter.

Making Cove Molding

Cove molding fits under the cap to trim the planter. The molding is 5/8 inch wide and 3/4 inch high, shaped with a 1/2-inch cove bit. Rout the profile on the edge of a wide board; then rip off the strip. To produce the right amount, crosscut two or three 28-inch-long boards. Rout the profile on the two long edges, rip off the 5/8-inch-wide molding, and rout and rip again. **(Photo 10)** Cut the strips to fit, mitering the ends, and glue and screw them in place. I used three 3/4-inch-long 6-gauge stainless-steel screws in each strip, and drilled and countersunk pilot holes so that the slender molding wouldn't split.

Cutting Bench Parts

The bench has six seat boards, two aprons, two mounting cleats, and four brackets made from 5/4 stock. Two seat battens are cut from one-by stock. Rip and crosscut all these parts except two of the seat boards to the cutting-list dimensions. The outer two seat boards are nosed along one edge. You can rout this profile in two passes with a roundover bit, using an edge guide to control the second cut. **(Photo 11)** Without a guide for the second cut, the bit's pilot bearing will ride on the roundover profile you've already cut and produce a different profile on the second side of the board. You need to hold off on cutting these two boards so that you can clamp them for the routing operation. After nosing the edges, you can rip and crosscut the boards to final size.

Shaping Brackets

The four brackets are 6 x 6 inches with a 5½-inch-radius arc. For maximum strength you'll want to shape them so the grain of the wood runs diagonally. To this end start by making a 45 degree cut on one end of a length of 5/4x6 stock. Make a template of hardboard or MDF and use it to guide the arc cut. Make the template by cutting a piece of 1/2-inch MDF or 1/4-inch hardboard to the dimensions indicated in the drawing. Using a router and trammel, cut the arc and trim down the template to 6 inches wide, leaving it at the 12-inch length. To use the template, align it to the 45 degree cut you made, then clamp the template and the workpiece to your workbench with the area to be cut overhanging the edge. **(Photo 12)** Scribe along the bottom edge of the template on the stock, and mark along the tiny flat at the tip of the arc as well. Using a saber saw, cut close to the edge of the template; then trim the bracket edge to match the template using a pattern bit in your router.

After all four brackets have been partially shaped, square them. Then swing the miter saw back to 0. Nip the tip of the arc on each bracket. Measure 6 inches from that tip, and square a cut line across the bracket to finish.

Mounting Cleats

Before you incorporate the cleats into the bench assembly, bore three holes for the mounting bolts, and use them as templates for drilling matching holes in the planter boxes. The cleats will overlay the top rail on the planter box frames, with the ends flush with the seam between rails and stiles. Lay a strip of 5/4 stock to represent the thickness of the seat boards on top of the mounting cleat, and set it against the rail with the scrap tight against the cove molding. When you have each hole started, remove the cleat, and extend each hole through the box side. It's a good idea to label matching cleats and planters during this stage.

Building the Bench

The bench is composed of the seat boards, cleats, mounting cleats, aprons, and brackets. The seat boards are joined by the seat battens and mounting cleats. The brackets are attached to the aprons, and the aprons to the seat assembly.

Lay out the six seat boards with the nosed edge on the outsides with 1/16-inch gaps between boards. I used spacers, aligned the ends of the boards, and applied a couple of clamps. Set the two seat battens in place, and mark around them, positioning each one 6 ½ inches from the center of the seat board length. Remove the battens, apply dots of adhesive to the seat boards inside the marks, and replace the battens. Drill pilot holes, and drive 1¼-inch stainless- steel screws into the seat boards.

Glue and screw the mounting cleats to the seat. I used 2¼-inch finishing screws to secure the cleats, driving them in pilots

Shape brackets *by aligning the bracket template with the mitered end of the stock to rout the arc. Use several clamps (set free of the router path) to secure the work so that it won't chatter under the cutting action.*

With the apron flat on your bench *and the bracket on a scrap of ⅛-in. hardboard to create the offset, predrill through the edge of the apron, and drive a long stainless-steel screw into the bracket.*

Assemble the bench *by locking the bench to the planters one bolt at a time. With one bolt in place, you can align the bulky assembly to insert the other bolts through the planter into the bench mounting cleat.*

with ½-inch-deep counterbores. Be sure you orient the cleats with the appropriate faces out, so you can align them with the holes you drilled in the boxes.

Next, attach the brackets to the aprons. The brackets are positioned flush with the ends of the aprons and are inset about ⅛ inch from the face to create a shadow line at the seam. Fasten them using adhesive and one 2¼-inch finishing screw and one 1⅝-inch screw. The long screw is driven through the apron into the bracket. You need to drill at least a 1-inch counterbore so that a 2¼-inch screw will penetrate the bracket. **(Photo 13)** Drive the short screw through the edge of the bracket into the apron.

Lastly, join the apron-and-bracket assemblies to the seat assembly. Use construction adhesive and six screws driven though the bottom edges of the aprons into the seat boards, and a single screw driven

on an angle through the face of each cleat into the back of the apron.

Drill and counterbore pilot holes, and run a bead of adhesive on the top edge of the apron and onto the ends of the cleats. Set the apron, flush up the ends, and snug it against the seat and the ends of the cleats with clamps. Drive the screws. After you've installed both aprons, the bench is ready for a test-assembly.

Assembling the Planter Bench

Prepare the planters by sliding a 4-inch carriage bolt through each hole in the planter. The heads should be inside the planter. Fit one end of the bench into the projecting bolt shanks. Get just one bolt all the way through into its hole in the cleat, and you are on your way. **(Photo 14)** That one bolt will support one end of the bench, allowing you to support the other end while you slide the second

planter into final position.

Once the bench is well supported, focus on fine adjustments that lead to getting all the bolts pushed through the planter and the mounting cleat. Slip a washer over the bolt shank, thread the nuts, and tighten.

Finishing

I finished the planter bench with marine spar varnish. After cleaning off all the beads of squeezed-out adhesive using a chisel and utility knife, do whatever touch-up sanding seems appropriate. Use a shop vacuum and a tack cloth to mop up every bit of sanding dust.

Following the manufacturer's directions, apply the finish. In most cases, you should apply a slightly thinned first coat, followed by two full-strength top coats. I allowed each coat to dry at least one day and sanded lightly between applications.

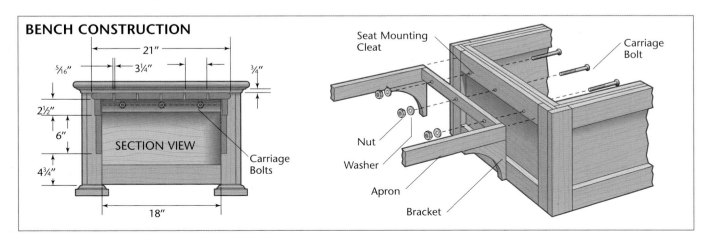

BENCH CONSTRUCTION

21"

5/16"   3¼"   ¾"

2½"

6"

SECTION VIEW

4¾"

Carriage Bolts

18"

Seat Mounting Cleat

Carriage Bolt

Nut

Washer

Apron

Bracket

Planter Bench

Outdoor Chair

This basic sturdy and comfortable chair can be a staple of any set of outdoor furniture. The straightforward design has an ample seat and a backrest frame supported by bolted-on legs. The economy version of this design is shown in stores with plump cushions on spring-metal supports. The top-of-the-line version is built of redwood. But if you look closely at some of these chairs, you'll see that the wood is construction fir or some other medium

grade disguised to look like redwood with a coat or two of stain. More and more, you also see pressure-treated stock used in all its gray-green glory. I used cypress in this project. The attractive wood is well suited to outdoor use and looks handsome on the slatted seat and backrest. Also, cypress is relatively light, so it's easy to move the chair around your deck or patio. The frame is made from sturdy 2x6 stock ripped into 2½-inch-wide pieces, while the slatted seat and backrest are made from thinner slats. But you can cut them out of the same stock. You'll see many variations of this basic design, and you may want to make small alterations. If you are an experienced woodworker, for example, you can create a more distinct, concave-shaped curve in the back and the seat. And, of course, you can use a router to dress up the main pieces with details such as a roundover or beaded edge.

EXPLODED VIEW

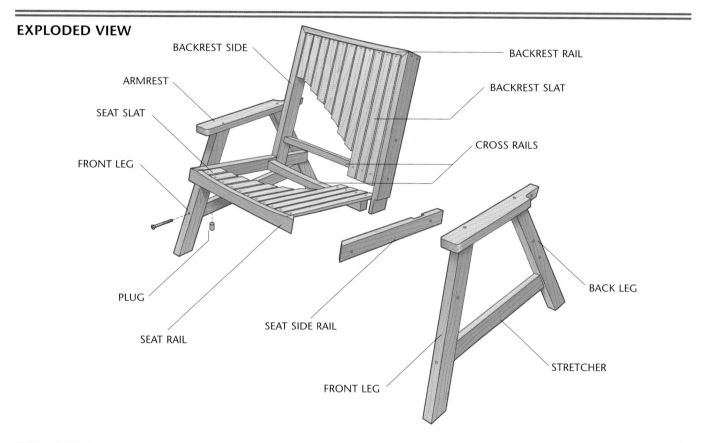

Part	Number	Thickness	Width	Length	Cypress Stock
Front legs	2	1½"	2½"	22⁷⁄₁₆"	2x6
Back legs	2	1½"	2½"	24³⁄₈"	2x6
Armrests	2	1½"	2½"	24"	2x6
Backrest sides	2	1½"	2½"	28⁹⁄₁₆"	2x6
Seat side rails	2	1½"	2½"	24"	2x6
Backrest and seat rails	2	1½"	2½"	22½"	2x6
Cross rails	2	1½"	2½"	21"	2x6
Stretchers	2	1"	1½"	21⅝"	2x6
Seat slats	11	⅝"	1½"	17"	2x6
Backrest slats	11	⅝"	1½"	22"	2x6
Plugs	4	½" dia.	—	1¼"	birch dowel

CUTTING LIST (Some parts are left long during construction.)

SHOPPING LIST

- 3 pcs. 2x6 8' cypress
- 1 pc. birch dowel, ½"dia.x36"
- 4 galvanized lag screws, ¼"x4"
- 3" galvanized deck screws
- 4 galvanized carriage bolts, ¼"x3", with washers and nuts
- 2 galvanized carriage bolts, ¼"x2½", with washers and nuts
- 2½" galvanized deck screws
- 1¼" galvanized deck screws

CHAIR ELEVATIONS

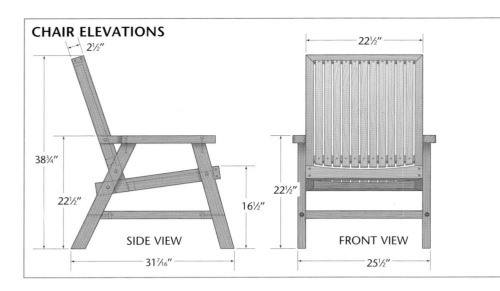

2½"

38¾"

22½"

16½"

22½"

SIDE VIEW

31⁷⁄₁₆"

22½"

22½"

FRONT VIEW

25½"

PLAN VIEW

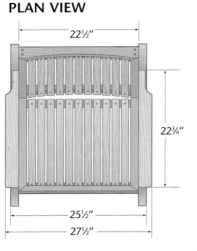

22½"

22¾"

25½"

27½"

BUILDER'S NOTES

This sturdy outdoor chair may have many parts, but it has a straightforward design that you can build using fundamental carpentry techniques and basic power and hand tools.

Materials
Although this style of chair can be made of redwood or pressure-treated lumber, I used cypress. While 2x3 stock seemed to look best, I found that it was not a common size. So I purchased 2x6s and ripped them into 2½-inch-wide pieces on a table saw.

Many weather-resistant adhesives are available, but for this project I used polyurethane glue. The odd thing about this glue is that it produces a waterproof bond when hard but actually needs moisture to cure. Construction-grade lumber often has enough moisture content to ensure proper curing, but it's a good idea to dampen one of the mating surfaces and apply glue to the other before closing the joint. Use a wet rag to wipe the surfaces; then spread the glue and clamp the joint before the

wood has a chance to dry.

As it cures, polyurethane glue expands, and in this sense it is a gap-filling glue. By filling gaps and crevices, it keeps moisture from collecting in exposed joints. Unlike epoxies, however, it won't strengthen a poorly fitted joint.

Tools and techniques
While you will use several tools to assemble the chair, you'll find that a table saw is very handy when it comes to the essential up-front work: ripping the raw stock to the widths and thicknesses needed. There isn't another tool that will do the work nearly as well or as easily.

You may think of the table saw as a professional-level tool that requires an investment of $800 or more. But bench-top models, which are smaller and lighter (and yes, less powerful and less capable than floor models), will do all the work required on this project. And a bench model is easy to move from a storage shelf to a workbench, where you can make a few cuts, then store it to make more room in your shop for assembly.

Another useful power tool for this project is a miter saw. There are several types: the straightforward miter saw, the compound miter saw, and the sliding compound miter saw. The simplest form is often called a chop saw. What these saws do best is cut miters, a fair number of which are required in this chair. Of course, you can always adjust the blade angle and use your trusty circular saw.

One key process used in this project, aside from mitering, is concealing fasteners and strengthening joints with cross-grain plugs. I used this process because one of the basic rules of woodworking is that screws don't hold well in end grain, and you certainly want the joints on an outdoor chair to be secure. (This lack of holding power in the end grain may not be as true as it once was because of subtle improvements in screw designs.)

A traditional response to the problem is to drill a hole perpendicular to the grain, close to the end of the piece, and glue a plug into it. That

way, the plug's grain will be perpendicular to the end grain of the piece, and a fastener driven into it will provide more security by grabbing the long grain.

Joining the stretchers to the legs presented a design challenge. Mortise-and-tenon joints are the natural choice, but cutting those joints is not simple. The simple joint would be a fastened butt joint, but because a screw driven into end grain doesn't hold well, my solution was to reinforce the butt joints with cross-grain plugs.

Finish
The finish you apply depends on the look you desire and the materials you've used. Any outdoor project needs a finish to help protect it from the weather. I used premium materials, selecting them for their color as much as their durability, so I used a clear finish. If you want to color the wood you select, it's best to use a penetrating stain.

Yard and Garden Furniture

STEP-BY-STEP

Side-Frame Parts

Before you start measuring and cutting, take a few moments to concentrate on power-tool shop safety, even if your temporary setup is a pair of sawhorses outside on the lawn. This is a good idea before you start any project.

The following are just a few reminders. First, be sure that you use power tools that have a grounded electrical supply. The safest situation is a grounded tool plugged into a ground-fault circuit interrupter (GFCI). Wear safety glasses, and put on a dust mask if you're cutting or sanding. To reduce the chance of a kickback accident with a circular saw, support your work so that the cut can open and the waste piece can fall away.

Once you are safely set up, begin work on the legs, stretchers, and armrests by ripping and crosscutting the parts to the dimensions specified on the cutting list. Cut the armrest somewhat longer than indicated in the drawings. An extra inch or two will allow you to adjust the position of the seat before you trim the armrest flush with the backrest.

Miter the legs next. Note that the front and back legs are mitered at different angles. These cuts are easy if you have a power miter saw. If you don't, lay out the angles with a sliding T-bevel and protractor, and cut to the line with a circular saw. **(Photo 1)**

Also miter the ends of the stretchers. Note that the front-end angle of each stretcher is mitered the same way as the front leg, and the back-end angle matches the angle cut on the back leg.

To improve the joint between the leg and stretcher, I drilled holes near the ends of the stretchers and glued dowels into the holes. Simply drill a 1¼-inch-deep hole, centered about 1 inch from the end of the stretcher. Drill into the bottom edge so that the dowel is hidden. I found that the typical ½-inch dowel fits best in a 1⁵⁄₃₂-inch or 3¹⁄₆₄-inch hole. Glue a piece of dowel into each hole, and belt-sand it flush after the glue sets.

Finally, shape the armrest. Cut the notch at the back of the armrest with a saber saw, and round off the front corners with a belt sander.

Side-Frame Prep

To lay out the holes in the side frames, set the parts on your workbench with all the parts supported. **(Photo 2)**

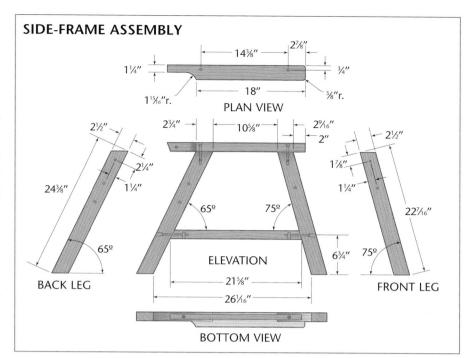

SIDE-FRAME ASSEMBLY

PLAN VIEW

ELEVATION

BACK LEG

FRONT LEG

BOTTOM VIEW

You can cut the miters for the side-frame parts with the help of an angle square. This model has a pivoting fence and a protractor scale. Clamping it to the work frees your hands to operate the saw safely.

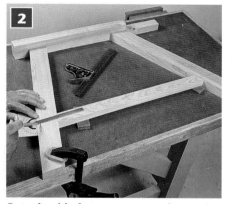

Butt the side-frame parts together, and clamp them down on the workbench before laying out the pilot holes for the screws. Note that the stretcher is shimmed up on scraps of ¼-in. hardboard.

Following the drawing, measure and draw lines indicating the paths of the shank and pilot holes for the screws. You can use a protractor head on a combination square to scribe the axis lines across the legs and onto the stretchers.

Drill the counterbores for the lag-screw heads first. Because the lags that fasten each leg and stretcher together are more or less level, the bottom of the counterbore must be plumb. That means you have to bore at an angle. I strongly favor the use

of a Forstner bit for doing the counterbores, although this bit can be difficult to control if it isn't square to the work.

You can overcome this drawback by making yourself a simple guide. Start with a piece of the 2x3 stock. Use a square to lay out a line across the butt end, extending it down the sides. Bore a ¾-inch-diameter hole into the end of the piece, aligning it with the layout lines down the sides. Drill about 2 inches deep, and miter-cut a piece 1 to 1½ inches

Clamp a wooden guide to the leg to help align and control the bit as you make the angled counterbore. Align the axis of the hole in the drilling guide with the axis of the pilot hole marked across the leg.

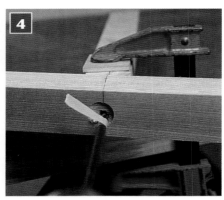

Drill the pilot holes through the legs into the stretchers using a long bit, and sight along it to help keep the bit lined up with the line marked on the parts. The masking-tape flag marks the cut depth.

DRILLING GUIDES

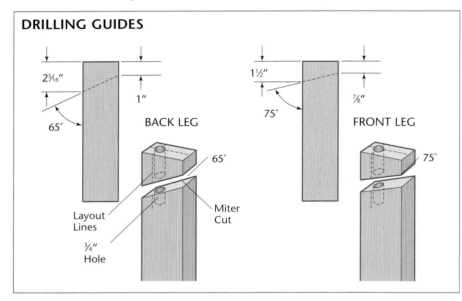

extend the holes into the stretcher and into the leg tops. As before, try to align the hole with the layout line. You need to repeat this process for every side frame assembly you are making.

Side-Frame Assembly

Once you have aligned the holes, apply some glue and screw the side-frame parts together. The joints derive some strength from the glue but depend on the screws because wood glued this way (end grain to long grain) can be weak.

Attach the legs to the stretchers with ¼-inch lag screws that are 4 inches long. Drive the hex heads with a wrench. Use a flat washer under the screwhead.

Fasten the armrests to the legs with 3-inch deck screws. Cut plugs to cover the heads, glue the plugs in place, and sand them flush. Take care to square up the assembly and align the parts before snugging the fasteners.

Backrest and Seat Frame

Cut the backrest and seat sides, the backrest and seat rails, and the cross rails to the dimensions on the cutting list.

You need to cut a concave curve on each of the rails. In addition, the curved edge of the seat and backrest rails have a rabbet cut in for the slats. This rabbet is ⅝ inch wide and ½ inch deep. Because the same arc is used on all four rails and is also the shape of the rabbet's shoulder, it's convenient to make a template.

Make the template of ¼-inch hardboard, ¼-inch or ½-inch void-free plywood, or ½-inch MDF. You can easily lay out the arc on the template stock using a flexible strip of wood, metal, or plastic. Mark the endpoints and the midpoint of the arc on the template stock. Flex the strip so that it connects the points, and trace along the strip onto the pattern. Cut the template carefully using a saber saw, and work the edge with a half-round file to smooth the curve.

The challenge is to secure the template to the workpiece in a way that will also secure the workpiece while you use your router. With the jig I made, the workpiece is set between a trap fence on either end and tucked back against a broad fence. **(Photo 5)** The fences are attached to the template. You secure the workpiece by driving screws through each trap fence into the end of the rail so that it can't move. The fence is wide enough to clamp to the workbench with the template edge

long from the workpiece. Cut the same 75-degree angle that you used to miter the ends of the front legs. Make a second guide for the back legs, and miter it at a 65-degree angle (25-degree miter).

To use one of the guides, set the miter-cut surface on the edge of the leg, and align the guide's layout mark with the mark on the leg. Clamp the guide, put the bit into the guide hole, and start drilling into the leg. **(Photo 3)** You can drill a deep hole if the lag will be concealed under a wooden plug, or drill a shallow flat area the size of the lag washer. To prevent moisture from collecting on the mounting screws, you can cover them with wood plugs. That will require ½-inch-diameter counterbores approximately ⅜ inch deep. **(Photo 4)**

With all the counterbores drilled (including those for the armrests), drill the shank and pilot holes. For the lags, drill a hole the same diameter as the lag's shank through the leg; then drill a pilot into the stretcher. I used a ³⁄₁₆-inch drill bit for the pilot.

For the shank holes, shim up the stretcher so it is centered on the thickness of the legs, and clamp the legs so they can't shift as you drill. You need a long bit to penetrate the leg. Use the dimple left by the Forstner bit to locate the ¼-inch shank hole. As you drill, line up the bit with the layout line. Drill through the end and just a fraction of an inch into the stretcher. In the same way, drill through the armrest into the top of the legs. Then switch to a ³⁄₁₆-inch bit, and

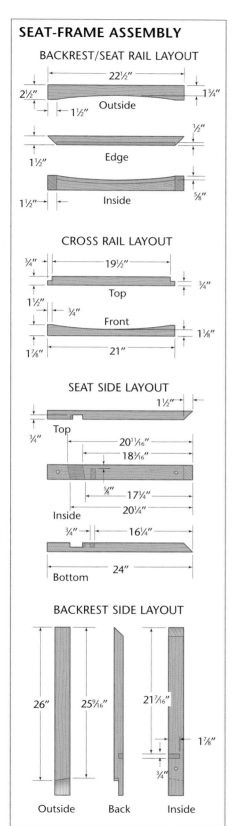

SEAT-FRAME ASSEMBLY

BACKREST/SEAT RAIL LAYOUT

Outside
22½"
2½"
1¾"
1½"

Edge
½"
1½"

Inside
1½"
⅝"

CROSS RAIL LAYOUT

Top
¾"
19½"
¾"

Front
1½"
¾"
1⅛"
1⅞"
21"

SEAT SIDE LAYOUT

Top
1½"
¾"

Inside
20¹¹⁄₁₆"
18³⁄₁₆"
⅝"
17¾"
20¼"

Bottom
¾"
16¼"
24"

BACKREST SIDE LAYOUT

26"   25⁹⁄₁₆"   21⁷⁄₁₆"
1⅞"
¾"

Outside   Back   Inside

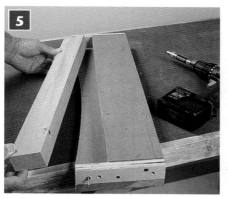

Make the curves in the seat rails with a router guided by a template. The curved shape is cut into the board attached to the base of this jig. It's large enough that clamps won't obstruct the router.

Cut the rabbet for the slats with the template that you used to shape the rail edge. You need to insert a spacer between the main fence and the workpiece and reposition the work.

overhanging the edge of the bench.

To shape the rails, fasten a rail into the jig, and clamp the jig to the workbench. Rough-trim the shape with a saber saw; then rout the final contour. Using a flush-trimming bit, place the template on the bottom. With a pattern bit, the template must be on top. To shape the cross rails, which are narrower and shorter than the backrest and seat rails, fit a ⅝-inch-thick

spacer between the fence and the work-piece and ¾-inch-thick spacers between the rail and the trap fences.

To cut the rabbets in the backrest and seat rails, use the ⅝-inch-thick spacer between the rail and the fence. Orient the jig so that the template is on top, and use a dado-and-planer bit, which has a shal-low cutting depth and a shank-mounted bearing. **(Photo 6)** Lay out the length of

RAIL TEMPLATES AND JIG

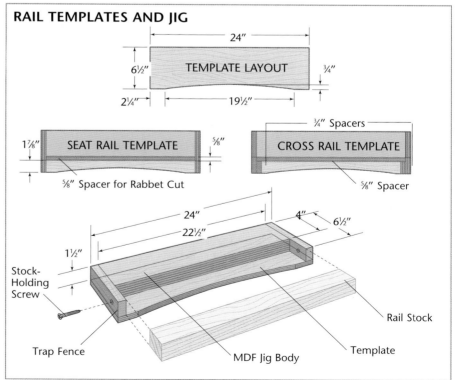

TEMPLATE LAYOUT
24"
6½"
¾"
2¼"
19½"

SEAT RAIL TEMPLATE
1⅞"
⅝"
⅝" Spacer for Rabbet Cut

CROSS RAIL TEMPLATE
¾" Spacers
⅝" Spacer

24"
22½"
1½"
4"
6½"

Stock-Holding Screw

Trap Fence

MDF Jig Body

Rail Stock

Template

Join the seat and backrest sides *using half-lap joints. The joint provides long-grain to long-grain faces to make good gluing surfaces and interlocking shoulders that give the joint good strength.*

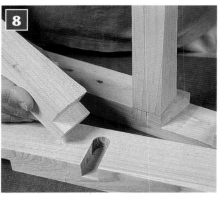

Rout slots called stopped dadoes *into the side pieces where the cross rails join the seat and backrest sides. To make the joint snug, you need to round the top corners of the tenon or square the corners of the slot.*

Join the seat sides with the cross rail, *and glue and screw the seat rail. I clamped a support block to each side, set the rail in position, and applied another clamp at right angles to pull it against the block.*

Join the backrest sides to the seat, *apply water-resistant glue to the tenons on the cross rail, and slide it into the dadoes. When the tenons are seated, tighten a bar clamp to secure the assembly.*

the rabbet on the rail, and monitor your cut carefully.

Seat-Frame Joinery

Begin the joinery cuts by laying them out on the side pieces in mirror-image pairs. The backrest sides are joined to the seat sides with half-lap joints. The angle between the seat and backrest is 100 degrees. Set a sliding T-bevel to that angle from a protractor and use it to lay out the shoulder of the lap on the backrest sides. Use it to also lay out one of the shoulders of the lap on the seat side. Then lay a piece of the working stock on the seat side, line it up along the scribed shoulder, and mark the second shoulder line along its opposite edge.

Form the laps by making repeated cuts with a circular saw to remove half

the thickness of the stock. **(Photo 7)** It's best to cut a little shallow and clean the surfaces with a chisel than to cut too deep and have to start over.

Next, cut the dadoes and the bare-faced tenons that join the cross rails to the sides. Lay out the stopped dadoes on the side pieces, and cut them using a router and ¾-inch straight bit. To guide the router, clamp a shop-made T-square to the workpiece. Cut up to your mark, and then either back out of the cut or switch off the router and, when the bit stops spinning, lift it off the work.

To complete the joint, cut what are called barefaced tenons on each end of the cross rails. In this case, you form the tenon by cutting a rabbet across one side of the rail. To fit the tenons into the dadoes, you have to either round off the

upper corners of the tenons or square up the corners of the dado. **(Photo 8)** Cypress is fairly soft, so a file makes quick work of rounding off the corners.

The last of the joints that tie the frame parts together are the miters between the sides and the backrest and seat rails. I cut them with a sliding compound miter saw. You can use a power miter saw, circular saw, or table saw.

Assembling the Frame

Use a water-resistant glue to fasten the cross rail between the seat sides, and clamp each joint. (If you use a pipe clamp, protect the wood with cauls.) Then apply glue to the mitered faces of the seat rail, and fit it between the seat sides. Clamp the rail and the sides to temporary alignment blocks. **(Photo 9)** The miter joint looks good but needs to be reinforced with a couple of 2-inch-long screws. After you drive the screws, you can remove the clamps and alignment blocks.

Now add the backrest. Apply glue to the half-laps, and join the backrest sides to the assembly. Apply a clamp over each joint, slide the cross rail into place, and clamp it securely. **(Photo 10)** Lastly, tilt the assembly so that the backrest rests flat on the workbench, and glue and screw the backrest rail to the assembly.

Set the clamped assembly aside until the glue sets. (The polyurethane glue I used took about 24 hours.) Then trim the bottom edges of the backrest sides flush with the bottom edges of the seat sides.

Seat and Backrest Slats

Altogether, the chair has 22 slats, each measuring 5/8 inch thick and 1 1/2 inches wide. I made them by ripping 2x6 stock on a table saw.

The backrest requires 11 slats that are a maximum of 22 inches long, while the seat requires 11 17-inch slats. You will probably get six slats from each piece of 2x6. Cut two 17-inch lengths of 2x6 and two 22-inch lengths. You want at least one smooth surface on each slat. But sanding the slats themselves to remove saw marks would be time-consuming. Instead, I planed the working edge of the stock before each rip cut. Set the rip fence to produce a 5/8-inch-thick ripping. Use a push stick, and rip one strip from each of the four 2x6s. **(Photo 11)** Plane each 2x6, rip another slat from each, and plane the newly cut edge. Keep repeating this cycle until all the slats are

ASSEMBLY BOLT LAYOUT

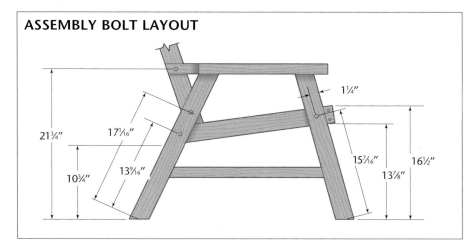

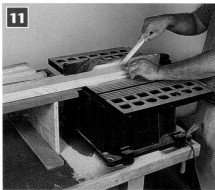

Position an outfeed table behind the saw to keep the slats flat and make ripping easier. On this saw, I removed the blade guard to use a push stick, which is essential for feeding the thin slats past the blade.

Clamp the side frames to the seat, and test the arrangement for comfort before bolting the final sections together. You can adjust the final pitch of the sections and customize the project to suit your needs.

To cut an arc on the backrest slats that matches the concave seat, tape a pencil to a scrap of wood, and slide it across the seat. This scribing process will transfer the contour to the ends of the backrest slats.

cut. Then sand them and round-over the edges with a router and roundover bit.

Install the slats with screws, but only temporarily, for two reasons. First, the backrest slats have to be marked for trimming, and you can't do that until they are installed. Second, you want to be able to do a test-sitting in the chair before actually drilling the assembly bolt holes, and to counterbore the holes you have to remove some of the slats.

I used scraps of ¼-inch hardboard as spacers to position each slat before driving the screws. Be sure you drill and counter-sink a pilot hole for each one.

Joining the Frames

This is when the chair comes together, simply by installing the bolts. Note that the two holes in the back leg and a hole in the front leg are centered across the legs' widths. Lay out the holes in the legs only. I marked the points on the legs intersected by the seat side, and lightly scribed a line across the two legs with the help of a yardstick.

You have an opportunity, at this point, to adjust the chair to suit you. You can raise or lower the seat level and change the tilt, too. It pays to clamp the parts together for a test-fit. Tip the seat assembly onto one side, align the side-frame assembly on it, and apply clamps. When you have clamped the other side in place, try the chair and adjust to suit. **(Photo 12)**

When you are happy with the chair, drill the bolt holes. Use a long bit so that you can drill into the leg and on through the seat-frame assembly members at the same time. While the chair is clamped together, scribe along the backrest sides onto the armrests and along the back legs onto the extensions of the seat sides. You

want to trim these parts flush.

You will need to drill counterbores on the inner surfaces of the seat-frame parts for the washers and nuts. To do this, remove most, if not all, of the slats. Then you have room to drill counterbores with a ¾-inch spade bit.

However, before removing the slats, mark the bottom edges of the backrest slats for their final trim. These slats are cut in an arc matching the concave shape of the rails. You must transfer the arc from the seat to the slats.

Tape a pencil to a scrap of wood, and slide this marking jig across the seat, scribing lines across the lower ends of the backrest slats. **(Photo 13)** This line defines the gap between the seat and the backrest slats.

After you have marked the arc, remove the slats, lightly marking each one so that you can return it to the same spot. Cut them with a saber saw, and sand the edges. Drill the counterbores in both the seat and backrest sides. Then reinstall the slats, this time with glue as well as the screws.

Next, trim the excess length from the armrests and the seat sides, and bolt the side-frame assemblies to the seat frame.

Finishing

After you've glued plugs into the counterbores to cover the bolt heads, sand the chair. Be sure to sand the plugs smooth and level relative to the wood surrounding them. Apply the exterior finish of your choice. If you have selected an attractive grade of wood for the project, consider a clear, oil-based wood finish formulated for outdoor use. The oil preserves the wood and allows the natural color and beauty to show through.

Outdoor Lounger

You can find traditional wooden chaise longues on the windy decks of elegant cruise ships and the sunny patios of exotic tropical resorts. But you don't have to take a vacation to enjoy the kind of relaxing, stretch-out comfort this type of chair provides. Of course, you could spend several hundred dollars to buy a reproduction. But now you can make your own, and tailor the dimensions to suit. This lounger uses the same simple design motifs built

into the Outdoor Chair project on page 92. You will find several similarities, including the heft of the stock, the angle of the legs, the slatted seat and backrest construction, and the roomy proportions. Overall, the construction is clean and elegant. But there are a few extra twists and turns in this project, such as the gentle curve built into the seat support rails. It will take you more time to cut them than it would to make a flat-backed surface, but the extra work will pay off in extra comfort. The seat is wide, and the backrest is ample. This project is also adjustable. Just bring the back support closer to or farther from the pivot points, and you can find a position where it's comfortable to read or to lie back and doze off in the sun. Although there are no cushions included in the project plans, you can certainly make some or buy a long pad made for loungers.

EXPLODED VIEW

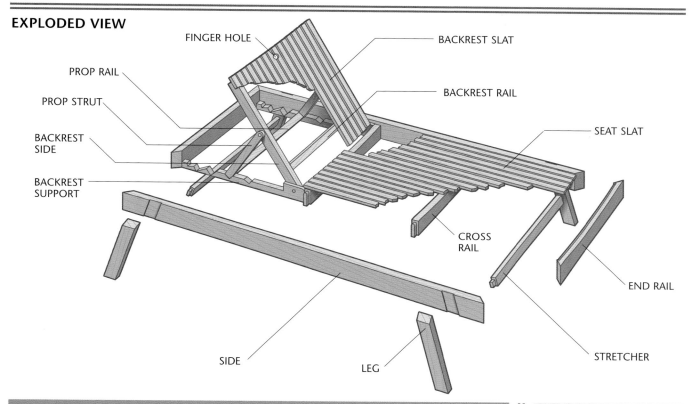

FINGER HOLE
BACKREST SLAT
PROP RAIL
PROP STRUT
BACKREST RAIL
BACKREST SIDE
SEAT SLAT
BACKREST SUPPORT
CROSS RAIL
END RAIL
SIDE
LEG
STRETCHER

CUTTING LIST (Some parts are left long during construction.)

Part	Number	Thickness	Width	Length	Cypress Stock
Sides	2	1½"	3½"	78"	2x4
End rails	2	1½"	3½"	29"	2x4
Cross rails	2	1½"	2⅞"	27½"	2x4
Legs	4	1½"	2½"	13⅛"	2x6
Stretchers	2	1"	1½"	29½"	¾x6
Backrest sides	2	1½"	1½"	28"	2x6
Backrest rails	2	1½"	1½"	22⅞"	2x6
Prop struts	2	¾"	1½"	14¾"	2x6
Prop rail	1	1"	1½"	26"	¾x6
Backrest supports	2	1"	2¾"	27½"	¾x6
Seat slats	16	⅝"	1½"	47¼"	2x6
Backrest slats	16	⅝"	1½"	28¼"	2x6

SHOPPING LIST

- 2 pcs. 2x4 8' clear cypress
- 1 pc. 2x4 10' clear cypress
- 4 pcs. 2x6 8' clear cypress
- 1 pc. ¾x6 8' clear cypress
- 2" deck screws
- 1¼" deck screws
- 4 galvanized carriage bolts, ¼"x3", with washers and nuts
- 2 galvanized carriage bolts, ¼"x4"
- 2 weather-resistant (galvanized, stainless steel, or brass) stove bolts, ¼"x2½"
- 8 galvanized flat washers, ¼"
- 4 weather-resistant stop nuts (galvanized, stainless steel, or brass)

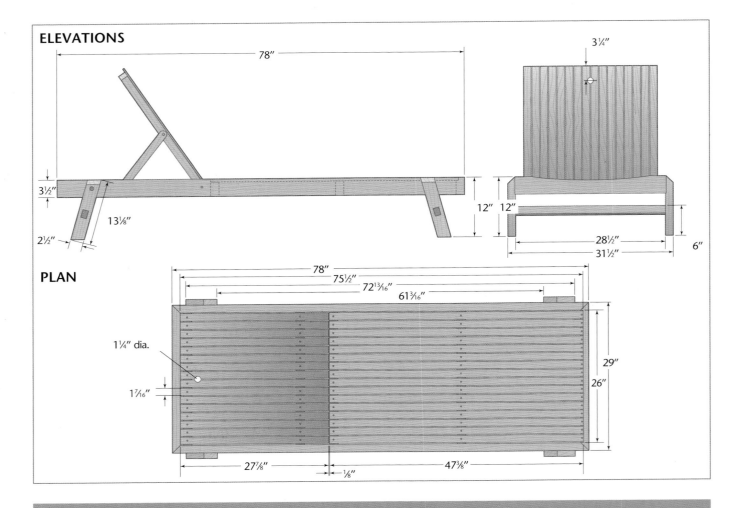

ELEVATIONS

PLAN

BUILDER'S NOTES

The construction of the outdoor lounger closely resembles that of the chair and the side table in most important respects. If you are building only this lounger, by all means read over the builder's notes for the chair on page 92 and the side table on page 110 before you start cutting.

Materials
I selected cypress for the lounger simply because I used it to make the chair and side table. But any of the outdoor woods will serve. For the templates used in shaping the lounger parts I chose medium-density fiberboard, or MDF, to which it is commonly referred. As the name implies, this material is manufactured by pressing a light batter of glue and fine wood fibers into dense sheets. MDF is flat and heavy—often half again as heavy as a comparable sheet of plywood. It comes in precisely thicknessed ½-inch 4x8-foot sheets, and generally costs no more than a sheet of good plywood. You'll find it in stock at most lumberyards and home centers.

Why MDF for the templates? Because it is flat, stable, and inexpensive. It's so dense that the edge can't be compressed by a router bit's pilot bearing, although it can be worked with a file and sandpaper. The material is void-free too, so you don't have to be concerned about the bearing dipping into a hollow spot along the edge.

Tools and Techniques
Essential tools are a table saw—a benchtop model will do—and a router. A fixed-base model works better for some cuts, but you'll need a plunge router as well. You can always use a circular saw for ripping, but a table saw will do a better job of making the legs and the slats from the 2x6 stock. The router is such a versatile tool that you will use it for a variety of tasks on this project. Fitted with a good pattern bit (a straight bit with a pilot bearing mounted on the shank rather than the tip), the router shapes the rails. With a straight bit, it cuts the dadoes that join the frame and backrest rails to the sides. With a roundover bit, it softens the edges of the lounger. A power miter saw is also handy—for cutting the miters that join the frame parts and for cutting the slats to length and mitering their ends. If you don't have one, use a saber saw rather than a circular saw.

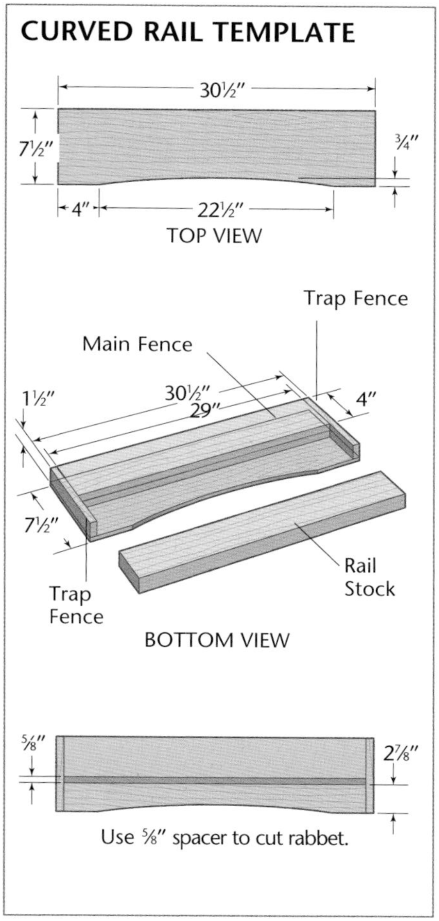
CURVED RAIL TEMPLATE
30½"
7½"
¾"
4"
22½"
TOP VIEW
Trap Fence
Main Fence
1½"
30½"
29"
4"
7½"
Trap Fence
Rail Stock
BOTTOM VIEW
⅝"
2⅞"
Use ⅝" spacer to cut rabbet.

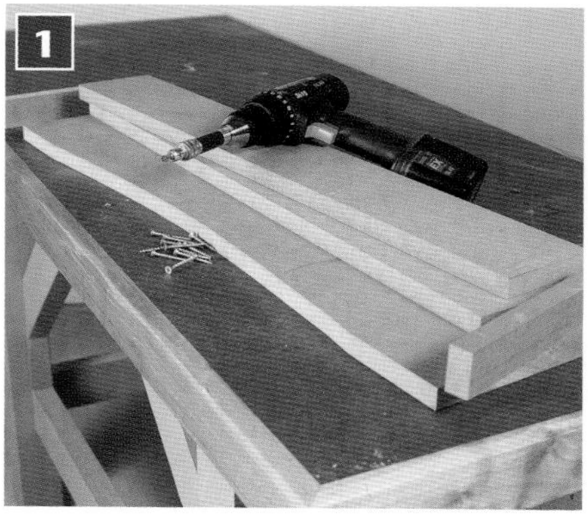
1

***This jig will help you shape** all the curved rails. It consists of the template, a fence, and two trap fences. Line up the two fence plies and screw them together. Screw a trap fence to each end; then screw on the template.*

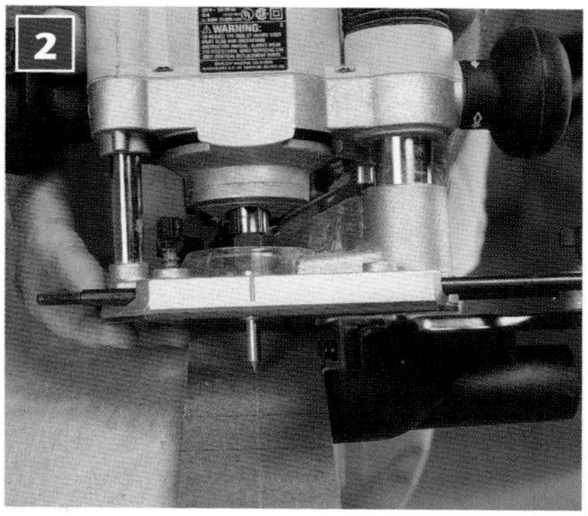
2
WARNING

***Align your router** with the centerline mark using a special accessory called a centering pin. Hand-tighten the pin; then bring the edge guide into position against the edge of the leg template, and lock it down.*

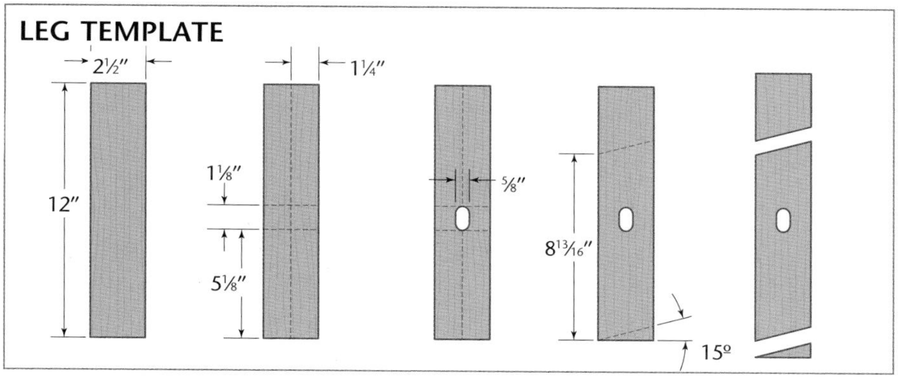
LEG TEMPLATE
2½"
1¼"
12"
1⅛"
5⅛"
⅝"
8¹³⁄16"
15º

STEP-BY-STEP

Making the Curved Rail Template

All of the rails, including the end rails, the cross rails, and those used in the backrest, have a curve cut into them. The curves make the lounger comfortable. In addition, the curved edge of the front end rail has a rabbet in it for the slats. This rabbet is ⅝ inch wide and ½ inch deep. Because you use the same arc on all these rails and the shape of the rabbet's shoulder, it's sensible to make a template you can use on all the pieces.

The challenge is to secure the workpiece to the template and your bench in a way that does not impede your router. With the jig I made, the workpiece rests against a broad fence that's as high as the workpiece is thick and captured between two trap fences, one on each end. (See "Curved Rail Template" drawing and Photos 1, 3, 4, and 5.) All the fences are attached to the template. **(Photo 1)** You drive a screw through each trap fence into the end of the rail so it can't move. The fence is wide enough to clamp to the workbench with the template edge overhanging the bench edge.

You can make the template itself from ¼-inch hardboard, ¼-inch, ½-inch, or ¾-inch (void-free) plywood, or ½-inch or ¾-inch MDF. I used ¾-inch MDF for the template, as well as for the fences. You can lay out the arc on the template stock using a flexible strip of wood, metal, or plastic. Mark the end points and the midpoint of the arc on the template stock. (The locations of these points are shown in the drawing.) Flex the strip so it connects the points, and trace along the strip onto the pattern. Cut the template carefully using a saber saw, and work the edge with a half-round file to smooth and fair the curve. Be sure to eliminate flat spots and small bumps so that the curve is smooth and continuous.

After the template is completed, attach the main fence and the two trap fences.

Making the Leg Template

Although it's not that difficult to make the legs, even with mortises and laps, a simple template makes the job even easier. I'd suggest using ¾-inch MDF; if you used it for the curved rail template, you should have a lot of it left over.

To make the template, follow the "Leg Template" diagram, above. Cut a blank of the correct width, but make it somewhat longer than the final length. This template ends up shorter than the legs it will shape—it defines the half-lap shoulder, the mortise, and the bottom of each leg.

Lay out and cut the mortising slot next. Begin by scribing the centerline and lines marking the ends of the mortise slot. Rout the slot with a ⅝-inch straight bit, using a plunge router and edge guide. **(Photo 2)** To cut the ½-inch-wide mortise, the guide slot needs to be both wider and longer than the mortise. The smallest template guide you can use with a ½-inch straight bit is ⅝-inch outside diameter. Thus the

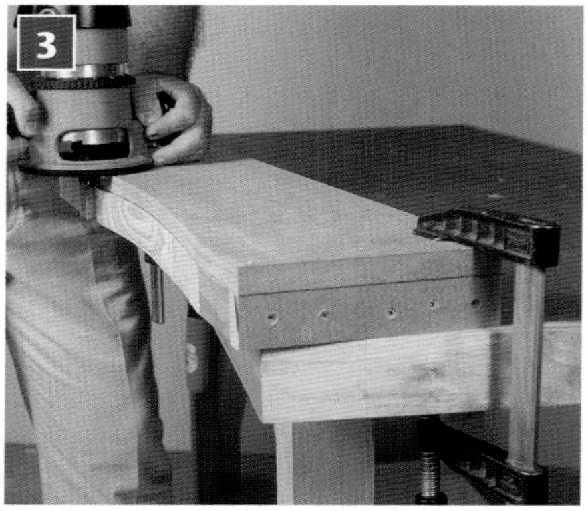

Use a router and template *to shape the lounger rails. Screw the workpiece into the template jig, trim with a saber saw, then use a pattern bit to trim the edge of the rail flush with the template guide edge.*

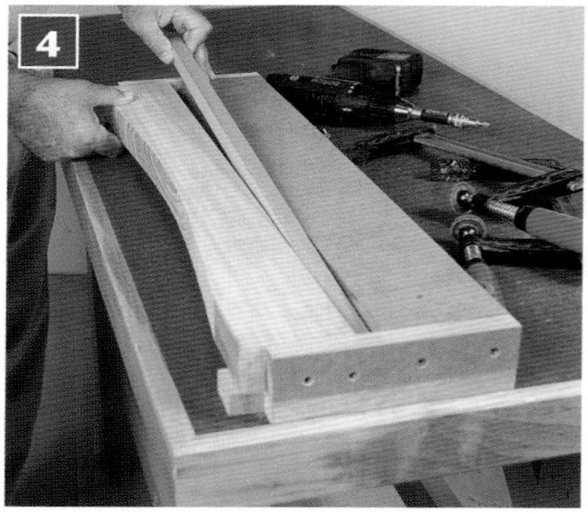

To rout the rabbet for the slats, *shift the rail forward in the jig ⅝ in. You can easily do this by fitting a ⅝-in.-thick shim between the rail and the jig fence, and refastening the rail into the jig.*

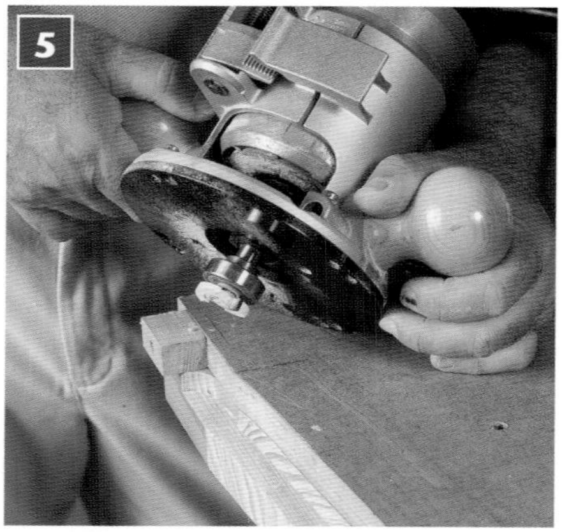

To cut the final rabbet, *use a rabbeting bit with a shank-mounted bearing. Run the router along the template edge from stop to stop. Make as many passes as needed to cut the rabbet a ½ in. deep.*

guide slot must be ⅝ inch wide and, to get a 1-inch-long mortise, 1⅛ inches long. You can eyeball the length, cutting from mark to mark, or clamp stops to the template to keep the router from moving too far and making the slot too long.

After the slot is completed, miter the ends of the template, reducing its length to the final dimension.

Cutting the Frame

The frame includes the sides, end rails, cross rails, legs, and stretchers. You can cut the stretchers from 5/4 stock, the legs from 2x3 stock, and the rest from 2x4 material. Because 2x3 stock is rare, you may need to rip down a 2x6 to make the legs. If you do this, also rip the stretchers from the same material. However, you will need a small amount of 5/4 stock later on to make the backrest supports. Be picky when you select stock for these parts. The sides, which are more than 6 feet long, need to be dead straight. If you can, avoid pieces with big knots, which can weaken the frame and detract from its appearance.

Cut the parts to the dimensions specified by the cutting list. Remember, several parts are initially cut longer than the specified lengths, including the cross rails and legs.

Miter the foot-ends of the legs by 15 degrees. Shape the end rails and the cross rails using the template. Fit the workpiece into the jig. Secure it by driving a screw through each trap fence into the end of the workpiece. Turn the jig over so that the template is up, and clamp it at the edge of the workbench with the working edge cantilevered past the workbench. **(Photo 3)** Set the clamps where they won't interfere with your tools.

Use a saber saw to trim away the stock that extends beyond the template edge. Then switch to a router and a long pattern bit with the pilot bearing mounted on the bit shank. Guide the bearing along the template edge, trimming the workpiece flush. Both end rails and both cross rails are shaped this way.

But you have to rabbet one end rail for the slats. Secure the workpiece in the same jig for this cut, shifted forward ⅝ inch. To do this, back out the screws holding the workpiece, shift it, and slip a ⅝-inch-thick shim between the workpiece and the fences. **(Photo 4)** Push the work back against the fences and redrive the screws. The rabbet is stopped at both ends, and while it is easy enough to eyeball this cut, it is less risky to screw small stop blocks to the template edge to help control the cut. If you use a bit with a shank-mounted bearing that matches the bit's cutting diameter, you need to position the stops where the cut begins and ends.

Now change router bits. You need a short pattern bit that will cut no more than ½ inch deep into the rail as its shank-mounted bearing rides along the template. Adjust the depth-of-cut and rout the rabbet. **(Photo 5)**

Cutting the Rail-to-Side Joints

This part of the project includes miters that join the end rails and the sides, as well as the dadoes and barefaced tenons that join the sides and cross rails.

Cut the miters first, adjusting your saw to cut a 45-degree bevel. Assemble the basic frame without glue to judge the fit of the joints, and if need be, adjust the bevel angle and retrim the cuts to achieve slightly tighter joints.

Lay out and cut the stopped dadoes for the cross rails next, referring to the "Frame Side Layouts" drawing, opposite, for dimensions. **(Photo 6)** I used a router and ¾-inch-diameter straight bit for these cuts, guiding the router along a home-made T-square. (See page 15 for plans.)

Before cutting the next round of joinery—the barefaced tenons on the cross rails—those rails must be trimmed to their final size. First, rip them to the proper width. On a table saw, set the rip fence so that the shaped edge falls to the outside (or left side) of the blade. Rip the two cross rails; then lay out the trimming crosscuts from the center of the piece so that you take an equal amount off each end to produce a piece 27½ inches long.

A barefaced tenon is simply one that's offset so that one cheek is flush with the surface of the workpiece. In this case, the key is to get a tenon that's ¾ inch thick, so it will fit the dado. Rout the tenons to size. (You can use the tenoning jig shown on page 18.)Then round off the top corners using a file so that they will seat properly in the routed dadoes.

Assemble the frame without glue to ensure that everything fits properly. You may need to trim a little. I used this test assembly as an opportunity to drill pilots and drive screws into the miter joints. I ran two screws through each end of the rails into the sides, and through the sides into the rails. A power drill/driver makes it easy to run the screws in, then back them

Lay out and rout the dadoes for the cross rails in one side, and align them with the marks on the other side. When you dado the second side, guided by the homemade T-square, the cuts in the two sides will align.

Use scraps of template stock to support the router at the start of the cut. Clamp the scrap on the leg and against the template. Use a 3-in. strip to begin, a narrower strip to widen the lap, and the template to finish.

Rout the mortise in the leg in several passes, stopping periodically to vacuum or blow out the chips in the template slot. After only a single pass, the template slot packs with chips except where the bit turns.

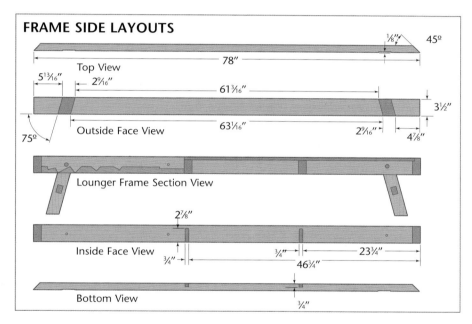

FRAME SIDE LAYOUTS

Top View — 78″ — ⅛″ 45º
5¹³⁄₁₆″ 2⁹⁄₁₆″
61³⁄₁₆″
Outside Face View — 63¹⁄₁₆″ — 2⁹⁄₁₆″ 3½″
75º 4⅞″
Lounger Frame Section View
Inside Face View — 2⅞″ — ¾″ — 23¾″
¾″ 46¼″
Bottom View — ¾″

FRAME RAIL LAYOUTS

END RAIL
26″ ⅝″
1½″ 45º ½″
29″
22½″ 3¼″
¾″ 3½″
29″

CROSS RAIL
¾″ 27½″ ¾″
¾″ 2⅞″
¾″ 26″

out. Just be careful not to let the bit skip onto the wood surface.

Cutting the Leg Joints

The legs join the sides in shallow lap joints. Because the laps provide a mechanical lock between the parts and prevent the legs from pivoting, you need only a single bolt at each joint.

I made both the mortises and the laps in the legs using the template. To cut the laps, use a very short pattern bit or a dado-and-planer bit with a shank-mounted pilot bearing. The process is like routing tenons. Begin by marking the inner face of the legs. That will help to prevent confusion as

you make two pairs of mirror-image legs. Bond the template to the first leg blank with carpet tape, aligning the foot-end of the template flush with the foot-end of the blank; then clamp the leg and template to the benchtop. Cut the ⅛-inch-deep lap beginning at the top of the leg and working toward the edge of the template. **(Photo 7)** The shoulder of the lap is established when the shank-mounted pilot bearing reaches the edge of the template and stops the cut.

While the template is still clamped to the leg, switch to the plunge router and rout the mortise. Cut it ¾ inch deep. **(Photo 8)**

Cut the laps in the outer faces of the sides next. Use the same router and bit to make this cut that you used to lap the legs. To guide this cut, use two pieces of MDF (each about 6 inches square) clamped directly to the lounger side.

Use a protractor or sliding T-bevel and pencil to lay out one shoulder line of each of the four laps. Align one of the MDF fences on an angled shoulder line, and clamp it.

Butt a leg against the MDF, then the second piece of MDF square against the opposite edge of the leg. Clamp that MDF square, and remove the leg. You don't need to cut deeper than an ⅛ inch.

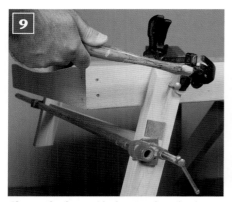

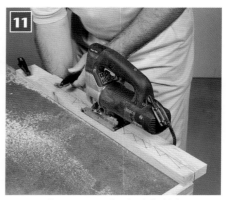

Clamp the legs with the stretcher glued between them, and install the bolts. You need only one bolt in the lap between the leg and the frame. Recess the nut in a counterbore, and cut the bolt shank flush.

To rout the recesses in the supports, clamp the blanks edge to edge, and position your homemade T-square to stop the router travel at the shoulder layout. That way you can rout freehand, sweeping edge to edge.

Use a saber saw to rip the full-thickness extension that will house the sawtooth piece. I've cut in from the end and will extend the rip cut to the shoulder of the recess, but not until I reposition the clamp behind the saw.

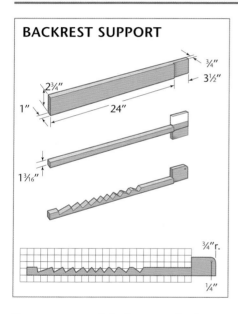

BACKREST SUPPORT

3/4"
3 1/2"
2 3/4"
1"
24"
1 3/16"
3/4" r.
1/4"

Because you used the leg to set the fences, you should have a perfect fit.

Assembling the Frame

The lounger will begin to take shape as you join the sides to the two cross rails, then glue and screw the end rails in place. Join the legs to the stretchers and these subassemblies to the frame. Along the way, you must make the stretchers and trim the legs to their final length and shape.

Begin by softening the exposed edges of the frame parts. I used a 1/8-inch-radius roundover bit for this.

Glue the cross rails into their dadoes in the side, and clamp this assembly. Then glue the end rails to the sides, and drive the assembly screws. Make sure the assembly is flat and square.

Now install the legs and stretchers. (I clamped the frame across the workbench so that it wouldn't slide or rock.) One by one, test-fit each leg into its lap, and trim the legs so that the tops are flush with the top edge of the frame. Also chamfer the top end of the leg as indicated in the elevation drawings.

With the leg clamped in place, drill a hole for the mounting bolt through the leg and frame side. Also drill a counterbore on the inner face of the frame side for the washer and nut.

Make the stretchers next. While the legs are clamped in place, measure to confirm the shoulder-to-shoulder length of the stretchers. Add 1 1/2 inches to that measurement, and cut two pieces of 1x1 1/2-inch stock to that length. Form tenons on the ends of the stretchers, using your router and a tenoning jig. (See page 18 for jig details.) Size the tenons to fit the mortises in the legs.

When you unclamp the legs, radius their exposed edges and the edges of the stretchers. Sand, assemble the legs and stretchers with glue, and join them to the frame with glue. Lastly, you can install the mounting bolts. **(Photo 9)**

Making Backrest Supports

These sawtoothed strips attach to the inner faces of the frame sides. They support the adjustable backrest and its prop piece. The prop can rest in any of several sawtooth notches to provide a range of backrest angles. They are thick enough to support both the backrest and prop rail when the assembly is lowered flat. And the supports have thinned areas that project up between the backrest sides and the frame sides at the pivot points, ensuring that the backrest will pivot smoothly without wiggling from side to side.

To make the supports, start by cutting two blanks to the dimensions on the cutting list. You can lay out the leg shape by enlarging the grid on the "Backrest Support" drawing, at left. Next, rout the recesses. The easiest approach is to clamp the two workpieces edge to edge; then clamp your homemade T-square across them to limit the cut. **(Photo 10)** Use either a large-diameter straight bit, a mortising bit or a dado-and-planer bit. Set up the router to cut 1/4 inch deep. Begin cutting at the ends of the boards, and work back and forth, cutting edge to edge, until the router base contacts the T-square. One final sweep with the base riding along the T-square will establish the shoulder of the recess and complete the cut.

Now rip down the width of each support, beginning at the end and cutting to the shoulder of the recess. Use a saber saw to cut along the recess shoulder to the rip line. Then clamp the workpiece at the edge of the workbench, and rip along the line. To keep the work secure, you'll have to use two clamps, and stop cutting temporarily to move one. **(Photo 11)**

Lay out and cut the sawtoothed notches with a saber saw to complete the supports. Note that the angles of the notches change slightly from one end of the support to the other. That's because the angle of the back-

Shape the prop rail using the template and jig you constructed in the first step. Press the blank against the template and the fences. Work with an oversize piece, and cut it down after you shape the curved edge.

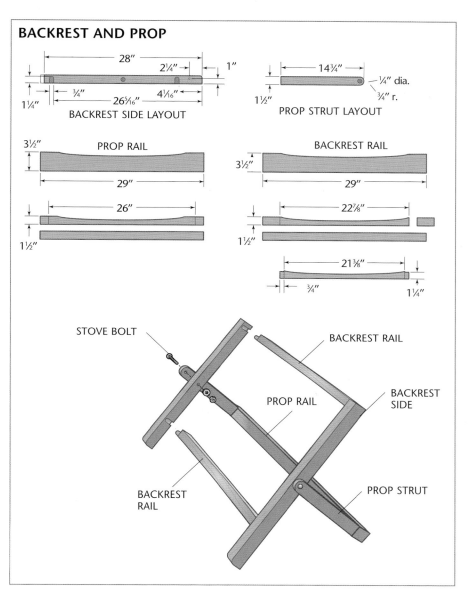

BACKREST AND PROP

BACKREST SIDE LAYOUT

28" 2¼" 1"
¾" 4¹⁄₁₆"
26⁵⁄₁₆"
1¼"

PROP STRUT LAYOUT

14¾" ¼" dia. ¾" r.
1½"

PROP RAIL

3½"
29"
26"
1½"

BACKREST RAIL

3½"
29"
22⅞"
1½"
21⅜"
¾" 1¼"

STOVE BOLT

BACKREST RAIL

PROP RAIL

BACKREST SIDE

BACKREST RAIL

PROP STRUT

rest prop varies according to the attitude of the backrest.

The final operation is to round off the upper corner of the recessed section. This will provide clearance for the outermost backrest slats when the backrest is adjusted. If the corner is left square, the slats bind on it, and you can't raise the backrest. Make a ¾-inch radius arc using a file or belt sander.

Finally, screw the completed supports to the inner faces of the sides. Align them flush with the bottom edges of the sides, so the ends butt against the end rail. Then drill pilot holes, and drive screws through the supports into the sides.

Cutting the Backrest

The backrest frame has two sides and two rails with the same curve that's featured on the rest of the rails. This frame is scaled to rest flat on the edges of the sawtoothed sections of the backrest supports and to hold the backrest slats flush with the top edges of the lounger frame. Its sides fit between the thin sections of the supports and pivot on bolts that pass through the frame sides, supports, and backrest sides.

Nesting between the lounger frame and the backrest frame is the prop assembly, which consists of a rail and two struts. This is attached to the backrest with bolts, on which it pivots. When the backrest is tilted up, the prop rail swings down, dragging on the supports. You simply move the backrest to the position you want, and the prop rail will settle in one of the notches, holding the angle you want.

While dimensions are provided for the parts that make up these two subassemblies, it is important to tailor them to the lounger frame you've assembled. You should measure your lounger frame and adjust the prop and backrest dimensions as needed. When you do cut the parts, bear in mind that all the rails—the two backrest rails, as well as the prop rail—must be cut 3½ inches wide and 29 inches long to fit the template jig. After you have shaped the curved edge in the jig, you can rip the rails and crosscut to the desired final dimensions.

Cut the two prop struts next. Scribe the rounded shape on one end of each piece with a compass. Trim the corners using a saber saw, and use a file or sander to round

to the scribed line. At the center point of the arc, drill a ¼-inch-diameter countersink hole for the pivot bolt.

Now shape one end of each backrest side, and drill a ¼-inch hole for the pivot bolt. For now, leave these parts oversize, and plan to trim them after assembly is complete. (I shaped the sides after the backrest frame was assembled, but doing the job before is probably better.)

You'll shape all the rails with a router and a rail-template jig the way you shaped the frame rails. **(Photo 12)** Mount the blank in the jig with screws, trim away most of the waste with a saber saw, then rout the edge to match the template with a router and pattern bit. After you have

Clamp the backrest frame, *and make sure it is square by measuring the diagonals, which should be equal. Then turn the assembly over, and clamp it to the benchtop to ensure that it will be flat.*

Set the backrest assembly *in place between the lapped ends of the supports. You need to make sure that both parts of the assembly can move without binding in the main lounger frame.*

shaped all the rails, rip them to the specified final width. To do this, you need to set the table saw rip fence so that the shaped edge falls to the outside (or left side) of the blade. To crosscut, lay out the trimming cuts from the center of the piece, and take an equal amount off each end to produce the specified lengths. Bear in mind that the prop rail is 3 inches longer than the two backrest rails.

Fitting the Backrest and Prop

Assemble the prop strut and prop rail with rabbet joints. You can cut the 3/4-inch-wide rabbets in the prop with a straight bit in a router that's guided along a T-square. To prevent tearout as the bit enters and exits the workpiece, clamp scrap stock against both faces. Set the router's depth-of-cut to 3/8 inch, position the T-square, and cut a rabbet in each end of the prop.

Assemble the prop strut and prop rail using glue and a few screws.

Turn to the backrest sides next. Lay out and cut the stopped dadoes for the cross rails, referring to the "Backrest and Prop" drawing on page 107 for positions and dado dimensions. Be sure to lay out the dado positions in relation to the shaped ends of the sides, not the opposite ends, which will be trimmed after assembly. I used a router and 3/4-inch-diameter straight bit for these cuts, guiding the router along the T-square.

Next, cut the barefaced tenons on the ends of the backrest rails. Rout each tenon using the tenoning jig, then round off the top corners with a file so that they will seat properly in the routed dadoes.

To assemble the frame, apply glue to the joints, and fit them together. As you clamp the frame, make sure it is both square and flat. Apply pipe clamps parallel with the rails, bearing directly on the joints. Next, check frame squareness using a try square or by measuring the diagonals, and make any necessary adjustments. **(Photo 13)** Then turn the assembly over and make sure it's flat on the benchtop.

After the glue has set, remove the clamps, and trim the extensions of the sides so that they are flush with the outer face of the rail.

Mounting the Backrest

Before you bolt the prop assembly to the backrest and the backrest to the frame, you should set the backrest into place to be sure that it fits with enough clearance for the assemblies to move. This part of the lounger needs to move easily without binding.

If everything fits, drill the prop mounting holes in the backrest sides using the holes drilled earlier in the props as guides. Counterbore the holes for the washers and nuts; then bolt the two assemblies together. I used stainless-steel flathead machine screws with stop nuts. The stop nut has a nylon insert that makes it resistant to loosening. It is an important characteristic in this situation because it allows you to leave the nut loose enough for the prop assembly to move freely without worrying that the nut will come off the bolt. I used one stainless-steel washer between the prop and the backrest side, and another between the side and the stop nut.

Now you can set the unit into the lounger frame. Place the backrest frame so that there's a bit of a gap—no more than 1/8 inch—between the frame's end rail and the prop rail. **(Photo 14)** You want enough clearance to allow the backrest to move without catching or binding. Apply a clamp on each side near the pivot hole, pinching the backrest to the sides of the lounger. Using the pivot holes in the backrest as guides, drill through the supports and lounger sides. Clamp or hold a scrap block against the side so that the drill bit doesn't tear out the wood as it exits.

Bolt the backrest to the lounger frame with a commonplace galvanized carriage bolt. But instead of matching it with a standard hex nut, use a stop nut. When you install the bolt, use a galvanized washer between the support and the backrest side, as well as between the frame and the nut. (I couldn't find a galvanized stop nut so I used a stainless-steel version.)

One tip: it's a good idea to hold the head of the bolt with locking-grip pliers. The underside of a carriage bolt head is supposed to dig into the wood and prevent it from turning, but cypress is soft and a stop nut turns hard. So unless you hold the bolt head, it will probably turn with the stop nut.

Making the Slats

Preparing the slats is a time-consuming task because there are so many of them. You need 32 altogether; 16 for the seat and 16 for the backrest. You can't take shortcuts on the preparation because the slats make up the contact surfaces of the lounger. You want them to be smooth, straight, and free of defects that might compromise their strength. You need to rip the slats, sand them, round over the edges, trim and miter the ends, and drill pilot holes with a special jig. When that work is done, you'll be ready to screw them into place.

Begin by ripping the slats from pieces of 2x6 stock. Crosscut the blanks at least 1/2 inch longer than the final size of the slats. Rip the slats on the table saw, making them 5/8-inch thick. Allowing for the saw kerfs, you should be able to get seven slats from each piece of 2x6. You might discover that some of the slats twist and turn as soon as you cut them from the blank. This can be caused when moisture held in the center of the stock is suddenly able to escape, and when eccentric grain patterns in the wood are not held in check by surrounding wood. If the warping is severe, you will have to toss the piece, so be prepared to cut yourself a few extra slats.

Sand the slats with a belt sander to smooth them and remove saw marks. To make the job easier, clamp a ½-inch-thick batten across one end of your workbench as a stop. When you lay a slat on the benchtop with its end against the batten, the movement of the sanding belt will push the slat against the batten, eliminating the need for a clamp. Sanding the edges is another matter, and you may want to use a random-orbit or pad sander, which is easier to control.

After you have sanded the slats, round-over the edges using a ⅛-inch-radius roundover bit in your router.

Now trim and miter the slats. The seat and backrest slats meet in a scarf, which is an end-to-end joint formed by mitering the two pieces. I left a gap of about ⅛ inch between the mitered ends of the two slats, though you may find that a tight scarf is possible. Determine the exact lengths of the two slats by setting them on the lounger frame and trimming them to fit. When you have settled on a length for each slat, set up a stop block on your miter saw, and miter-cut each backrest slat and seat slat to length.

Screw placement has a big impact on the appearance of the lounger. To get a consistent and visually pleasing placement, I made simple jigs—one for the seat slats, one for the backrest slats—to govern the hole placement. **(Photo 15)** To make similar jigs, you need a strip of ¼-inch plywood or hardboard several inches longer and wider than the two kinds of slats. Tack thin scrap blocks to the plywood strip—one at each end and several along the sides—to position the slat being drilled. Lay out and drill through the plywood at each place you need a pilot hole in the slat. To use the jig, fit a slat against the blocks so that it can't move, and turn the jig over. Drill through the jig into the slat. When you install the slats, you can redrill at each spot with a combination pilot-hole bit to extend the pilot into the lounger rail and countersink the pilot in the slat.

Installing the Slats
The most trying part of the slat installation is working out the overall spacing. I cut up several scraps of ¼-inch plywood, which is really about ³⁄₁₆ inch thick, ¼-inch hardboard, and ⅛-inch hardboard, both of which are dead-on in thickness, and used them to make spacers to fit

between the slats. **(Photo 16)** Through trial-and-error, I worked out a satisfactory slat layout that allowed for an even, over-all pattern.

After sanding, all the slats were less than 1½ inches wide. So I created ³⁄₁₆-inch gaps between the frame and the outermost slats, and between the four middle slats. The other gaps are ¼ inch. Some of the slats were a little crooked, but I was able to force them into position using a flat pry bar, and hold them with spacers.

Be sure to work the slats so that the long side of the miter at the backrest end of each one faces down.

With all the seat slats wedged in place with the spacers, drill and countersink through the pilot holes. Then drive a galvanized 1¼-inch deck screw through each slat into each rail, and remove the spacers. You don't need any glue.

You install the backrest slats basically the same way, aligning them with the seat slats, of course. **(Photo 17)** You can tape a strip of ⅛-inch hardboard to the lounger-frame end rail to establish an appropriate and consistent clearance gap between the rail and the ends of the slats. The miters here should be facing up and should project under the miters on the adjoining seat slats.

Complete the installation by drilling a finger hole in the backrest. Because the center point of the hole will likely fall between slats, you need to make a simple guide to help make a clean hole. Do this by boring a 1¼-inch-diameter hole through a small scrap of plywood or MDF. Use a clean-cutting Forstner bit to drill the guide hole and the finger hole. You can clamp the drilling guide to the slats even though it won't seat completely on the concave surface. Clamp a second scrap of material to the underside of the slats to back up the work and prevent the bit from blowing out splinters as it breaks through. Drill the hole; then round-over the edges with a ⅛-inch-radius roundover bit.

Finishing
After you've sanded the chair to eliminate any possible rough edges, apply a finish. I used an exterior clear penetrating oil finish. The oil preserves the wood along with its natural color and beauty. Best of all, the application is a straightforward, one-step process. That pays off when it comes time to recoat the lounger and prepare it for another season out on your patio or deck.

Use a placement jig to set screws evenly and improve the look of your lounger. A slat is held in the jig against end blocks. Then you flip it over and drill through the jig and slat, using the same placement each time.

Clamp the lounger frame on a bench, and distribute the slats, inserting spacers between them to establish an overall fit. You can straighten slightly crooked slats with the spacers before fastening the slats in place.

Use the seat slats at left to guide your installation of the backrest slats. You can align them by eye. But you may need some spacers to keep the new slats straight as you drill and drive the screws.

Outdoor Side Table

If you have a chair on your deck or patio, or on a nice piece of lawn, you surely will need a table beside it. This little table is designed specifically to accompany two other projects, the Outdoor Chair and the Outdoor Lounger. You can tailor one piece to match another exactly. But many of the fundamental design and construction motifs used in the table are borrowed directly from the other pieces. You'll find a distinct similarity in the cant of the legs, the

way the frames are mitered to make the top and shelf, and how the slats are used for the shelf. The top of the table is designed to be the same height as the chair's armrest, and the shelf is designed to be the same height as the lounger seat. You'll find that an ample surface—for your iced-tea glass, morning newspaper, or cell phone—can be reached conveniently from either the chair or the lounger. Should you decide to make the table to accompany one of the chairs, it pays to plan ahead and buy enough stock for both pieces at the same time. You are likely to find that wood quality varies greatly from one supplier to another and even within one batch of lumber at the same yard. To make the best possible match with the overall hue and grain of the wood you choose, it's wise to buy your stock from one supplier for both (or all) project pieces at the same time.

EXPLODED VIEW

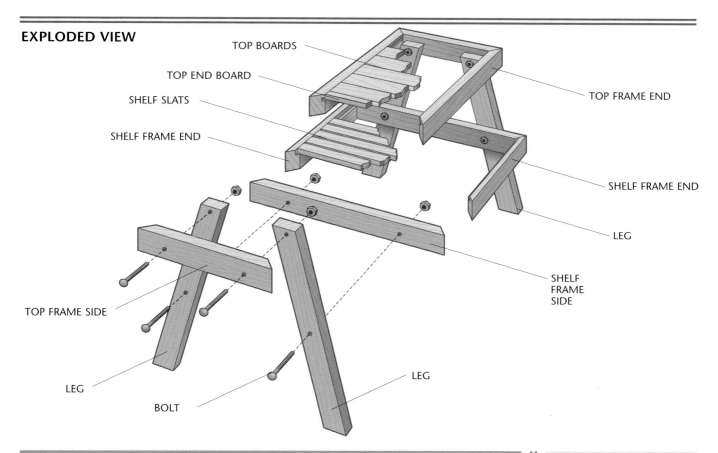

CUTTING LIST (Some parts are left long during construction.)

Part	Number	Thickness	Width	Length	Cypress Stock
Legs	4	1½"	2½"	23¼"	2x6
Top frame sides	2	1½"	2½"	17¼"	2x6
Top frame ends	2	1½"	2½"	23¼"	2x6
Top boards	6	¾"	3¼"	15¼"	1x4
Top end board	1	¾"	1⅝"	15¼"	1x4
Top end board	1	¾"	1⅞"	15¼"	1x4
Shelf frame sides	2	1½"	2½"	28"	2x6
Shelf frame ends	2	1½"	2½"	17¼"	2x6
Shelf slats	8	⅝"	1½"	26"	2x6

SHOPPING LIST

- 2 pcs. 2x6 8' cypress
- 1 pc. 1x4 12' cypress
- 8 galvanized carriage bolts, ¼"x3"
- 8 galvanized flat washers, ¼"
- 8 galvanized hex nuts, ¼"
- 1⅝" galvanized deck screws
- 2" galvanized deck screws

Outdoor Side Table

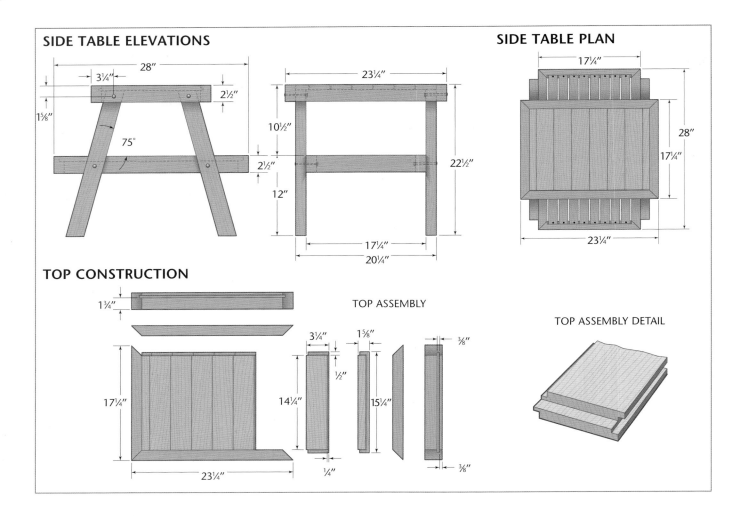

SIDE TABLE ELEVATIONS

SIDE TABLE PLAN

TOP CONSTRUCTION

TOP ASSEMBLY

TOP ASSEMBLY DETAIL

BUILDER'S NOTES

The construction of this side table mimics that of the chair and the lounger in most important respects. It makes a good match with each one. Even if you are building only this table, by all means read over the builder's notes that accompany the chair and lounger projects before cutting any wood. But there are a few items that apply just to the table.

Materials
The top to the table is made of a 2x3 frame with an insert of ¾-inch-thick boards joined with tongue-and-groove joints.

The ¾-inch stock I used was smooth on one face, rough on the other. It was also ⅞ inch thick. Some lumberyards have the facilities to surface lumber and will plane the stock for a fee. Surfacing the stock smooths both faces and reduces its thickness to a uniform ¾ inch. If you don't have surfacing equipment and the supplier doesn't provide this service, you can ask them for the name of a local shop that can dress the stock to a uniform finish.

Tools and Techniques
One unusual router bit used

on this project is the slot cutter. The typical slot cutter consists of a plate, roughly 2 inches in diameter with two or more cutting tips. The cutter bolts onto an arbor, which has a shank that's secured in the router's collet, as well as a threaded extension for the pilot bearing and the cutter. The cutter and the arbor are usually sold separately, so you can use a single arbor with different cutters. It's the height of the cutting tip that establishes the cutting size. For example, the ¼-inch cutter used for this project has cutting tips ¼ inch high that cut a slot that's ¼

inch wide. The depth of the cut is controlled by the pilot bearing. On some slot cutters, you can change the bearing size to alter the depth of cut.

With a slot cutter, the cut is made at right angles to the face on which the router rests. The router rides on one surface of the workpiece, while the cut is made in the edge. That means you can groove or rabbet narrow edges without having to balance the router on the surface being cut. It's much safer (and more accurate) with the router resting on the broad face of the board.

STEP-BY-STEP

Making the Parts

The legs and the frames for the top and the shelf are all made of 2x3 cypress ripped from 2x6 stock. Because all these pieces will be mitered, you ought to cut those parts ½ to 1 inch longer than needed. Later, as you miter the parts, you will reduce them to the desired final measurement.

After ripping and crosscutting the parts to rough length, sand all the faces and edges using a belt sander. **(Photo 1)** If desired, you can soften the edges with a router and an ⅛-inch roundover bit.

The top surface is formed from strips of one-by cypress. If necessary, have the stock planed flat and smooth on both faces to ¾ inch thick. I broke down the one-by cypress into four blanks, each 32 to 33 inches long. After cutting the grooves and tongues on the pieces, I crosscut all the top boards to the final length specified on the cutting list.

Top Frame

The top is formed of narrow boards that are captured in a frame made of 2x3s. The frame members are joined with glued-and-screwed miter joints. Each frame member is grooved for tongues cut on the edges of the top boards.

Begin making the frame by cutting the groove. The first thing you want to do is look over your parts and identify the best surfaces. On each piece, mark the top edge and the inside face.

The grooves can be cut on a table saw, but I chose to use a slot cutter in a router. Fit a ¼-inch slot cutter in your router, and adjust the router to place the edge of the groove ⅜ inch from the reference surface, which in this case is the top edge of the frame member. (You want to cut the groove on the inside face.) Make the initial cut in each of the four frame members before readjusting the router's depth setting to widen the groove to ⅜ inch. Then make a second cut on each frame member. **(Photo 2)**

Now miter the ends of the frame members. The goal, of course, is to make a frame that's square. To that end, test-fit the frame and clamp it; then drill the pilot holes and actually drive the assembly screws. Measure the diagonals to check whether the assembled frame is square. When you are satisfied, mark the members so that you can reassemble it as it is

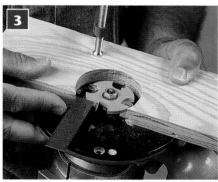

Make belt-sanding easy by clamping a cleat across the end of your workbench. This way, the action of the sander will push the workpiece against the cleat and keep it from shifting or flying off your work surface.

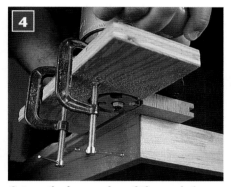

Use a router and slot cutter to produce the grooves in the top frame for the top boards. In this case, you will need to make two passes to produce the desired ⅜-in.-wide cut with the ¼-in. cutter.

Make an edge guide from plywood or MDF to help cut grooves in the top boards. Cut a hole in the scrap for a slot cutter, clamp it to the router base, and adjust the scrap so that the cutter makes a ¼-in.-deep slot.

Cut on the lower edge of the workpiece to form the tongue in the top boards. Cut one edge; then turn the work over and reclamp it. Make a second cut, as shown here, to complete the tongue.

now; then back out the assembly screws, and set these parts aside.

Top Boards

Assemble the top boards edge to edge with tongue-and-groove joints. The perimeter of the panel made of these boards is rabbeted, forming a tongue that fits the groove in the top frame. You need to cut a groove on one edge of each top board and a tongue on the other.

The first task is to set up the router and cutter. Here you want a groove that's only ¼ inch deep. To set up the router, you can either change the pilot bearing or make a fence to override the bearing. **(Photo 3)** To make a fence, use a scrap of ¾-inch plywood or medium-density fiberboard (MDF). Cut a hole in it somewhat larger than the slot cutter, locating it so that it breaks through one edge of the scrap. (If

you don't have a hole saw, just cut an opening with a saber saw.) With carpet tape or, even better, a couple of small C-clamps, attach the scrap to the router baseplate, exposing ¼ inch of the cutter.

Now adjust the router's depth setting to center the cut on the edge of the top boards. Get the setting as close as you can. To cut the grooves, rout from one end of the board to the other. Then turn the board over and reroute the same groove. Whatever your setting, this will center the groove, though the router may make the groove slightly wider than ¼ inch.

Use the same router, cutter, and makeshift fence to cut the tongues. **(Photo 4)** The only change in the setup is the router's depth setting. To adjust it, rest the router on a top board with the cutter beside the groove, and lower the cutter so its edge is flush with the wall of the groove. To prove the setup, make test cuts on a scrap of the working stock. Make a pass along the edge; then turn the piece over and make a second cut. Test the fit of the resulting tongue in one of the grooves. If the fit is too tight, raise the cutter very slightly. If it is too loose, lower the cutter very slightly. When the setup is dead on, cut tongues on all the boards.

Prepare the Top Panel

Crosscut the top boards to the length specified on the cutting list. Assemble them without glue to produce the most attractive arrangement. Instead of using full boards with one odd size at the end, for example, split the difference with two narrow but similar boards on each end. Pull the boards together, get the ends flush, and measure the diagonals to ensure that the assembly is square.

Next, trim the width of the two boards that will be at the ends of the panel so that you'll have a panel that will fit in the frame you've prepared. Ultimately, the edges of the individual top boards will be slightly chamfered, making the seams between boards a design element. You want the assembly to be symmetrical. Measure the overall panel (remembering to include a ½-inch-wide tongue on each end of it), and mark the two end boards for ripping. Each will eventually have the same width exposed, but because of its tongue, one will be ¼ inch

Test-fit the top boards, and cut tongues into the edges where the boards will be joined to the top frame. Use a bar clamp to hold the boards together and short clamps to hold the panel flat on the bench.

Use a block plane to make a narrow chamfer on the edges of the top boards. This adds handcraftsmanship and interesting detail to the table. Tilt the plane slightly, and make several passes.

wider than the other. Rip the two boards; then rejoin them to the assembled panel.

Check both sides of the panel, and decide which will be the exposed surface. This is the face that should be down as you rout the tongue. Square up the panel once again, and apply a pipe or bar clamp across it. Tighten it enough to pull the boards tightly together. **(Photo 5)**

The tongues that join the top boards to the frame can be cut using the same slot cutter used for the tongue-and-groove joints. Pry the makeshift fence off the baseplate. Adjust the router's depth so that

the cutter will make a rabbet just under ¼ inch deep in the bottom face of the workpiece. (In other words, measure from the baseplate to the cutter, and set the gap to about 9/16 inch.) Be sure to position the panel where the edge to be routed will be clear of the bench.

Make an initial cut along the panel edge, producing a shallow rabbet on the underside. Adjust the router to bring the slot cutter closer to the router baseplate. This will increase the depth of the rabbet and simultaneously reduce the thickness of the tongue being formed on the panel's edge. The goal is a tongue that is snug—not tight, not loose. Reach that goal with incremental cuts, and use a frame member to check whether the tongue fits the groove. Keep cutting and test-fitting until you have a good fit.

Once you have the correct setting, cut the other three edges of the panel. When you do this, you'll be cutting a slot rather than a rabbet. After you've made a cut on the other three panel edges, adjust the router to move the slot cutter away from the baseplate. Now cut along each of the three edges, removing the waste and opening the slot so that it becomes a rabbet like the first edge.

Assembling the Top

Assemble the top boards and frame without glue initially. You want to be able to close the miter joints of the frame tight with the top panel in place. If you can't, you probably need to trim the panel. Trimming the panel will necessitate recutting the rabbets that form the perimeter tongue.

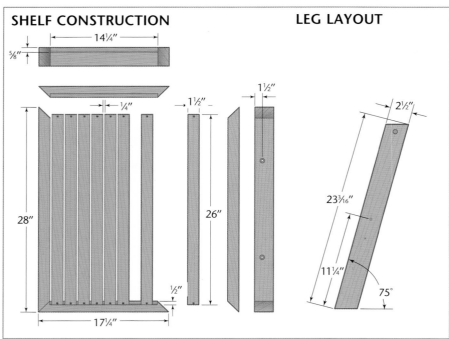

SHELF CONSTRUCTION

14¼″
⅝″
¼″
1½″
28″
26″
½″
17¼″

LEG LAYOUT

1½″
2½″
23³⁄₁₆″
11¼″
75°

Yard and Garden Furniture

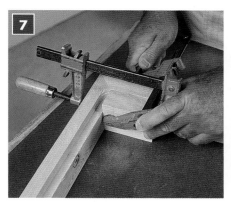

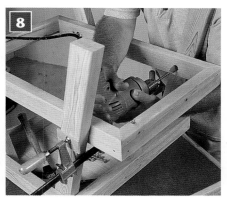

Cut four small blocks with faces and edges square to each other to glue-up the mitered corners. Clamp them to the sides at the miter, and as you join the frame pieces, clamp them to the blocks, too.

Clamp the shelf frame between the legs, and drill pilot holes for the 3-in.-long assembly bolts. Use a spade bit to make a $\frac{3}{8}$-in.-deep counterbore for the washer and nut in the inner side of the shelf frame.

Use a chisel to square the ends of the stopped rabbets after the shelf frame is assembled. With a soft wood like cypress, you need to use a sharp chisel. A dull edge will pull chunks out of the end grain.

Once you have the proper fit, you should decide whether or not you want to detail the tabletop boards. I opted to chamfer the edges of each board—in essence, calling attention to the seams between the boards and between the boards and the frame members. I used a block plane, holding it at about a 45-degree angle and just skimming it along the arris of the edge. Three or four passes along each edge should do it. **(Photo 6)**

Final assembly should be pretty straightforward. Use glue and screws to assemble the miter joints. The top boards are captured in the groove and shouldn't be glued to the frame.

Assembling the Shelf Frame

Like the top, the shelf is framed with 2x3 stock assembled with miter joints. The shelf slats are set into stopped rabbets cut in the frame ends. At this point, you should have the blanks for the frame parts cut to rough length and sanded. You need to do two things before cutting the miters and assembling the joints.

First, double-check the size of the shelf you need. This design has the shelf fitting between the legs, and that distance is determined by the size of the top. So measure the inside dimension of the top frame, and subtract from it twice the thickness of the legs. The remainder is the width of the shelf frame.

Second, lay out the miters and the stopped rabbets on the end pieces. Then, rout the rabbets, $\frac{1}{2}$ inch wide by $\frac{5}{8}$ inch deep, using a rabbeting bit. Be sure you begin and stop the cut exactly at or shy of

the marks. After the frame is assembled, you'll square the ends of the rabbets with a chisel. For now, leave them as the router cut them.

Cut the miters, and assemble the shelf frame with glue and screws. **(Photo 7)** Don't install the slats yet, because they'll be in the way when you drill and counterbore the holes for the bolts that fasten the top, shelf, and legs together.

Attaching the Legs

Miter the legs; then lay out the holes for the bolts that mount the legs to the shelf. It's better not to drill these holes until you've got the legs and shelf clamped together because you may want to fine-tune the shelf placement

Lay out the locations of the bolt holes on the table's top assembly. Turn the topside down, stand the legs in place inside the top assembly, and clamp them. Now drill holes through the top and the legs for the bolts that join them. Unclamp the legs, and use a $\frac{3}{4}$-inch spade bit to drill a counterbore on the inner face of each leg. The bit's point goes into the $\frac{1}{4}$-inch-diameter hole, and the cutter excavates a recess for the nut and washer.

The counterbore bit might wobble in the hole and make a slightly ragged cut, but it will be hidden on the inner face of the joint. The technique of counterboring first, then drilling through could cause problems here because the $\frac{1}{4}$-inch bit might damage the outer face of the joint as it exits the wood.

Bolt the legs to the top. Then rest the table on its top, and fit the shelf frame

between the legs. Center the frame, and make sure it is the same distance from the top all around. Clamp the frame to the legs, leaving room to drill the holes. **(Photo 8)** Drill the pilot holes through the legs and the frame; then drill counterbores on the inner faces of the frame. You still need to install the slats, so don't bolt the frame in place yet.

Installing the Shelf Slats

The shelf slats are $\frac{5}{8}$ inch thick, and ripped from 2x6 stock. Avoid stock with obvious knots, because slats with big knots will be weak. Avoid swirling grain patterns, too, because the slats may warp or bow. After cutting the slats, sand them well and round-over the edges with your router and the $\frac{1}{8}$-inch roundover bit.

Clamp the shelf frame to your workbench, and use a chisel to square the ends of the rabbets. **(Photo 9)** The assembled joints provide support for the fragile wood between the end of the rabbet and the miter. Set all the slats in the shelf frame now, and adjust them to equalize the spacing. Drill pilot holes, and drive a screw through each end of each slat, fastening it to the frame. Do any touch-up sanding; then bolt the shelf to the legs.

Finishing

After sanding the table lightly, apply the finish of your choice. Presumably, you'll use the same finish on the table that you used on the chair or lounger. Because I used a clear penetrating oil finish on those other projects, I used it on this one.

Tree Bench

The tree bench is a classic piece of outdoor furniture that evokes visions of English country landscapes and graceful gardens. This version is built of western red cedar and finished with spar varnish to stand up to the elements. Despite its rugged construction, the pleasing design will create a surprisingly comfortable place to relax under the shade of your favorite tree. You can build only part of the bench, of course, or complete the hexagon to surround a tree. But

the bench is designed in two parts so that you can build each one in a shop, then cart it to the tree for final assembly. The split design also allows you to vary the placement. You can site the halves facing each other, for example, each nestled against its own tree. Or you could place one half against a garden wall to set off an espalier or some other ornamental feature of your yard. You'll also appreciate a built-in fixture of this project: a hinged section of the backrest that

drops down to serve as a little table for afternoon snacks. You can incorporate this table in both bench halves if you like, or leave it out altogether and stick with the fixed-slat design. You may also want to vary some overall dimensions because this bench is designed to fit around a pretty large tree. You can scale back the plans just a bit to work with a somewhat smaller tree.

EXPLODED VIEW

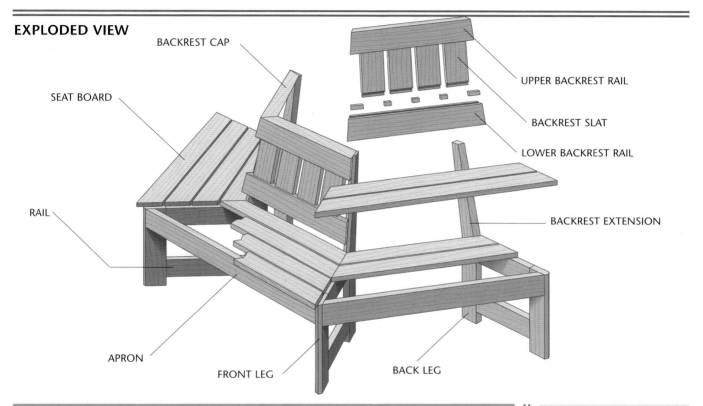

BACKREST CAP

SEAT BOARD

UPPER BACKREST RAIL

BACKREST SLAT

LOWER BACKREST RAIL

BACKREST EXTENSION

RAIL

APRON

FRONT LEG

BACK LEG

CUTTING LIST (Some parts are left long during construction.)

Part	Number	Thickness	Width	Length	Cedar Stock
Front legs	4	1½"	3½"	16½"	2x4
Back legs	4	1½"	5½"	36"	2x6
Rails	8	1½"	3½"	16"	2x4
Apron	1	1"	3½"	39¾"	⁵⁄₄x4
Aprons	2	1"	3½"	39"	⁵⁄₄x4
Seat boards	3	¾"	3½"	42"	1x4
Seat boards	3	¾"	3½"	37⅝"	1x4
Seat boards	3	¾"	3½"	33⅜"	1x4
Seat boards	3	¾"	3½"	29"	1x4
Upper backrest rails	2	1"	3½"	23"	⁵⁄₄x4
Upper backrest rail	1	1"	3½"	22¾"	⁵⁄₄x4
Lower backrest rails	2	1"	3½"	25½"	⁵⁄₄x4
Lower backrest rail	1	1"	3½"	25⅝"	⁵⁄₄x4
Backrest slats	12	¾"	3½"	11"	1x4
Backrest caps	2	¾"	2½"	23"	1x4
Backrest cap	1	¾"	2½"	22¾"	1x4

SHOPPING LIST

- 12 pcs. 2x4 8' clear cedar
- 2 pcs. 2x6 12' clear cedar
- 2 pcs. ⁵⁄₄x4 10' clear cedar
- 4 pcs. ⁵⁄₄x4 8' clear cedar
- 9 pcs. 1x4 12' clear cedar
- 1⅝" stainless-steel screws
- 2" stainless-steel screws
- 6 stainless-steel carriage bolts with washers and nuts, ¼"x3½"
- 2 pair stainless-steel or brass butt hinges, 1½"x3" (with screws)
- Stainless-steel or brass chain, 24" long

Tree Bench

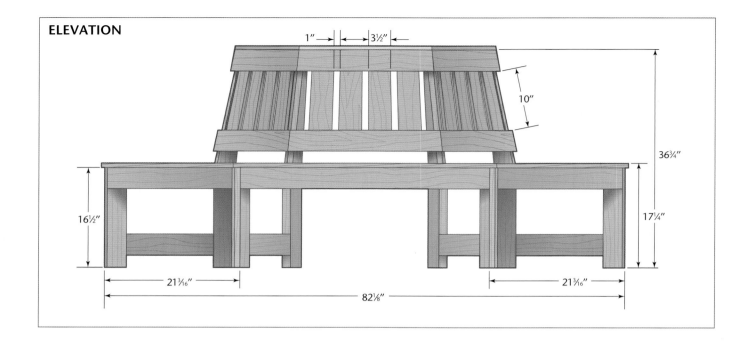

ELEVATION

BUILDER'S NOTES

It pays to start the project with a particular tree in mind. Measure it carefully, and note the root layout to make sure the legs will fit.

This one is set up around a big evergreen that fit the bill. The roots weren't a problem, and the lowest branches were above head height.

I measured the tree circumference at several spots to check for clearance, divided the largest measurement by 3.14 to compute the diameter, and used that number to scale the bench. But I test-fit a set of the seat frames on-site to be sure the paper plans would work. It may seem like obvious advice, but double- check to be sure that your basic layout will work before you cut up a lot of lumber.

Materials

I used high-grade, clear cedar for the bench. But most other prime outdoor woods would be suitable. For example, redwood would be a good choice in

areas where the lumber is readily available.

If you want to paint the bench, you could build the seat frames of pressure-treated stock because they are in constant contact with the ground, and use a wood such as pine for the seat boards and backrests. A good paint job would prolong the life of the entire bench and would conceal that you used different woods in the construction.

To help secure the seat frames and the backrest assemblies, I used poly-urethane glue. It expands as it cures and fills gaps in your joinery, which helps to seal out moisture. This product is popular with woodworkers because it is easy to apply and offers reasonable assembly time while providing a strong, waterproof bond.

You'll also need some construction adhesive. I used it to bond the seat boards, aprons and backrest assemblies to the seat frames. You don't need a lot. Just be sure you use a vari-

ety rated for outdoor use.

With cedar or redwood, use stainless-steel or ceramic-coated fasteners and hardware. With other woods, stainless-steel, galvanized or brass fasteners are fine.

Tools and Techniques

The tree bench is a straight-forward project except at the joints, which take the form of bevels, miters, and compound miters.

You make a bevel by tilting the saw blade and cutting the edge of a board at an angle. You make a miter by cutting at an angle across the face of a board. Combine the two, and you have a compound miter. As you look down onto the face of a board, it creates an angle left to right, and an angle along the edge up and down. To make angle cuts, you need a highly adjustable saw—and for this project you make several such cuts.

You can make some of the straight-line bevels on a table

saw by sliding the workpiece along the fence into the tilted blade. But with the bevels on the tapered back legs, you have to use a saber saw with a tilting base instead, and guide it along a straightedge clamped to the leg.

You can make the miters and compound miters on a table saw using the miter gauge to guide the workpieces. But it's better to use a compound miter saw or, even better, a sliding compound miter saw because the workpiece remains stationary and the blade moves.

Finish

I used spar varnish on the bench (three coats sanded in between), which enhanced the appearance of the cedar. Even then, you'll have to reapply it almost every year. But you could paint your bench or use another outdoor finish. With any clear finish, the cedar will gradually weather to an elegant silver-gray hue.

PLAN VIEW

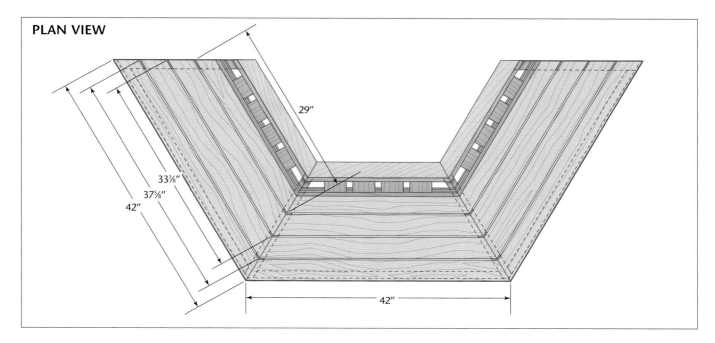

STEP-BY-STEP

Even though the basic bench design is intended to completely encircle a tree, the plans here cover only half the circle. This way you can build the project as is to use against a wall, for example, or build a second section and bolt it in place with the first. If you do want the full circle, you'll save time by ganging up some of the parts, running them through cutting operations, and making the benches simultaneously.

If you are building the two sections, one good approach is to assemble each half frame with the first seat board—just enough to establish the shape—then bolt the two halves together. This way you cut and fit the remaining seat boards and other parts with the bench halves bolted together in their final position. That's a good way to ensure that everything fits together, even at the two seams where the frames join.

Either way you do the work, bear in mind that you can reduce the visual impact of small misalignments between the two bench halves by beveling or rounding-over all the parts. Treating both halves with the same finishing detail helps your eye look right past a problem joint.

Cutting the Seat Frame Parts

Begin construction of the tree bench with the seat frames. Each one has a back leg, a front leg, and two rails, and each bench requires four leg frames as well.

Select straight and true stock for the parts. Then crosscut the back legs from 2x6 stock and the rails and front legs from 2x4 stock, all according to the cutting list dimensions.

Routing the Leg Mortises

The seat frame parts are joined using mortise-and-tenon joints. Use a plunge router, an edge guide, and the mortising jig detailed in "Routing Mortises," page 16, to make the mortises.

You need to lay out only one of the mortises completely. You can locate the others with a registration line equidistant from either end of the desired mortise.

Lay out the full mortise on a front leg blank, and mark the registration line for the second mortise. Stack all the legs together, and use a square to extend the

SEAT FRAME CONSTRUCTION

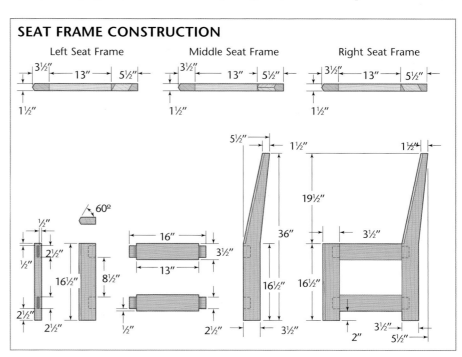

Set a 2-in. block into the mortising jig to raise the front legs to the proper height. You need to make the adjustment because the jig is built to accommodate the back legs, which are 5½ in. wide.

Slip the light-color tenoning jig over the ends of the boards, clamp the work and the jig firmly, adjust the cutter depth, and start routing. It's wise to make a sample tenon and test it for fit in the mortise.

With the router bit guide riding against the template, you can trim away any rough edges left by the initial cut of your saber saw. The template-router combo also can eliminate the need for sanding.

registration lines across the edges on them all. Then set up the router and jig using the leg with the full mortise layout and following the procedure described in the tools and techniques chapter.

As you rout the rest of the mortises, remember that you want them centered across the edge of each leg. To do this, you rout a first pass to full depth, turn the leg around, and rerout. This will widen the mortise slightly, but it will unerringly center it. The jig is built to accommodate the wide back legs. To use it on the narrower front legs, you need to raise the leg blanks by resting them on a 2-inch block. **(Photo 1)**

Cutting Tenons on the Rails
All the rails are the same length, and all of them have tenons on both ends. Once you've completed the mortises, you can cut the tenons on the rails to fit them.

There are many ways to cut tenons using store-bought jigs or even freehand. I used a homemade jig (described in "Routing Tenons," page 18). Make sure the jig fence is slightly thinner than the rail stock, that the top is large enough to support the router and accommodate a clamp, and that the top and fence are at right angles to each other. To save time, make the jig big enough to allow you to do two rails at a time. **(Photo 2)**

It's wise to make a test tenon, so you can adjust the position of the stop in the jig and the cutting-depth setting of the router. When you're satisfied with the fit, cut all the tenons on the rails. Round the corners using a file or a chisel so that they will fit the round-end mortises.

Cutting the Back Legs to Shape
I made a medium-density fiberboard (MDF) template to expedite the job of shaping the legs and improve the quality and consistency of the finished product.

To make the template, cut a piece of ½-inch or ¾-inch MDF to the same dimensions as the back leg. (That should be 5½ inches by 36 inches, but if the cedar you are working is more like 5⅜ or 5¼ inches wide, cut the MDF to that width.) Lay out the cut lines; then cut them with a saber saw. I clamped a straightedge to the template blank to guide these cuts and used a saber-saw version of the T-square setup gauge to position the straightedge. (You can find plans for the setup gauge in "Tools and Techniques," page 15.) Sand the edges if necessary to remove saw marks, particularly on the back edge to

smooth the transition from leg to backrest.

Stick the template to a leg blank with patches of carpet tape, cut close to the template with a saber saw, and trim it flush with a router and long pattern bit. **(Photo 3)** If you're confident with a saber saw, you can skip the work of making a template and simply lay out the shape on each leg and cut to the lines.

Beveling the Edges of the Legs
The bevels on the front legs are primarily cosmetic, carrying the converging planes of the seat rails to a pointed edge down the center of the leg. If you want, you could skip this operation and leave the front edges of the legs square. But the bevels on the back legs provide a bearing surface for the backrest boards. Because you have to make them, you might want to do the front legs too.

The backrest bevels extend from the top down to the intersection with the top side rail: two legs have double bevels, one has a single bevel angled to the left, and one has a single bevel angled to the right. All pieces are beveled by 30 degrees, leaving 60-degree angles. I used an engineer's protractor to lay out the bevels on the top of each leg **(Photo 4)**, and extended the cut line down to the base of the bevel using a straightedge. **(Photo 5)**

You can cut the bevels on both front and back legs using a saber saw, although it's easier to shape the front legs on a table saw. Tilt the blade of the saber saw right or left, depending upon the cut. You can cut from either end of the front legs, but you must start each backrest cut at the top of the leg and stop it before cutting all the way through. Clamp a straightedge to the workpiece to guide the saber saw, or better yet, make a saber saw version of the the circular saw guide described on page 9. **(Photo 6)** On the back legs, stop the cut just shy of the base mark, and use a chisel to pare way the last bit of waste between the end of the cut and the mark.

If you cut the front leg bevels on a table saw, tilt the blade by 30 degrees (to leave you with a 60-degree cut), and adjust the fence so that the blade cuts through the lower half of the edge, leaving the upper half square. Rip the leg, flip it end-for-end, and rip it again to bevel the other edge.

Gluing Up the Seat Frames
You'll find that this is a straightforward part of the project. First, assemble each frame without glue to make sure each set

Lay out the bevel angle and cut lines on each back leg to eliminate confusion when you cut. The single bevel extends across the leg from a corner, and the double bevel extends from the center of the edge.

Once the angles are marked, extend a line from the bevel down the leg face. Make the line parallel with the leg's tapered edge using a straightedge and pencil.

Use a straightedge guide so that the saber saw can't wander off course, and keep the saw base squarely on the work as you cut. If your saw has the adjustment, it may also help to dial back the rate of oscillation.

of legs and rails does, in fact, go together. Then apply waterproof glue to the mortises and tenons, assemble the parts, and clamp the assemblies. After the glue has set, remove the clamps and sand the frames. (Check the label for manufacturer's recommended clamping time.)

Joining Seat Frames and Boards

In this step, the bench really begins to take shape. You begin by lightly scribing a centerline on the rails of the two interior seat frames (the two with the double bevels on the backrest extensions). You can use a marking gauge to scribe the line, or just a pencil and ruler. The seat boards will butt end-to-end on this line. On the outside seat frames, the seat boards will completely overlap the rails.

Next, stand up the four seat frames that support the bench. To make them a little more stable until you get the first seat boards attached, apply a hand screw to one leg of each frame, or clamp on a few blocks of wood. **(Photo 7)**

Cut the three front (and longest) seat slats. Miter the ends of these boards at 30 degrees. As you attach these and the other seat boards, be sure that they butt end-to-end over the centerline of the middle seat frames, but overlay the outer frames.

Position one board on the two middle seat frames with the ends on the scribed centers and the front edge overhanging the front legs by about ½ inch. Drill pilot holes for two screws in each end of the board, and attach it to the seat frames with 1⅝-inch-long stainless-steel screws. Attach the other two boards in the same

manner, using each one to join an outer frame to the bench assembly.

Cut and miter the remaining 12 seat boards, and attach them to the frames the same way. To establish a consistent gap between them, mount the rearmost boards next. To fit them tightly to the backrest extensions of the back legs, bevel the back edges by approximately 8 degrees. You can cut this bevel on a table saw, or use a hand plane. Once you attach the rearmost boards, set the others in place to work out a consistent gap. (Remember, you need some space for drainage the same way you do with deck boards.) When your spacing layout is set, screw all the boards in place.

Cutting and Attaching the Aprons

The aprons fit under the front seat boards and between the legs. They are cut from ⁵⁄₄ stock, and the ends are mitered at 30 degrees. The middle apron is ¾ inch longer than the two outside aprons because the two middle frames are slightly farther apart.

Cut the aprons to length, miter the ends, and test them for fit. Apply a thin bead of construction adhesive along the ends and the top edge of the apron. Press the apron into place, and apply soft-jawed clamps to secure it to the seat board. Then drill pilot holes, and drive two 1⅝-inch-long stainless-steel screws through the face of the apron into each front leg. **(Photo 8)** Drive the screws; then remove the clamps.

Making the Backrest Rails

To give yourself a margin for error on these

Attach a hand screw to one leg of each seat frame to keep it stable as you start the assembly. (You could also clamp on blocks of wood.) This lets you jockey the frames into position as you attach the front seat boards.

Apply construction adhesive to the top edge and miters of the apron, and clamp it using cauls or soft-jawed clamps to avoid denting the cedar. Drill pilot holes, and drive stainless-steel screws to secure the piece.

Tree Bench

To cut the first compound miter on the rail, tilt the saw blade left to cut a 30-deg. bevel, and rotate the saw table 6 deg. to the right. Set the workpiece face down on the table, extending to the left of the blade.

To mark your cuts accurately, hold the rail in place on the bench. Butt it tightly against the adjoining rail, which has been temporarily screwed in place. Use shim blocks under the rail to hold it in position.

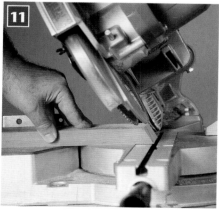

Rotate the saw 6 deg. to make the second rail cut. Position the workpiece the same way, face down, tightly against the fence. Cut shy of your mark, check the fit, and make skimming cuts to perfect the joint.

parts with compound angles, it's wise to crosscut the pieces a bit longer than the specification on the cutting list. You can trim them back to fit your bench. To make the cuts, you need either a compound miter saw or a table saw, although with patience and a couple of angled T-squares as guides you can use a saber saw or circular saw as well.

On the upper backrest rails, cut compound miters by tilting your saw blade by 30 degrees and rotating the miter gauge of a table saw (or the saw table of a compound miter saw) by 6 degrees. **(Photo 9)**

Cut the compound miter on one end of an outside rail that will mount to a middle seat frame. Clamp the piece in place with the unmitered end extending well beyond the outside seat frame to mark the next cut. **(Photo 10)** Then swing the table or miter gauge in the other direction and make the cut. **(Photo 11)** As you work your way from one frame to another, check your cuts for fit. If the joint isn't tight, adjust the bevel and miter slightly and recut the pieces, just skimming the wood with the blade. Take the time to get the angles just right at the start, and record the settings so that you can duplicate them on the other compound cuts. Even after you've fine-tuned the settings, test-fit each joint for best results.

I found it helpful to screw the upper backrest rails in place as I cut them—and it's easy enough to back out the screws and remove the rails for any additional cuts that may be needed later. I installed the first rail with its free end overhanging the outside seat frame. This made it easy to hold the middle rail against it to mark the opposite end for cutting. Once I made that cut, I screwed the middle rail in place, then cut the second outside rail. Finally, I cut the outside ends of the two outside rails.

Cut the lower rails in the same fashion. I cut some scraps of MDF into 2-inch-wide by 6-inch-long shims to rest the lower rails on as I fitted and temporarily installed them. Once all the rails are cut and mounted, measure the distance between them to confirm that they are 10 inches apart. If this distance is more or less, you need to adjust the length of the backrest slats. Then unscrew the rails for the next operation.

The top rails need to be beveled along their top edge so that the cap will seat flat on the legs and rails. Use a sliding T-bevel or an engineer's protractor to capture the angle from the back leg's backrest extension (between the beveled surface and the

BACKREST CONSTRUCTION

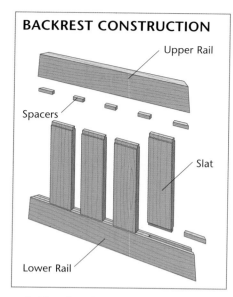

Upper Rail
Spacers
Slat
Lower Rail

top). Then bevel the rails accordingly on the table saw or using a saber saw.

Lastly, rout a slot in each rail for the backrest slats. Use a ¼- or 5/16-inch slot cutter to produce a cut that's ½ inch deep and approximately ½ inch wide. Chuck the cutter in the collet, and adjust the router so that the cutter will produce a shoulder a hair over ¼ inch wide. Dog or clamp each rail flat on the benchtop, make an end-to-end pass with the router, and roll the rail over to make the second pass. This will widen the slot and center it. (In the next step, you'll cut tenons on the slats that will fit the slot, however wide it turns out to be.)

Making the Backrest Slats

Cut the backrest slats from 1x4 stock. To determine how long to cut the slats for your tree bench, measure between the rails. Add one inch for the two tenons. Next, cut 1/2--inch tenons on the ends of the slats. Make them as thick as the rail slots are wide. You can use a router and rabbeting bit matched with a pilot bearing to produce a cut that's exactly 1/2 inch wide and as deep as you set your router to cut. Make a few test cuts on scrap wood to get a tongue that fits snugly in the slots. Then make a cut on each face of the slat to produce a centered tongue, or tenon.

Because you have to make four cuts on each of 12 slats (24 if you are making the full-surround bench), you may want to set up a custom jig for the operation. To make one, cut a strip of working stock to use as the fence, and trim it 4 to 6 inches longer than the slats. Screw a small stop

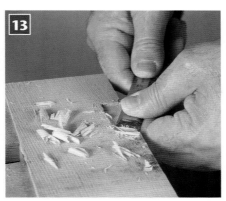

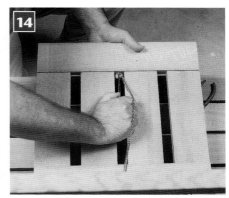

Glue the spacers between slats on the bottom rail, apply glue to the upper connections, and nestle the top rail into place, sliding one slat after another into the rail slot. Check for square before clamping.

Use a sharp chisel at a flat angle to slice away the wood inside the borders of the hinge mortise. If you cut the perimeter lines deeply enough with your utility knife, you won't tear out wood around the edges.

Suspend the drop-down table from the backrest with a brass chain fastened at one end to the edge of the rail and at the other end to the back of a slat. Adjust the chain so that the table will be level when it's extended.

to the edge of this fence to register the length of your slats. Use two deep-throated bar clamps to secure this fixture at a corner of your benchtop. Then place a slat against the fence and stop, clamp it with a C-clamp, and rout a rabbet across the end. The router should slide smoothly across the workpiece onto the fence, and the fence should back up the cut. Pop open the clamp, roll the piece over, reclamp, and make the second pass to complete the tenon.

Assembling the Backrests

Make the backrests by gluing the slats between the rails. To space the slats and plug the slot sections between them, you need several 1-inch-long pieces of cedar to fit between the slats, and 4- to 5-inch-long pieces for the spaces between the slats and the ends of the rails. Produce them by ripping scraps into strips just wide enough to fit the slots. Crosscut the strips into pieces that you can hold between bench dogs or a bench vise, and use a block plane to shave down the width to the depth of the slot. Then crosscut the spacers to size.

Assemble the backrests one at a time, but try a test run to prove that the spacers and tenons fit the slots. Mark a vertical centerline on each rail to use as reference during assembly. Glue a short spacer into the center of both slots, and glue a slat into the bottom rail slot on either side of the center spacer. Add spacers and slats in turn until you glue long spacers in the remaining open slots. Let them run long, and trim them flush with the end of the rail after the glue dries. Then apply glue

to the top rail slot, and fit it over the slat tenons. **(Photo 12)** Upend the assembly, press opposing sets of short spacers into the gaps between the slats, and glue in the long spacers.

Check the overall alignment of the assembly using a square on the centerline and between the rails and the slats. Apply clamps carefully to avoid damaging the wood and racking the frame out of square. After the glue has set, remove the clamps, and drive stainless-steel screws through the pilot holes to secure the backrests to the bench.

Optional Drop-Down Backrest

If you want use one of the backrests as a drop-down tray-table, you need to cut a few extra parts, cut up the backrest, and install hinges, a support chain, and a latch.

First, cut and mount two auxiliary rails. Like the aprons, these extra rails fit between the legs and are secured with construction adhesive and screws, and they sit directly behind the backrest rails. Cut these from ⁵/₄ stock with compound miters on the ends just as you did the backrest rails. These auxiliaries should fit tight between the legs, flush with the beveled surfaces.

Cut the backrest apart next. Use a saber saw, and crosscut the rails at the two outer slats. As you cut each projecting rail end from the unit, mark its position (upper left, lower right, etc.) on the back. One by one, hold these ends in place on the bench, and scribe across their ends on the auxiliary rails.

Remove the lower auxiliary rail from the bench. Align the backrest-tabletop on it, centered between the scribed lines, with its bottom rail aligned directly over the auxiliary. On the bottom edges of these rails, mark the locations of the hinges.

Use the hinges themselves to lay out the mortises. Run a sharp utility knife along each edge of the leaf, and make several passes to deepen the cuts. Then set your chisel blade in the cut with its bevel toward the mortise, and strike the handle with a mallet. Deepen the cut around the perimeter of the mortise; then work on flattening out the base **(Photo 13)**, checking your progress with the hinge leaf.

Then remount the auxiliary rail on the bench using adhesive and screws, and mount the rail ends using adhesive and driving screws through the original pilot holes. Mount the backrest-tabletop to the auxiliary rail with the hinges. Attach the brass support chain to the bottom edge of the upper auxiliary rail so that the tabletop will be level when open. **(Photo 14)** Lastly, mount the latch.

The Backrest Cap

The cap covers the tops of the legs and finishes off the entire bench backrest. Cut the cap pieces from one-by stock, and miter the ends at 30 degrees. Cut them to fit. Then attach them to the bench with adhesive and stainless-steel finishing screws. As a final touch, you may want to spend some extra time sanding this piece smooth. Then sand the rest of the bench as needed, vacuum off all the dust, and apply your choice of finish.

Garden Bench

You will probably be able to build this garden bench over one weekend, and maybe in one day. But that doesn't mean it's a slap-together piece of furniture you'll want to keep out of sight. The basic lines and straightforward construction combine to create a versatile and functional piece. You'll find that the ample seat and wide-set legs make the bench exceptionally stable—strong enough to hold a cat, obviously, and a few people, too. The

flat seat is a generous 15 inches wide for comfort. You'll be able to use it as a seat, a coffee table, a work surface, all without worrying about it tipping over. That's because of the double angles on the legs. First, the sides of each piece are angled out to create a wide footprint that prevents rocking from front to back. Second, each leg is splayed toward the end of the bench to prevent rocking from end to end. The three main pieces (the top and legs) are fastened together using basic joinery, a few screws, and a stretcher pinned with dowels. This last detail is a rustic bit of carpentry that is well suited to a piece of outdoor furniture. Overall, the basic construction will go quickly. That will free you to concentrate on finishing the edges, sanding, and sealing. You'll find that the bench will look good in a garden, in the shade of a favorite tree, or on your front porch.

EXPLODED VIEW

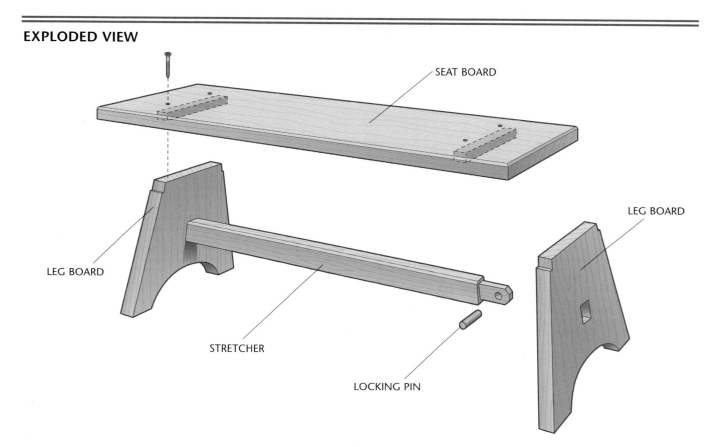

SEAT BOARD

LEG BOARD

LEG BOARD

STRETCHER

LOCKING PIN

CUTTING LIST (Some parts are left long during construction.)

Part	Number	Thickness	Width	Length	Stock
Seat board	1	1½"	15"	54"	2x10 cypress
Leg boards	2	1½"	15"	14¼"	2x10 cypress
Stretcher	1	1½"	2½"	46³⁄₁₆"	2x10 cypress
Locking pins	2	¾" dia.	—	4"	birch dowel

SHOPPING LIST

- 2 pcs. 2x10 8' cypress
- 1 pc. ¾"x36" birch dowel
- Water-repellent wood preservative
- 3" galvanized deck screws

Garden Bench

FRONT ELEVATION

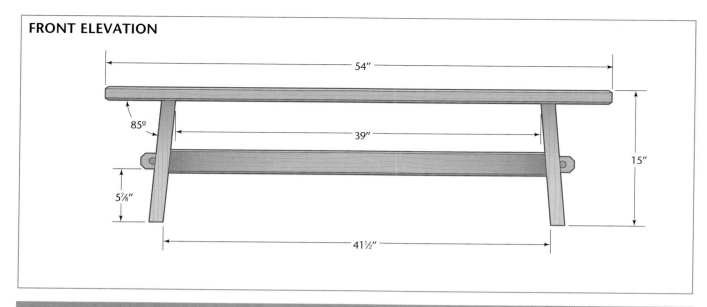

BUILDER'S NOTES

This bench project is a good example of what a nice piece of furniture you can produce with a saw, a router, and only basic woodworking skills.

Materials

The style of the bench calls for a heavy-duty wood with enough thickness and weight to root it to the ground. Rough-cut boards might do the job, although you could have a tough time locating something like 2-inch-thick oak. I surveyed the stock at several building-supply centers and settled on cypress.

It's heavier and generally denser than redwood and cedar, and comparable to Douglas fir in weight and hardness. It is a good wood for outdoor projects, naturally weather resistant, and good looking. And it is commonly available—though sometimes via a special order—in the eastern part of the country.

I used two 2x10 boards to form the seat and each of the legs. Because the actual width of nominal 10-inchers is 9¼ to 9½ inches (and you will lose a

bit more wood in ripping and jointing them for glue-up), the final width will be between 18½ and 19 inches. This size worked out well because I was able to rip off a piece to use as the stretcher.

You could try to get by with gluing together two 2x8s. But the final actual width of this assembly won't be quite enough for the project. Often a 2x8 is only 7¼ inches wide. And once you mill ⅛ inch off each board to prepare it for gluing, you're down to 14¼ inches. That didn't seem quite wide enough to suit me, though it might be the right choice if you are minding a tight budget.

Tools and Techniques

I used a fixed-base router on many parts of the bench: preparing the edges of boards for gluing, trimming and chamfering the ends of the legs, cleaning up the mortises, forming the tenons on the stretcher, and creating the foot cutout. To perform all these tasks, you need a model that will take ½-inch-shank bits. The router doesn't have

to be particularly powerful; 1½ horsepower is more than adequate.

You will need a three special bits if you handle a lot of the work with a router. But you'll find that they will be useful on many other projects as well. One is simply a long straight bit that you'll use to joint the edges of boards prior to glue-up. It should have cutting edges at least 1½ inches long, although 1¾ inches would be better, and be at least ½ inch in diameter. I used a ½-inch-diameter bit with 2-inch-long cutting edges.

You have two choices for the second bit. You can use a pattern bit or a flush-trimming bit with 1½-inch-long cutting edges. This bit is used to rout the foot cutout following a template. The difference between the two types is the location of the pilot bearing. On a pattern bit, it's mounted on the shank; on the flush-trimmer, it's on the tip of the bit. If you use a pattern bit, position the template on top of the workpiece. If you use a flush-trimming bit,

position the template under the workpiece.

The last bit you need is called a dado-and-planer bit, or bottom-cleaning bit. You'll use it to make the tenon on the stretcher. The bit is available in a number of sizes, with and without a shank-mounted bearing. You need the version with the bearing. I used a 1¼-inch-diameter model.

You also need a selection of router jigs, all of which you can make yourself. There are plans for several helpful jigs in Chapter 1, "Tools and Techniques," page 6.

Finish

I used the same kind of water-repellent wood preservative on the bench that you use on a deck. It allows the natural beauty of the wood to show but offers resistance to decay that enhances the natural resistance of the cypress. Eventually, ultraviolet rays will fade the wood and erode the surface somewhat, so you should plan on adding a fresh coat periodically.

END ELEVATION

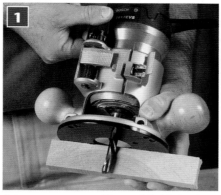

11"

1½"

13½"

10" 2½"

15"

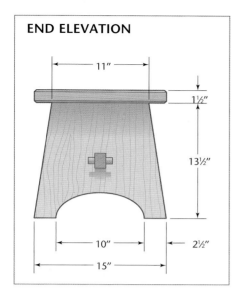

1

Set up your router with a straight bit that is at least 1½ in. long, with a diameter of at least ½ in. Set the depth so the cutter bit is just a hair deeper than the stock you are edging. A spiral cutter like this one is fine.

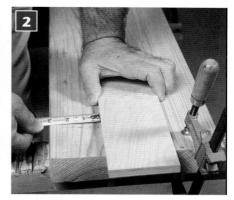

2

Use the factory edge on a strip of plywood to guide your cut with the router. To locate the fence, measure back from the cutter to the edge of the router base. The bit should trim no more than ⅛ in. off the board.

STEP-BY-STEP

Gluing Up Seat and Leg Stock

Both the seat and the legs are 15 inches wide, which is a size you can find in plywood, but not in a heavy-duty wood that's suitable for this bench design. But you can still build to that ample dimension by gluing together two boards.

Because stock boards from a lumberyard or home center seldom have edges suitable for gluing, you'll need to "joint" them. In this process, you true up edges that may be rough, out of square, and marred with dents and dings.

You can use a jointer, a stationary power tool with a long, solid table and large blades that can put a true edge on lumber. But it's an expensive piece of equipment that many do-it-yourselfers

don't own. Instead, use your router to rout the mating edges as positive and negative images, ensuring a virtually invisible joint.

Begin by selecting flat boards for the seat and trimming them an inch or so longer than the actual final size specified on the cutting list. This common practice gives you a little more lumber to work with, for instance, when you need to clamp a board for cutting or sanding. And it's easy enough to trim off the excess when tenons, joints, and other details are completed.

Set up your router with a straight bit. For best results, use a bit that is at least 1½ inches long, and a router rated at 1½ horsepower or more. If the stock you use is thicker than standard two-by lumber, you'll need a longer bit. You should proj-

ect the bit ¹⁄₁₆ to ⅛ inch below the lower surface of the wood. **(Photo 1)**

Next, select a straightedge to use as a guide for your router. A strip of plywood is fine. Remember, because you are creating a positive-negative match, the fence doesn't need to be absolutely straight. It does need to be at least 6 inches longer than the stock, so it can guide the router at the very beginning and end of the cut. Clamp the fence to the stock so your cutter will just skim the edge. You can determine where to place the fence by measuring from the edge of the bit to the edge of the router base plate and adding ¹⁄₁₆ inch. **(Photo 2)**

You'll get the cleanest edge by moving the router steadily but slowly. If you hear the rpm on your motor start to drop, you're probably going too fast. Slow down, and

PLAN VIEW

54"

6¾"

5"

15"

3

To create a clean edge, be sure that the router motor is up to speed before the bit engages the wood. Use the extensions on the fence to guide the router into the cut, and keep the router moving along the fence.

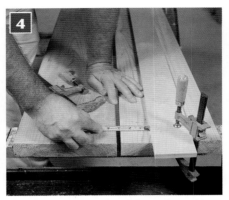

4

Leave the first board and fence clamped in place, and bring the second board into position leaving about a ⅛-in. gap. To joint the second board, the gap must be slightly less than the diameter of the router bit.

5

Clamp the second board securely in position. Make sure it is parallel to the first board. Then make another pass with the router using the original fence, and you'll have two boards that mate perfectly.

let the cutting bit do the work.

Once the setup is ready, make one continuous pass with the router, working from right to left. **(Photo 3)** When the first edge is done, move the second board into place. Make the gap between the two boards just ¹⁄₁₆ inch less than the bit diameter. **(Photo 4)** When you rout the second board, you must feed the router from left to right. **(Photo 5)**

Glue the jointed edges together using waterproof glue and pipe clamps.

If you have enough clamps, you can set the seat assembly aside and glue up stock for the legs. You can save some time by doing one glue-up for both legs, and cutting them after the glue sets.

Ultimately, you have to chamfer the top and bottom edges of the legs, so it's a good idea to add about 6 inches of length to the leg blank.

Preparing the Seat Blank

Remove the clamps from the seat blank, and scrape off any dried glue that has been forced out of the joint. Then you can rip and crosscut the blank to the length specified on the cutting list. Save the off-cuts—you'll use them later to make the stretcher. Chamfer the edges of the seat using a chamfering bit, and belt-sand the panel using a coarse-grit belt.

Making the Leg Dadoes

The legs fit into stopped dadoes cut into the underside of the seat. Although the bench's legs are canted outward at 5 degrees, the dadoes are not. Instead, they are cut slightly wider than the legs are thick, as indicated in the "Dado Layout" drawing, below.

To set up for the cut, clamp fences to the seat to guide your router and prevent the cut from being too wide or too long. You can use two T-squares, one on either side of the cut, and two stops, one at either end of the dado. To determine how far away from the edge of the dado to place the T-squares and the stops, subtract the radius of the bit from the radius of the router base. Measure that distance from each of the dado layout lines, position the guides, and clamp them. Then rout along one T-square and back along the other.

LEG-TO-SEAT JOINERY

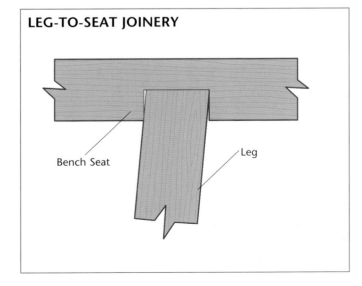

Bench Seat

Leg

DADO LAYOUT

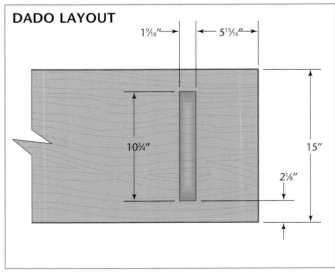

1⁹⁄₁₆″

5¹⁵⁄₁₆″

10¾″

15″

2⅛″

LEG LAYOUT

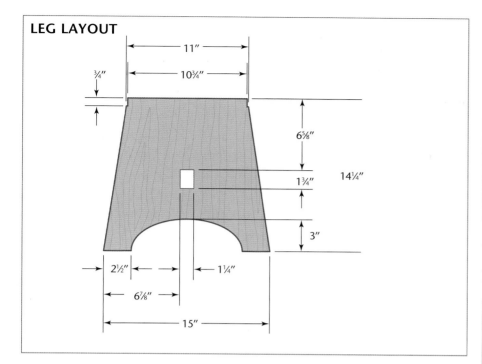

Finally, trim out any waste between the two cuts to open the dado to the required width. **(Photo 6)**

Preparing the Legs

The top and bottom edges of the legs are beveled at a 5-degree angle. You can create this angle by adjusting the bevel on your circular saw and introducing the bevel as you cut the legs from the glued-up blank. Plan the cuts so your circular saw will be well supported. Be careful also to orient the cuts properly. The top edge must be parallel to the bottom edge when you are done. Lastly, sand each piece with the belt sander.

Making the Stretcher Mortises

Follow the above "Leg Layout" drawing to pencil in the mortise outline on each leg blank. Then you can make the basic mortise with a drill and use a chisel to complete the rectangular shape. Instead, I drilled a hole to get the blade started and then roughed out the opening using a saber saw. **(Photo 7)** I finished the mortise using a router and a long straight bit. **(Photo 8)** The corners will be rounded, but you can leave them that way because the tenon fits loosely.

Cutting the Foot Arches

You can cut the arches in the legs a couple of different ways. The simplest way is

to scribe the arch onto the leg, cut to the line with a saber saw, and clean up the cut with sanders. The trick to this kind of layout is to scribe circles at the bottom corners of the arch, and combine those shapes with the segment of a more shallow circle to complete the shape.

The alternative method is probably more accurate because it relies on a template to guide your router through the curving cut. This will take a little longer, of course, but the arches on both legs will end up exactly the same.

To make the template, cut a piece of ¼-inch hardboard to the same dimensions as the leg blank, and follow the steps shown in the "Foot Arch Template" drawing, page 130. To make the curved cuts that make up the arch, you need to use a trammel-guided router.

When you make any cuts on the template, be sure to clamp it on scrap plywood so you don't mar your workbench top.

First, locate the pivot points for the short-radius arcs, and drill holes in the template for the trammel pivots. The radius of each arc is less than the radius of most router baseplates, so you'll have to make the baseplate itself serve as the trammel by drilling a pivot hole in it. Lay out the location by measuring from the bit, incorporating the full diameter of the bit.

Use a short nail as a pivot, inserting it

To control the dado cut, *set up fences and stops that limit the travel of the router. You can use a homemade T-square or a series of straight-edges. Be sure they are clamped securely to the work surface.*

Drill a hole to provide access *for a saber saw blade, and rough out the four sides of the mortise for the stretcher. Nibble away the waste with the saber saw, but stay just shy of your pencil layout lines.*

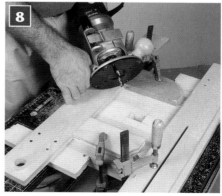

To finish the mortise, *clamp T-squares to the leg and stops between the squares. You can also use straightedges. To position them accurately, you need to measure carefully from the edge of the router base to the bit.*

Garden Bench

To make a trammel that can guide the router along the two short-radius arcs, drill a small pivot hole in the router baseplate that allows the router to travel on the pivot pin driven into the template.

You need to cant the tenoning jig for your router to align with the shoulder. On this cut you should minimize tear-out by taping backup scraps to the stretcher before clamping the jig in position.

Secure the legs by inserting the stretcher tenons into the leg mortises. Then lock up the position by tapping the locking pin into place. If the pin is too loose, make a new one with a smaller flat.

through the pivot hole in the template and setting the router onto it. **(Photo 9)** Set the cut depth to about $\frac{1}{8}$ inch for the first pass, then increase it to complete the cut on the second pass.

To make the long-radius arc, extend the centerline of the template onto the scrap plywood and locate the pivot point. To help keep the router level while you make the cut, you may want to clamp a scrap of hardboard to the plywood where the pivot

will be. Set up the trammel, adjust the radius, and begin the cut with the bit set into one of the first arcs you cut. Swing the router on its pivot until the cut intersects the second arc. Complete the template by sanding the rough edges.

When the template is done, place it on the leg blank and transfer the arch layout to the leg.

The next step is to use a saber saw to trim away most of the waste, which

means cutting to within $\frac{1}{8}$ inch of the line. This step makes it easier to finish the piece with your router.

Be sure that your template is in the right position and firmly clamped to the working stock—and that the assembly is clamped snugly to the workbench in at least two places.

Set up your router with the long, straight pattern bit described in the Builder's Notes, on page 126. Take the time to adjust the bit so the bearing will ride along the edge of the template edge, and the cutting edges trim the full thickness of the leg stock. It's also important to make the rout in a continuous pass, applying constant control through the cut.

Tapering the Legs

With the mortise and the foot arch cut, you can taper the leg. Note that you must cut small notches into each top corner of the leg to allow it to fit into the stopped dado in the seat. You should use a backsaw to cut the notch, sawing the shoulder at a 5-degree angle. Check the fit of the leg in its dado, and if necessary, pare the notch until the leg seats in the dado.

Make the straight-line taper cut with a circular saw. Even a sharp blade will leave the fresh cut edges a bit rough, so you should mill the sawed edges with the router the same way you did with the initial glue-up of the seat and leg blanks. This operation yields a smooth, square surface more reliably than sanding with a belt sander.

Lastly, chamfer the exposed edges of the leg. Use a chamfering bit in your router,

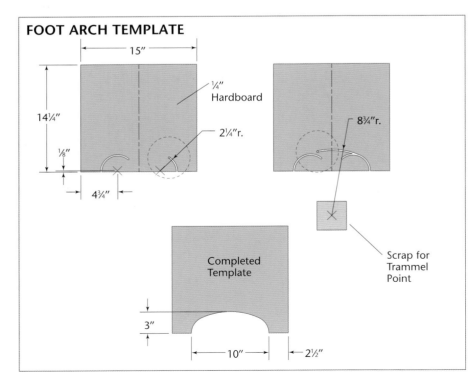

FOOT ARCH TEMPLATE

15"

$\frac{1}{4}$" Hardboard

14$\frac{1}{4}$"

2$\frac{1}{4}$"r.

8$\frac{3}{4}$"r.

$\frac{1}{8}$"

4$\frac{3}{4}$"

Scrap for Trammel Point

Completed Template

3"

10"

2$\frac{1}{2}$"

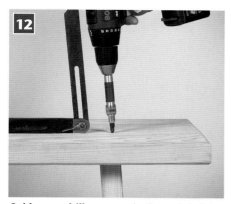

Guide your drill as you make the angled pilot holes for screws that fasten the seat to the leg assemblies. You can set a sliding T-bevel to match the leg angle, and simply rest it on the seat as you drill.

and mill the tapered edges and the edge of the arched cutout. Do this on both faces of each leg, of course.

Creating the Stretcher
Make the stretcher from the piece of wood you ripped from the seat blank. Cut this piece to size, and sand it smooth. Trim the ends at an 85-degree angle to match the cant of the legs. With a combination square and a sliding T-bevel set to 85 degrees, lay out the shoulders of the tenons on each end of the stretcher.

Cutting the Stretcher Tenons
To cut an accurate tenon, use your router with the tenoning jig described in "Routing Tenons," page 18. Cut the side cheeks of the tenon first. This will establish the angle, and you can use the shoulders as a guide when you make a cut with a backsaw to establish the canted shoulders for the top and bottom surfaces of the tenon.

Align the platen of the jig directly on the angled shoulder layout line, and clamp the jig and workpiece to the workbench. Use a dado-and-planer bit, and adjust the cut depth. The bearing must have good contact with the jig's platen, and the cut should be just a hair over ⅛ inch deep. **(Photo 10)**

It's good practice to creep up on a perfect fit. You start with shallow cuts on both cheeks of the tenon, and test it for fit in one of the mortises. Then increase the depth of cut accordingly.

With the side cheeks cut, move on to the top and bottom cheeks. Use a backsaw to

cut the shoulders, canting the blade to follow the angle of the side shoulders. Then use the tenoning jig and router to cut the top and bottom cheeks. It may take you a bit longer to fit the top and bottom cheeks. The tenon has to be smaller vertically than the mortise, so the legs can be tilted.

Completing the Stretcher
Start by drilling the locking-pin holes. You need to position each hole so that the leg cuts across it slightly. To lay out the center point, fit the tenon through the mortise, and measure ¼ to ⁵⁄₁₆ inch from the face of the leg. Then drill the hole.

Trim off the corners of the tenons, as shown in the layout drawing, below, and chamfer the edges of the stretcher body.

Making the Locking Pins
To start work on this unique feature of the bench, cut a 2-inch length of ¾-inch dowel to make the two locking pins.

Use a block plane to create a flat edge on each dowel. This flat faces into the surface of the leg as you drive the dowel into the hole through the tenon.

To create a tight fit, plane or file a slight ramp on each end of the flat. This will allow the pin to ride up onto the leg surface as it emerges from the hole. Chamfer the end edges of the dowel with a file to finish.

Assembling the Bench
Ideally, the leg assembly will take just a bit of coaxing to fit together with the seat. Start with the seat upside down on the workbench, and fit the legs onto the stretcher. Toe-in the leg tops and align them at their respective dadoes. You should be able to get both legs started into the dadoes more or less simultaneously. If you can't get both legs into position, the stretcher is probably a bit too long. To remedy this, trim the shoulders on one tenon.

Now insert the locking pins. Use a few light hammer blows to center each pin so it projects equally on both sides of the tenon. **(Photo 11)** Do this carefully, because the pin may tend to tear the wood of the leg.

Set the bench on its feet to lay out the locations of the four screws that fasten seat to the leg assembly. Drill pilot holes, and drive a 3-inch galvanized deck screw into each one. **(Photo 12)**

Finally, apply the exterior finish of your choice. I used a water-repellent wood preservative. Following the directions on the can, I brushed it on liberally and kept the surface flooded for 10 to 15 minutes to allow the finish to penetrate. After 10 minutes, you stop replenishing and allow the excess to penetrate or evaporate, which can take up to 24 hours.

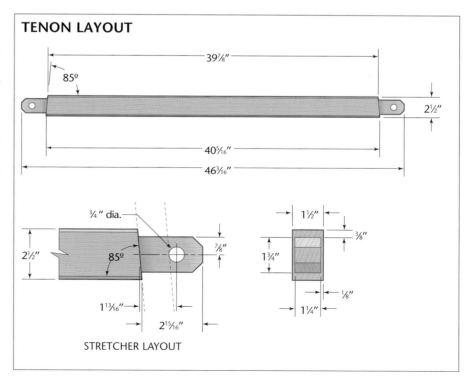

TENON LAYOUT

39⅞"

85º

2½"

40⁵⁄₁₆"

46³⁄₁₆"

¾" dia.

2½"

85º

⅞"

1¹³⁄₁₆"

2¹⁵⁄₁₆"

1½"

⅜"

1¾"

⅛"

1¼"

STRETCHER LAYOUT

Park Bench

However small your yard may be, if you think of it as parkland, you may see just the right location for this park bench. The best spot may be under a spreading shade tree, beside a fence or wall, or next to a planting bed. Of course, benches in public parks tend to have concrete legs for durability with wooden slats forming the seat and backrest. More often today, the legs are plastic that is colored and textured to look like concrete. At the other end of the

Yard and Garden Furniture

spectrum, some very costly benches are made of solid teak. This project represents a middle ground that is a very doable furniture project for the home do-it-yourselfer. It's a simple model, but this bench fulfills the demands placed on a park bench. It is a sturdy and comfortable place to sit, requires only modest maintenance, and is reasonably attractive. What this bench offers that most others do not is straightforward and relatively easy construction. You can handle the simple tapers using a circular saw and tackle the one curve using a saber saw. Also, the joints are basic butt joints secured with screws and bolts, so you won't have to do a lot of fancy joinery work. The bench is attractive, comfortable, durable, practical, easy to build, and it is one piece of outdoor furniture that you can complete in a day.

EXPLODED VIEW

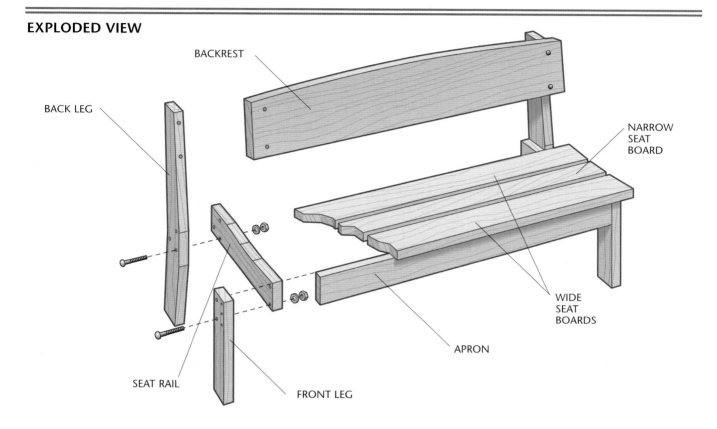

BACKREST

BACK LEG

NARROW SEAT BOARD

WIDE SEAT BOARDS

APRON

SEAT RAIL

FRONT LEG

CUTTING LIST

Part	Number	Thickness	Width	Length	Douglas Fir Stock
Front legs	2	1½"	3½"	14½"	2x4
Back legs	2	1½"	5½"	32"	2x6
Seat rails	2	1½"	5½"	19"	2x6
Apron	1	1½"	5½"	48"	2x6
Wide seat boards	2	1½"	5½"	55"	2x6
Narrow seat board	1	1½"	3½"	55"	2x4
Backrest	1	1½"	11¼"	55"	2x12

SHOPPING LIST

- 1 pc. 2x12 8' Doug fir
- 3 pcs. 2x6 8' Doug fir
- 1 pc. 2x4 8' Doug fir
- 10 galvanized carriage bolts, ⁵⁄₁₆"x3½", with washers and nuts
- 2 galvanized carriage bolts, ⁵⁄₁₆"x4", with washers and nuts
- 2 galvanized carriage bolts, ⁵⁄₁₆"x4½", with washers and nuts
- 3" galvanized deck screws

ELEVATIONS

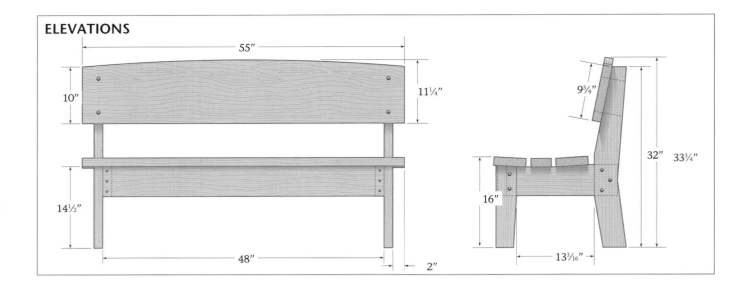

55"
11¼"
10"
14½"
48"
2"
9¾"
32" 33¾"
16"
13³⁄₁₆"

BUILDER'S NOTES

This isn't the fanciest project in the book by any means, and it may not stack up against some of the solid teak benches you can buy. But you can have the satisfaction of building this one yourself, and save a lot of money in the process. It's an excellent weekend project. And you don't need an array of tools or a lot of workshop space. You don't even need glue.

Materials

When I think of park benches, I think first of the benches with concrete ends and planks for seat and backrest. But these heavyweight models that use cast concrete are too cumbersome-looking for most yards. And exotic woods such as teak can drive your materials costs out of line. White oak is a possibility, but it isn't readily available to the do-it-yourselfer because the thicknesses needed are stocked only by specialized lumber dealers. Also, you would need a jointer and a thickness planer to prepare the oak.

Of the most-available woods, I elected to go with Douglas fir. It doesn't weather as well as redwood or cedar, but it will fair well enough outdoors if you apply a good finish—to start with and at least once again every year. What it has that redwood and cedar do not is weight. Douglas fir is substantially heavier and will make your bench a middleweight instead of a flyweight.

While Douglas fir is available, it may not be stockpiled on the racks of your local lumberyard in a variety of widths. When I built this park bench, I could find only 2x12 stock, so I had to rip the boards to the widths needed. This is possible even with a benchtop table saw, though you've got to use a very moderate feed rate to avoid stalling the saw. Douglas fir is a lot denser than pine or cedar.

There are several other alternatives, including cedar, redwood, cypress, or even pressure-treated pine.

Tool and Techniques

If you need to rip the parts from wide boards, you may feel that you need a table saw. Not true. Using a circular saw with a rip guide (or the homemade guide shown on page 9), you can make all the rip cuts.

The essential power tools are a circular saw, saber saw, drill-driver, and belt sander. You might prefer to use a router for some operations, and if you do, you need a long, flush-trimming bit.

Finish

I used a clear penetrating oil finish. Penetrating oils are popular among fine furniture makers because they provide good protection and let the wood show through. Painting is always an option, but exposure can cause cracking and lead to regular repainting. In general, penetrating finishes require less upkeep than coatings that rest on the surface, like paint

The details of applying penetrating oil are laid out in the final step of the project. But it's worth noting that some penetrating-oil fumes are noxious, so you should apply the material outdoors, if possible, or in an extremely well-ventilated area. To deal with oil-laden rags and prevent a fire hazard, immerse them in a bucket of water, or spread them out over a washline outdoors until dry.

One other advantage of a penetrating oil finish is that it's easy to renew. No finish, even one with a UV-inhibiter, can stop the inexorable graying of wood left outside. Makers of penetrating finishes tout its ability to remove at least some of the weathered look and return the wood close to its natural color. Simply brush it on, allow it to penetrate for a short time; then wipe off the excess. A thorough application every year should keep your park bench looking good for decades.

PLAN VIEW

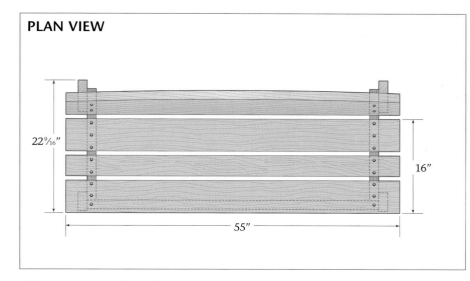

22⁹⁄₁₆″ · 55″ · 16″

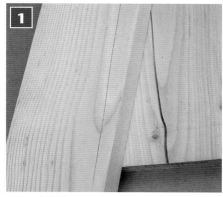

Leave inferior lumber at the yard, including boards with deep or long splits like the one on the right. Don't worry about checking. These are shallow surface tears that don't go through the wood.

BACK LEG LAYOUT

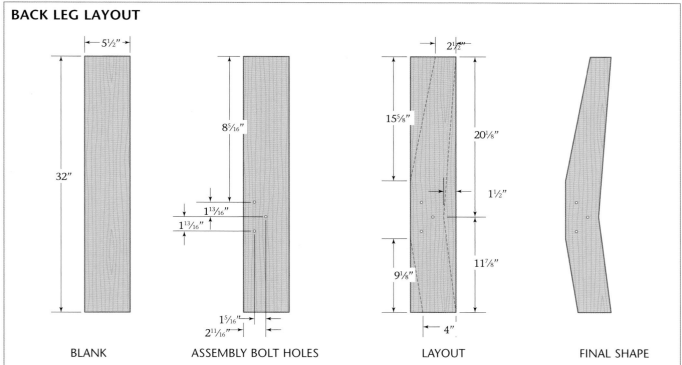

BLANK	ASSEMBLY BOLT HOLES	LAYOUT	FINAL SHAPE

STEP-BY-STEP

Assessing Lumber

Construction-grade lumber is never quite as good as you'd like it to be, and, if anything, quality has taken a turn for the worse in recent decades. The lumber has been dried to some degree, but isn't as stable as the wood you would generally use to make furniture. Thus, when you bring it into your shop, it will probably continue to dry, and as it does, it may cup and twist and crack. Picking through piles at the lumberyard or home center will help, particularly if you avoid the very heavy pieces that are laden with excess moisture. Even then, it's wise to evaluate what you have and look for the best way to work around the most severe defects and get the parts you need. **(Photo 1)** You'll want to avoid large, weak knots and deep splits, although minor versions may be difficult to avoid altogether. It is construction lumber, after all. This selection process should not be too difficult on the bench because you'll cut only a few parts to size, and the design does not call for furniture-quality joints.

Making the Back Legs

The first thing to do is to lay out and drill the holes for the assembly bolts, a job that is easiest before you have cut the legs to shape. The holes should be ⁵⁄₁₆ inch in diameter.

FRONT LEG LAYOUT

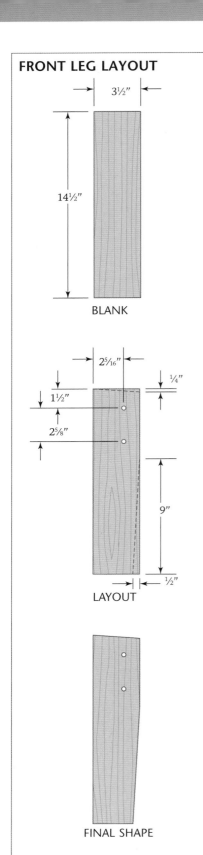

3½"

14½"

BLANK

2⁵⁄₁₆"

1½"

¼"

2⁵⁄₈"

9"

½"

LAYOUT

FINAL SHAPE

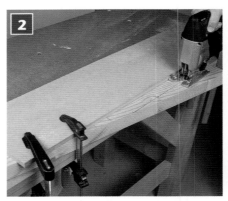

I used a piece of MDF to make a cutting guide for the back legs. The idea is to make a rough cut running the saber saw shoe along the guide. Then you can use a router to make the final, smooth-edged cut.

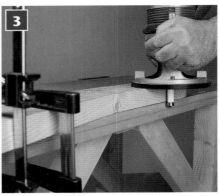

To make room for your router (fitted with a large flush-trimming bit), leave the work-piece long, and set two clamps side by side at the end. Tighten them up, and they will keep the work from twisting.

With that task completed, lay out the cuts following the pattern drawings. You can make these cuts using a saber saw. For best results, clamp a straightedge to the work to guide the saw. The idea is to position the work at the very edge of the workbench to provide clearance under the cut line for the saw blade. To secure the guide and the work so that neither moves in mid-cut, each needs at least two clamps. It is possible to make each clamp serve double duty, clamping both the guide and the work. In any event, the clamps have to be out of the way of the tool making the cut. **(Photo 2)**

When you're done, smooth out the cut edges with a belt sander, then a pad or random-orbit sander. Use a ⁵⁄₁₆-inch-radius or ⅜-inch-radius roundover bit to shape all the edges of the back legs. This extra step makes the legs look more finished.

Cutting two-by lumber with a saber saw—provided it is a good one—is not difficult, but the cut edges left are often rough and slightly out of square with the adjoining faces. What you might do, if you have the right router bit, is freehand the cuts using the saber saw, then trim the edges to the desired line with a router and long flush-trimming bit or long pattern bit. Of course, you need a guide to direct the cut, and where you put the guide—on top of the work or beneath the work—is a function of where the pilot bearing is on the bit you use. **(Photo 3)**

This approach provides some advantages. The routed edge is smooth and square to the faces, and it needs only a light finish sanding. But the router's foot-print is larger than a saber saw's, so you have to locate clamps where they won't interfere with the router.

Making the Front Legs

The bench's front legs are made from 2x4 stock and cut with a slight taper on the

SEAT RAIL

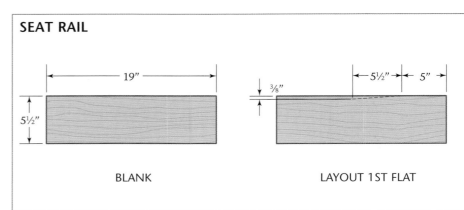

19"

5½"

BLANK

⅜"

5½"

5"

LAYOUT 1ST FLAT

It's always easier to sand the parts *before assembly, using a belt sander to start and a pad sander to finish. The top edges of the seat rails can remain rough because they'll be covered by the seat boards.*

Lay out the rail and legs *on a scrap piece of plywood to keep from drilling into your work surface. Then line up the short vertical edge of the leg perpendicular to the bottom edge of the rail using a square.*

Drill through the holes in the leg *into the seat rail. A tape flag on the bit can help you judge the depth so that you bore completely through the rail but not also through the scrap into your benchtop.*

back edge, which adds a touch of elegance to the bench.

As with the back legs, you should first lay out and drill the $5/16$-inch-diameter holes for the assembly bolts. Then lay out and cut the tapers. Sand the legs; then round-over the vertical edges and the feet edges with the same roundover bit used on the back legs. During assembly, the tops of these legs are trimmed flush with the seat rails

Making the Seat Rails

Begin the bench assembly by cutting the two seat rails. If necessary, rip your stock to width, and then crosscut the blanks for the rails to the dimensions specified on the cutting list.

Each rail has a concave shape cut on the top edge. This shape is made up of three flats to accommodate the seat boards. Following the seat-rail drawing, mark the top edge of the two rails, then cut to the

lines with a saber saw. Remember, you need to sand the faces and edges of the rails **(Photo 4)**; then round-over just the bottom edges using a router fitted with a roundover bit.

Assembling the Legs and Rails

The next step is to bolt together the rail and the legs. To do this you need to line up the legs on the rail and, using the holes bored in the legs as guides, drill the holes in the rail. Then assembly is a simple matter of installing and tightening the $3\frac{1}{2}$-inch galvanized carriage bolts.

To protect the benchtop when you drill the bolt holes, lay out the parts on a sacrificial scrap of plywood. Measure $1\frac{3}{4}$ inches from the front end of the rail, and square a line across it. Square a second line across the rail $141\frac{5}{16}$ inches from the front end. Carefully align the legs at these lines, and use a square to make sure that

the short vertical edges on each leg are perpendicular to the bottom edge of the rail. **(Photo 5)**

Use scraps of the working stock to support the legs and keep them in the correct relationship with the rail. If possible, configure the assembly so that you can clamp the legs in place. When the parts are securely squared up, you can go ahead and drill the bolt holes through the rail. **(Photo 6)**

When you have bored the holes, sand the seat rails to remove the layout lines. When you bolt the parts together, remember that you need a left and a right assembly for the bench.

Attaching the Apron

The apron is the first part installed that ties the two leg-and-apron assemblies together. It is a 48-inch-long 2x6. After you cut the apron to size, sand it thoroughly and round-over the bottom edges.

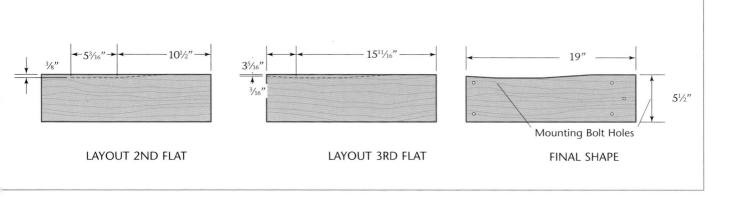

$\frac{3}{8}$" | $5\frac{3}{16}$" | $10\frac{1}{2}$"

LAYOUT 2ND FLAT

$3\frac{5}{16}$" | $\frac{3}{16}$" | $15\frac{11}{16}$"

LAYOUT 3RD FLAT

19" | 5$\frac{1}{2}$"

Mounting Bolt Holes

FINAL SHAPE

Stand the leg-and-rail assemblies on their backs, and use a clamp to hold the sections in position. Position the apron, make sure it is square to the end assemblies; then drill pilot holes and drive the screws.

Use a thin, flexible strip of wood to create your curve. You can pin the flexed ends with nails or clamps at each end. Then raise the center of the strip at midspan and carefully mark the curve.

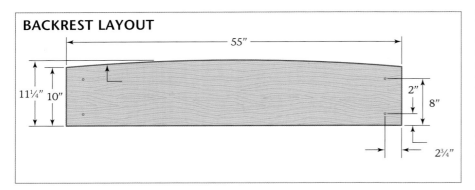

BACKREST LAYOUT

55"

11¼" 10"

2"

8"

2¾"

On a piece of furniture such as this one you'll want to smooth semi-concealed edges as well as the exposed surfaces to make it more comfortable for the people who might use it.

Butt the apron against the front ends of the rails so that they are tight against the inner faces of the front legs, and fasten it with three long deck screws. **(Photo 7)** Be sure to drill and countersink pilot holes so that you don't split the ends of the apron. Also check the screw locations, and position them so that they don't collide with the assembly bolts.

Attaching the Seat
The seat is composed of three square-cut, unadorned boards. Two are 2x6s, one a 2x4. These boards should have been already cut to length. Sand them and round-over all their edges with the bit used throughout the project. You don't want to risk a splinter on the seat boards.

With the bench standing on its feet,

set the boards in place. There should be a flat spot on each rail for each board. There's no specific spacing of the boards; simply align them so that they are parallel, and try to make them look good. Drill pilot holes through the seat boards into the rails, and drive 3-inch deck screws to secure them in place.

Making the Backrest
A single 2x12 forms the backrest. The upper edge is arch shaped. That means you need to cut a smooth, fair curve, which can be the biggest challenge of this project. You can do it in one of several ways.

The fastest and, if you are skilled and experienced, completely satisfactory approach is to lay out the cut line and make the cut with a saber saw. Assuming the cut is a soft, even curve, a little clean-up work with a belt sander is all you have to do to make the backrest ready to install. The problem for many woodworkers is getting the curve

cut without introducing high spots, low spots, and flat areas. Forming such a cut into a fair curve takes a lot of belt sander work.

An alternative approach is to make a template to guide a router as it cuts the backrest. Of course, you still have to rough-cut the curve with a saber saw. But a template material like ¼-inch hardboard is a lot easier to work than 1½-inch-thick lumber. Hardboard is inexpensive, and you can cut the template into smaller pieces for other uses (like other templates) after the backrest is cut.

With either approach, you can first lay out the curve using a thin strip ripped from the working stock. It needs to be about 5 feet long and no more than ½ inch thick. The strip can't have any knots because you are going to flex it into the curve you want. The flex would likely break the strip at a knot. Hold the strip on edge against the face of the backrest (or against the template), and flex it into the arch you want. You can use nails to hold the ends while you create the curve with a block at midspan and trace your cut line. **(Photo 8)**

Cut the curve, and sand the cut edge smooth. Then sand the backrest and round-over its edges. If you are using a template, clamp it to the backrest and rough-cut the curve. Then rout the curve to its final shape, guided by the template, and sand the part and round-over its edges. **(Photo 9)**

Mounting the Backrest
Lay out and drill the mounting bolt holes in the backrest, referring to the backrest drawing for the hole locations. These holes are 5/16 inch in diameter.

Now lay out the position of the backrest's bottom edge on the back legs. Measure 9¾ inches down from the top of each back leg and square a line across the leg. To help hold the backrest while you extend the mounting bolt holes through the legs, clamp a support block to each leg on this layout line. Set the backrest on the blocks, and clamp it to the legs. **(Photo 10)**

Using the holes in the backrest as guides, extend the holes for the bolts through the legs. Remove the backrest and the support blocks, and sand out the layout lines. Then bolt the backrest to the legs. Use the 4-inch-long bolts in the upper holes and 4½-inch-long bolts in the lower holes.

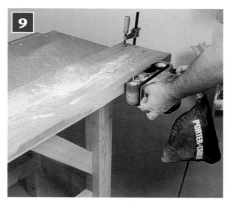

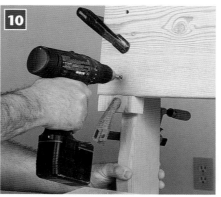

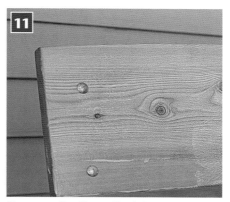

Use a belt sander to sand the curved cut on the top of the backrest. You also may want to round-over both top edges with a router, and finish this visible edge by hand, using progressively finer grits of sandpaper.

Use temporary blocks on each leg to support the heavy backrest board. When the board is properly aligned on the legs, clamp it in position, and extend the mounting bolt holes into the legs.

Use a small roller to flood the wood surfaces with the clear penetrating oil and a brush to smooth out an even film. You generally need to let the oil penetrate for 20 to 30 minutes before wiping.

Finishing

While paint would be a reasonable choice for a finish, Douglas fir is such an attractive wood that it seems a shame to conceal it. Consequently, I used a clear penetrating oil finish formulated for outdoor use. The finish darkens the wood somewhat but brings out the grain and allows you to see and appreciate its beauty. **(Photo 11)**

Bear in mind, due to the vapors that are given off, all penetrating oils need to be applied in a very well ventilated area. The great outdoors is ideal. In the first days of spring, carry the bench out onto the driveway or terrace, and apply the finish there.

This process also produces oil-laden rags that can spontaneously combust. Avoid any dangerous surprises. When you are done, either unroll the oily rags and hang them outside to dry, drop them into a water-filled bucket, or simply burn them yourself.

To finish the wood, flood the surfaces with the oil finish, and allow it to penetrate for 20 to 30 minutes. (Be sure to check the manufacturer's instructions on the product you use.) You can apply the finish with a brush, or load on the oil with a small roller and use the brush to smooth out the finish.

Check the surface periodically, and as areas begin to lose their surface sheen, apply more oil. After about half an hour, use rags to wipe any remaining oil from the wood. With most products, it will take 48 hours or more for the finish to dry completely.

BITS FOR TEMPLATE WORK

There are a few options for cutting the curve in the backrest, but you'll want to avoid the technique that's usually used—the trammel. Because of the subtle curve on the backrest, this trammel would be over 26 feet long! Unless you've got an unusually large shop, you'll probably be better off using a router with either a pattern bit, which has a bearing above the cutters, or a flush-trimming bit, which uses a bearing mounted below the cutters. Either will cut accurately.

When routing with a flush-trimming bit, attach the template to the underside of the workpiece with double-sided carpet tape, hot-melt glue,

Flush-Trimming Bit

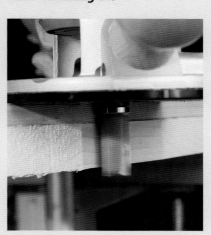

Pattern Bit

or clamps. The bearing rides along the template, and the cutter automatically cuts the work to match.

A pattern bit works the same way, but you attach the template to the top of the workpiece. In either case, you should cut the workpiece to within $1/16$ inch of the final size with a saber saw before routing. Also, be aware of what is under the workpiece as you rout. You don't want to cut into your workbench.

Hammock Stand

There's nothing like a spacious, comfortable hammock for relaxing outside on a summer day. You seem to float in the air, gently rocking, with breezes wafting over and under you. Just lie there and let the cares and stresses of your busy life drain away. But there's always a hitch, isn't there? You know the perfect spot for the hammock, but now you have to figure out how to support it. Generally, you need to hang the hammock from hooks set 12 to

15 feet apart, and 4 to 5 feet off the ground. Set the supports too close together or too far apart, and you'll sag into the hammock, or flip right out of it. You also need to find support trees or posts that are pretty stout. A hammock stand is often a better solution. You can make the proportions just right for comfort and move the assembly wherever you want it. Build your own in only a few hours, customizing it, if need be, to fit your hammock. Once the frame is built, you can screw in your hooks just the right distance apart and just the right height off the ground. The sturdy main struts on this stand have enough capacity to handle just about any hammock on the market, or even one that you make by hand. And if that perfect site in your backyard gets too sunny, the solution is simple: just move your new hammock stand to a better location.

EXPLODED VIEW

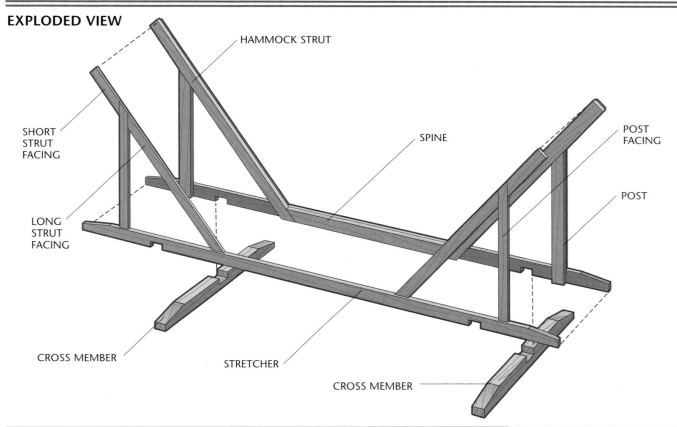

HAMMOCK STRUT

SHORT STRUT FACING

SPINE

POST FACING

POST

LONG STRUT FACING

CROSS MEMBER

STRETCHER

CROSS MEMBER

CUTTING LIST

Part	Number	Thickness	Width	Length	PT Stock
Stretchers	2	1½"	3½"	168"	2x4
Spine	1	1½"	3½"	62"	2x4
Cross members	2	3½"	3½"	60"	4x4
Hammock struts	2	1½"	3½"	78"	2x4
Posts	2	1½"	3½"	36½"	2x4
Long strut facings	4	1"	3½"	48⁹⁄₁₆"	⁵⁄₄
Short strut facings	4	1"	3½"	22¾"	⁵⁄₄
Post facings	4	1"	3½"	37³⁄₈"	⁵⁄₄

SHOPPING LIST

- 1 pc. 4x4 10' PT southern yellow pine
- 2 pcs. 2x4 14' PT southern yellow pine
- 2 pcs. 2x4 10' PT southern yellow pine
- 1 pc. 2x4 8' PT southern yellow pine
- 4 pcs. ⁵⁄₄x6 10' PT southern yellow pine
- 2" deck screws
- 3" deck screws
- 2 screw eyes, ⁵⁄₁₆"x3"
- 2 repair links

Hammock Stand

ELEVATIONS

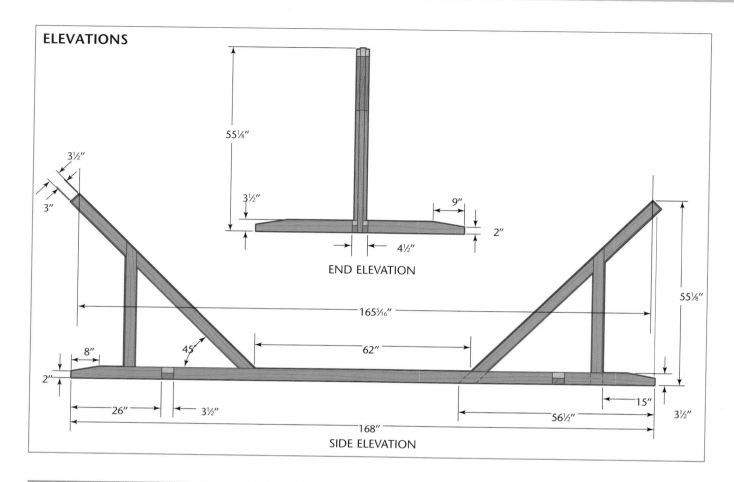

55⅛"

3½"

3"

3½"

9"

2"

4½"

END ELEVATION

165⁵⁄₁₆"

55⅛"

8"

45

62"

2"

26"

3½"

168"

56½"

15"

3½"

SIDE ELEVATION

BUILDER'S NOTES

The hammock stand is a plain and simple project that even a novice woodworker can tackle with success. But it's a good idea to build the stand outside because you wind up with a long and cumbersome piece of furniture that may be too big to work on conveniently in a home shop.

I supported the assembly on a pair of sawhorses and used an extra 16-foot 2x4 to help support the upper ends of the posts and struts during the assembly process.

Materials

You may be able to pull your hammock stand under a porch roof. But it's wise to choose materials based on the idea

that it will be left out in the weather day in and day out. Over the winter you could partially dismantle the stand by turning out the screws from the cross members and storing the major sections in the garage.

To stand the exposure, the best plan is to use pressure-treated (PT) wood. It is strong and durable, and widely available in the stock sizes you need for this project. It may not be the most attractive wood on the market, but you can dress up the finished piece with stain.

You need to take special precautions when working PT wood and to protect yourself against sawdust that is infused

with chemicals that make the wood rot-resistant by poisoning the microbes that break down wood. While manufacturers insist that PT wood is safe, it's wise to wear a dust mask and eye protection when cutting it. Also, sweep up the sawdust, and make sure the debris gets carted away with the trash (where permitted by local ordinances). Don't burn scraps of PT wood in your fireplace or woodstove.

Tools and Techniques

You need two power tools to build the stand: a circular saw to crosscut and miter the frame parts and to make the facings; and a drill-driver to fasten the parts together.

A 7¼-inch circular saw

will handle all the 90- and 45-degree crosscuts. (Use a square to guide your circular saw as you make the cuts.) You also can use the circular saw with a guide to rip the ⁵⁄₄ stock. If you have access to a table saw for the rips and a power miter saw to handle the crosscuts and miters, the cutting will be easier and faster.

Finish

I used a water-repellent solid-color stain on the hammock stand—just to conceal the green tinge of the wood. The water-based stain spread smoothly and made it easy to clean up the brush with soap and water.

Yard and Garden Furniture

STEP-BY-STEP

Measuring

The first thing to do is to determine how far apart the suspension hooks need to be set for your hammock. There's no point in making the stand a lot larger than necessary. **(Photo 1)**

Typically, a new hammock will include printed instructions (and warnings) that indicate a range of measurements for properly positioning the suspension points. The printed material with the hammock I bought indicated the suspension points should be 13 to 15 feet apart and 4 to 5 feet above the ground. This stand is designed around those guidelines, with the final suspension points just 13 feet apart and 4½ feet above the ground.

Altering the stand's dimensions to accommodate your hammock is not difficult. Examine the side elevation drawing, noting the distance between the hangers and between the ground and each hanger. To increase the distance between hangers, increase the length of the stretchers and spine, and move the posts and struts out.

Making Cross Members

Begin the woodworking by cutting the 4x4 cross members, shaping the ends and cutting the laps for the stretchers. I cut both cross members from a 10-foot-long 4x4. You can make overall cuts while squaring up the ends, if necessary, and then simply cut the post in two.

Because the girth of the cross members exceeds the cutting capacity of the typical circular saw, you need to cut the 4x4 in

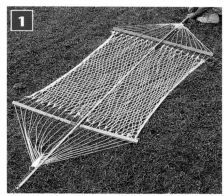

Stretch out your hammock on the ground, and measure it from end to end before you start construction. That dimension will determine how far apart the suspension points must be on your stand.

two passes. Normally, you make these cuts using the full depth of the blade. That way, cuts from opposite sides of the piece will meet up. The trick is to get the two cuts level. You need to follow your square lines very carefully.

Lay out and cut the tapered ends next. Follow the layout shown in the drawing, and mark out cut lines on both sides of the cross member, connecting them with lines across the ends and the top surface. Make the cuts in the same way you cut the cross members. Cut a little more than halfway through the stock from one face; then roll the piece over and make a second cut. Use a power planer or belt sander to smooth the sawed surface.

The laps are located equidistant from the ends of each 5-foot-long cross member, and are cut into the top surface. Following the drawing again, mark the laps on the cross members. The depth of the laps is 1¾ inches, which is half the stock width. The width of the laps is 4½ inches, which is the thickness of three 2x4s stacked face-to-face.

Cut the laps using your circular saw. Adjust the cutting depth to the layout line on one of the cross members. The two critical cuts on each lap are the shoulder cuts. Guide the saw with a square as you cut them so that you produce crisp, square cuts. You want the stretcher-and-spine assembly to fit tightly between the shoulders. Having cut the shoulders, set the square aside, and make repeated, closely spaced cuts to waste the material between them.

Making Stretchers

The next step is to shape the ends of the stretchers and cut the laps in them for the cross members.

The 2x4 stretchers are 14 feet long. Select two straight 2x4s, trim them to equal lengths, and, in the process, square the ends. (Note: You should be able to make these cuts without altering the cut-depth setting on your circular saw. You want to cut laps in the stretchers at the same setting used to lap the cross members.) Lay out the tapers on the ends, and saw to the cut lines with your circular saw. Clean up the freshly cut tapered edges with a power planer or a belt sander.

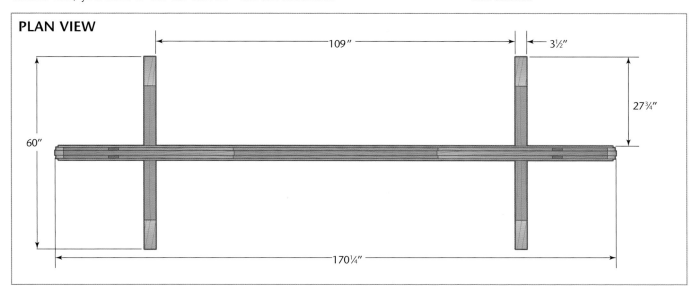

PLAN VIEW

109″   3½″
27¾″
60″
170¼″

2

Cut the lap pockets for the stretchers and cross members with a circular saw. Clamp the stretchers together, and make repeated, closely-spaced passes to clear the pocket. Clean up the edges with a planer or sander.

3

Use a guide with your circular saw to make true cuts for the spine, posts, and struts. This speed square can be adjusted to any angle between 45 and 90 deg., and is useful on the many miter cuts.

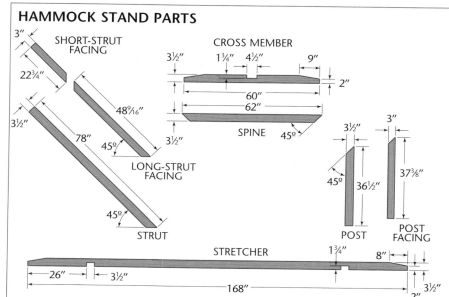

HAMMOCK STAND PARTS

SHORT-STRUT FACING — 3", 22¾", 3½"

CROSS MEMBER — 3½", 1¾", 4½", 9", 2", 60", 62"

SPINE — 45°

LONG-STRUT FACING — 48⁹⁄₁₆", 78", 3½", 45°

STRUT — 45°

POST — 3½", 45°, 36½"

POST FACING — 3", 37⅜"

STRETCHER — 26", 3½", 168", 1¾", 8", 2", 3½"

Now make those laps that are cut into the bottom edges of the stretchers. The depth of the laps is 1¾ inches (which is half the stock width). The width of the laps is 3½ inches, which is the width of the 4x4 cross members. Clamp the two stretchers together, and lay out the laps as shown in the drawings above.

Cut the laps with your circular saw. As before, the critical cuts are the shoulder cuts. Once you make them, continue with repeated, closely spaced cuts to waste the material between them. **(Photo 2)**

Cutting Major Supports

The spine and the posts are the only parts you need to cut to a specific length at this time. Cut the spine to the length specified on the cutting list. Miter both ends at 45 degrees. **(Photo 3)** Cut each of the two posts for the stand from a different 10-foot 2x4. Lay out each post, and make the miters. The remaining length of stock, with one end miter-cut at 45 degrees, is the strut. You will need to trim each strut to final length late in the assembly process, but for now, each strut is a piece roughly 7 feet long.

Basic Assembly

Screw the spine, posts, and struts to one of the stretchers, beginning with the spine. Mark the centerpoint on both the stretcher and the spine, lay one piece on the other, align the marks, and flush-up the edges. Then drive three or four 2-inch deck screws through the spine into the stretcher.

Next, position one of the struts. It should angle off the stretcher at 45 degrees. One edge should be tight against the end of the spine, and the mitered end should be flush with the bottom edge of the stretcher. To make things easier, support the free end of the strut on an extra 2x4 laid on the sawhorses, parallel with the stretcher. To fasten the assembly, drive several 2-inch screws through the strut into the stretcher

Work on the post next. Don't be too concerned about positioning it at this stage. Align the post so that the mitered end is tight against the underside of the strut and the square end is flush with the bottom edge of the stretcher. When the post is perpendicular to the stretcher, drive several 2-inch screws. Also drive a 3-inch-long deck screw through the post edge into the strut. **(Photo 4)** Use this approach to install the other strut and post at the other end of the assembly.

Then set the second stretcher in place and screw it down, using 3-inch-long screws. Drive four screws through the stretcher into each post and strut, and drive several screws through the stretcher into the spine. Carefully roll the assembly over and drive 3-inch screws through the top stretcher into the assembly.

Cross Members

You've already cut the laps in the stretchers and the cross members, but this is the first opportunity to fit the parts together. Ideally, it will take only modest persuasion to close the joints. Seat the cross members;

4

Set the stretcher across sawhorses along with an extra 2x4 to support the free ends of the posts and struts and keep them level. Here, I'm driving a screw through the post into the strut.

Yard and Garden Furniture

then drive 3-inch screws through the 4x4s into the stretchers. **(Photo 5)**

At this point, you can right the stand and complete the assembly, or you can leave it on its side across the sawhorses while you fit and attach the facings.

Facings

The facings are strips of $5/4$ stock screwed to the faces of the struts and posts. The critical pieces are the ones that face the posts because they overlap the butt joint between the post and strut and lock the pieces together. To create a little visual interest, I ripped the facing strips to a 3- inch width, leaving a $1/4$-inch reveal bet-ween the edges of the struts and posts and their facings. This looks better than leaving the edges flush.

The first job is to rip the stock to width. Pressure-treated $5/4$ is typically stocked in the form of $5/4$x6 decking. It is $5 1/2$ inches wide, with radiused edges. To use the material as facing in this project, you should rip off the radiused edges, which will reduce the width to 3 inches. You need to rip down the four 10-footers specified on the shopping list to make the facings. You can handle the job with a table saw, or use a circular saw with a sturdy rip guide. It's best to first crosscut each 10-footer into three pieces: a 52-inch-long piece, a 40-inch-long piece, and a 28-inch-long piece; then rip them.

The individual facings should be cut to fit. To begin, miter one end of a 52-incher at 45 degrees. Set the 40-incher on the post, and line it up with the $1/4$-inch reveal along the edges. Set the 52-incher on the strut with the miter against the stretcher and the square end overlapping the post-facing. Line it up, and mark it (and the post facing) for trimming where they meet. **(Photo 6)** Miter the ends of these pieces, and screw them to the post and strut. Ultimately, you will drive several 3-inch screws through the upper end of the post facing into the post and strut. But don't do it until a facing piece has been applied to both sides of these parts. **(Photo 7)**

Lastly, cut and install the four post facings and long-strut facings. Wait to apply the short-strut facings until you've installed the suspension hardware and trimmed the strut.

Hardware

Before cutting and attaching the last four pieces of facing, you need to trim the struts. Before you do that, you need to

Settle the cross members and stretchers into the lap joints, and secure with 3-in. screws driven through the bottom of each cross member. Use a clamp to squeeze the stretchers together.

Fit the facings by centering the rough-length facing and the strut facing on the post. Mark and scribe the edges of the strut facing where it overlaps the post facing; then miter the two pieces.

Attach the mitered facings to the frame with screws. Lock the post and strut together with 3-in. screws. They will penetrate the facing and frame and extend into the facing on the opposite side.

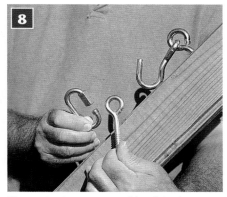

Use a stout screw eye with a 3-in.-long shank, and use a beefy repair link to connect the hammock to the screw eye. The hammock I bought included screw eyes and hooks. You may need to buy hardware.

find where you must locate the hardware. **(Photo 8)**

For my hammock, the hooks needed to be 13 feet apart and at least 4 feet above the ground. To start, I measured and marked the spot on each strut that was just 4 feet vertically from the ground. Then I measured horizontally from point to point of my vertical marks and found them to be less than the required 13 feet apart. To meet the required horizontal measurement, I simply slid the attachment points toward the ends of the struts. (This is one place where it pays to measure carefully, and more than once.)

The attachment hardware I used was supplied with the hammock. If that's not the case for you, use a pair of screw eyes and repair links. With the points located and marked, simply drill pilot holes to avoid splitting, and turn the screw eye into the struts.

Now mark and trim the struts. I crosscut the struts $3 1/2$ inches from the screw eye. With the struts trimmed, you can lay out and cut the remaining pieces of facing and attach them. Now the hammock stand is ready for finishing.

Finishing

If you use pressure-treated wood, you don't really need a finish. Decks and outdoor furniture made of unfinished pressure-treated wood can be left as is. I toned down the greenish tinge and the pronounced grain by applying one coat of a solid-color exterior stain.

Plant Cart

otted plants add seasonal beauty. We love to have them in the house, especially during the sometimes long and awfully dreary winter. But once spring rolls around and the days start getting longer, we want them out on the deck or patio. They probably want to be out on the deck or patio, too! But it's a lot of work to truck them all out there, then truck them all back in again when that first taste of spring gives way to a late frost. Here's the perfect

solution: a plant cart. The cart has two wooden crates, each of which will hold three or more potted plants. Back the cart into an indoor corner for the winter, and the blooms and foliage of lush plants can virtually obscure your creation. Come spring, you can wheel a batch of sun-loving plants outdoors to chase the sun, and in doing so, display your handiwork to its best advantage. Once you find the cart a permanent outdoor spot, you can also hang a few plants from the handle for an even better show of foliage. With its large front wheels and ball casters, the plant cart is easy to maneuver over the threshold and through the doorway, out into the sunlight flooding the deck or patio. This isn't your usual boxy cart but a sleek and curvy show-off. It's the perfect project to wow both the plant lovers and hobby woodworkers in your acquaintance.

EXPLODED VIEW

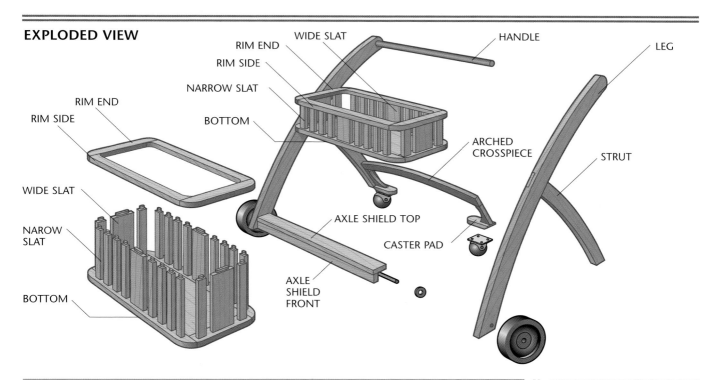

CUTTING LIST (Some parts are left long during construction.)

Part	Number	Thickness	Width	Length	Cypress Stock
Leg/strut blanks	2	1"	10"	48"	5/4x6
Axle shield top	1	3/4"	2 3/4"	29"	1x6
Axle shield front	1	3/4"	1 1/2"	29"	1x6
Arched crosspiece	1	3/4"	4"	29"	1x6
Caster pad-and-bracket strip	1	3/4"	2"	24"	1x6
Handle	1	1 1/4" dia.	—	29 1/2"	birch dowel
Lower crate					
Rim sides	4	1"	2"	29"	5/4x6
Rim ends	4	1"	2"	15 5/8"	5/4x6
Wide slats	4	3/4"	3 1/2"	9 3/4"	1x6
Narrow slats	20	3/4"	1 1/4"	9 3/4"	1x6
Bottom	1	3/4"	13 1/2"	28"	1x6
Upper crate					
Rim sides	4	1"	2"	29"	5/4x6
Rim ends	4	1"	2"	12 3/8"	5/4x6
Wide slats	4	3/4"	3 1/2"	6 1/4"	1x6
Narrow slats	20	3/4"	1 1/4"	6 1/4"	1x6
Bottom	1	3/4"	11"	28"	1x6

SHOPPING LIST

- 4 pcs. 5/4x6 8' cypress
- 4 pcs. 1x6 8' cypress
- 1 pc. 1 1/4" dia.x36" birch dowel
- 2 steel-rim, solid-tire wheels, 8" dia.x1/2" bore
- 1 pc. 1/2" dia.x36" steel rod
- 2 push caps, 1/2" dia.
- 2 flathead locking screws, #6x3/4"
- 2 ball-type swivel casters, 2" dia.
- 8 panhead screws, #8x5/8"
- 2" galvanized deck screws
- 3" galvanized deck screws

ELEVATIONS

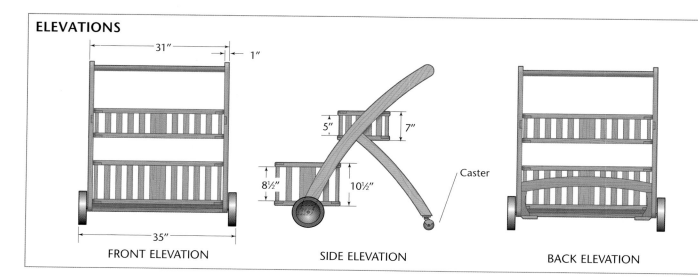

FRONT ELEVATION

SIDE ELEVATION

BACK ELEVATION

Caster

BUILDER'S NOTES

This is a pretty challenging woodworking project. The cart's framework consists of curved parts assembled with curved lap joints. The containers for the potted plants each have 48 mortise-and-tenon joints. The frames of these containers are contoured with a template, and a bottom is fitted into one of the frames using what is really an inlay technique.

Any hobby woodworker who works carefully, uses jigs and fixtures, and has a good assortment of power tools should still be capable of acheiving beautiful results.

Materials
Cedar and redwood seem to be a bit soft for a knockabout project on wheels, probably bumping door jambs and railings as you move it in and out of the house. Cypress seems just a bit more durable to me.

An additional factor is the standard stock thicknesses. The project calls for ⁵⁄₄ and one-by stock, and both are available in cypress. In the nominal one-by thickness, cypress typically is a bit "heavy," meaning that the thickness is in fact 1 inch.

Redwood and cedar, in that nominal thickness, tend to be "light," or closer to ¹¹⁄₁₆ inch. You can plane the cypress, smoothing both faces and reducing the thickness to the conventional ¾ inch. Planing redwood or cedar to smooth both faces would make them too thin for the project.

The wheels I used are 8 inches in diameter, have a ½-inch-diameter bore for the axle, and have solid-rubber tires on metal rims. Such wheels are nondescript, generic items, and the width and tread pattern will vary. You can use larger or smaller wheels simply by altering the elevation of the caster pads to keep the cart level.

I used a standard ½-inch-diameter steel rod for the axle. The push caps used to lock the wheels onto the axle look similar to miniature broad-brimmed hats. Look for them in the aisle lined with drawer-after-drawer of fasteners and miscellaneous hardware. The caps have barblike tabs inside the crown, which dig into the axle to prevent the cap from coming off.

Casters vary widely. I exam-ined and rejected 2-, 3-, and 4-inch industrial swivel casters made from rubber, as well as a score of smaller and flimsier plastic casters. I settled on sturdy swivel casters with 2-inch-diameter balls instead of wheels. The ball is mounted on an axle, so it rolls like a wheel. But the spherical shape allows it to traverse irregular surfaces easily, and it is much less likely to get hung up in a seam or crack. The balls are hard rubberlike plastic; the cowls are brass-plated steel.

Tools and techniques
It is essential that you have a plunge router for the project, and it is good to have a fixed-base router, as well.

Beyond a good selection of straight bits, it is essential to have a 1¼-inch-long pattern bit, which has a pilot bearing that matches the bit's cutting diameter mounted on the shank, or a similar-size flush-trimming bit, which has a pilot bearing on its tip. Either of these bits can be used (in conjunction with a template) to shape the legs, struts, cross brace, and crate rims. To shape and rabbet the bottom rims,

as well as cut the half-laps and tenon the slats, you'll need a large-diameter mortising bit—often called a dado-and-planer bit. To soften the edges of the project parts, you need a couple of roundover bits; I used a ¼-inch-radius bit to do the side assemblies and crate rims, and a ³⁄₁₆-inch-radius bit on the crate slats.

You need three template guides; ½-inch o.d., ¾-inch o.d., and a 1-inch o.d. guide.

In this project, we use two guide/bit combinations with one template to cut the bottom's outer edge and the rim's inner edge. The edges should mate perfectly, with the bottom fitting tightly inside the rim.

If you are experienced, you may opt to skip the tem-plate-making steps and simply cut the sides and struts with the router and trammel. The templates represent a low-risk approach. If you have any trouble getting the trammel set up, and you botch the cuts, you've lost a relatively inexpensive piece of MDF; not some expensive, high-quality lumber.

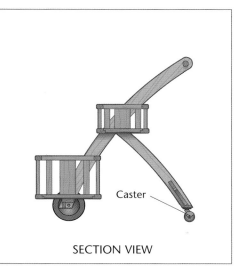

Caster

SECTION VIEW

PLAN VIEW

29"

37³/₁₆"

35"

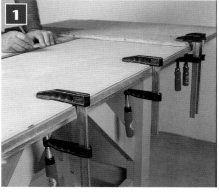

Clamp an auxiliary top *to your benchtop. The MDF on the bottom supports the work, while the plywood on top protects the MDF from the router bit. Mark a centerline to aid in aligning the pivot point and template.*

STEP-BY-STEP

Gluing up stock for the Legs and Struts

If you edge-glue two 48-inch pieces of ⁵/₄x6 stock, producing a board roughly 10 inches wide, you'll be able to take both a leg and a strut from it.

Select the flattest boards you can find. Cut two pieces 48 inches long for each leg and strut. Joint the edges with your router. See the sequence in the Garden Bench project ("Glueing up Seat and Leg Stock," page 127) for pointers on jointing. Glue and clamp the boards.

When the glue has cured, remove the clamps and sand the panels with a belt sander to smooth them.

Setting Up the Staging for Curved-Template Cuts

If you look at the layout drawings, you'll see that the curve of the legs and struts has radius of about 72 inches. Surprised? It is big, but you cut these parts with a router and a simple trammel made from a strip of ¹/₄-inch plywood. The most time-consuming part is setting up the staging.

The work surface must support the workpiece and, 72 inches away, the pivot for the trammel. The workbench I used as the basis for my staging was just over 60 inches long and 24 inches wide.

To expand the benchtop, as well as make the trammel, templates, and a lapping jig, I used a sheet of ³/₄-inch medium-density fiberboard (MDF) and a sheet of ¹/₄-inch lauan plywood (the really cheap stuff).

Begin with the MDF. Cut a 10-inch-wide

by 96-inch-long strip from the sheet. This will yield the blanks for the templates and the lapping jig. Lay the remainder of the sheet on the benchtop.

Cut the lauan plywood next. The trammel is an 8-inch-wide by 96-inch-long strip of this. Cut the trammel strip; then lay the remainder of the sheet on top of the MDF. Clamp the two-layer auxiliary top to the benchtop at a couple of spots. **(Photo 1)**

With the base set, locate where you will place the blank to be routed, and from that, locate the pivot point. I centered the blank on the lauan plywood base, aligning it flush with the plywood's edge. First, measure from side to side, and mark the centerline of the plywood base. Next, measure and mark the spot 1 inch from the edge of the plywood on the centerline.

Lastly, from that spot, measure 72⁹/₁₆ inches along the centerline, and mark it. That distance is the longest of the radii that you will cut, and the mark is the pivot point for the trammel. To elevate the pivot to the same plane as the surface of the template blank, lay a scrap of ³/₄-inch plywood across the lauan-plywood base, centered over the pivot, and clamp it. Measure again, and mark the pivot point; then drill a pilot hole in the plywood at that spot.

Making the Trammel

The trammel is the 96-inch-long strip cut from the sheet of lauan plywood in the previous step. All you have to do to "make" it is to mount the router at one end, and then lay out pivot points.

While a plunge router seems like the natural choice for routing the arcs, you're making through-cuts, so a fixed-base router will work just fine.

Attach the router to one end of the plywood trammel strip with several patches of carpet tape. (If you can get a clamp on the base to squeeze the plywood and the router base together very hard for just a moment, you can vastly improve the bond of the tape.) Once the router is attached, use a ¹/₂-inch straight bit to bore a hole for the bit through the plywood. With a plunge router, this is easy.

With a fixed-base router, it is a little more involved: First, loosen the clamp that secures the motor in the base. Get a good grip on the motor, switch it on, and then plunge the bit into the plywood and bore on through it. Switch off the router, and reclamp the motor.

To make the templates, you will cut arcs of six different radii, two for the edges of the leg template, two for the edges of the strut, and two for the half-lapping jig. Some radii include the bit; some exclude it. Here they are:

- 72⁹/₁₆ inches, with the bit outside the radius (leg)
- 69⁹/₁₆ inches, with the bit inside the radius (leg)
- 72³/₁₆ inches, with the bit outside the radius (strut)
- 69¹⁵/₁₆ inches, with the bit inside the radius (strut)
- 72³/₁₆ inches, with the bit inside the radius (half-lapping jig)
- 69¹⁵/₁₆ inches, with the bit outside the radius (half-lapping jig)

Plant Cart

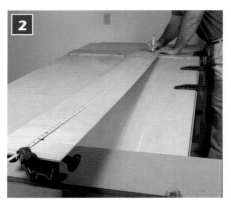

Use a spring clamp to hold the hook end of the measuring tape lined up with the correct side of the bit, which frees up both your hands to position the tape, and mark the pivot point on the trammel's far end.

Before you cut the template, use a pencil to scribe the arc's edges. Use the actual pivot points and be sure to hold the pencil on the correct side of the bit hole. This is easier with a removable, fixed-base router.

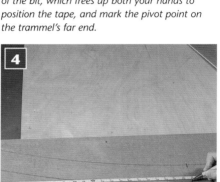

Measure from the end of the template blank, and mark where the half-lap's lower shoulder intersects the arc. It's important to do this before you cut the template because you'll trim off the reference edge in doing so.

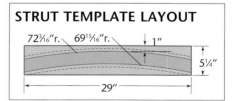

Cut the template by swinging the router back and forth on its plywood tether. Cut only about ⅛ in. of material on each pass. It will take six passes to cut through the ¾-in.-thick template material.

LEG TEMPLATE LAYOUT

Half-lap Shoulder — 48" — 1"

9"

22⅞" — 72⁹⁄₁₆"r. — 69⁹⁄₁₆"r.

STRUT TEMPLATE LAYOUT

72³⁄₁₆"r. — 69¹⁵⁄₁₆"r. — 1"

5¼"

29"

Measure from the bit and lay out all 6 pivots needed in the trammel. To do this, lay the router (and the trammel) upside down, and measure with a measuring tape. If you don't have a helper to hold the tape measure at the bit, enlist the aid of a spring clamp. **(Photo 2)**

Position the measuring tape's hook at the bit and tape it to the trammel. Then play out the measure, locate the pivots, and mark and label them. Finally, drill a pilot hole for a screw through the trammel at each pivot point.

Using a Trammel when Routing Templates

Begin by cutting the strip of MDF into the proper-size blanks for the various templates. The blank for the cart leg is 9x48 inches. For the strut, the template blank measures 5x28 inches. The blank for the half-lapping jig parts is 9x16 inches.

Do the leg template first. Measure and mark the midpoint between the ends of the blank on its edge. Align that mark on the centerline marked on the lauan plywood auxiliary benchtop, and position the blank flush with the edge of the plywood. Drill pilot holes through the back corners of the blank and drive a screw into each, attaching the blank to the auxiliary benchtop.

Set up the trammel next. Drive a screw through the appropriate pivot hole in the trammel itself into one of the holes drilled into the pivot base of the auxiliary benchtop. The router should be able to swing in an arc across the blank. You can now clearly see the cut's arc across the blank, and you can drive a couple of more screws through the blank into the auxiliary benchtop. You must position them where they won't conflict with the bit, but where they will secure the template itself (as opposed to the waste).

Before you make the cut, lay out the location of the half-lap joint that will join the strut and the leg. The idea is to mark the template, then transfer the layout to the workpieces. The dimensions are shown in the leg template layout drawing. Use the trammel and a pencil to draw the leg's edges on the blank. **(Photo 3)** Then measure from the blank's end to mark the intersections of the strut with the leg. **(Photo 4)**

Use a ½-inch straight bit to cut the templates. With a fixed-base router, set the cut depth to ⅛ inch. With a plunge router, set the total cut depth to ¾ inch, but cut no more than ⅛ inch of material per pass. The proper feed direction for this cut is counterclockwise, so begin cutting with the router at the left end of the blank, feeding the router to the right. After making the first pass, return the router to the starting point. Increase the cut depth by ⅛ inch, and make another pass. Repeat and repeat until you have cut completely through the blank. **(Photo 5)**

Shift the trammel position to cut the second arc, cutting it the same way you did the first.

Vacuum up all the dust, back out the mounting screws, and remove template and waste from the auxiliary benchtop. Don't toss the waste; some of it will be used later in making the jig for the half-lap.

Mount the blank for the strut on the auxiliary benchtop. Shift the trammel as required, and cut the strut template the

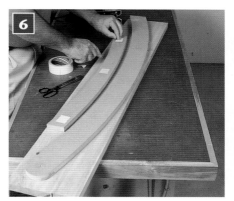

***With carpet tape,** bond the leg and the strut templates to the panel. Nest them very close together to minimize the width of panel needed. Trim the pieces with a router and pattern bit or flush-trimming bit.*

***Assemble the half-lapping jig in place.** Clamp the support rails to the leg. Set the fence platform on the fences and leg, and align it with the shoulder layout marks transferred to the leg from the template.*

***Screw the first fence to the rails;** then set the strut against the fence, and clamp the second fence tight against the strut. Drive screws through the fence into the rails. Remove the strut, and the jig is ready.*

same way you did the leg template.

Lastly, mount the half-lap jig blank on the benchtop, and cut those pieces.

Rounding the End of the Leg template

The top end of each side is rounded, and the axis of the round handle is the center point of the arc. If you round the end of the template, and drill a ⅛-inch hole through the template at the center point of the arc, you can use the template to incorporate these features in the sides when you cut them.

Locate the centerpoint—and you don't have to be overly precise in doing this. Swing a compass set to a 1½-inch radius around the point, laying out the rounded end. Then drill a ⅛-inch-diameter hole through the template at the center point. Trim as close as possible to the line with a saber saw; then file and sand the edge smooth.

Cutting the Legs and struts

As I mentioned earlier, you can cut both a leg and a strut from each 10x48, glued-up panel of ⁵⁄₄x6 boards.

Lay the two templates on one of the panels. If necessary (and possible), shift them around to avoid knots or blemishes. When you are satisfied with the positions, scribe around the templates with a pencil, then remove them. With a saber saw, cut outside the lines, separating the two blanks from the workpiece.

Bond the leg template to the leg blank with several patches of carpet tape. **(Photo 6)** With a router and either a pattern bit or a flush-trimming bit, trim the blank to

duplicate the template. To avoid having the bit cut into the benchtop, you'll have to clamp the work so that a part of it overhangs the bench edge. Once that part is cut, you'll have to unclamp the work, shift it so you can rout the remaining uncut edges, and reclamp it.

Drill through the hole in the top end of the template, boring through the leg. Lastly, extend the half-lap layout marks across the edges of the template and across the edges of the leg. Then pry the template and the leg apart.

Now stick the strut template to the strut blank. Trim the workpiece to match the template the same way you did the leg.

Repeat the entire process to cut and shape the second leg and strut.

Cutting the Half-laps

Join the strut to the leg with a half-lap joint. The leg is dadoed, and the strut is rabbeted. Because the strut is trapped between the shoulders of the lap in the side, it can't twist, so it stays put.

The tricky part of cutting a half-lap joint usually is getting the cut depth just right. Here, you have that challenge, but even more, you have to cut the shoulders on a curve. This is where you use the scrap produced when cutting the templates. The jig is essentially the tenoning jig described in detail on page 18, but with curved edges. You make one jig to cut the lap in the leg, another for the strut. Then you take both jigs apart and reassemble them to cut the other joint.

Lay out the parts, aligning the strut with the layout marks transferred to the

leg from the template. Scribe along the edges of the strut on the leg; then scribe along the leg onto the strut. These layout lines mark the shoulders of the laps.

Take a long piece of the scrap from cutting the template, and clamp it against the leg at the joint location. This is the jig's rail.

Lay one of the fence pieces—cut specifically for this purpose—on the leg, and align it flush with the shoulder line. Clamp it to the rail, and drive three screws through the fence and into the rail. **(Photo 7)** Remove the clamp.

Next, lay the strut on the leg, tight against the fence. Add the second fence, pushing it tight against the strut. Clamp the second fence temporarily while you screw it to the rail. **(Photo 8)** Remove the clamp and the strut, and clamp the jig to the leg.

Set up a similar jig on the strut so you can lap it together with the leg. The lap in the strut is at the end, so there's no second shoulder, but you need a fence out there to support the router.

Adjust the cut depth to ⅛ inch, and make a pass on both the leg and the strut. Readjust and cut again on both parts. Keep track of how deep you are cutting with a rule, and as you approach the proper depth—before you cut too deep—remove the jigs and test-fit the parts together. Make the final depth adjustment, and finish the cuts. Repeat the process for the other leg and strut.

Joining the Sides and Struts

Glue and clamp the strut to the leg. When the clamp is off, trim and sand the tip of the strut flush with the leg's edge. Sand all

CART ASSEMBLY

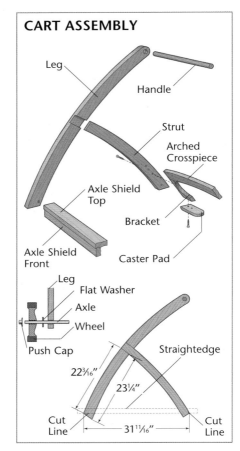

Leg

Handle

Strut

Arched Crosspiece

Axle Shield Top

Bracket

Axle Shield Front

Caster Pad

Leg

Flat Washer

Axle

Wheel

Push Cap

Straightedge

22³⁄₁₆"

23¹⁄₄"

Cut Line

31¹¹⁄₁₆"

Cut Line

CASTER BRACKETS

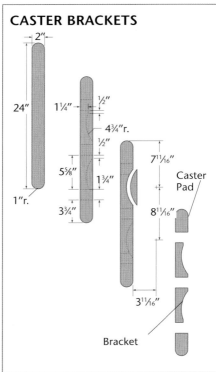

2"

24"

1¹⁄₄"

¹⁄₂"

4³⁄₄"r.

¹⁄₂"

5⁵⁄₈"

1³⁄₄"

7¹¹⁄₁₆"

Caster Pad

1"r.

3³⁄₄"

8¹¹⁄₁₆"

3¹¹⁄₁₆"

Bracket

To help align the caster pad, *clamp a scrap of the working stock with the bracket in the bench vise. Apply glue to the beveled end of the bracket, set the pad in place, and drive two 2-in. screws through the pad.*

With the handle *and axle shield in place, glue and clamp the caster pads to the struts. Fit the cross brace in place, and mark along the brackets's top edges. Trim the brace, glue and clamp it, and secure with screws.*

the surfaces; then round-over the edges using a roundover bit.

Cutting the Crosspieces, Handle, and Caster Brackets

Rip and crosscut the pieces to the sizes on the cutting list. Lay out the caster brackets and pads on a single board, and cut it apart only after you shape the pieces.

Round-over the exposed edges of the axle shield, and glue it together, as shown in the "Cart Assembly" drawing at left.

Cut the rounded ends on the bracket-and-pad strip, and smooth them with a finishing sander. Lay out the parts on the strip, as shown in the caster brackets drawing. Cut the arcs in the brackets, using either a router and trammel or a saber saw and trammel. Then crosscut the parts from the strip, cut the flats in the brackets, and sand all the parts. Radius the exposed edges.

Use the strut template to cut the arched crosspiece. Sand the piece and radius the exposed edges.

Chamfer the ends of the caster pads at 45 degrees, and bevel the lower end of the brackets at 32 degrees. Clamp the bracket, beveled end up, and apply a thin coat of glue to the end grain. Then press the pad into place while you drill holes. Drive 2-inch screws through the pad and into the bracket. **(Photo 9)**

Assembling the Cart

A large, level working surface is crucial for this step. I laid a half-sheet of ³⁄₄-inch MDF on my benchtop and leveled it with shims. Use a straightedge to scribe a line connecting the bottom front corner of the leg with

the bottom back corner of the strut. Trim on these lines. Mark a parallel line for the upper crate through the lower junction of the strut and leg.

Install the handle next. This will keep the side assemblies upright, though they'll be wobbly. Using the centerpoint holes as guides, drill ¹⁄₄-inch-deep recesses on the legs' inner faces with a 1¹⁄₄-inch Forstner bit. On the outer face, drill a ³⁄₈-inch counterbore and a pilot hole. Glue the handle into place and drive 3-inch screws to secure it.

Attach the axle shield next. Drive 3-inch screws through counterbores in the legs and into the ends of the shield.

Drill ¹⁄₂-inch holes for the axle, positioning them clear of the shield. Install the axle and mount the wheels temporarily. Either use ¹⁄₂-inch threaded rod and secure the wheels with stop nuts, or use ¹⁄₂-inch steel rod with press-on caps to secure the wheels.

Cap one end of the axle. Fit a wheel and a washer onto it, feed it through the holes, then add another washer and wheel. Measure the extension to fit the second cap or nut, and mark the rod for cutting.

While the axle is still in place, drill the locking-screw holes. Drill into the back edge of the leg and into the axle rod. You don't need to penetrate the metal deeply, just enough for the tip of a screw to extend into it to keep it from sliding right or left (and from turning).

Remove the axle, and cut it to your mark using a hacksaw. File off sharp edges left by this cut.

You can reinstall the axle and wheels, but don't press the second cap onto the

Make a tenoning jig with only one rail to cut the half-laps on the rim frames. Set the jig over the workpiece, tight against the end and the edge. A single C-clamp secures the jig and work to the benchtop for the cut.

axle yet. The caps don't come off easily, so wait until the project is completed.

Apply glue to the joining edge of a pad-and-bracket assembly, align it on the strut's inner face, and clamp it. Drill ⅜-inch counterbores, then pilot holes, and secure with 2-inch screws.

Hold the arched crosspiece in place and scribe the top of the brackets on the crosspiece. Cut the crosspiece to size, and glue the crosspiece in place. Clamp it to the pad-and-bracket assembly, and apply a pipe clamp to pinch the crosspiece across the struts. Drill counterbores and pilot holes, and drive 3-inch screws through the struts and into the ends of the crosspiece. **(Photo 10)**

Cutting the Crate Parts

Cut the parts for the crates according to the cutting list. If you use a power miter saw, use a stop block to position the stock for the cuts. This ensures that every slat will be the same length, and every rail the same length.

The bottom is formed by gluing narrow boards edge to edge to form one wide one. You will use a template and router to cut the panel to its final dimensions and contour. It's a good idea to cut the stock you use an inch or two longer than needed, and glue up a panel that's 1 or 2 inches wider than specified.

Cutting the Joinery and Assembling the Rim Frames

Join the frame members with half-lap joints. Because the ends are lapped for joining, this is sometimes called an end lap. Cut and glue these laps the same way

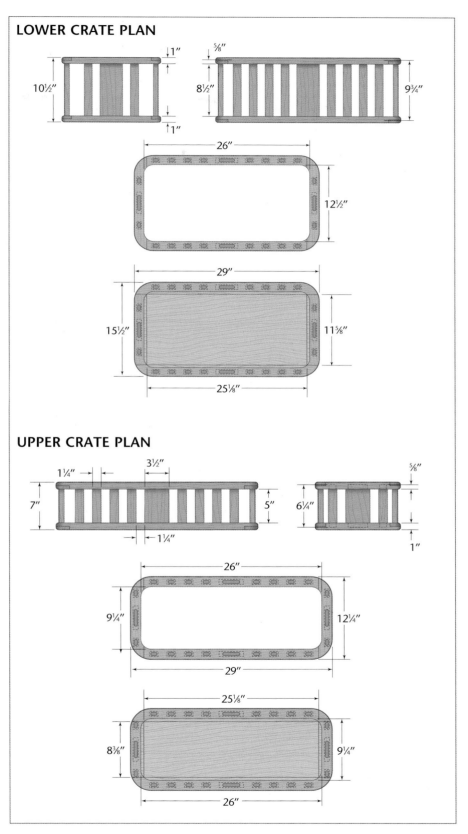

LOWER CRATE PLAN

UPPER CRATE PLAN

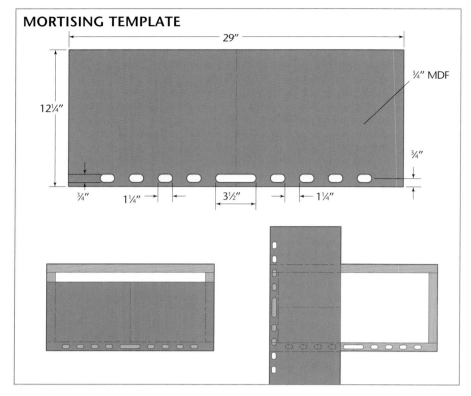

MORTISING TEMPLATE

29"

12¼"

¾" MDF

¾"

¾"   1¼"   3½"   1¼"

you did the ones that join the legs and struts, but use a jig with straight edges to guide the cuts. **(Photo 11)**

Mortising the Rim Frames

Each rim frame has 24 mortises. That's a total of 96 in the cart, but don't worry. Using a plunge router and a simple template, you can knock out all those mortises in very short order, and with no layout.

After cutting the MDF to size, lay out the centerline of the mortises, as indicated in the drawing—¾ inch from the edge—and the slot for the long mortise in the middle. Then set a compass or dividers to 1¼ inches and step off the slots for the mortises on either side of the long one. Mark the slots clearly.

Cut the slots with a plunge router set up with an edge guide and a ¾-inch straight bit. Use stop blocks to avoid cutting too far.

To cancel out the impact of minor alignment errors, have one face of the template facing up when you mortise the bottom frames, and the same face down when doing the top frames. This will keep the spindles and slats aligned vertically. Mark one face "Up for Top," the other "Up for Bottom."

The completed template is used with the plunge router, a ¾-inch-outside-diameter template guide, and a ⅜-inch straight bit. All the mortises are cut ⅝ inch deep.

For the mortises in the rim-frame rails, simply align the template flush with the edges. Run a finger along the front edge of the template to ensure that it is really flush with the frame; then check the ends. Clamp the template and frame to the benchtop, and rout each mortise. Before you move the template, vacuum the chips out of the slots; then rerout to ensure that each mortise is really cut to full length and full depth. **(Photo 12)**

Lay out a centerline on the template edge and another on the rim frame; then match them up and flush the front edge. Clamp the template and rim down, and you are ready to rout. Rout just three mortises in each end, regardless of the frame size.

Making the Rim Templates

Shape the rims using a router and templates. Because the crates are different sizes, you need two sets of templates.

Make the external template first; then use it to make the internal template and to shape the bottom. You'll use the internal template to define the top rim's inner edge and to rabbet the bottom rim's inner edge.

To shape the corners of both external templates, you need a 1⅛-inch-radius corner-rounding template. To shape the outside corners of all the rims, you'll need a corner-rounding template with a 3-inch radius.

Cut the template blanks from either ½- or ¾-inch MDF. With a compass, lay out the desired radii on the two corner-rounding template blanks. Cut and fair the templates one at a time. Cut as close to the line possible using a saber saw, and use a belt sander or rasp to smooth the curve. Finish up with a file and sandpaper.

Next, cut the external templates to size. Use the 1⅛-inch-radius corner-rounding template and a pattern bit in your router to round the four corners of each template. Just align the corner-rounding template at a corner of the external template, edges flush. Clamp the two pieces to the workbench, with the corner to be worked clear of the benchtop. Nibble at the corner with the router, working away the waste a little at a time, until the bit's pilot bearing is in full contact with the guiding template. Unclamp the work and shift the guiding template to the next corner. Keep going until you've rounded all the corners on both external templates.

Make the internal templates next. Use a plunge router fitted with a ½-inch-outside-diameter template guide and a ¼-inch straight bit to make the cut. Using carpet tape, bond the external template to the blank for the internal template. To protect the benchtop, stick the work to a scrap piece of plywood; place patches of tape in the corners and the center so neither the template nor the waste will shift as the cut is completed. Clamp this "workpiece" to the bench.

Feed the router around the external template, moving only counterclockwise, keeping the guide tight against the template's edge. Make three to five laps around the template, cutting slightly deeper each time, until you cut completely through the internal template. Pry the pieces apart, and save the external and internal templates for later use. **(Photo 13)**

Shaping the Rims

You shape the inside edges of the rims by using the internal template, and then you shape the outside corners, one by one, using the 3-inch radius corner-rounding template.

Mortising the crate rims is fast and easy with the template, because you can rout as many as nine mortises in quick succession. Clamp the template to the work, and use a bushing to guide the router bit.

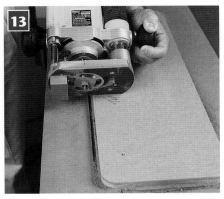

Attach a scrap to the router's base with carpet tape when you make the internal template. With the router supported on both sides of the bit, it's easier to plunge the bit or increase the cutting depth.

Cut away as much of the waste as you can using a saber saw before you pick up the router. Clamp the work overhanging the workbench at a corner so you can do a full side and a full end without stopping.

To form the top rims, you use a straight pattern bit long enough to trim the full thickness of the stock flush with the internal template. I used a ³⁄₄-inch-diameter, 1¹⁄₂-inch-long straight pattern bit for this.

Use the same internal template on the bottom rims, but cut only ³⁄₈ inch into the rim, forming a rabbet to accept the bottom board. I used a router and a dado-and-planer bit with a shank-mounted bearing, but you can use any pattern bit that is short enough.

Attach the template to the rim with carpet tape. You want the template squarely aligned with the workpiece, its edges parallel with those of the rim. This isn't an easy task to accomplish. It helped me to line up the template before applying tape, tracing around its inside edge onto the rim.

With tape stuck on the rim, it was easier for me to align the template and press it down. Squeezing the template and rim together with a quick-action bar clamp at each patch of tape improves the bond between the pieces.

To rout the top rims, you need to work one section at a time. Clamp the work at the benchtop edge, with as much of the top overhanging as you can manage. **(Photo 14)**

Trim away most of the waste with a saber saw, and rout the rim's edge flush to the template. Do as much as you can, shift the position of the work on the bench, and repeat the sawing and routing operations.

Continue to work and shift the rim workpiece until you shape the entire inner edge.

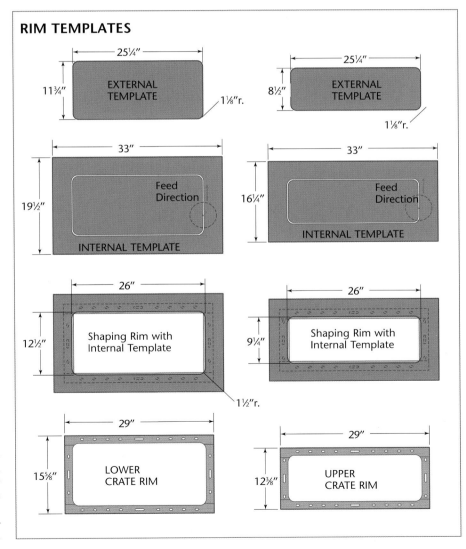

RIM TEMPLATES

EXTERNAL TEMPLATE — 25¹⁄₄″ — 11³⁄₄″ — 1¹⁄₈″ r.

EXTERNAL TEMPLATE — 25¹⁄₄″ — 8¹⁄₂″ — 1¹⁄₈″ r.

INTERNAL TEMPLATE — 33″ — 19¹⁄₂″ — Feed Direction

INTERNAL TEMPLATE — 33″ — 16¹⁄₄″ — Feed Direction

Shaping Rim with Internal Template — 26″ — 12¹⁄₂″

Shaping Rim with Internal Template — 26″ — 9¹⁄₄″ — 1¹⁄₂″ r.

LOWER CRATE RIM — 29″ — 15⁵⁄₈″

UPPER CRATE RIM — 29″ — 12³⁄₈″

You can clamp the work right on top of the bench when rabbeting the bottom rims because the bit doesn't cut through the work. Use a large-diameter pattern bit with very short cutting edges for this operation.

The process of routing the bottom, guided by the external template, is similar to routing the internal template, but you use a large-diameter template guide with a small-diameter bit to make the cut.

Use a router with an edge guide and a straight bit to rabbet the crate bottoms. Don't try to guide the router around the corners, just keep the router moving straight, and let the rabbet disappear at the corner.

Because the cut you make into the bottom rims is a rabbet and not a through-cut, you don't need to cantilever to work off the benchtop edge. **(Photo 15)**

Once the inside edges are routed, remove the template, and round off the outside corners of the rims using the corner-rounding template, the router, and the long pattern bit. Align the template flush with the rim edges, and clamp the work at a benchtop corner (so the bit can cut the work but not the benchtop). Use a saber saw to cut close to the template, and trim it flush using the router.

When you have shaped the rims, radius their edges with a ¼-inch roundover bit. You won't round-over the top inner edges of the bottom rims. You want a flush transition from the rim to the bottom panel. Sand carefully to remove all mill marks and layout lines.

The Crate Bottoms

The bottoms are shaped using the external template and rabbeted with a router and edge guide.

You need to edge-glue narrow boards to create blanks for the bottoms. Crosscut pieces of one-by stock, and joint the edges with a router and straight bit. Glue and clamp the boards using waterproof glue.

When the glue cures, remove the clamps, sand the faces smooth, and clean up all the sanding dust so the carpet tape used next will stick well.

Attach the external template to the blank next. To shape the bottom, use a 1-inch-outside-diameter template guide and a ¼-inch-diameter straight bit. The operation is similar to cutting the internal template. Move the router counterclockwise around the external template, and make several passes, cutting slightly deeper on each lap. **(Photo 16)**

The bottom should fit snugly into the bottom rim, even before it gets rabbeted. You may need to sand the edges a bit.

Rabbet the perimeter of the bottom panel next, so the bottom will drop into the rim with its top surface flush. You can use a rabbeting bit or a straight bit and an edge guide to cut the rabbets.

Make the first pass at about half the final depth of the rabbet, and then adjust to the final depth. Experiment on a scrap piece of the working stock to set the depth precisely, so the scrap fits into the rim with the top surfaces flush, and then cut the rabbet on the bottom to final depth and width. **(Photo 17)**

Glue the bottoms into the rims with waterproof glue. If you use polyurethane glue, don't overspread it, because the excess will foam up out of the joint, making extra cleanup work. A nifty trick is to apply clear packing tape onto the top-surface seam between the bottom and the rim. This will seal the seam and prevent the glue from foaming out of it. Clamp the assembly and set it aside until the glue sets. After the glue has set, you just peel off the tape.

The Crate Slats

Each crate has 24 slats, all cut from one-by stock. Four are 3½ inches wide, the rest 1¼ inches wide. The only difference between the slats in the upper and lower crates is the slat length.

Rip the stock to width, sand all the faces, and then crosscut it to the lengths required. Set up a stop block on the fence of your power miter saw or an auxiliary facing attached to your table saw's miter gauge to position each piece so that each one will be the same length.

Make a tenoning jig next, as detailed in "Routing Tenons" on page 18. One jig will serve for all of the slats. I made mine using a strip of ¾-inch fir plywood for the fence, ¾-inch MDF for the top and auxiliary top, and a piece of ½-inch MDF for the stop (all pieces mined from the scrap pile). I used only a single fence for this jig.

While the jig isn't attractive, it is square and true. The top is perfectly square to the fence, and the stop is parallel to the top's guide-edge. Plywood is typically ¹⁄₃₂ or so under ¾ inch in thickness, so the jig rests on the work, not on the fence. As described in "Routing Tenons," cut the tenons with a fixed-base router with a dado-and-planer bit that has its pilot bearing on the shank. The bearing rides along the edge of the jig's top to guide the cut. You should be able to make a cut of the necessary depth in a single pass.

Make test cuts on a scrap of the working stock to establish the proper depth of cut. As always, creep up on the setting, cutting the opposite cheeks and testing the fit of the resulting tenon in a mortise. In the end, making a cut on each of a slat's four surfaces should produce a tenon that, once the corners have been rounded off, will fit the mortise.

I found that to cut the cheeks I could gang three of the narrow slats in the jig and secure the works to the benchtop with a single locking C-clamp.

Make a tenoning jig big enough to handle three slats for the cheek cuts and five for the edge cuts. Butt the ends of the workpieces tight to the stop, and clamp it to the bench. Keep the clamp out of the router's path.

Before you open the glue, do a dry-run assembly to make sure everything fits. Sliding a slat partway out of one rim's mortise as you engage it in the other rim's mortise helps keep it engaged in both.

Use temporary cleats to support the upper crate while you adjust its position. When the position pleases you, clamp the crate itself; then drill counterbores and pilot holes, and drive the mounting screws.

To make the edge cuts, I could gang five slats in the jig, though I had to use a deep-throat bar clamp to secure this setup. **(Photo 18)** Be sure the ends of the slats are tight against the fence and the stop; then clamp the work and make the cut. Just repeat the process to cut all the cheeks and edges.

To fit the routed mortises, with their rounded ends, the corners of the tenons need to be rounded or knocked off. While I usually round tenons with a file, in this case I pared the corners with a chisel. Either approach works fine.

Lastly, radius the edges of the slats with the ¼-inch roundover bit that you used on the rim edges.

Assembling the Crates
A straightforward job, you assemble each crate by fitting a slat into each mortise in the bottom assembly, then setting the top rim in place, with a tenon sliding into each mortise. The trick is to accomplish this without dribbling glue all over or having the parts seize before they are fully seated.

Begin with a test fit, so you understand what's involved. Joining all the slats to the bottom is easy. You will probably find that getting all the tenons engaged in the top rim is a not as easy. The first few engage easily enough, and the last few the same. It's the many in between that are troublesome. Pressing down on one corner of the rim may lift another corner, allowing tenons already started to pop out of their mortises. What worked for me was to pull the slats partially out of the bottom mortises as I got them engaged in the top mortise. **(Photo 19)** This way, the work is

not strictly a matter of pressing the top rim down onto the tenons.

I used polyurethane glue for this job for several reasons. First, it is waterproof. It also expands to fill gaps and seal out moisture. You apply the glue to only one surface, rather than both, so the work of applying it is halved. And it isn't as tacky as type 2 yellow glue, so tenons are less likely to seize while you align and engage others in the assembly.

To assemble a crate, first dampen all the tenons with a wet rag. Next, don latex gloves (to protect your hands from glue stains), and judiciously apply glue to all the mortises in both the top and bottom rims. Don't overdo it; you don't want fillets of polyurethane foam around each slat. And you don't want excess glue dribbling out of the top rim's mortises when you set it into place. Try to place the glue around the top of each mortise wall so that the tenon will smear it down the mortise walls as it seats.

Insert a slat into each mortise in the bottom assembly. Upend this assembly, and set it on top of the upper rim. One by one, get the tenons engaged in the top rim. When all are engaged, apply clamps to pull the two rims together, seating all the joints. The unit should pull together square and true, unless your mortises or tenons have somehow been cut out of square. Leave the clamps in place for several hours.

Mounting the Crates
The lower crate rests flat on the axle shield; this ensures that it is level when the cart is resting on a level surface. The fore-and-aft position can be varied to suit you. The posi-

tion depicted in the section view drawing on page 149 has the centerline of the crate aligned on the centerline of the axle-shield.

Position the crate and clamp it. At the top and bottom rims, drill counterbores; then bore pilot holes through the leg into the crate. Drive a 2-inch screw in each pilot. Locate two screws side by side at each spot.

To mount the upper crate, first clamp cleats below the layout lines drawn as you began assembly of the cart. Rest the crate on these cleats, and slide it forward and backward to determine the alignment you like best. Consider the height of the plants you plan to put in the lower one. You can push it forward to slightly overhang the the lower crate or pull it back to be clear of it. The position depicted in the side elevation drawing has it clear of the lower crate. Install the crate in the same manner as the lower crate, and remove the cleats. **(Photo 20)**

Applying a Finish
The first operation in the finishing process is to plug all the counterbores in which screws are seated. Using a plug cutter, make the required plugs from scraps of the working stock. Glue a plug into each counterbore. After the glue sets, pare or saw the plugs flush, and sand them smooth.

Apply the finish of your choice next, following the manufacturer's directions. When the finish is dry, install the casters, axles, and wheels. Drive the locking screws through the legs and into the holes you drilled in the axle. Slip the washers and wheels into place, and press the push caps onto the ends of the axle.

Folding Table-Stool

Here's a handy outdoor companion—a combination table and stool that is self-contained, lightweight, and easy to carry with its own built-in handle. Open it up, and it's a sturdy stool. Set between a couple of chairs, it is a handy side table. The table-stool is designed around a nifty concept. In a nutshell, the design has two pairs of sturdy legs joined by a pivot to form an X. The legs naturally tend to move in opposite directions around the pivot. And

without anything to hold them back, the leg tops would spread farther and farther away from one another until the assembly collapsed. The design takes advantage of this tendency by linking halves of the seat to opposite halves of the legworks. When the halves meet, they interlock, which holds the legs in the proper position. To collapse the table-stool, you simply lift the outside edges of the seat and pull the two halves away from each other.

That allows the legs to close up and the seat sections to swing down flush on either side. (See "Folding Sequence," page 163.) This unusual, easy-to-store design is a great weekend project. Depending on the type of lumber you use, you should be able to build a couple of tables for less than $20, including hardware. And you won't need more than a couple of afternoons or evenings in the shop to make them.

EXPLODED VIEW

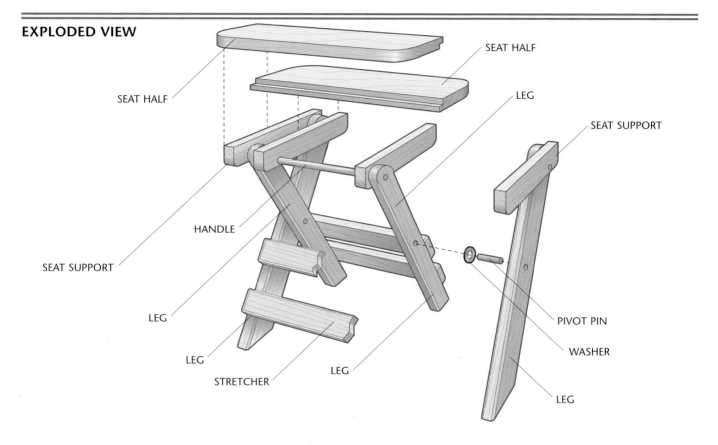

CUTTING LIST

Part	Number	Thickness	Width	Length	Stock
Legs	4	¾"	2"	18¹⁄₁₆"	1x4 Douglas fir
Seat supports	4	¾"	1½"	11¼"	1x4 Douglas fir
Stretchers	2	¾"	1½"	12⁷⁄₁₆"	1x4 Douglas fir
Stretchers	2	¾"	1½"	10⅞"	1x4 Douglas fir
Handle	1	½" dia.	—	11"	birch dowel
Pivot pins	4	½" dia.	—	1½"	birch dowel
Seat half	1	¾"	6⅜"	16"	1x4 cypress
Seat half	1	¾"	6"	16"	1x4 cypress

SHOPPING LIST

- 2 pcs. 1x4 6' Douglas fir flooring
- 1 pc. 1x4 6' cypress
- 1 pc. ½"x18" birch dowel
- 2" deck screws
- 1⅝" deck screws
- ½" nylon washers
- Brads

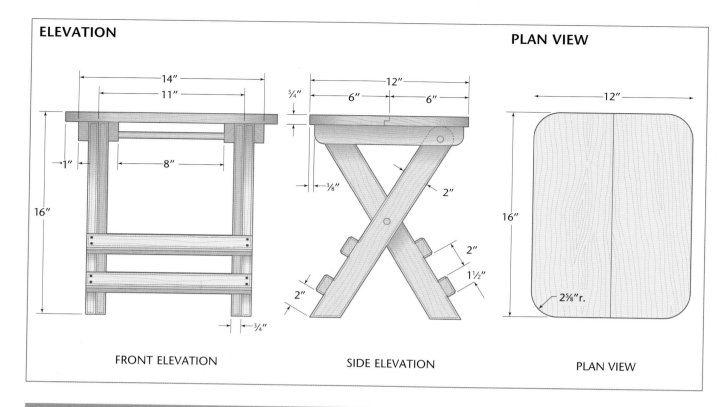

ELEVATION

PLAN VIEW

FRONT ELEVATION

SIDE ELEVATION

PLAN VIEW

BUILDER'S NOTES

This great weekend project requires only a modest amount of material. The resulting project has a bit of novelty to it and a whole lot of practicality. Let's consider the materials you need, as well as the tools you ought to have.

Materials

The table-stool has a cypress top mounted on leg assemblies made of Douglas fir. You can make the whole project from cypress or from any other exterior-grade wood.

The stock at your local lumberyard may be run-of-the-mill. But you might find tongue-and-groove stock intended for porch flooring that will work. In one of my trips to the yard, I came across 1-inch-thick quarter-sawn Douglas fir. I removed the tongue and groove to make the final stock just under 3 inches wide.

In the past, I have found flooring cut from Philippine mahogany, oak, and other woods that are perfect for outdoor projects like this table-stool. Of course, you can use two different woods to provide some contrast—for example, using a wood with a darker hue for the leg assemblies and one with a lighter hue for the top.

On the pieces that pivot, I eased the connections with nylon washers. These washers are thick enough to provide a little clearance for movement and are smooth enough to ease the pivot action. This assembly is an important part of the project because it makes the piece easy to set up and use—and easy to store in a small space.

Tools and Techniques

Because you need to rip the tongue-and-groove stock to remove the milled edges and get the widths needed, you ought to have access to a table saw for this project. I used an inexpensive bench-top model.

A power planer, which is a motorized version of the traditional hand plane, can slick the edges of your just-ripped stock. If you don't have one, that hand plane will do just nicely, as will a sander.

In this project (and most others in the book), I used templates for making the parts. The value of the template lies primarily in having holes for pivot bolts consistently placed. A natural-born woodworker might be able to knock out these parts via the eyeball method, but anyone who is not an expert will benefit from using templates. Once you've used the template for the holes, you might as well use it to form the contours as well. In this project, the

contour amounts only to rounded-off corners.

These templates fall into the category of jigs because they have fences to register the workpiece easily. Just place the workpiece in the jig, and apply a clamp. You can then drill the necessary holes and trim the corners with a router and flush-trimming bit.

Finish

Rather than risk having the folding action gummed up by a finish that builds up a coating on the wood surface, I used an application of clear penetrating oil finish. This type of finish is specially formulated for outdoor use. Use one with an ultraviolet (UV) inhibitor to prolong the life of the wood.

STEP-BY-STEP

Selecting Stock

Cut the parts to the sizes specified on the cutting list. Unless you have a table saw with a substantial outfeed table, it's best to crosscut the parts to rough length before ripping them to width. **(Photo 1)** Remember the basic safety rules about wearing safety glasses and using a push stick. Give yourself an extra $\frac{1}{16}$ inch in width so you can plane each cut edge to remove saw marks. Miter one end of each leg, as specified in the drawings.

The cypress stock specified on the shopping list is narrower than the seat halves. To form the seat, you will need to edge-glue two panels, one 6 inches wide, the other $6\frac{3}{8}$ inches wide.

Use two pieces of the 1x4 stock specified for each panel. Joint the edges with a power planer (or with a hand plane). Lay out two pipe clamps with strips of scrap, called cauls, to prevent jaw damage. Finally, cut the various pieces of dowel.

Making Templates

For the sake of appearance, the legs and seat supports should be uniform. That means using templates for the seat support and legs that incorporate fences to capture and align the working parts.

Use $\frac{3}{4}$-inch-thick material for the templates: either plywood or medium-density

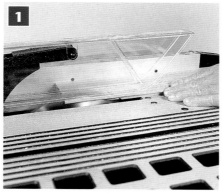

Rip the tongue and the groove from the flooring by first crosscutting the stock into the lengths needed for the project. For safety, feed the end of the stock along the rip fence using a push stick.

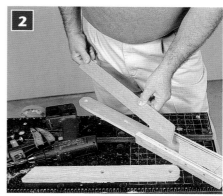

Fit the leg into the jig, and clamp it to a backup scrap and your workbench. The scrap prevents chipout when you drill the pivot holes. Turn the jig over, and reclamp to rout the radii on the leg top.

fiberboard (MDF). For the leg template, begin with a strip the same width as the leg, but 24 inches long. Lay out and drill the holes. Radius the top end. Nail fences to either side, as shown in the drawing on page 162. The foot-stop establishes the length of the legs. It is mitered at the same angle as the leg's foot. Cut it and nail it to the template. For the seat support, use a piece for the template that is longer and wider. Drill the guide hole for the pivot hole. Radius the corner. Nail the fences in place.

Legs and Seat Supports

This part of the project is largely a matter of clamping a part in the appropriate jig, then drilling the holes and trimming the edge with a router and flush-trimming bit. **(Photo 2)** When you drill the holes, clamp the work tightly against backup scrap so the bit doesn't lift chips from the margins of the hole as it exits. Also make sure that the holes are perpendicular. You'll find that the thickness of the template offers some help here. Once the holes are drilled and the edges shaped,

LEG ASSEMBLIES

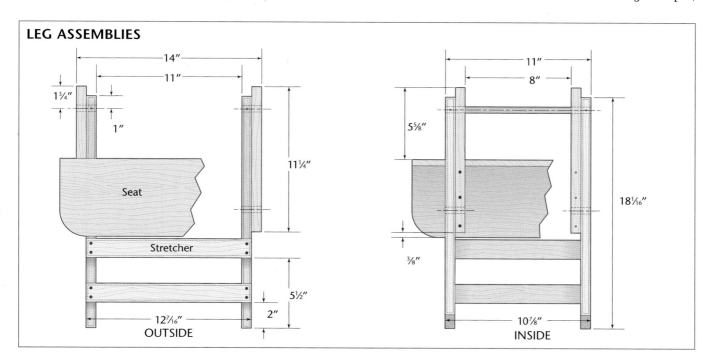

OUTSIDE

INSIDE

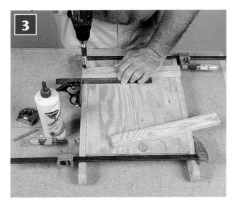

Clamp the legs to the jig so they are parallel, measure from corner to corner to check for
square; then attach the stretchers. Use a small
bead of glue on each leg; then drill pilots and
drive screws.

Place a nylon washer on the pivot, and
tape a second to the leg to align the seat
support and provide clearance for movement.
When the supports are positioned, clamp the
assembly to attach the seat.

Attach the seat panel to the supports for
the inside leg assembly by clamping the supports to the assembly jig. The pivot ends of
the supports rest on scraps of seat stock. Drill
pilots and drive screws.

sand the parts. I chamfered the edges of
the legs to make them more finished looking using a router and chamfering bit.
Another option is to use a block plane or
even a sander to ease the edge.

Seat Halves
Remove the clamps from the panels glued
up for the seat halves, and scrape away
any dried glue. Trim the panels to size,
and cut the rabbets that lock the two
halves together when the table-stool is set

up. I cut them with a router with a ³/₈-inch
rabbeting bit. Set up as if you were cutting
a half-lap, removing half the thickness
from each piece. When you are done,
radius the corners with a saber saw and
finish-sand the panels.

Stretchers
Once the parts have been ripped and
crosscut to size, chamfer the edges. I used
an awl to mark the centerpoint of each
pilot hole and put two screws in each end.

Outside Legs
Make two leg assemblies, which I'll call
the inside and the outside, by assembling
the parts around a scrap of plywood—an
assembly jig. **(Photo 3)** Start with the
wider of the two assemblies, and finish
with the narrower. This way you can
start with the full-size jig and simply cut
it down later. Start with an 11x16-inch
plywood jig. Set it on your workbench,
and place a leg against each side. Align
the feet flush with the bottom edge of the

LEG ASSEMBLIES AND SUPPORT LAYOUTS

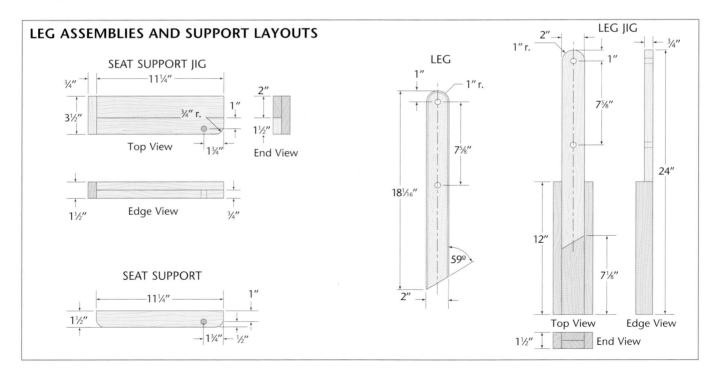

SEAT SUPPORT JIG

¾″ |— 11¼″ —|

3½″   ¾″ r.   1″

Top View   1¾″

2″

1½″

End View

1½″   Edge View   ¾″

SEAT SUPPORT

|— 11¼″ —| 1″

1½″

1¾″ — ½″

LEG

1″   1″ r.

7⅝″

18¹/₁₆″

59°

2″

LEG JIG

2″

1″ r.   1″

¾″

7⅝″

24″

12″

7⅛″

Top View   Edge View

1½″   End View

Lock the pivot pin into the leg with a finishing nail so it can't turn or pull out. The support pivots on the pin. Predrill for the nail to be sure that it will penetrate the pin without splitting the wood.

Nylon washers on the pivot pins offset the legs so they won't bind. Holding the washer while you insert the pivot pin is a challenge. Because tape might stick too well, I used a 3M Post-It Note to lower it in place.

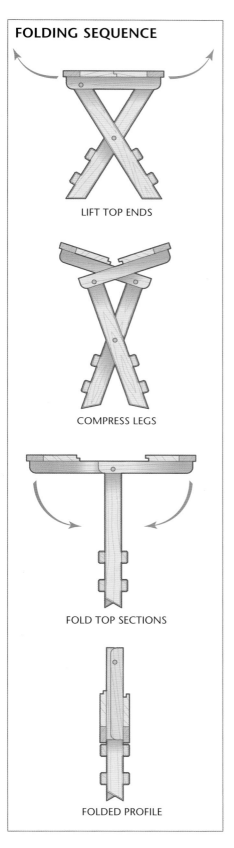

FOLDING SEQUENCE

LIFT TOP ENDS

COMPRESS LEGS

FOLD TOP SECTIONS

FOLDED PROFILE

plywood, and clamp the parts together. Turn the work over and glue, and screw the stretchers to the legs.

Add the seat half and its supports. Insert a pivot dowel in the holes at the tops of the legs. Drill a pilot hole, and drive a 4d finishing nail through the leg edge into the pivot, locking it. Make sure the pivot protrudes to the outside of the leg. Slip a nylon washer over each pivot, then a seat support. **(Photo 4)**

At the opposite end of the stretcher, tape a spacer washer to the side of the leg. Clamp the supports. Turn this assembly over, and align it on the appropriate seat half. Drill pilot holes, and drive 2-inch deck screws through the support into the seat. Be sure to test the action; the seat should swing easily.

Inside Legs

For the inside leg assembly, cut down the plywood assembly jig to 8 inches by 11¼ inches. Use it to position the seat supports while you attach them to the appropriate seat half. Set the plywood on the workbench, and butt a support against each side. Then you can line up the support ends flush with the top and bottom edges of the plywood, and clamp them together. **(Photo 5)**

Now place this on the seat half, align it, and mark it. Lift the supports off the seat, apply beads of glue, and reposition the supports. Drill pilot holes, and drive 2-inch deck screws through the supports into the seat. Next, add the legs and stretchers. Then insert the handle through the pivot holes in the supports. Place a nylon washer

over each end of the handle; then add a leg. Position the stretchers on the legs. Drill pilot holes, and drive two 1⅝-inch deck screws through each end of both stretchers. Finally, drill a pilot hole, and drive a 4d finishing nail through the edge of each leg into the handle. **(Photo 6)** You will need a very small-diameter pin-drill bit for this operation. The finishing nail locks the handle in the legs and traps the seat supports between the legs.

Leg Assemblies

The inside assembly should drop easily—but not too easily—into place between the legs of the outside assembly. Insert the remaining two pivot pins, and lock each one by driving a finishing nail through the inside leg edge. To position the nylon washers, try sticking them to a 3M Post-It Note and lowering them into the seam between the legs so you can slide the pivot pin through. **(Photo 7)** The iffy part is getting the Post-It to hold the washer long enough. When the assembly is complete, the table-stool should fold and unfold as shown in the folding sequence drawing at right.

Finishing

I applied a clear penetrating oil finish rated for outdoor use. Apply it liberally. Then allow about 20 minutes for it to work into the wood, and wipe off the excess with rags. It will take another two or three days for the finish to cure. Because the fumes present a hazard, work outdoors if at all possible. At minimum, open windows and ventilate the work area for safety.

Picnic Table & Benches

This easy-to-build picnic table is just the ticket for anyone who enjoys a backyard cookout. It is roomy enough to accommodate platters of burgers, barbecued chicken, huge salad bowls, and pitchers of iced tea, while the benches fill up with famished picnickers. And it is sturdy enough to take whatever an active cookout can dish out. The traditional sawbuck design has been around forever. There's nothing particularly fancy about it, but it

Yard and Garden Furniture

works well. If you maintain the set—limiting out-of-season exposure to the weather, renewing the finish every couple years—it could be around for a couple of generations. The bench's legs are farther apart than those on the table, which allows you to store the benches almost completely under the table and out of the way when the table and benches aren't in use. Another benefit is that the benches are much less likely to tip up when someone sits too close to the end of an unoccupied bench. The screwed and bolted construction is sturdy, but it allows you to get by with only basic tools for the project. Depending on your tastes, you can make this table of redwood or cedar. Or you can use construction-grade fir, which is what I did. Whatever you choose, you'll get a light but sturdy table that will be a favorite outdoor dining spot for years to come.

EXPLODED VIEW

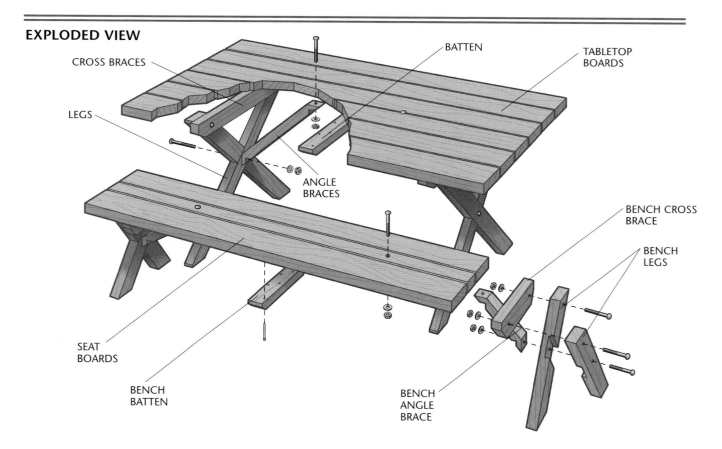

CUTTING LIST (Some parts are left long during construction.)

Part	Number	Thickness	Width	Length	Fir Stock
Tabletop boards	6	1½"	5¼"	70"	2x6
Batten	1	1½"	2½"	30"	2x3
Legs	4	1½"	2½"	41"	2x3
Cross braces	2	1½"	2½"	30"	2x3
Angle braces	2	1½"	2½"	22⁵⁄₁₆"	2x3
Seat boards	4	1½"	5⅜"	70"	2x6
Seat boards	2	1½"	2½"	70"	2x3
Bench battens	2	1½"	2½"	11¾"	2x3
Bench legs	8	1½"	2½"	19⅛"	2x3
Bench cross braces	4	1½"	2½"	11¾"	2x3
Bench angle braces	4	1½"	2½"	11¹¹⁄₁₆"	2x3

SHOPPING LIST

- 5 pcs. 2x6 12' Doug fir
- 8 pcs. 2x3 8' Doug fir
- 2" galvanized deck screws
- 3" galvanized deck screws
- 12 galvanized carriage bolts, with washers and nuts, ⁵⁄₁₆x3"
- 12 galvanized carriage bolts, with washers and nuts, ⁵⁄₁₆x3½"
- Water-repellent wood preservative

Picnic Table & Benches

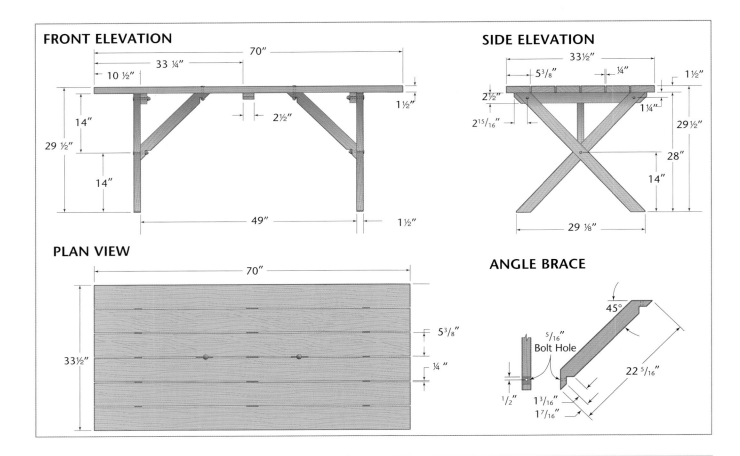

FRONT ELEVATION

70"
33 ¼"
10 ½"
1 ½"
14"
29 ½"
14"
2 ½"
49"
1 ½"

SIDE ELEVATION

33½"
5³/₈"
¼"
1 ½"
2½"
1¼"
2¹⁵/₁₆"
29 ½"
28"
14"
29 ⅛"

PLAN VIEW

70"
33½"
5³/₈"
¼"

ANGLE BRACE

45°
5/16"
Bolt Hole
22 ⁵/₁₆"
½"
1³/₁₆"
1⁷/₁₆"

BUILDER'S NOTES

This picnic table is a particularly good project for a handyman or novice woodworker because it doesn't take too long to make, and you don't need an extensive tool collection to build it. You can also build it with fairly inexpensive, construction-grade lumber. The finished project is handsome and practical, and your family will use it for years and years to come.

Materials
The table and benches pictured here are made of Douglas fir, a material commonly used to frame houses. Construction-grade lumber usually has lots of knots, cracks, and other defects. But if you choose your boards carefully, you can use it to build this project.

Look for straight flat boards with no loose knots. Inspect the edges for big splinters, dents, or other defects. Avoid boards with knots on the edges, wane, or major checks at the ends. Finding boards with no end checks is nearly impossible these days, but you cut a bit from most of the boards before you install them, so plan to discard the ends.

Tools and Techniques
Only a modest tool collection is needed to construct the picnic table and benches. A circular saw will handle most of the cutting, though you may want to use a gauge or homemade guide for some of the cuts, especially the miters.

You'll use a router primarily to "break" the edges of the boards, eliminating the hard edges that often are left after you've crosscut parts and sanded them smooth. Rout these edges with a ¹/₈-inch or ³/₁₆-inch roundover bit or a chamfering bit.

You'll also use the router to refine the cross-lap joints that join the legs into pairs. When doing this job, it's helpful to have a dado-and-planer bit, also called a bottom-cleaning bit, or mortising bit. Lacking this bit, you can use a chisel to pare the bottom of the laps smooth and flat.

Finally, you need a good drill-driver, because there are lots of screws to drive. A common accessory called a drill-and-drive assembly

is especially handy on this project. It's a two-piece unit. The socket base chucks into your drill, and the second piece has a predrill bit on one end and a screwdriver bit on the other. It locks quickly into the socket at either end. Drill a pilot hole, and then pop the bit holder out of the socket, flip it end-for-end, and reinsert it. Now you're ready to drive the screw.

Finish
I used ordinary water repellent as the only finish on my table and benches. It is easy to apply, but doesn't last. Scrub with a bleach solution occasionally, let the wood dry, and then reapply the finish.

Lay the boards *across a pair of pipe clamps. Align the ends; use spacers to set the gaps; then tighten the clamps to hold everything in place. Set the batten in place, and fasten it to each board with two screws.*

To lay out the miters on the legs, *use a sliding T-bevel, also called a bevel square. Set the blade of the T-bevel to the correct angle using a protractor. Then scribe along the blade to mark the cut line.*

Set one board on top of the other, *the tops flush against a straight board. Set the distance between the feet to 29⅛ in., and scribe along the edge of the top leg with a knife, marking the leg that's underneath.*

STEP-BY-STEP

Cutting the Tabletop Parts

The tabletop is made of 2x6 boards joined by a batten and cross braces. The main job here is preparing the boards—sanding them and perhaps rounding- over or chamfering all their edges.

Begin by cutting the tabletop boards and batten to length. With a roundover bit or a chamfering bit in your router, rout the edges of the boards to soften them. Be sure you work the ends as well as the long edges. Rout the "exposed" edges of the batten as well; the edges that will be against the tabletop boards need not be routed.

Sand the surfaces, especially the top faces, with a belt sander equipped with an 80-grit belt. Brush all the sanding dust from the boards; then hit them again with a 120-grit belt.

Assembling the Tabletop

Lay out the boards across a pair of pipe clamps. Leave gaps of approximately ¼ inch between them. Make spacers from scraps of ¼-inch plywood to ensure the boards are spaced uniformly. Tighten the clamps, and lay the batten across the center of the boards. Drill pilot holes; then drive 2-inch galvanized deck screws through the batten into the boards. Be sure that the batten is fastened to each board using two screws. **(Photo 1)**

Mitering the Legs

The legs are made of 2x3s. They cross in the familiar sawbuck style and are joined with a cross-lap joint.

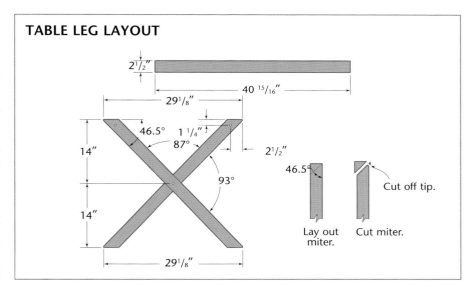

TABLE LEG LAYOUT

2½"

40 15/16"

29⅛"

14"

46.5°   1¼"
87°

14"

2½"

93°

29⅛"

46.5°

Cut off tip.

Lay out miter.

Cut miter.

Begin by cutting the four legs to the rough length specified on the cutting list. Miter the ends at 43.5 degrees (leaving a 46.5 degree angle). If you have a power miter saw, cutting these miters is quick and easy. With a handheld circular saw, however, you need to lay out the cut line. **(Photo 2)** The precise length of the legs is not crucial as long as they are all exactly the same length. Also, be sure the cuts on each leg are parallel with each other. After making the cut, nip off the sharp point formed, as shown in the illustration above.

Laying Out the Cross-lap Joints

Lay out the legs in an "X" shape. The leg on top may tend to tip, so prop it with 2x4 scraps. Place the angled ends of the boards on a straight board or a wall, and keep them flush to it while you adjust the legs. Slide the legs sideways until the feet are 29⅛ inches apart.

Use a utility knife to mark the shoulders of the cross-lap joint on the bottom leg. **(Photo 3)** By using a knife to score the cut line and then cutting exactly to the mark, you will get tight-fitting joints. Slicing through the surface fibers of the wood before cutting with a saw also ensures that you'll get a crisp, splinter-free shoulder. Now turn the boards over, adjust the spacing as before, and mark the other half of the joint.

Cut laps and Assemble the Legs

Rough-out the cross lap with a circular saw, then clean it up with a router fitted

Picnic Table & Benches

A router fitted with a dado-and-planer bit will level and smooth the bottom of the laps, ensuring a strong joint. The bit's shank-mounted bearing rides on the shoulder of the lap, preventing the bit from overcutting.

With the half-laps test-fitted, mark the edges of each joint on the opposite leg. Use these marks to guide your router as you round over the edges of the legs—skip the portion that falls within the half-lap joint.

holes through the legs and the brace at the same time. If your bit isn't long enough to penetrate both the leg and brace, drill through each leg far enough to mark the brace, then remove the leg assembly, and complete the holes in the brace. Don't fasten the legs to the braces yet.

Install the Legs and Cross Braces
Position the cross braces on the bottom of the tabletop. Drill pilot holes and drive 3-inch galvanized deck screws through the brace into the tabletop. A drill-and-drive accessory makes this job easy. **(Photo 6)** Bolt the legs to the braces.

Make and Install the Angle Braces
The angle braces lock the legs at right angles from the tabletop and keep it from wobbling. They run from the cross-lap joint of the legs up to the underside of the tabletop.

Cut the braces to the dimensions specified on the cutting list. Miter the ends, as shown in the "Angle Brace" layout drawing, and cut the notches with a saber saw. Drill a $5/16$-inch-diameter hole in each notch, as shown in the illustration on page 166.

To install one of these braces, hold it in place against the leg and the tabletop. Be sure the mitered ends sit flush with the surfaces they contact. Using the holes in the brace as guides, start drilling into the leg assembly and into the tabletop. **(Photo 7)** The bolt hole on the tabletop is centered on a gap between two tabletop boards, and the brace is very helpful in getting the hole started properly. Take away the brace and complete the holes.

Use 3-inch-long $5/16$-inch galvanized carriage bolts to fasten the braces to the tabletop and through the cross lap joints in each leg assembly.

But for a finish, the table is now complete, so set it on its feet and admire your handiwork!

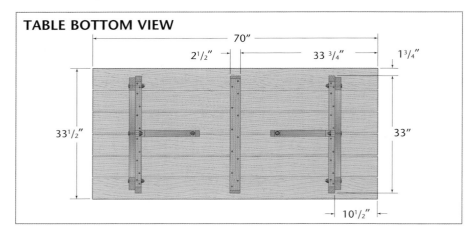

TABLE BOTTOM VIEW

70"
2½"   33¾"   1¾"
33½"   33"
10½"

with a dado-and-planer bit. To do this, set the circular saw's cutting depth to just under $3/4$ inch. Cut the shoulders of the lap first, being very careful to skim the inner edge of the cut line. Then hog out the waste between the shoulders with repeated cuts. When you are done, the bottom of the lap most likely will be rough and uneven. The router will take care of that.

The dado-and-planer bit has a bearing mounted on the shank above the cutters. Run along the shoulder of the lap, this bearing will prevent the bit from widening the cut. **(Photo 4)** The bit's cutting edges are designed to clean the bottom of the cut. Adjust the depth of cut just a little shy of $3/4$ inch. Resting the router on the face of the leg, sweep through the lap, leveling its bottom surface. Rout both laps; then fit the joint together. If necessary, adjust the router's depth of cut and make another pass over each leg to refine the fit of the joint.

Be sure the leg pieces fit together well, but don't fasten them together yet. Mark the edges of the half-lap joints so you don't round-over that part of the leg when you round-over the rest. **(Photo 5)**

Make the Cross Braces
The cross braces have the same dimensions as the batten and serve a similar purpose. They're screwed to the underside of the tabletop, near the ends, and help maintain the board spacing. They are installed on edge, though, rather than flat like the batten, and once the cross braces are installed, you'll bolt the leg assemblies to them.

Cut the braces to the dimensions on the cutting list. Rout the exposed edges, and bevel the ends of the braces, as shown in the table bottom view drawing.

To drill holes for the assembly bolts, start by clamping the cross brace to your workbench. Then clamp a leg assembly to the brace, just as it will be when assembled. Mark the hole locations; then drill the

Build the Benches
The benches are built in the same way as the table. The parts you make, the sequence of steps, the assembly approaches are all the same as they were in constructing the table. Only the dimensions are different. And of course you'll build two of them, one for each side of the table.

Here is a work-sequence checklist for building the benches:

Yard and Garden Furniture

- Cut the seat boards. Sand them and "break" the edges.
- Cut the battens. Use them to assemble the seats.
- Lay out the legs.
- Cut the joinery, and assemble the legs.
- Make the cross braces.
- Fasten the braces to the seats.
- Bolt the legs in place.
- Make and install the angle braces.

Finishing

You can use whatever finish appeals to you on this project, but be sure to finish the table and benches promptly. Although Douglas fir is a strong, durable wood, your picnic set will last years longer if you finish the wood and remember to maintain the finish over the years.

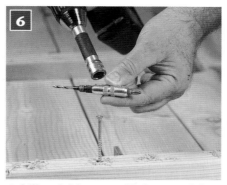

A drill-and-drive assembly has a predrill bit with a countersink on one end, and a Phillips bit on the other. You drill a pilot hole and countersink, then flip the bit assembly to expose the driver and drive the screw.

To help get the bolt holes started in the right spots and in the correct alignment, hold the angle brace in position. Use the holes in it to guide the drill bit as you bore into the tabletop and leg assembly.

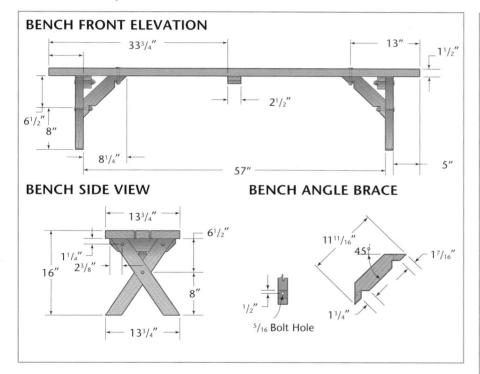

BENCH FRONT ELEVATION

33³/₄″   13″   1¹/₂″
6¹/₂″   8″   8¹/₄″   57″   5″   2¹/₂″

BENCH SIDE VIEW

13³/₄″   6¹/₂″
1¹/₄″   2³/₈″   16″   8″   13³/₄″

BENCH ANGLE BRACE

11¹¹/₁₆″   45°   1⁷/₁₆″   1³/₄″
¹/₂″   5/16 Bolt Hole

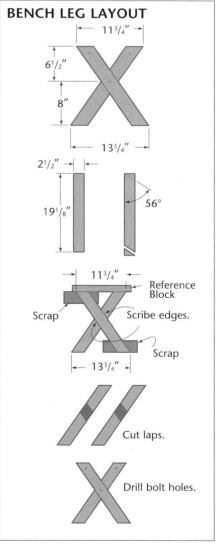

BENCH LEG LAYOUT

11³/₄″   6¹/₂″   8″   13³/₄″
2¹/₂″   19¹/₈″   56°
11³/₄″   Reference Block
Scrap   Scribe edges.   Scrap   13³/₄″
Cut laps.
Drill bolt holes.

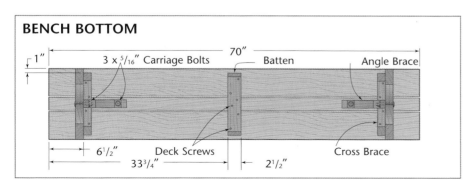

BENCH BOTTOM

1″   70″
3 x 5/16″ Carriage Bolts   Batten   Angle Brace
6¹/₂″   Deck Screws   Cross Brace
33³/₄″   2¹/₂″

Picnic Table & Benches

Porch Swing

If you live in a house that actually has a front porch instead of a sunny deck, here's a valuable and rewarding accessory for it: a porch swing. The swing is wide enough for two adults, or an adult and a couple of kids. Though the finished project is a fairly large piece of furniture, it doesn't take too long to make, and your porch swing will continue paying you back for years and years. In past generations, before people had so

Yard and Garden Furniture

many demands placed on their time, they knew about quiet relaxation—houses had porches and porches had swings. You could get out of the sun and into the shade, catch a passing breeze, chat with your spouse, and maybe even let the gentle rocking motion lull you into a doze. The design of this swing adapts well to several different house styles. It won't look out of place hanging on the porch of a Victorian mansion, an Arts and Crafts–style bungalow, or a turn-of-the-century row house. While the simple elegance of hanging the swing from the rafters has great appeal, you might not have the ideal spot to hang this project. If you run into this problem, you can build a pair of well-braced A-frames supporting a single beam and hang the swing from that, or build the glider stand I've included at the end of this chapter. It sits nicely on a deck or even the lawn.

EXPLODED VIEW

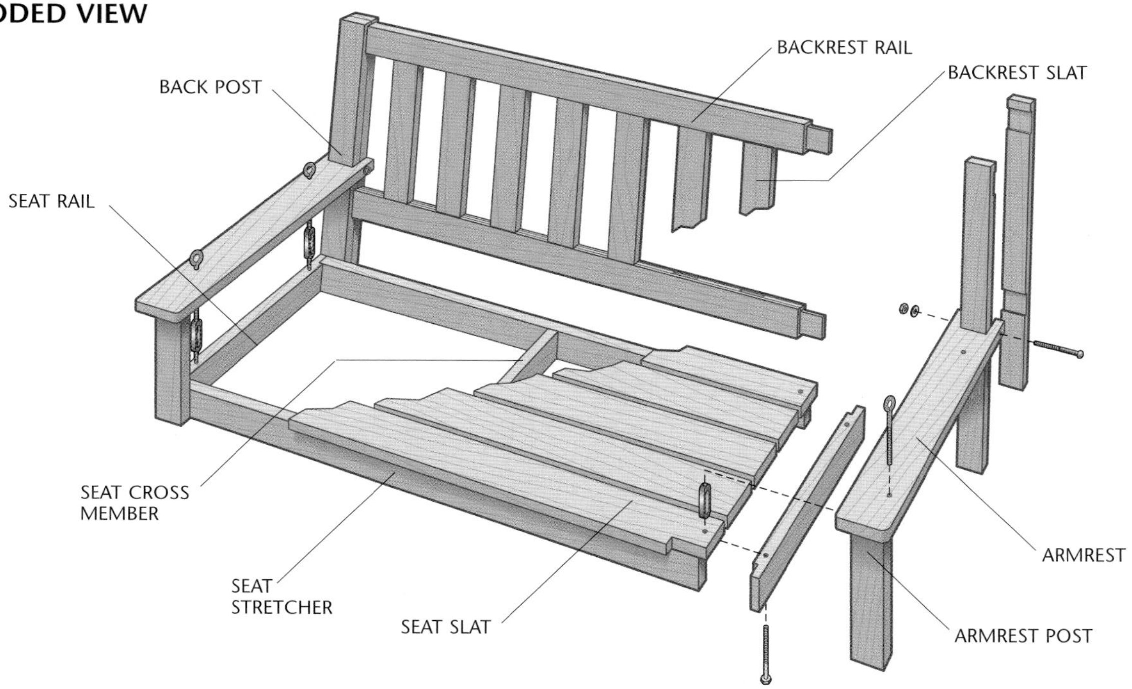

CUTTING LIST (Some parts are left long during construction.)

Part	Number	Thickness	Width	Length	Cypress Stock
Seat rails	2	1″	2½″	19¼″	5/4x6
Seat stretchers	2	1″	2½″	48″	5/4x6
Seat cross member	1	1″	2½″	17¼″	5/4x6
Back posts	2	2″	2½″	30″	5/4x6
Backrest rails	2	1″	2½″	49″	5/4x6
Backrest slats	7	1″	2½″	10⅝″	5/4x6
Armrest posts	2	1″	2½″	12″	5/4x6
Armrests	2	1″	4½″	25½″	5/4x6
Seat slats	5	1″	3¾″	50″	5/4x6

SHOPPING LIST

- 7 pcs. 5/4x6 8′ cypress
- 2½″ galvanized deck screws
- 3″ galvanized deck screws
- 2 galvanized carriage bolts, 5/16″x2½″, with nuts and washers
- 2 galvanized carriage bolts, 5/16″x3½″, with nuts and washers
- 2 galvanized carriage bolts, ¼″x5″, with nuts and washers
- 4 galvanized carriage bolts, 5/16″x8″, with nuts
- 4 galvanized eyebolts, 5/16″x4″, with nuts
- 4 galvanized coupling nuts, 5/16″
- 4 galvanized screw eyes, 5/16″x3″
- 6 snap links
- Chain

ELEVATIONS

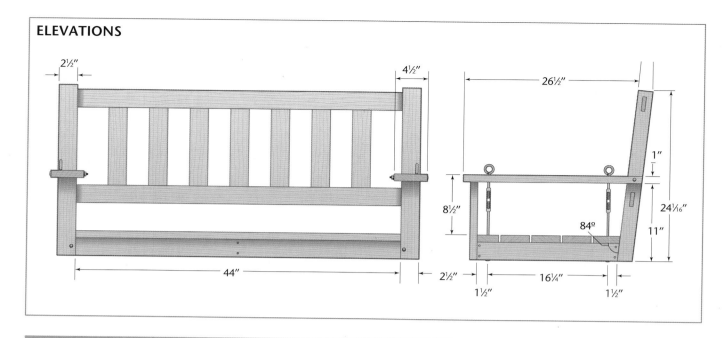

BUILDER'S NOTES

Even for a modestly experienced woodworking hobbyist, this Porch Swing is a manageable project.

Materials

You'll build your porch swing out of wood, fasteners, and glue. To hang the swing, you'll need lengths of chain and a few specialized pieces of hardware to link the chain to the swing and to the suspension points on your house or deck.

Let's look at the wood first. The optional glider stand was built of cypress. You can use any "outdoor" wood available to you: redwood, cedar, pressure-treated, white oak, or even exotics like ipé, jarrah, and teak. You can use any wood, as long as it is available in ⁵⁄₄ stock (pronounced "five-quarter"), which is really about 1 inch thick. Typically, ⁵⁄₄ cypress is stocked in a nominal 6-inch width with radiused edges, intended for use as decking. Most of the stock in this project is 2½

inches wide, so if you rip a ⁵⁄₄x6 board in half, then re-rip each half to 2½ inches, you'll slice off the radiused edges in the process.

Where I used glue in this project, I chose polyurethane glue. This is a good waterproof glue that tends to expand as it cures, filling all the gaps in a joint. In certain spots in the project, I wanted that to happen. I don't want moisture to penetrate the mortise-and-tenon joints between the back posts and the backrest rails, or the joints between the backrest slats and the lower rail.

The glue has two drawbacks, one of which is a direct consequence of the glue's foamy nature. It tends to well up out of joints as it cures, so you do have some cleanup work to do in inside corners. A chisel works well.

The other drawback is that the glue will stain your hands. The stains do wear off, but it'll take a week or more, so wear latex gloves when you use the stuff.

If you can find galvanized fasteners in the sizes specified, use those, but some of the larger bolts are hard to find. On the swing shown, the entire suspension system is composed of zinc-plated hardware. My experience is that zinc-plated hardware doesn't rust quickly, and I suspect it will easily last a decade or two.

I used repair links to hang the swing so I wouldn't have to pry links of the chain open, then squeeze them closed. On the glider, I used S-hooks. Examine both and decide for yourself which is more appropriate for your application.

Tools and Techniques

A table saw is essential for this project. You'll use it for all sorts of sawing operations, but the one it does best is the one needed for this project: ripping. An inexpensive bench-top model is fine.

Another very useful tool is a long drill bit. To bore some of the bolt holes, the conventional 2- to 3-inch-long

bit is inadequate. The bolt that fastens the armrest to the back post is 5 inches long. You can't drill this hole without a 7- or 8-inch-long bit, and the extra length makes it easier to keep the bit aligned as you drill. The long bit also helps carry hanger-bolt holes from the seat frame up to the armrests.

Finish

I used a semitransparent water-based stain on the swing and glider, which provided fast drying time and easy cleanup. To me, the color provided by the stain punched up the appearance of the project.

In addition to providing color, the pigment in the stain shields the wood from the sun's harmful ultraviolet rays. This is especially worthwhile if you place the swing and glider in a sunny spot.

Other outdoor finishes, ranging from paint on down to a simple water-repellent preservative will also finish this project nicely.

STEP-BY-STEP

Making the Seat Frame

The seat frame consists of the two stretchers, two rails, and a cross member. All are cut from stock that's been ripped to 2½ inches wide. One end (the back) of the rails and the cross member is mitered at 6 degrees (leaving an 84° angle).

Except for the fact that the back stretcher is canted, the seat frame is a simple box. Use rabbet joints at the four corners and butt joints between the stretchers and cross member. Glue the joints with waterproof glue, reinforcing each one with two 2½-inch galvanized screws.

The challenge here is cutting the rabbets. While the rabbets are only ⅜ inch deep, they are 1 inch wide, which is wider than the cut made by the typical rabbeting bit for a router.

To begin, put the two rails together, and mark the outside faces. You will cut the rabbets in the unmarked, inner faces. Use a straight bit to rout these rabbets, guiding the router along a T-square or other straightedge clamped to the rail. Be sure you don't cut the back rabbets square to the rail edges if you use a T-square; the rabbet's shoulder must be angled. **(Photo 1)**

Drill countersunk pilot holes in the rails, and screw the rails and stretchers together without glue to check the fit of the cross member between the stretchers. It should fit snugly without bowing the stretchers out or pulling them in. Make it fit; then mark and drill countersunk pilot holes through the stretchers. Dismantle the frame, and then put it all back together using waterproof glue in each joint.

Before moving on, lay out and drill the 5/16-inch-diameter holes for the hanger

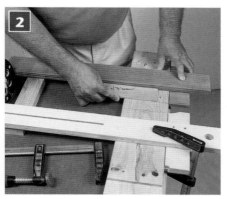

Clamp a fence *across the workpiece to cut the 1-in.-wide rabbets that join the seat frame. Use a spacer between the fence and the router on the first cut, a thinner spacer on the second, and none for the final cut.*

With two fences *guiding your router, there's little chance of overcutting the dado. Use a setup gauge like the one shown on page 15 to position the fences in relation to the dado layout, as shown here.*

bolts in the seat rails. It's important that these holes be perpendicular. The hole locations are shown in the "Elevations" drawing, at left.

Making the Back Posts

The backrest assembly consists of the posts, rails, and slats. You'll need to make the posts first.

Despite the large through-mortises, making the back posts is a relatively simple job. First cut dadoes across a piece of 5/4x6 stock; then rip the board in half and glue the pieces together face-to-face. The dadoes combine to form through-mortises. After the glue has cured, rip the post to its finished width, and crosscut it to the finished length.

It is common practice to cut the mortise for a joint first and then cut the tenon to fit the mortise. And that's the technique you'll use here. The width of the tenon shoulders

is important, however, because of the slot you'll cut in the rails for the backrest slats. The slot needs to be ¼ inch deep to provide a strong joint between rail and slat, and you don't want to cut into the tenon. So size the dadoes with care, and if you do make an error, it's better if the dadoes are slightly undersized.

The workpieces should be about 3 or 4 inches longer than the finished posts; the idea is to leave an equal amount of waste on each end to be trimmed away. Lay out the dadoes from a centerline, making sure that they are the correct distance apart.

Cut the dadoes using a router and a straight bit. Make several passes to complete the 2-inch-wide cut. Clamp a guide on both sides of the cut. **(Photo 2)** This eliminates the need to keep moving the guide, and the chance that a feed error will result in cutting the dado too wide.

After the dadoes are cut, rip the work-

PLAN VIEW

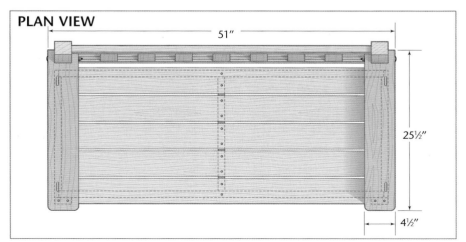

51"

25½"

4½"

SEAT FRAME

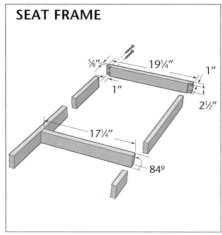

5/8" 19¼" 1"

1"

2½"

17¼"

84°

To cut the grooves in the backrest rails, set the fence and cut the shoulders of the groove, as shown here. To complete the groove, move the fence about 3/16 in. farther away from the blade, and make two more cuts.

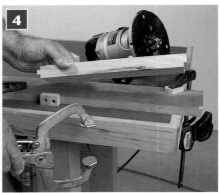

Make a fixture to hold the slats. Screw a stop to a piece of MDF, and clamp it to your bench. Butt the end of the workpiece against the stop, with the side against the MDF. Secure with a locking C-clamp.

piece in half; sand the gluing surfaces well; and use waterproof glue to bond the two pieces face-to-face. Be sure the pieces align to give you proper mortises and that you clean up glue squeeze-out inside the mortises. After the glue cures, rip the posts to finished widths. Crosscut them to finished length, based on the final positions of the mortises.

Before moving to the next step, drill holes in the posts and the seat frame for the mounting bolts. Bolt the posts to the frame so that you can attach the rails to the assembly as you make them.

Cutting the Backrest Rails

Rip and crosscut the two backrest rails to the dimensions specified in the cutting list. As you do this, be sure you rip away any radiused edges. You want square edges on the rails.

Cut a slot in one edge of each rail for the backrest slats. The slot is 3/8 inch wide and 1/4 inch deep. Because these slots are cut end-to-end, the table saw is the best tool for the job. To make this cut, you need to remove the blade guard from the saw. Be sure to replace the guard as soon as you have completed the cuts.

Adjust the blade height to 1/4 inch, and position the rip fence 5/16 inch from the blade. Make the first cut; then flip the board end for end, and make the second cut on the same edge. These cuts will form the shoulders of the slot. Adjust the fence so that it is about 3/16 inch farther away from the blade, and make two more cuts in each rail. (Photo 3) If necessary, adjust the fence a third time, and make two more cuts.

Lastly, cut the tenons on the ends of the rails. To lay out the tenon shoulders, hold the rail against the posts, which are mounted to the seat frame. Doing this will ensure that all the parts fit together. (If you cut the tenon shoulders too far apart or too close together, the backrest mounting bolts won't line up with the holes in the frame when you attach the glued-up backrest assembly.)

Cut the tenons next, using a router and the tenoning jig shown on page 18. Take your time and get a good fit. Remember that the tenon ends will be visible in the assembled backrest.

The Backrest Slats

Rip and crosscut the seven slats to the dimensions specified by the cutting list. Use a rabbeting bit in your router to cut stub tenons on the ends to fit the grooves in the rails. Cut a rabbet across one face of the slat; then turn it over, and rabbet the second face. The wood that remains between the rabbets is the tenon.

Install a pilot bearing that will give you a 1/4-inch-wide rabbet. (Photo 4) Put the bit in your router, and adjust the depth of cut to 1/4 inch. Cut two rabbets to form a test tenon and check how it fits in one of the grooves. If it's too tight, increase the depth of cut. If it's too loose, decrease the depth of cut. When the setting is just right, cut all the rabbets.

Sand the slats; then round the edges using a 1/4-inch-radius roundover bit.

Assembling the Backrest

Before gluing up the backrest parts, do a complete test-fit without glue. Collect all the parts; adjust your clamps; and be sure that all the parts fit—tenons in grooves, tenons in mortises—and that everything really does align properly.

You also need to work out how far apart you want to space the slats; then cut spacers that both locate the slats and plug the groove in the lower rail. Filling the groove in the lower rail, between the slats, will extend the life of the swing by keeping out water. Rip a strip of stock that just fits the groove. After you settle on a slat spacing, crosscut the strip into pieces that just fill the gaps.

Once you are fully satisfied that the assembly works and that you can fit all the parts in place easily, open the glue and get started. I used polyurethane glue for this assembly. It is waterproof and expands as it

BACK POST

2"
2½"
11½"
2"
1"
30"
¼"
5½"
2¹¹⁄₁₆"
¹³⁄₁₆"
24³⁄₁₆"
84°

BACKREST

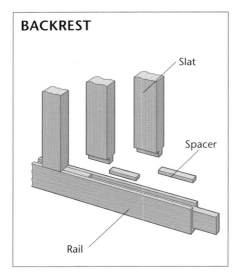

Slat

Spacer

Rail

cures—so it will fill seams and small gaps—keeping moisture from penetrating into the joints. Wear latex gloves during glue-up.

Apply the glue to only one of the mating surfaces. The other surface should be dampened with a rag, because the glue needs moisture to set. Use a disposable brush to spread the glue in the groove of the lower rail. Dampen an end spacer and press it into the groove, with its end flush with the rail tenon's shoulder. Dampen the end of a slat and press it into the groove, up against the spacer. Insert another spacer, then a slat, and continue filling the lower rail. **(Photo 5)**

Now dampen the upper rail's groove. Spread glue on the tenons of all the slats. Fit the top rail over the slats' stub tenons; then apply three pipe or bar clamps across the rails. **(Photo 6)** Be sure to use cauls between the clamp jaws and the rails so that the wood isn't crushed as you tighten the clamps. This is a good time to take a break, if you need one.

If you want to keep going, apply glue to the tenons at one end of the backrest; dampen the mortises in one of the posts; and join the two. **(Photo 7)** Apply glue on the other end of the rails, and add the second post. Apply clamps, at least one across each face of the assembly, and set the unit aside while the glue cures.

Joining the Backrest to the Seat Frame

After the glue has cured, remove the clamps. It's likely that some glue will have foamed out of the joints here and there. Slice it off with a utility knife, and then sand it smooth.

When the touch-up sanding is done, glue and bolt the backrest assembly to the seat frame. Use galvanized carriage bolts, orienting the bolts so that the washers and nuts are inside the seat frame.

Installing the Armrest Supports

Cut the armrest supports to the dimensions on the cutting list. Round-over the long edges using a router and ¼-inch-radius roundover bit. Mount the supports to the front of the seat frame, using glue and a ⁵⁄₁₆-inch by 2½-inch carriage bolt. Orient the bolt so that the washer and nut are inside the frame.

Making the Seat Boards

The seat consists of five identical slats, which are glued and screwed to the seat frame rails and cross member. You have

Begin with the lower rail clamped in the workbench vise with the groove up. After spreading polyurethane glue in the groove, dampen the mating parts with a wet rag before pressing them into place.

Dampen the mortises in the post, and apply glue to the tenons on the rails. Work the tips of the tenons into the mortises; then drive the parts together. When both posts are joined to the rails, apply pipe clamps.

Apply glue to the upper tenons of each slat, and dampen the groove in the upper rail. Align the first tenon, then lower the rail as you align the rest. Then apply two clamps, one parallel with each end slat.

The front seat board must fit closely where it fits around the armrest supports. Center it; then transfer the support locations directly to the slat. Use a utility knife to mark the slat; then cut inside the knife cuts with a saber saw.

to install them before the armrests, which restrict your ability to drive screws into the ends of the seat boards.

Cut the slats to the dimensions on the cutting list. Lay out and countersink pilot holes for the mounting screws. Plan for two screws at each rail and at the cross member. Using that ¼-inch roundover bit, radius all the edges of all five slats.

Fitting the two outer slats at the posts and armrest supports requires a little extra work. The front slat overhangs the front seat stretcher by about ¾ inch. To mark the slat for notching, put it on the seat frame, centered end-to-end. Butt it against the back of the armrest supports, and mark the slat using a square. **(Photo 8)** Make the cut using a saber saw.

With the front slat fitted, lay the others in place, spacing them about ⁵⁄₁₆-inch

to ⅜-inch apart. Use temporary wooden spacers inserted between the slats to get consistent spacing. You'll probably need to trim the back slat about ⅛ inch at the posts to make it fit.

When the slats are fitted, drive the screws in the previously drilled pilots.

Lastly, extend the hanger bolt holes you drilled previously in the seat rails, boring them on through the seat boards.

Shaping the Armrests

Cut the armrests to the dimensions on the cutting list, and lay out the notch for the post. Clamp a block temporarily to the front of the post. Rest the arm on the front support and this block; center it on the post, and then extend cut lines from the post sides along the arm. **(Photo 9)**

Cut the lines using a saber saw. Drill a

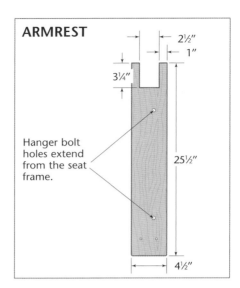

ARMREST

2½"
1"
3¼"
4½"
25½"

Hanger bolt holes extend from the seat frame.

Clamp a temporary support block to the post. Set the armrest on the block, and center it on the post. Butt a rule against the side of the post, and scribe along its inside edge on the armrest, as shown here.

Drill a large hole that is just touching the baseline. Use your saber saw to cut first to one kerf, then the other. Refine the fit by chiseling or filing the cut edge to an angle that matches the cant of the post.

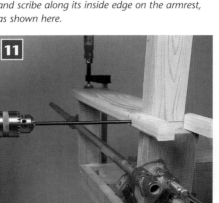

Draw a straight line across the back of the post, representing the axis of the hole. Then start drilling the hole. Before you penetrate too far, stop and check the angle carefully both from the side and from above.

Drop an eye bolt through the hole in the armrest, and slide a carriage bolt up through the hole drilled in the seat. Spin nuts onto each, then join with a coupling nut. Tighten the machine nuts against the coupling nut.

hole in the center of the waste, just touching the baseline. Use the saber saw to cut from the hole to either side. **(Photo 10)**

When the armrest fits around the post, undercut the sawed base line using a chisel (or a file), so the arm will fit tight to the post on top.

Lastly, round the corners of the armrest using a belt sander, and round-over the edges using the roundover bit.

Mounting the Armrests

Countersink pilot holes for the screws, and drill the hole for the bolt before applying glue. **(Photo 11)** Place the bolt hole where it will pass through the meat of the armrest and the post.

Insert a long drill bit or dowel up through the hanger bolt holes in the seat, and mark the underside of the armrests. Remove the armrests, and drill the holes.

Now you're ready to attach the armrests. Apply the glue to the tops of the front supports and to the inner edges of the cutout at the back of the armrest. Dampen the mating surfaces. Install the armrests, and drive the screws into the front supports. Insert the bolts through their holes, with the heads to the outside. Add the washer and nut; then tighten it as much as you can.

If the shank protrudes from the nut by more than ¼ inch, cut it off with a hacksaw. File any sharp burrs from the cut end. Remove the alignment blocks, or they'll end up glued to the swing.

Applying the Finish

You can apply any finish you want to the swing. The one shown in this chapter has

a semitransparent stain.

Apply the finish to all surfaces, not just the upper ones. Brush it on the underside of the armrest and the seat slats, and coat the edges of the seat slats.

Assembling the Swing

Each hanger bolt assembly consists of a ⁵⁄₁₆-inch carriage bolt 8 inches long, a ⁵⁄₁₆-inch eyebolt 4 inches long, two ⁵⁄₁₆-inch nuts, and a ⁵⁄₁₆-inch coupling nut. Insert the carriage bolt up through the seat board, and the eyebolt down through the armrest. Thread a nut onto each, then join the two with the coupling nut. **(Photo 12)** When the coupling nut is tight, jam the other nuts against it so that everything is locked together.

Suspend the swing from substantial frame members, like the porch's ceiling joists or roof rafters—after all, it has to support the dynamic weight of two or more "swingers." Pick a pair of joists or rafters that are at least as far apart as the width of the swing. Make sure the two points are on the same level. Drill pilot holes, and turn screw eyes into them.

Attach the chain to the swing's eyebolts using snap clips or repair links. Run chain from the eyebolts to the screw eyes, and use more repair links to connect the chains to the screw eyes.

From time to time, check that the screw eyes are still securely anchored in the joists or rafters.

GLIDER STAND

If you don't have a suitable porch for a rafter-hung swing, consider building this optional glider stand. In a glider, the seat is suspended so that it moves back and forth in a linear motion. You don't find your feet lifting off the floor.

To build the glider stand, you need a few extra boards, and a slightly different selection of hardware. When you're building the swing itself, you can skip the parts that involve installing the hanger bolts.

Cutting the Parts

With the exceptions of the arms and the swing beams, all the glider stand parts are crosscut from 2x4s. Cut the feet, legs, stretchers, and blocks to the lengths on the cutting list.

Lay out the tapers on the foot pieces, as shown in the "Glider-Stand Elevations" drawing, and cut them with a circular saw. Sand the cut edges.

Cut the arms from the 2x6; then rip the remaining piece in half, forming the two swing beams, which are mounted under the swing bench. If necessary, crosscut these beams to length.

Using a roundover bit in a router, soften all the edges of the beams and the arms. You can radius the edges of the stretchers, but wait until after test-fitting the stand to round the legs and feet.

Cutting the Leg Joinery

You'll cut both edge-laps and cross-laps cut into the legs. The edge-laps join them to the feet, while the cross-laps join them to the stretchers. As a part of the cross-lap joint between leg and stretcher, the stretchers are lapped, too.

Nowhere to hang your swing? Build this portable glider stand for the deck or lawn.

EXPLODED VIEW

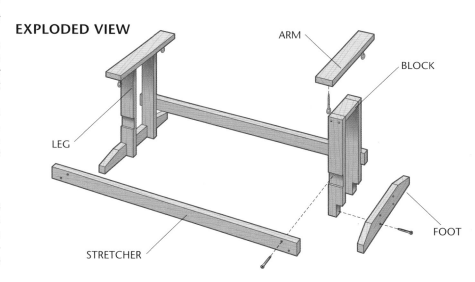

ARM

BLOCK

LEG

STRETCHER

FOOT

CUTTING LIST

Part	Number	Thickness	Width	Length	Cypress Stock
Feet	2	1½"	3½"	28"	2x4
Legs	4	1½"	3½"	25½"	2x4
Stretchers	2	1½"	3½"	67"	2x4
Blocks	2	1½"	3½"	5"	2x4
Arms	2	1½"	5½"	26"	2x6
Seat beams*	2	1½"	2½"	65"	2x6

*Not shown. See elevation drawing, p. 193

SHOPPING LIST

- 2 pcs. 2x4 8' cypress
- 1 pc. 2x4 10' cypress
- 1 pc. 2x6 10' cypress
- 8 screw eyes, $^5/_{16}$"x2½"
- 8 S-hooks
- chain
- 3" galvanized deck screws
- 2" galvanized deck screws

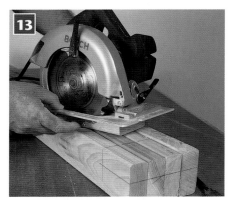

Clamp the legs together, and set your circular saw to cut the thickness of a 2x4. The first cut will be just inside the shoulder line. Shift to the foot end, and make repeated cuts to remove all the waste.

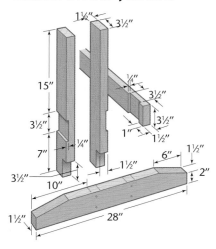

Screw an MDF base to two strips, spacing the strips just far enough apart to fit a 2x4 between them. When you align the resulting jig on a layout line, you will always cut a lap that's exactly the correct width.

GLIDER-STAND ELEVATIONS

GLIDER STAND JOINERY

This joint is a lot simpler to make than a mortise-and-tenon joint, and it provides solid contact between the joint's shoulders to help the assembly resist the stresses of the swinging.

To cut the edge laps, you have to remove a pretty big block of wood. You can use a band saw or saber saw, a radial-arm or sliding-compound miter saw, or even a circular saw.

If you use a saw with a circular blade, cut the edge laps all at once by stacking the legs together. Mark the line for the shoulder cut. Set the depth of cut equal to the thickness of a 2x4. **(Photo 13)** Cut just inside the shoulder line first; then shift to the opposite end of the lap, and start making closely spaced kerfs. Clean up the cut with a chisel.

Cutting the Cross Laps
The cross-lap cuts in the legs and in the stretchers are exactly the same. Because you're making eight of these cuts, it is worthwhile to make a jig, like the one used for cutting tenons, and do them with a router. **(Photo 14)** You will need to lay out only one shoulder for each lap, and the jig will control the cut width from there. Fit the jig over the workpiece; align it with your layout mark; then cut the lap in one pass.

To simplify layout as much as possible, set the two stretchers side by side. Measure 1 inch from each end, and extend a line across the face of both stretchers. This is the shoulder of the lap.

Mark the legs in pairs. Butt two of them edge to edge, with the laps facing out.

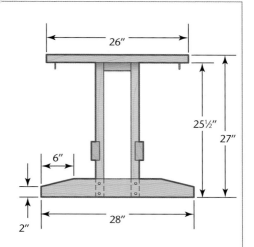

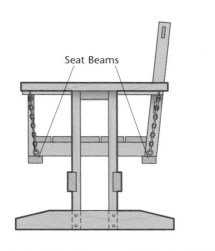

Seat Beams

Measure up 7 inches from the foot, and extend the line across both. Make an X on the far side of the line so that you cut on the correct side. Lay out the second pair of legs in the same way.

The depth of these laps isn't critical, by the way. I cut mine ¼ inch deep, but a ¹⁄₁₆ either way isn't a problem. Just make sure they are all the same.

Assemble the Stand

Before gluing and screwing the stand together, assemble the legs and feet, and mark edges that you want to round-over. Mill these edges using the router and roundover bit used earlier.

Set out two of the legs on edge, with the edge laps up. Be sure the cross laps face out. At the top, fit the 5-inch-long

To assemble the stand, clamp the blocks between the legs, and be sure it's square and flat. Position the foot in the laps, align it, clamp it all to the bench, and drill the pilot holes and install the screws.

block in place, and clamp the legs, pinching the block between them. Lay the second block flat, and fit it between the bottom ends of the legs. Apply a clamp to hold it in place. Measure diagonally from corner to corner to ensure that this unit is square. Apply construction adhesive to the edge laps; then set the foot in place. **(Photo 15)** Drill pilot holes, and then drive two 3-inch-long deck screws through the foot into each of the legs.

Free the blocks, and use them to join the second leg-and-foot assembly. Then use four 3-inch-long deck screws to permanently install one block at the top of each set of legs.

Now stand the leg-and-foot assemblies up and install the stretchers. Apply adhesive to the laps in the stretchers, then join them to the legs. Clamp each joint, and then screw each one together, using three or four 2-inch-long deck screws. Assemble one joint at a time, drilling pilot holes and driving the screws.

Test-fit the arms, but don't install them permanently yet; they will be in the way when you need to place the seat in the stand. Be sure everything fits; then apply the finish.

Install the screw eyes on the arms. Lay out the locations (centered between the sides and 1½ inches from the front and back edges), drill pilot holes, and turn the screw eyes into place.

Cypress is pretty soft, so don't use too large a bit to drill the pilots. It may be a bit more difficult to turn in the screw eyes, but they will hold better. If needed,

With the swing seat mounted on the seat beams and the unit set into the stand, you can cut the chains to length and hang the glider. You can use either S-hooks or repair links to connect the chain to the screw eyes.

wax the threads with beeswax, and use a screwdriver for leverage.

Hanging the Seat

Now it's time to hang the swing. The swing rests on the two seat beams, which have screw eyes at each end. Chains extend from the screw eyes in the arms to the screw eyes in the seat beams.

First, install the screw eyes in the seat beams the same way you installed the screw eyes in the arms. Then attach the beams underneath the seat. Turn the seat over, and align the front beam so that an equal amount extends beyond the seat on either end.

Line up the front edge of the beam flush with the front faces of the seat's armrest posts. Drill pilot holes, and drive 3-inch deck screws through the beam and into the seat framework. Align the back beam in the same way, with the back edges flush to the back faces of the backrest posts. Screw it in place.

Put the seat between the legs, resting it on the stretchers. Install the arms by driving two 3-inch screws through each arm into each leg. Then drive a pair of 2- or 2½-inch screws up through each block into the underside of each arm.

The seat is suspended from the arms with short pieces of chain. Link the chain to the screw eyes with S-hooks or repair links. **(Photo 16)** The suspension chains, including the S-hooks, should measure between 10 and 11 inches in length. Cut the chain, and hang the seat from the stand's arms. Now it's time to hop in to see how your new swing feels, and how it swings.

Porch Rocker

The porch rocker is an American classic and an icon of leisurely small-town life. You can picture a set of these handsome models on an old-fashioned front porch, but they will do just as well today on a brand new patio or deck. And who knows, you may find yourself rocking there peacefully on summer evenings the way people used to, waving hello and chatting with neighbors who happen by. Times have changed, but a rocking chair is still about

the most comfortable way to spend time outside. There are many different designs, of course, because most furniture makers built rockers as well as tables, chairs, and cabinets. You'll find ornate rockers made with hardwoods and delicate finishes, and those made from simple designs, such as Shaker style. This ample-sized version is built for comfort, and it's rugged enough to survive outside. You'll really appreciate how it rocks so smoothly and quietly.

And the best part is that you can build this model yourself with common materials found in most local home centers. Everything is planned out and measured on this project as it is on all the pieces. But bear in mind that you can adjust some of the dimensions to suit your needs. Because this piece is proportioned on the large side, it has more than enough room for a few cushions, if you want them.

EXPLODED VIEW

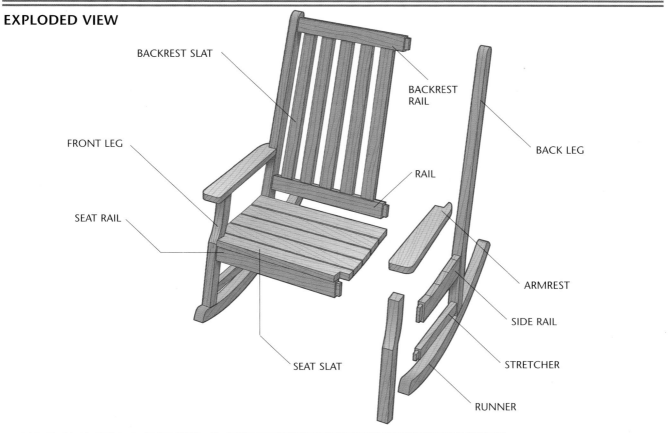

BACKREST SLAT

BACKREST RAIL

FRONT LEG

BACK LEG

RAIL

SEAT RAIL

ARMREST

SIDE RAIL

STRETCHER

SEAT SLAT

RUNNER

Part	Number	Thickness	Width	Length	Meranti Stock
Back legs	4	1"	5"	46"	⁵⁄₄x6
Front legs	4	1"	3½"	23"	⁵⁄₄x6
Side rails	2	1"	3"	18½"	⁵⁄₄x6
Stretchers	2	1"	1½"	18½"	⁵⁄₄x6
Seat rail	1	1"	3"	23½"	⁵⁄₄x6
Backrest rails	2	1"	2½"	23½"	⁵⁄₄x6
Backrest slats	5	¾"	2¼"	23½"	1x6
Seat slats	5	¾"	3½"	25"	1x6
Armrests	2	1"	3½"	22½"	⁵⁄₄x6
Runners	4	1"	5½"	36"	⁵⁄₄x6
Runner mounting pins	4	½" dia.	—	4¼"	birch dowel

CUTTING LIST (Some parts are left long during construction.)

SHOPPING LIST

- 1 pc. ⁵⁄₄x6 10' meranti

- 4 pcs. ⁵⁄₄x6 8' meranti

- 2 pcs. 1x6 8' meranti

- 1 pc. ½" dia.x36" birch dowel

- 1¼" galvanized deck screws

- 3" galvanized deck screws

Porch Rocker

ELEVATIONS

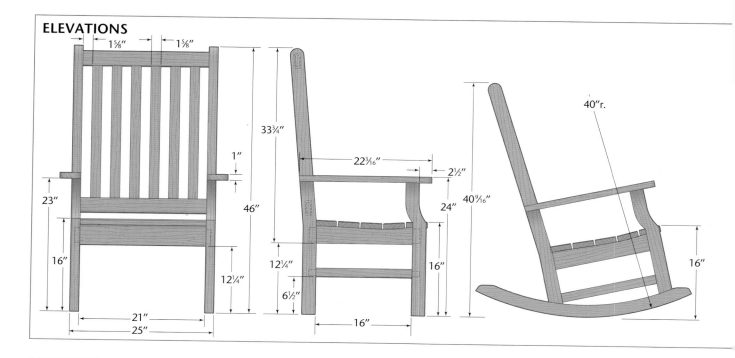

BUILDER'S NOTES

Building a rocker may seem difficult, but it's just like making a chair with the addition of runners.

Materials

I used meranti for the chair, and I was lucky enough to find dark-colored heartwood to use for the legs and rails. On paper, the rocker looked best with 2-inch-thick legs, so I made them by face-gluing two pieces of ¾ stock. In the meranti, true dimensions made the legs top out at 2⅛ inches thick. If you want a lighter appearance, by all means use two-by stock and reduce the depths of some of the mortises. This will save you the trouble of face-gluing the stock you'll use for the legs and runners.

To make the templates, use ½-inch MDF. Make sure the edges of the completed templates don't have voids; a problem you may have if you use plywood. The ½-inch thickness works because of

the deep mortises that you must rout in the front legs. The cut is near the outer limits of a router, and using ¾-inch-thick material for the template that guides the cut is pressing those limits.

Tools and Techniques

You'll need the usual array of tools, including a saber saw, drill-driver, a fixed-base and a plunge router, sanders, and perhaps a half-dozen pipe (or K-body) clamps. For face-gluing the boards that form the leg blanks, you can use any number of different clamps.

But the project, simple as it might seem, does have a number of tooling challenges in store for you. There are templates to use, so you need pattern bits and template guides to go with the routers. You'll need an edge guide to make the templates. The runners are curved, so a router and trammel is the best way to cut the template for them. When it comes to

power tools, a good 10-inch bench-top table saw will suffice for ripping stock for the rails and slats, and for ripping the glued-up blanks for the legs before you can rout the mortises and shape the legs. Once glued up, the stock is very thick, and feeding it too quickly can stall a bench-top saw. It's important that you square up these blanks after they are glued but before they are worked.

I cut the mortise for the side rail in the front legs with a router. Then, after the leg is cut (taking off the top of the mortise in the process), a 1¼-inch-deep cut will remain. Of course, routing a 2½-inch-deep mortise calls for an especially long bit. Among several manufacturers, Amana has a ½-inch diameter straight bit with 3-inch cutting height and an overall length of 5¼ inches. It's number 45477. Freud has a ½-inch straight bit (number 12-130) with 2½-inch-long cutting edges

and an overall length of 4⅜ inches. Both of the bits cited have ½-inch shanks. The generally accepted rule of thumb is that you should have a length of the shank equal to twice its diameter gripped in the collet. That means that with 1 inch of the shank in the collet, 3⅜ inches of that Freud bit can be projecting from the collet.

Finish

I used marine gloss spar varnish to finish the porch rocker. It's time-consuming to apply on some outdoor woods, but the appearance and protection make it worth the trouble. The meranti I used is such a variable wood that it took four coats to achieve a solid overall gloss. On the first couple of coats, some parts of the wood sucked up the varnish and remained dull. By the fourth coat, however, the pores of the wood were loaded up, and the surface really glistened.

PLAN VIEW

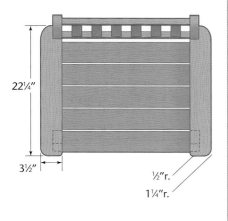

22¼"

3½"

½"r.

1¼"r.

STEP-BY-STEP

The rocker's four legs are 2 inches thick, which has more to do with appearance than strength. To get this thickness, you need to face-glue two pieces of ⁵⁄₄ stock, which is usually 1 inch thick.

Rip stock for the front legs. (The back legs are left at the standard width for ⁵⁄₄x6 stock.) It's wise to rip the stock ¼ to ½ inch wider than the 3½-inch width specified. Crosscut these parts ½ to 1 inch longer than the cutting list specifications to give yourself some leeway for planing and reripping the blanks to final dimensions after they are glued up.

To join the boards, spread glue on the mating face of one piece using a brush to make sure that you cover the entire surface. Set the mating piece on top and rub the two pieces together slightly to thoroughly smear the glue onto both mating surfaces. Slide the parts into the best alignment, and apply several clamps. Hand-screw clamps may be best for this sort of application, but use whatever clamps you have. **(Photo 1)**

After the glue has set and the clamps have been removed, clean up the edges of the blank and scrape off any dried beads of glue. Then rip about ⅛ inch of stock from one edge, turn the piece around and re-rip it to the desired width, cleaning and squaring the second edge, and making both edges parallel.

Back-leg Template

While the blanks for the legs are curing, move ahead by making the templates you'll use to shape the legs, and rout their mortises. First, make the template for the back leg according to the dimensions in the "Back-Leg Template" drawing at right. The template shown is intended to be used with a pattern bit, so it is exactly the same size as the leg. If you use a template guide with a regular straight bit, you will have to adjust the template dimensions to account for the offset.

For the back leg template, cut a blank 5 inches wide and 46 inches long. Lay out the leg shape, and use a saber saw to cut out the template, guiding it along a straightedge. Make sure the edges are smooth, straight, and free of dents, ridges, or saw marks. Any defects in the edge will telegraph into the legs themselves when you use the template to guide your router. A good saber saw, with a sharp blade guided along a straightedge, should yield a satisfactory edge. **(Photo 2)** Finish the piece with a few swipes of a sanding block.

If you want to ensure that the back edges of the template are parallel to the front ones, you can use a router outfitted with an edge guide to cut them. The guide slides along the front edges, while the router bit cuts a groove.

Next, make the mortising slots that will guide your plunge router in cutting the backrest mortises. The slots are ⅝ inch wide so you can use a ⅝-inch-outside-diameter template guide with a ½-inch straight bit to make the cuts.

Lay out the mortises on the template (following the drawing) and outfit your plunge router with its edge guide and a ⅝-inch straight bit. You should center the slots on the template, but if you reference the same edge with the guide as you rout them, it won't matter if they are slightly off-center. (All the mortises you cut with the template will be off the same amount from the same edge.) Set the edge guide to position the bit over the center of the template, and set the plunge stop at just a hair over ½ inch. Clamp the template at the edge of your workbench with a piece of scrap material inserted between the template and the bench. This extra step will keep the bit from cutting a groove in the benchtop. Finally, clamp a scrap to the template at each end of the intended slot to act as a stop and to prevent you from inadvertently making the mortise too long. Cut the slots in two or three passes each.

Use hand-screw clamps to secure the face-glued pieces. Tighten the inner screw, pinching the two pieces together with the bases of the jaws. Now turn the outside screw to close the tips of the jaws, squeezing the work evenly.

BACK-LEG TEMPLATE

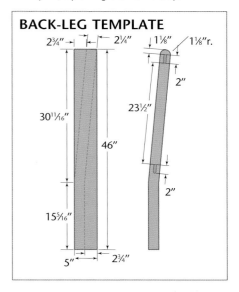

2¾" · 2¼" · 1⅛" · 1⅛"r.

2"

30¹¹⁄₁₆"

23½"

46"

15⁵⁄₁₆"

2"

5" · 2¾"

Position a straightedge with a setup gauge that represents the distance between the edge of the saw's shoe and the blade. Clamp the gauge on the cut line. Then you can clamp the straightedge against it.

FRONT-LEG TEMPLATE

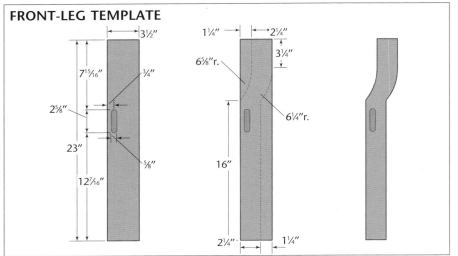

To lay out the front leg, clamp a block on the straight line above the knee, holding one end of a flexible strip such as a metal yardstick or thin wood ripping. Bend it to the desired arc, and trace the curve on the template.

Front-Leg Template

The template for shaping the front leg is made in much the same way as the back leg template, according to the dimensions and layout of "Front-Leg Template" drawing.

Cut a piece of the template material to 3½ inches by 23 inches. Then rout the slot for the mortising operation using your plunge router still outfitted with the edge guide and the ⅝-inch straight bit.

Adjust the edge guide to position the centerline of the cut ¾ inch from the edge of the template. Remember that this slot is wider and longer than the actual mortise you'll make. You'll use a ⅝-inch guide in the slot, with a ½-inch bit passing through it to cut the mortise in the leg stock.

Clamp the template stock overhanging the end of your workbench, again, with a piece of scrap between the template and the bench. Position and clamp stops to the work to control the start, end, and overall length of the slot. When everything is ready, rout the slot.

Lay out the shape of the leg next. Draw the straight lines with a ruler, then use a compass or bendable guide to draw the curves. **(Photo 3)** Cut the shape using a saber saw; then sand the cut edges to fair the curves and remove any rough or uneven spots.

Making the Mortise Template

You'll use this template to mortise both the front and back legs. If possible, make the template from ½-inch material. The mortises in the front legs have to be routed 2½ inches deep, but shaping the leg makes the location for the side-rail mortise inac-

cessible to a router. That means you have to rout the mortise before the leg is shaped. And because shaping removes a lot of stock at the mortise location, you have to rout a mortise that's twice as deep as it will be in the finished leg.

Using a ½-inch template instead of a ¾-inch template reduces the total distance your bit has to reach by ¼ inch, which can be a significant amount in this situation.

The dimensions and layout of the template are shown in the "Side-Rail Mortise Template" drawing at right. The template is the same width as the legs, so you can use it for both lefts and rights. (Attaching fences to position the template would prevent that.) As you lay out the mortising slots, work from the foot of the template. It doesn't matter where you trim the top.

Lastly, cut the slots in this template the same way you did with the front and back leg templates.

Routing the Leg Mortises

You should cut these mortises before the legs are shaped. They will eventually be 1¼ inches deep. But remember, you need to cut these mortises in the front legs to a depth of 2½ inches because of the leg's final shape. After the leg is cut to shape, the remaining mortise will be 1¼ inches deep.

The first thing to do is to use your three templates to lay out all the legs. You want to be absolutely certain you produce a right and a left of each leg. It seems simple enough, but once the router starts shrieking and the chips start flying, you can get mixed up. Align the shaping template on

the blank and trace around it with a pencil, including inside the mortise slots. Then position and trace around the side-rail mortise template, making sure the mortise layouts are offset away from the face of the blank that has the shape layout.

Mortise the back legs first. Align the template on the workpiece by feel, making it flush with the edges and the foot. Use clamps large enough to secure the template to the work and the work to the benchtop.

Outfit your plunge router with a ⅝-inch-outside-diameter template guide and a ½-inch-diameter straight bit. Set up the router to produce a mortise that's 1¼ inches deep. Set the router on the template with the guide captured in the slot. Bottom the bit against the leg blank, and set the plunge control to stop at 1¼ inches.

Rout the mortises by plunging the bit about ¼ inch into the wood and moving the router back and forth to the limits allowed by the slot in the template. After a couple of passes, you'll need to stop, remove the router, and vacuum the chips out of the slot. If you don't take the time for this operation, the chips pack in the ends of the template slot and in the cut, limiting the router's movement. As a result, you won't get a mortise of the proper size.

After you've routed to the full depth, take the time to do one last vacuuming, followed by one last full-depth plunge and end-to-end cut.

You mortise the front legs basically the same way. But you need to work with an unusually long bit to do the job, and you will have to stop part way through the

SIDE-RAIL MORTISE TEMPLATE

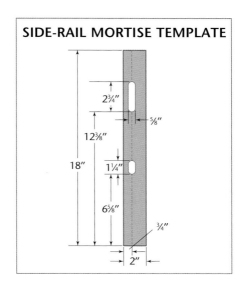

Depending on the router setup and the length of the plunge travel, you may need to start the mortises with a relatively short bit. After excavating the mortise, you can switch to a longer bit of the same diameter.

To finish routing the mortises, after they are excavated to about 1½ in. deep, switch bits and adjust the depth stop by plunging the router and aligning the bit's tip with a mark on the outside of the workpiece.

operation to rechuck the bit, extending its reach.

Depending on the brand and model of your router, you may need to begin the cut with a short bit, then switch to the long bit. **(Photo 4)**

Begin the operation with the bit set in the collet so that it is clear of the work when the plunge is retracted. Set the router to plunge as deep as possible. Rout the mortises progressively deeper until you reach that maximum depth.

Then you need to unplug the router and reset the bit in the collet. (That's basic safety procedure whenever you adjust or change bits.) You must have a minimum of 1 inch of a ½-inch-diameter shank gripped in the collet, and you better be using a ½-inch shank bit for this operation. With a bit that's slightly over 4 inches long and a template that's only ½ inch thick, you should be able to cut to the desired 2½ inch depth.

To reset the depth stop, put a mark on the outside of the leg that's 3 inches from the top of the template. With the router still unplugged, back off on the depth stop and plunge the bit until it aligns with the mark. **(Photo 5)**

Lock the plunge and set the depth stop to arrest the plunge at this depth. Now the bit will project from the template guide even with the plunge lock off. You must have the router squarely on the template, with the guide in the slot and the bit extending down into the mortise before you switch it on.

When you are done, be sure not to lift the router from the template until the bit stops spinning. This may seem like an

FRONT-LEG-RAIL MORTISE LAYOUT

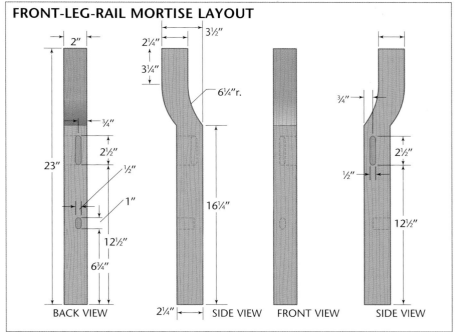

BACK VIEW   SIDE VIEW   FRONT VIEW   SIDE VIEW

annoying waste of time, but it will keep you from inadvertently damaging the template and the work.

When you resume the mortising operation, make incrementally deeper cuts until you achieve the desired depth. Stop periodically to vacuum chips from the cut, and always remember to wait until the bit stops spinning before lifting the router clear of the work.

Lastly, cut the mortises for both the rail and the stretcher in each front leg in this manner.

Because it takes such a long bit to rout a mortise 2½ inches deep, and the razor-

sharp bit extends well beyond the router's base even when the plunge mechanism is fully retracted, you'll want to take some extra safety precautions during this operation.

The best protection is to work methodically, always planning ahead and thinking about where that bit is—and where it's going—every time you move the router. Short of actually cutting yourself, the main danger is gouging a divot from one of your expensive workpieces.

Shaping the Front Legs
Stick the template to the correct face of

Porch Rocker

If your longest pattern bit can't handle this job, make two cuts. In the first pass, the shank-mounted pilot bearing rides along the template edge, but the cut extends only part way through the edge of the workpiece.

Remove the template, so on the second cut the bearing will ride on the router-cut edge, while the cutting edges will extend the cut across the rest of the edge. You can sand away the streak where the cuts overlap.

along the curves where there is an abrupt transition from long grain into end grain. The bit can dig in and gouge chunks out of the edge very suddenly, which could be dangerous and spoil the workpiece. This is a situation where you may want to move the router back and forth, nibbling back toward the template with shallow cuts rather than simply powering into the work.

After one leg is completed, pry the template off of it and repeat the process when you make the second leg. Remember as you start the second leg, that you want them to be mirror images of each other, not duplicates.

Making the Back Legs

You make the back legs basically the same way you make the front ones. Stick the template to the blank with carpet tape, clamp the work to the workbench and rout the mortises. Then cut the legs to shape; first to rough shape with a saber saw, then to final shape using a router and a pattern bit, matching the template.

Cutting the Backrest Joinery

The backrest consists of the upper and lower backrest rails, which capture five vertical slats between them. The rails are joined to the legs with mortise-and-tenon joints (the mortises have already been cut). The slats are joined to the rails with tongue-and-groove joints, according to the specs on the "Backrest Joinery" drawing on the next page.

Before you can cut the joinery, you have to cut the parts, of course. So rip and cross-cut the rails and slats to the dimensions specified on the cutting list.

Work on the rails first. The initial job is to cut the slot for the slats. One good way to do this is by using a router and slot cutter. The router can rest securely on the face of the workpiece while the groove is cut into the edge.

You can be sure that the groove is centered by making two passes with the cutter, one referenced from each face of the board. **(Photo 8)** This will increase the width of the groove slightly, but that's OK. You will cut the tongues on the slats to fit whatever width of groove you cut in the rails.

The only hitch is that the standard slot cutter makes a ½-inch-deep cut. To remedy that, you only have to change the size of the pilot bearing. The typical slot cutter is an assembly in which the cutter and a bearing are bolted onto an arbor. Just replace the standard bearing with one

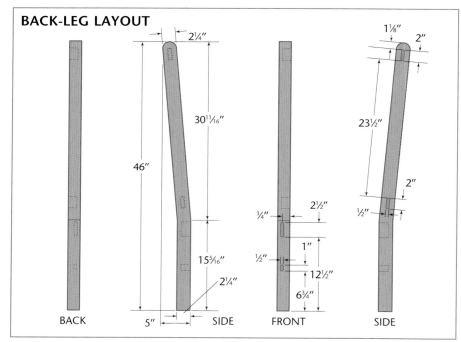

BACK-LEG LAYOUT

the leg blank—the so-called inside face on which you traced the mortise layout as well as the leg contour. Use carpet tape to securely bond the template to the blank.

Work on the mortise first, using the same ⅝-inch-outside-diameter template guide and ½-inch straight bit in your plunge router to make the cut. Cut the mortise 1¼ inches deep.

With the mortise routed, cut the leg to shape. Use a saber saw to trim away the bulk of the waste, cutting to within ⅛ inch of the template. (Just don't let your attention wander and cut into the template.)

Stock this thick can require some heavy-duty cuts with a saber saw. So adjust the oscillation to high speed, if possible, to improve the cutting rate. Remember that saber saws don't always produce perfectly square cuts; the blade can deflect and leave an angled edge—especially if you hurry the tool through the cut. Take it slow, and avoid leaving an undercut edge that can't be cleaned up with the router.

The next step is to use your router outfitted with a long pattern bit to trim the sawed edges smooth and flush with the template. **(Photo 6) (Photo 7)** Be careful that's ½-inch larger in diameter. This will reduce the cut depth to ¼ inch.

After cutting the grooves, cut the tenons on the rails. The basic dimensions for the tenons are shown in the drawing, but be sure to measure your mortises before actually starting on the tenons. What you must do is form a tenon that will fit the mortise.

The final operation is to cut the tongues on the slats. You can handle this operation using the slot cutter or a rabbeting bit. With the slot cutter, the bit is extended so it makes the cut on the underside of the wood because the bearing is between the router and the cutter. The bearing on the rabbeting bit is on the end, so the cut is made on the top of the wood.

Regardless of the bit, you need to cut two rabbets across the slat's end, sizing them so the tongue that's left is a nice, snug fit in the groove. It's wise to make some test cuts on scraps of the stock used for the slats, and creep up on the correct setting. Remember that any change you make in the bit's cutting depth will be doubled because you make two cuts to form the tongue. So make your adjustments in small stages.

Once you have the router set up, cut the rabbets on all five slats. The biggest part of the job is producing the five slats, which require 20 rabbet cuts. You can save time by clamping all five slats together and cutting a rabbet across them all in one pass.

While you still have the router set up for cutting the tongues, use it to make some filler strips for the rail grooves. To keep moisture from collecting in the grooves and to help position the backrest slats during assembly, you need strips of material that are the same size as the tongues. That means you need to use the router to cut tongues on the long edges of some scraps of the slat stock. Rip the tongues from the stock and test how they fit in the groove. Assuming they fit well, crosscut them into 1⅝-inch-long pieces. You need 12 altogether.

Shaping the Rails and Tenons

You have three rails left to make. The seat rail, which joins the two front legs, simply needs to be tenoned on both ends. The side rails also need tenons, but they must be shaped slightly to give the rocker seat a slight concave contour. This is the kind of extra detail that can really make a project worthwhile. Flat seats and backs are easier to fabricate, of course, but you'll appreciate the extra steps once the project is done and it's time to relax in your rocker.

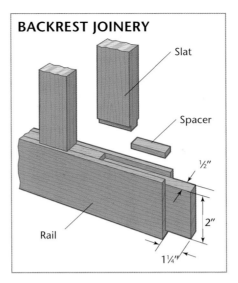

BACKREST JOINERY

Slat

Spacer

½"

2"

1¼"

Rail

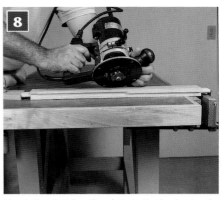

8

Rout the slot for the slats in the backrest rails using a slot cutter. Make the first pass; then turn the piece over and make a second cut (partially completed here). This two-step procedure centers the slot.

Cut the tenons on all the rails first. Use the jig made for tenoning the backrest rails, and cut these tenons in the same way.

The side rail contours are shown in the "Side Rail Layout" drawing, at right. The contour creates a bit of a hollow for the seat, yet provides a flat spot to attach each seat slat. Lay out each rail, carefully following the specs in the drawing. Cut to the lines using a saber saw and sand the sawed edges smooth.

Gluing the Backrest and Legs

If you have fit the joints carefully as you made them, the entire backrest assembly (which includes the rails, slats, and both back legs) should go together without a hitch. But to be sure, do a complete run-through without glue. This kind of dry run will prove that the parts do fit together. One of the important details to check during the dry run is the position of the tiny filler pieces. You need to be sure that they really do position the slats correctly.

Once you're satisfied, open the glue and begin assembly in earnest. Join the slats to one of the rails first. Secure the rail in the workbench vise with the groove up. Glue a filler into the groove with its end flush with the end of the groove. Glue a slat into the groove next, pressing it tightly against the end of the filler. Then insert another filler, followed by another slat. Continue to work your way across the rail, alternating filler pieces and slats.

Now apply glue to the upper rail's groove. Glue a filler into the groove at each end. Then apply glue to the tongue on each slat and fit the rail over the tongues. Apply a pipe or bar clamp across the rails near each

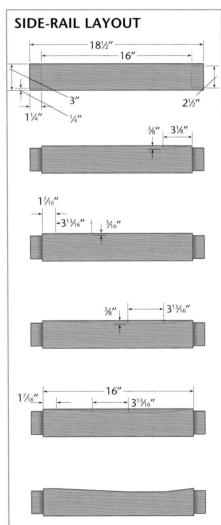

SIDE-RAIL LAYOUT

18½"

16"

3"

1¼"   ¼"   2½"

⅜"   3⅛"

1⁷⁄₁₆"

3¹³⁄₁₆"   ³⁄₁₆"

⅜"   3¹³⁄₁₆"

1⁷⁄₁₆"   16"

3¹³⁄₁₆"

Weather-resistant yellow glue *is very grabby, so as you join the top rail to the assembly, working the slats into alignment can require some persuasion with a block of wood and a hammer.*

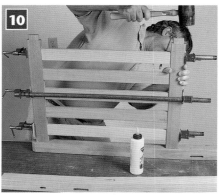

With glue on the mortises and tenons, *lower the backrest assembly tenons into the mortises in the back leg. Whack the ends of the backrest rails with a rubber mallet to seat the shoulders of the rails.*

Apply glue to mortise and tenon *using a brush to paint the surfaces so that you get a thorough, even—but thin—application. Using too much glue results in squeeze-out and a messy cleanup job.*

To complete the assembly, *join the front legs and the front rail. Glue the side rails and stretchers into the back legs, then hoist up the front and lower it carefully onto the rails and stretchers.*

to the two front legs. Apply glue to both the mortises and the tenons with a small brush. **(Photo 11)** Press the tenon into its mortise in one leg, then push the other leg onto the rail's second tenon. Apply a pipe or bar clamp across the legs, placing it on the outside, where it won't interfere with the assembly of the side rails.

Now join the side rails and stretchers to the back legs. Press the tenons into the mortises. If necessary, smack the end of the tenon with a mallet or hammer to seat the part.

Set the backrest assembly (with or without clamps) on the workbench. Apply glue to the appropriate elements and lift the front portion of the rocker framework into place. **(Photo 12)** As the joints are pressed closed, you can right the chair—it is still a chair at this point in its development—and apply clamps paralleling the side rails and stretchers. Don't dawdle, or the glue will grab, keeping the joints from closing properly. But use the clamps here, as elsewhere, to force the joints to close tightly. Check the assembly with your measuring tape and square to ensure that the chair is square and true. Then set it aside overnight, all clamped up, so the glue can cure.

Fitting the Seat Slats

With the frame assembled, cut the five seat slats to fit. You need to set the ends of the slats flush with the outer faces of the legs so they slightly overhang the side rails. After cutting the slats, sand them smooth, and round-over the top edges with a small-radius roundover bit.

Drill counterbores for the mounting screws, using a ⅜-inch Forstner bit, and use two screws on each end of the slats. The counterbores allow you to conceal the screws with wood plugs, and the Forstner bit should produce clean, chip-free bores for the plugs.

Even though some—probably many—of the plugs will be all but invisible, you will need to position the galvanized screws consistently on all the slats. So make a jig from a scrap of ¼-inch plywood or hardboard. Drill two ⅜-inch holes through it and attach blocks to position it on the end of a slat. Then go ahead and drill the counterbores.

Notch the front and back slats to fit around the legs. (Note that the notches in the rearmost slat involve little more than trimming the slat's back edge on an angle where it abuts the leg.) To lay

end, and just begin to force the rail down onto the slats. Quickly lay the assembly flat on the benchtop, and press fillers into the gaps between slats in the upper rail. This will force the slats into alignment. But you may find that some of them require a bit of persuasion with a small wood block and a hammer. **(Photo 9)** As you get the last slat squared and the last filler seated, tighten the clamps firmly, pulling all the joints closed. Flip the assembly over and measure the diagonals to ensure that it's square. If it is, add a third pipe clamp parallel to the center slat.

The last parts to add to this assembly are the legs. Apply glue to the tenons on the same end of both rails—and to the mortises in one of the legs—and join the two. **(Photo 10)** Repeat the glue application on

the other end of the rails and to the mortises in the second leg, and join the second leg to the assembly. Remove the clamps from the rails and apply them across the legs. Use three clamps, with two across one side of the assembly and the third between them but on the opposite side. This will prevent clamping pressure from twisting one or both of the legs. When the assembly is squared up and solidly clamped, set it aside while the glue cures.

Assembling the Chair

With the backrest assembly glued and clamped together, you can either take a break or press on. It's a natural stopping point that some do-it-yourself furniture builders will appreciate.

The next step is to join the seat rail

13

Cut plugs from your working stock. Apply glue, and as you insert the plug, orient its grain parallel to that of the workpiece. After the glue sets, pare the excess with a chisel and sand it flush.

14

Use a belt sander to shape the armrests. Lay out the corners and trim close to the lines with a saber saw. Then clamp the work in your vise and run the sander at slow speed, keeping it moving along the work edge.

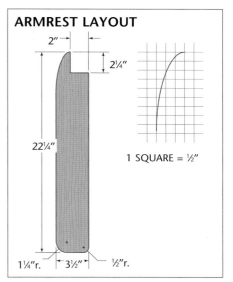

ARMREST LAYOUT

2″

2¼″

22¼″

1 SQUARE = ½″

1¼″r.   3½″   ½″r.

out the notches, set the slat in place, butt a small rule against the side of the leg, and scribe along it on the slat. Then reposition the slat so its end is against the inside of the leg. (Obviously, you have to tip up the slat sharply, or cock it slightly to do this before marking the slat.) Next, use a square to extend the mark. Cut to the line using a saber saw, paring as necessary with a chisel to achieve a nice tight fit.

After cutting and fitting the notches, install these two slats. Use the center point in the counterbores to locate your combination bit for drilling the pilot holes. Use 1¼-inch galvanized screws to secure the pieces. The front slat needs three additional counterbores drilled just back from the front edge so it can be screwed to the front rail.

Space the remaining three slats evenly between the front and rear slats. Then drill pilot holes and screw the slats to the side rails.

To make matching plugs, bore them out of scraps of the working stock. Glue a plug in each counterbore, aligning the grain in the plug parallel to the grain in the slats as you insert them. **(Photo 13)** When the glue has set, pare each plug almost flush with a chisel, then sand it perfectly flush.

Fitting the Armrests
Given the overall character of the chair, a fairly straight armrest will look best. (See the "Armrest Layout" drawing, above.) While you could make a template to shape these two parts, the goal is not a particular contour, only an attractive one.

So it works well to simply saw the corners close to layout lines, and then fair the curves on both pieces at the same time using a belt sander.

But to begin with, you need to notch the armrests to fit the back legs. Once this is done, you should have a left and a right piece. To mark up the armrests for notching (and later for installation), clamp a scrap to the back leg to support the armrest so it is square to the front leg. (You need the armrest to sit flat atop the front leg.) Mark the armrest (basically the same way you marked the seat slats), for the width and thickness of the legs. You also need to capture the angle of the back leg and transfer it to the edge of the armrest so you can make the crosscut for the notch at the correct bevel angle. You make the rip cut at 90 degrees.

Next, cut the notches using a saber saw. Now it's time to lay out the curves on the corners. First cut them close to the lines using the saber saw. Then set the armrests together face-to-face, line up the edges, and clamp them in your vise so you can belt-sand the edges. If you have a variable-speed sander, dial back the speed. Then sand the edges, particularly the corners, shaping them to smooth, graceful arcs. **(Photo 14)** You'll have to shift the armrests in the vise to give yourself good working access to each corner that needs to be worked.

When the edges are nicely shaped, sand the faces to remove mill marks and smooth the surfaces. Then break the edges using a small-radius roundover bit in your router.

Finally, join each armrest to the chair frame with a screw through the edge into the back leg, and a pair of screws through the face into the top of the front leg. Drill counterbores for the screws so they can be concealed beneath wood plugs. After fastening the armrests in place, plug the holes.

Cutting the Runners
The best all-around runner shape that provides the smoothest rocking action is a fixed-radius arc. Experienced builders often incorporate a flat or very gentle reverse arc at the rear of the runner for aesthetics (and sometimes to halt a tip-over). But if poorly placed, it can stop the movement too abruptly and spoil the ride.

A good radius for the runner is 40 inches. To better fit a short person, you might reduce the radius to 36 inches. If you want to customize a project for a particular person, try measuring the person when seated from chin to floor, and use that measurement as the runner's radius.

The runner should be no less than 34 inches long, and in this case, I made the runners 36 inches long. A longer runner would have outstripped the dimensions of the ⁵⁄₄x6 working stock.

Cut and face-glue two 36-inch pieces of ⁵⁄₄x6 stock for each runner blank. Do it the same way you glued up the blanks for the legs.

While the glue cures, make a template for the runner. Use ½-inch or ¾-inch MDF or void-free plywood for this template. Cut a blank 6 inches wide and 36 inches long. Fasten it to a scrap piece of plywood,

Porch Rocker

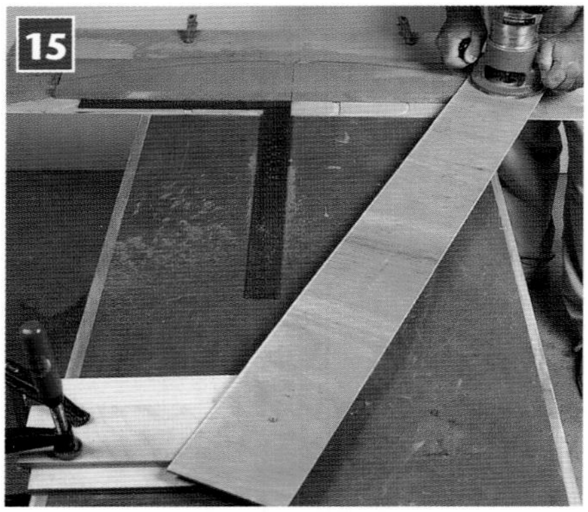
15

The custom trammel *is a strip of ¼-in. plywood bonded to the router baseplate with carpet tape. The pivot is a screw driven through the trammel into a scrap of wood clamped to the workbench.*

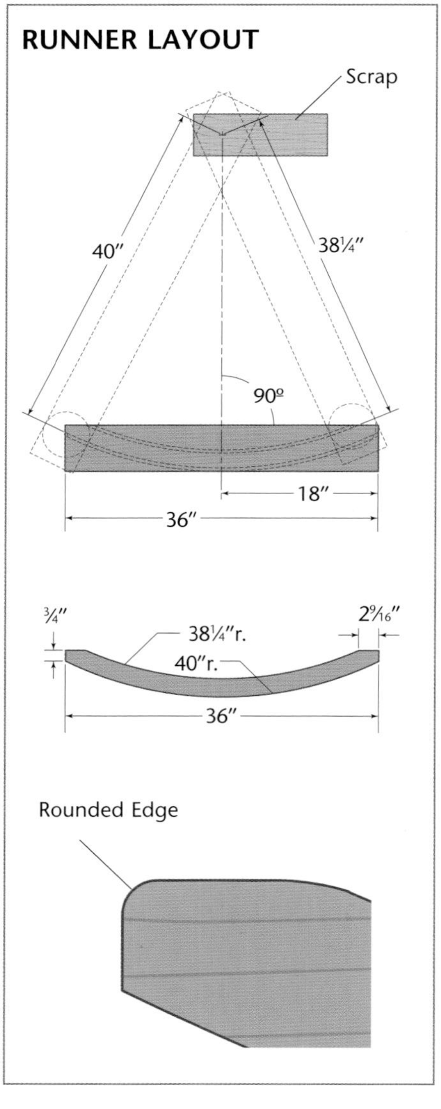
RUNNER LAYOUT
Scrap
40″
38¼″
90º
18″
36″
¾″
2⁹⁄₁₆″
38¼″r.
40″r.
36″
Rounded Edge

hardboard, or MDF that's a foot or more larger than the blank in each direction. By doing this, you can cut through the template blank without damaging the workbench beneath it, and you can clamp the work to the bench without having the clamps impede the swing of the router and trammel that will be making the cut.

Clamp the blank to one end of your workbench, find the centerline of the blank, and extend it off the template. You must locate the pivot point on this line, as indicated in the "Runner Layout" drawing at left. To avoid driving a pivot screw into your workbench top, firmly clamp a scrap to the workbench at the pivot point.

Use a strip of □-inch plywood for a trammel. Mount the router at one end using carpet tape to bond the plywood to the router's baseplate. You can use a fixed-base router for this because you can swing the trammel so that the bit is completely clear of the template blank on both the left and right, yet still have the router base supported. I used a ½-inch straight bit for the cuts. Next, measure from the bit to locate the pivot hole in the trammel. To cut the template, you will need two different pivot holes in the trammel. Establish the pivot for the bottom edge of the runner (the outside arc) by measuring 40 inches from the near side of the bit. This way, the ½-inch-wide cut made by the bit is outside the radius. The pivot for the top surface of the runner (the inside arc) is 38¼ inches from the far side of the bit so the cut is inside the radius.

Rout one arc, then the other. Set the bit to cut about ⅛ inch deep, and begin with the bit clear of the work. Switch on the router and swing it across the template. Be forewarned that routing MDF like this will raise a cloud of fine dust. Switch off the router, increase the cutting depth by about ⅛ inch, and make another pass. Keep repeating the procedure until you have cut completely through the template stock, but not the backup panel underneath it. **(Photo 15)**

With both arcs cut, free the template from the backup plywood, and use a file or coarse sandpaper to round the angular corners at the ends of the runner.

Cut the runners pretty much the way you cut the legs. Stick the template to the thick blank using carpet tape. Cut away as much of the waste stock as possible using a saber saw, and then use a router and a long pattern bit to trim the runner to match the template.

After both runners are cut, clamp them side-by-side in the workbench vise and sand the bottoms smooth and even. You want both the same, so the chair rocks straight. Then sand the tops and the sides to remove any mill marks, and round-over the edges with a small-radius roundover bit.

Mounting the Runners

To mount the runners, which is the critical step, you need to trim the legs—both to shorten them and to shape them to match the arc of the runners.

Begin by marking the legs for trimming. Set the chair on its side across a pair of sawhorses. Now follow the layout drawing, measure from the side rail on the front and back legs, and mark the inner edges of the legs. Lay a runner across the legs, and line it up on the marks. Trace your cut lines along the runner on both legs. Then use a saber saw to cut as close to the line as possible. **(Photo 16)**

To produce a tight joint, you need to refine the fit between the runner and the legs. To do this, stick coarse sandpaper to the top surface of the runner with carpet tape. Use half of a quarter-sheet at each of the contact spots. Then simply slide the runner back and forth, sanding the leg ends until they perfectly match the arc of the runner. **(Photo 17)** This takes some time, but it's more precise than using a belt sander.

you can mount the runners to the legs in several ways. One straightforward approach is to glue and screw the runners in place. Apply glue to the ends of the legs, then place the runner, and apply clamps between the runner and the stretcher. Drill a counterbore and a pilot hole through the runner into each leg, and drive a 3-inch-long galvanized screw. **(Photo 18)** If you can drill the pilot hole so that the screw just catches the stretcher's tenon in the back leg, you'll get some extra holding power.

Another approach, old-timey but very strong, is to dowel the runners to the legs. With this system, you glue and clamp the runner in place, and drill a 4-inch-deep hole for a ½-inch dowel through the runner and into the center of the leg. Because dowels often are undersized, use a 3¹⁄₆₄-inch-diameter bit to make the hole. Cut a 4¼-inch-long piece of dowel for each hole, and saw a 1-inch-deep kerf into one end. Cut a slender wedge to drive into the kerf.

RUNNER MOUNTING

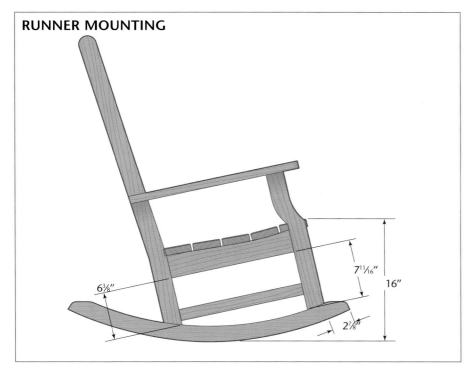

Cut the legs of the chair with a saber saw, guided by one of the runners. Offset the runner from the cut line to leave the line on when you cut. Clamp the runner securely to the legs; then cut them both.

Make a tight joint by using the runner as a sanding block. Bond two strips of coarse sandpaper to a runner with carpet tape, and slide it back and forth across the leg ends. Take the time to achieve a perfect fit.

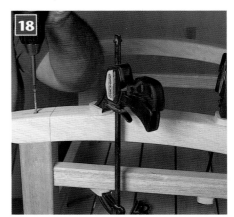

Apply glue to the legs; then clamp the runner. Drill a counterbore and a pilot hole through the runner into the center of each leg. Fasten each joint with a 3-in. galvanized screw.

Now apply glue to the dowel, and drive it into one of the holes, seating it so the kerf is oriented across the runner. Put a touch of glue on the wedge, and drive it into the kerf. Saw or pare the protruding dowel end and wedge; then sand it flush with the runner surface.

Now you can stand the chair on its runner and relax for a bit. The only job left is finishing.

Applying a Finish

Of the many finishes available for outdoor projects, the high-gloss look of clear varnish is just right for this one. For the outdoors, marine spar varnish is the most durable. I used a solvent-based product that needs to be applied in a well-ventilated place, dries slowly, and requires mineral spirits for cleanup. You also need to apply three or four thin coats for best results.

If you have been carefully sanding all the parts as they were readied for assembly, the rocking chair should not require much sanding at this stage. But you should run your fingers over the edges of the armrests, the legs, and the seat slats to make sure they are really smooth. Meranti doesn't sand particularly well; it tends to look and feel somewhat fuzzy. But working those edges with 220-grit sandpaper and some elbow grease will make

a difference.

After sanding, vacuum the rocker carefully. Move it to a clean, well-ventilated area, and dust every nook and cranny using a clean tack cloth. You'll be surprised at how quickly the tack cloth loads up with sanding dust.

Pop open the spar varnish, and apply it with a clean natural-bristle brush. Use thin coats to avoid runs, which can be difficult to spot and clean up.

The varnish typically takes a good 24 hours to dry. When it is dry, lightly sand the entire rocker. Use a fresh tack cloth to remove the sanding dust, and apply a second coat. Let it dry thoroughly, sand it lightly, clean it with a tack cloth, and apply another coat.

The initial coat will undoubtedly appear blotchy. The second coat may, as well. But by the third or fourth coat, you should see the uniform overall sheen of an elegant finish that also offers maximum protection against the weather.

INDEX